Progress Without Loss of Soul

Progress Without Loss of Soul

Toward a Wholistic Approach
to Modernization Planning

THEODOR ABT

Translation by Boris L. Matthews

Chiron Publications • Wilmette, Illinois

Originally published in 1983 as *Fortschritt ohne Seelenverlust: Versuch einer ganzheitlichen Schau gesellschaftlicher Probleme am Beispiel des Wandels im landlichen Raum.* Copyright 1988, Hallwag AG, Bern.

Translation © 1988 by Chiron Publications.

Library of Congress Catalog Card Number: 89-890

Printed in the United States of America.
Edited by Priscilla Coit Murphy.
Book design by Kirk Panikis.

Library of Congress Cataloging-in-Publication Data:

Abt, Theodor.
[Fortschritt ohne Seelenverlust. English]
Progress without loss of soul : toward a wholistic approach to modernization planning / Theodor Abt ; translation by Boris L. Matthews.
p. cm.
Translation of: Fortschritt ohne Seelenverlust.
Bibliography: p.
Includes index.
ISBN 0-933029-19-5 : $19.95
1. Rural development – Switzerland – Case studies. 2. Rural development – Switzerland – Psychological aspects – Case studies.
3. Switzerland – Rural conditions – Case studies. 4. Regional planning – Switzerland – Case studies. 5. Human ecology – Switzerland – –Case studies. I. Title.
HN610.Z9C615 1989
307.1'4'09494 – dc19
89-890
CIP

ISBN 0-933029-19-5 (paper)
ISBN 0-933029-36-5 (cloth)

Contents

Foreword

The outcry of mankind over the environmental disaster of pollution can no longer be ignored yet, except for minor completely insufficient measures, nothing has been done. The reason for this is that technical measures are not capable of preventing the disaster. A fundamental change of attitude of the masses is needed, similar to the great changes of attitude that characterized the birth of a new religion in the past. Dr. Abt's book, which draws its sap from his personal dreams, points out the direction from which the change will have to come. C. G. Jung had already pointed out, before his death, that our situation is so desperate we need the help of the unconscious to solve its problems. This "help of the unconscious" is often represented in dreams by the image of extraterrestrial beings and divine intervention. Following one's own dreams and putting what they say into action is therefore, in my view, even more important than purely technical measures. Dr. Abt's book is a convincing attempt to show us the where the great change ahead of us has to take place.

Marie-Louis von Franz

Foreword

There is, I believe, hardly a contemporary notion of progress which is not in desperate need of the sort of reappraisal that Dr. Theodor Abt gives it in this remarkable essay, *Progress Without Loss of Soul*. In this regard, as an Elizabethan sundial in a secluded English country garden one nostalgic autumn afternoon informed me: "It's always later than you think."

For in the vast proliferating empire of progress, in the technological fields of human endeavor and applied science and its consequences, in the conduct and spirit of man and his societies, it is not just the matter of increase it so plausibly purports to be, but also a mortal danger to almost all forms of natural life and even the earth itself. This profound ambivalence at the heart of progress is all the more awesome because it has been a dark potential since our conscious beginnings and implicit in the evolution of man from the moment the Promethean gift of fire came into his hands.

One of the earliest, and, for me, most striking images of its paradoxical role, is the story of the struggle between Jacob and Esau in their mother's womb. From then on, the Jacob in man, with a fearsome increase of power, has been joined in conflict with the Esau, with all that is natural in man and represented by the hunter who is close to his instincts, dependent on nature, and obedient to its urging and the wonder and reverence it evoked in his spirit, until we arrive at a moment when the triumph of Jacob in man, and the nations and cities it fathered, seems final and complete.

On the horizons where the great empires, the Ninevehs, the Tyres, Thebeses and Babylons, have gone down into the dust and rubble which is all that is left of themselves and the abundant world of nature which nourished them, there is a terrifying statement of its danger to man, beast, and flower. There were, for instance, the great forests of Central Asia which stretched from Istfahan eastwards to the Himalayas and the Hindu Kush, and north to the seas of the Caspian, and west to the wine-dark ocean of the Mediterranean. They have all gone. Humble woodcutters and charcoal burners feeding the needs and greeds of cities have left hardly a tree between Tehran and the Caspian. Where is the grass that Nebuchadrezzar ate? And where are the hanging gardens of Babylon? And what would not have been done sooner with the bulldozers and mechanical saws of today? North Africa from Nile to Atlas Mountains and the Pillars of Hercules, which was the granary of Europe, today is an impoverished fringe of earth on a man-made desert of the Sahara. The European shore of the Mediterranean, in spite of the vision of wealth and luxury it still holds for the weary industrial man, is a ghost of what it was in its Athenian day. Then, there was not a valley, a mountain, or a stream where men did not walk and commune with their gods, and dream in the company of satyrs, centaurs, nymphs, fauns, and the titanic forces of a world charged with magic and wonder. No one who has read his Homer, Thucydides and Vergil can be anything but terrified by what is left and in comparison looks like a scorched earth today.

At the same time as this devastation of the earth and plunder of its natural resources gained force, it was accompanied by an equal and opposite kind of radioactive fall-out in the soul of man. Pericles, in the course of one of his great orations during the Peloponnesian Wars, warned the Athenians how much of the desperation in which they found themselves was caused by the way wherein they had allowed their city-state to fall into the hands of men who had developed a slanted, soured and revengeful environment. He urged the Athenians therefore to go back to their ancient rule of choosing men who lived on and off the land and were reluctant to spend their lives in towns, and prepared to serve them purely out of sense of public duty and not like their present rulers who did so uniquely for personal power and advancement. He was already demarcating in his own context of time the danger of a growing imbalance between the Jacob and the Esau minds, between the separation of the spirit of man from its natural roots within and without, and a consequent loss for the reverence of the feminine values, our great mother earth and all her instinctive and caring heart that made life once so rich and productive. It is extraordinary how contemporary Pericles still sounds.

Euripides, having just failed in the great debate with Aeschylus in the Kingdom of Pluto to gain the right to return to life and speak for the true spirit of Greece, penned perhaps the most fearful warning of all in *The Bacchae*: the horrendous story of how Bacchus and his followers subverted and brought to ruin one of the greatest empires the world had ever seen, and how all the long-rejected, powerful energies in the soul of man rebelled and overthrew the law and order and power which had so long tyrannized them. Significantly in *The Bacchae*, the harbinger of the great catastrophe to come is "a city slicker with a smooth tongue," and all the stories and legends of the coming of Bacchus read almost like a report of the World Narcotics Bureau on the rising drug traffic of today, and the cry everywhere, the same old Theban call, for more police and for more and more law and order, without any inkling of how societies and their unlived selves are accessories before the act.

In the thousands of years between the moment when the King of Thebes was pulled limb from limb by his own wife and daughters, this great divide has continued to deepen faster. What we call "civilisation" has tended to become with geometric progression also a form of technological barbarism, invading not only what is left of rain forest, savannah, and virgin water, but every aspect of human endeavor, and even the genes of the human body. It is not for nothing that this difference between what I've called a city mind and a country mind was one of the first things that struck Jung when he went to school and university at Basel. Jung once told me how this town mind was to him daily more unreal and nightmarish, and how the longing for a return to the natural or the country mind became greater and more urgent. Already as a young boy, he said, as he became more familiar with life in the town, the stronger became his conviction that what he was getting to know as reality was not reality at all, but belonged to a totally different order, a disproportioned abnormality of man which passed itself off as the total reality. He longed for the view of reality which it seemed he lacked or had lost. He came to write:

> *I longed for the vision of the world as a country among rivers and woods, among men and the animals, and small villages bathed in sunlight with the rims of the clouds moving over them encompassed by clear dark nights—a world in which happily uncertain and unpredictable things can still happen and the surrounding world of nature would be the world of the country which is no mere locality on the map, but is God's world so ordered by Him that it would be filled with secret meaning. . . .* (Memories, Dreams, Reflections)

And he went on to write how trees for him were not just trees but rather represented the thoughts of Our Creator. He told how he walked through a forest as if he were looking at the act of creation itself and could feel the voice of creation speaking over his shoulder. This view, this vision, accompanied him to the end of his days and made him one of the greatest healers that life has ever known: a healer in the ancient religious sense of a person who unites that which has been divided and rejected, that which is hurt and wounded, and brings them together so that they achieve a wholeness which is greater than the sum of the parts.

This totality, this wholeness, it is important to remember, has the same origin, the same root in our language as the Saxon word for holy. Holiness and wholeness implied the same condition of mind and instinct, feeling and intellect, intuition and the transfigurative indefinable mysterious something which dreamt through human beings and ultimately maintained a vision beyond themselves and their societies.

So what Dr. Abt is after is on the trail of this indescribable dreaming element in life and time, which will restore man's wholeness and unify him, centered in the self where he is at last invulnerable and inviolate against the slanted and corrupting pressures which the life of our time would inflict on us. There is no dimension of contemporary life which is not threatened with fragmentation and so, incomplete, and it must not be thought that all I have been discussing is a universally orchestrated form of Greenpeace and conservation of the earth and its wildlife. I have chosen them only as examples because they are the most striking and represent the physical dimension in which the slanted man in his cities began to abuse the power conferred on him by science and its many technologies, in the world without, and as in the world without, so above, so below and so within. This corruption of power and this abuse of power over nature has indeed gone so far that not surprisingly everywhere there is the temptation to despair and feel all now is always too late. Moreover, in our centuries of the pursuit of reason and the indulgences of a hubris of a tyrannic rationalism, we have lost touch with this dreaming element which still, night and day, seeks to re-direct us to a destination where beginning and origin are one and whole. The desert and vast stretches of plundered earth which I have described as evidence of our devastation of nature therefore warn us also of the profound crisis of meaning which is bearing down on our spirit and producing what Dr. Abt so aptly calls a loss of soul. Or a state of "unbeing," as called by Thomas Berry, the remarkable historian of religion who, from his base in the Passionist monastery in Riverdale, has so profound an insight into the crisis of soul of which progress is so disturbingly symptomatic. For Berry, all the negations of progress were symbolized in the nuclear cloud concentrated once over Hiroshima. Dispersed, no longer easily discerned, for him the same cloud "shrouds in death the living earth." What he calls the comfortable disease of progress "leads on in a more generous time scale, to the same dead earth that the nuclear bombs produced in a moment." The result is always the same: only the efficiency changes. What the bomb does quickly, surgically, he says, progress will achieve more slowly if men continue to un-selve themselves and remain lulled in their cushioned unbeing.

Human beings, I believe, can endure anything except a state of meaninglessness, and ultimately what Dr. Abt is concerned about is bringing back meaning, and the sense of totality it confirms on all life on earth back to progress, and make it what it should not have ceased to be: a part, an instrument also, of man's dreaming self. He, too, set out on his journey in the way Jung had done by following first his own dreaming self and then the dreamer waiting unacknowledged at the door of the imaginations where excess of reason would lock it out. He serves it not only as a lecturer on the faculty of the Federal Institute of Technology in Zurich where Jung was a professor, but also as a working and training analyst at the Jung Institute in Zurich which, with my knowledge of all the admirable Jungian institutes I know all over the world, is still I think the best. And then more, he serves it in the world without, as an environmental engineer, on his own endangered and wounded piece of earth in Switzerland. So all that he says is based not just on diagnosis and analysis followed by some dogmatic judgment, but by synthesis and a process of trial and error in one of the oldest cantons in his native country, where man's continuity with his primordial beginnings is still intact in spirit. There he has proved how the dream can provide a clear, precise, and dynamic way of bringing man and his society back into creative partnership with the earth and nature, and a new sense of meaning and re-belonging. There he has a tested model, a pilot scheme of how the rest of the world must proceed if it is to save progress from itself. His brave and original work of pioneering may seem to some to branch out sideways from the main tree which is growing so steadily and high from the seed planted by Jung. One would not be surprised even if some orthodox Jungian would wonder at what he is about, and many a person in any case hostile to any thought of a nonchemical psyche would condemn him for just being another wild and wooly kind of mystic. But anyone who knows his history knows how in the beginning, on the very rim of the first horizon, man found a dreamer and a dream, and how from then this dreaming process was active at every unforgiving second of life, reminding the being chasing after his favorite partiality to pause and allow his shadow, lengthening behind him, to come up and join his bright and impatient other with the sun at last on his side. As he stands there with a horizon which still seems to hem him in, wondering how to go beyond, the dreamer abolishes it only to renew it endlessly ahead.

Africa's greatest poet has put it far better than I can, in a poem about the terrapin which, according to one of the oldest of old myths, supported the feet of the great elephant on whose back stood the pillars that hold the earth in position. This terrapin, in the poet's wild and volcanic epic, is the saving element that rises above the sea and flood to help the ark of Noah and its precious cargo of living things to survive. All done, the terrapin, the redeemer, sinks back into a dark,

unfathomed ocean, Dr. Abt would say back into the dreaming unconscious, leaving all living things on earth safe and free to scatter like
jewels over emerald grass, or move like flame through to the forests
and savannahs, still glistening and wet, and man reprieved and able
once more to listen to the "silent chanting of his soul," proclaims:

> *Though times shall change and stormy ages roll,*
> *I am that ancient hunted of the plains*
> *That raked the shaggy flitches of the Bison:*
> *Pass, world: I am the dreamer that remains,*
> *The Man, clear-cut against the last horizon.*
> —*Roy Campbell*, The Flaming Terrapin (1926)

This may bring no statistics or what the world would call facts to
measure the worth of this remarkable book, but it does convey in a
way no words of mine can, the sort of climate in which it was conceived and enabled Dr. Abt to serve so well the dream over all and
within himself.

Sir Laurens van der Post

Preface to the English Edition

Progress Without Loss of Soul grew out of my experiences as the project director of a comprehensive economic development plan for two Swiss mountain regions. Consequently, my reflections and my examples refer predominantly to Switzerland. Nevertheless, any other place in the world could just as well have given birth to this book, be that place urban or rural, be it a country of the first, second, or third world. But especially in rural areas and in countries of the third world—areas where the consumer mentality is not yet the pervasive common denominator among people—we can often see before our very eyes how our potent modern progress is capable of destroying essentially *nonmaterial* values. Thus, for example, money economy, new roads, mechanization, or television bring not only more freedom of movement and consumer possibilities, but also—depending on how we deal with these innovations—the destruction of the sense of village solidarity, a much more hectic pace of life, and eventually loss of identity. In urban areas, by contrast, we have already accustomed ourselves to a frictionless, matter-of-fact life style. Hence in metropolitan areas it is less noticeable if, for example, important open spaces vanish as a result of rapid change in the environment, even though a certain spontaneous *joie de vivre*, community feeling, and love of one's surroundings are consequently lost. In their place, the city offers more material advantages.

Progress has doubtless brought much that we value and would not like to do without, thus we cannot simply denounce progress. Rather, it is a question of becoming conscious of the *danger* that the domain transcending the material plane could be compromised by a viewpoint that embraces material progress alone. Attachment to place and to the soil, the sense of village community, of cultural heritage, and of a relationship to the beyond are acknowledged values for many people; yet in our everyday political and economic world, material views and considerations hold the foreground. The saying, "Money rules the world," is not entirely inaccurate. If, for example, we look at the collective problems of our times, these problems do all appear to be of a material nature. Hunger, distribution of resources, the assault on the environment, and political tyranny are such tangible unsolved challenges that it sounds almost absurd to want to set spiritual and emotional values in the foreground, too.

Yet nobody can deny that the way in which the individual masters his ever-present suffering despite his material well-being depends on his emotional tone, the mood of his soul. Neurotic dissatisfaction or the currently widespread inability to enjoy cannot be made to disappear magically, despite the availability of material goods. And the troubled individual is not capable of seeing the blossoming flower at the edge of the road. Despite this, we continue to act as though this fundamental fact were "only" psychic, and irrelevant in the light of our tangible contemporary problems.

Whether or not we experience our lives as meaningful and therefore worth living depends ultimately on our soul, on that unknown hinterland or background of our consciousness. For this reason people in all cultures throughout the ages have taken care to pay adequate attention to this unconscious realm. It has been only since the Enlightenment and the subsequent rationalizing-away of all things that cannot be measured and experimentally replicated that experiential knowledge, the life wisdom of our ancestors concerning man's relationship to this hinterland of the soul, has vanished from our field of vision. Unrestrained by all the bonds and ties that the reality of the soul impose upon mankind, material progress commenced its triumphal march.

Especially in recent decades we have lost sight of the reality of the soul in the face of imposing progress in the natural sciences and technology. Consequently, the word "soul" has, to a large extent, vanished from our political and scientific vocabularies. For example, not too long ago we spoke of five hundred souls living in a community; now we prosaically speak of five hundred *inhabitants*. Statistical thinking has bestowed upon us the pernicious habit of increasingly regarding the individual human being as an abstract, quantifiable unit. What is external mirrors what is internal: more and more we see our life as no more than that little line that someday will be engraved on our tombstone between the year we were born and the year we died. The idea and the experience of a soul that transcends our earthly existence and our known field of consciousness has vanished from the realm of most modern people's experience. The overwhelming possibilities of material progress obviously have a blinding power to fascinate us. And so we still believe that our happiness on earth depends *only* on our material circumstances. We seem to have forgotten that man does not live by bread alone!

In 1973, when I was given the task of working up a comprehensive economic development concept for Canton Uri in Central Switzerland, I shared the prevailing, generally materialistic attitude: it seemed to be a question of increasing the level of material prosperity of this mountain canton through the best possible regional development program, so as to create a counterforce to the depopulation of the mountain valleys. Material progress was to be promoted according to established goals corresponding to those set by contemporary social policy.

Then a series of noteworthy dreams that related to my work on the development concept made me aware of the spiritual-emotional realm. This inner dimension seemed to me, however, to be so widely separated from the concrete problems of development that I believed it could not possibly be linked with my "outer" work. Thanks to Dr. Marie-Louise von Franz, my analyst during my training as an analytical psychologist at the C. G. Jung Institute in Zürich, I accepted these utterances from the depths of my soul as serious reminders that the soul cannot be ignored in development planning. Those dreams and my interpretation of them were accepted as part of my dissertation at the Federal Institute of Technology (Abt, 1977).

This essay is an attempt, first, to expose this dimension of the unconscious emotional reality in our everyday social-political life and, second, to relate it to our various social problems. In this essay I have consciously limited my area of study in terms of geography and academic discipline: only those areas will be discussed in which I have personal experience. The work is limited to Switzerland and to the areas of rural and agrarian sociology, as well as regional and agrarian economics. I hope to make it evident that the hinterland of our soul, our emotional background, is a reality that absolutely must be given its full due when we set to work on collective problems. If this is not done, the background of our soul will make its demands felt in the form of all sorts of irrational disturbances and spiritual epidemics. Let the mythological fantasies of the Third Reich in Germany serve as an illustrative admonition.

In a book review I have been reproached for saying too little as to what should be done concretely in the realm of development policy and planning. In response to this I must counter with a question: has it not been the general solutions and approaches themselves that have rendered impossible specifically appropriate, unique, and hence organically natural solutions, to social problems? Doubtless the answer to this is "yes." Hence the goal of my essay is not that of presenting a successful solution that can simply be duplicated. Rather, my intention is to demonstrate that C. G. Jung's discovery of the collective unconscious can make decisively important contributions to our approach to working on problems in the area of social policy. However, only the individual confronted with a social problem can judge what that means in the specific instance and then act accordingly.

C. G. Jung's discovery of the collective unconscious brought about a fundamental shift in viewpoint in psychotherapy and consequently in the whole approach to therapy. But what this means in each individual case can never be formulated in general terms; for in each and every course of therapy, it is ultimately a question of discovering the meaning of the unique individual's life and hence also of the unique individual's suffering. Analogously we cannot avoid basing our modern theories of social change on the foundation of the discovery of the collective unconscious. With that as the basis, our guiding images for social policy will have to consider the *entire* human being and not only his biological needs—in other words, the human being *and* the human soul which, as will be shown in this essay, has its roots deep in inorganic matter. Thus, thanks to Jung's discovery, planning and development projects can no longer overlook nature in her entirety.

Theodor Abt
Zürich
December 1986

Preface to the First Edition

Mobility, technology, mass media, and money economy have fundamentally altered our life. True, this progress has brought more prosperity; yet at the same time we feel that a certain quality of life has been lost. It is not only tangible things such as the insidious destruction of the landscape or noise pollution. The deterioration in the quality of life appears also in the spiritual and emotional realm as alienation from the environment, from one's fellow human beings, and from oneself. The loss of this relatedness leads to a feeling of being no longer enveloped in something all-embracing. Nostalgia as a mood of our culture is the expression of this loss of soul.

In itself, every step of progress, every transition to something new, harbors the danger that the spiritual connection to what has gone before can be lost. Hence there is nothing new about the idea of progress entailing loss of soul. We see it in various folk sagas. According to a folktale from Uri, for example, the builder of the famous bridge over the Schöllenen Gorge in the Gotthard Pass was the devil himself. As payment for his work, he wanted the soul of the first person using his bridge. However, if soul substance is the price that has to be paid for progress, then the value of progress is questionable. According to the legend, the community of Uri pondered how they should deal with this devil of progress, who threatened their souls. The saga tells of some symbolic measures by which the danger of loss of soul could be avoided and progress consolidated.

Today, too, vast technological progress threatens to take over the soul. For this reason we, too, must reflect on how we can escape the threat of loss of soul. In examining this problem, the rural areas in Switzerland were chosen as the frame of reference. By looking at the changes in village and peasant life, we show where we must focus our attention if progress is not to be achieved at the cost of our souls.

We are indebted to the work of C. G. Jung for the decisive insights we have gained into the connection between external events and the reality of the soul. The results of his research into the nature of the collective unconscious paved the way for the examination of this social issue. This essay is thus also an attempt to elucidate the relevance of Jung's work in reference to contemporary social problems in general.

The writing of this work was supported from several sides. I am indebted to Prof. Dr. Albert Hauser and Hr. Prof. Jean Vallat for suggesting I undertake research in this direction. At their request, the work was accepted by the Agricultural Department at the Federal Institute of Technology (ETH) in Zürich as an *Habilitationsschrift.** Both scholars followed writing of this study attentively, critically, and helpfully; and I should like to express my heartfelt thanks to them here. Additionally I would like to thank the following officials, institutions, and people for their support and valuable suggestions: the Institute for Rural Economics of the Federal Institute of Technology (ETH) in Zürich, and particularly Dr. Charly Darbellay, Prof. Dr. Peter Rieder, the Research Group for Regional Economy, and the secretaries; the Government of the Canton of Uri, and especially the members of the Governmental Commission on Development and Council Member Josef Brücker; Dr. Erich Suter, president of the "Pro Züricher Berggebiete" Association, as well as the chairman of this association; Fritz Wezel, former director of the Heimatwerk School, Richterswil; Dr. Gotthilf Isler, Küsnacht; Prof. Dr. Paul Hugger, Zürich; Prof. Dr. C. A. Meier, Zürich; and Dr. Fritz Mühlemann, Bern. Likewise I would also like to thank numerous persons with whom I was able to discuss the topic, especially in the Canton Uri, in Haslital, in the Lötschen valley, and in the Zürich Oberland. They all made valuable contributions to the success of this work.

My most deeply felt thanks goes to Dr. Marie-Louise von Franz for numerous suggestions and her devoted concern. Without her informed guidance and support this work would not have come into being. Equal thanks is due my dear wife for her understanding and her support. Finally I would like also to thank the Hallwag Publishing Co. particularly Max Welter, for the close cooperation in the first printing. Thanks go to Roland Eberle and Hans Kissling for editing the manuscript.

Theodor Abt
September 1983

---

*The *'Habilitationsschrift'* is a thesis required of candidates wishing to qualify for lecturing at a university in German-speaking countries.

PART 1

THE STARTING POINT:
The Malaise in Rural Areas

Malaise in rural areas[1]—does that really exist in Switzerland? Our rural population, our farmers, indeed even our mountain farmers are relatively well off—in any case, better off than just a few years ago, and better off than in any of the surrounding countries. And often enough, whenever city dwellers drive through the country, they envy the idyll of a world supposedly still largely intact. In fleeting contact with people living in rural areas, moreover, it is seldom possible to ascertain a greater degree of dissatisfaction than among city folk. Is it not then erroneous to speak of a malaise in rural areas? At first glance, yes. We need to be more familiar with present-day conditions in rural communities and especially our agriculture. Only when we look behind the scenes of windows full of blossoming geraniums and Ländler music on Sundays does the harsh reality of the rural workaday world become visible. We then recognize the material, social, spiritual, and emotional difficulties that have been brought about by the rapid introduction of technology, rationalization, and secularization into rural life.

---

[1]In what follows, we understand the concept "rural area" in the sense delimited by Hans Elsässer: "Not a single criterion but rather a meaningful combination of various criteria permit us to demarcate the rural areas, for example, settlements considered small on the basis of population, low population density, number of jobs, infrastructure, predominance of agriculture or forestry, etc." (Cf. various authors, "The Rural Area—A Task for Regional Planning," ORL-Schriftenreihe, no. 28, Zürich, 1977, p. 64–77.)

Chapter 1

The Rural Social Problem

The Vicious Circle of Migration

The technological, economic, and social development of recent decades has fundamentally altered the living conditions in remote areas of the country. Concentration of the population in metropolitan areas[1] and the corresponding emigration of predominantly young people from geographically disadvantaged rural communities has resulted in these areas becoming less and less attractive. We can justifiably speak of this process of migration as a modern mass migration or *Völkerwanderung*, for it is taking place in virtually all industrial nations.[2]

In Switzerland, too, the population is becoming concentrated in central areas as a consequence of migration. Figure 1 depicts the extent of this process of concentration.

About one half of all the people living in Switzerland today live in urban areas, yet they occupy only about 2% of the land area.[3] This gives us an idea of the geographic concentration of the population. The consequences of this continuing shift in population are very far-reaching for rural communities. Many villages lose their local school, their post office, the milk collection station, the municipal hall, the train station, as well as private stores and skilled trade enterprises. For lack of suitable persons, the political offices can no longer be satisfactorily filled in many places; and the diminishing tax base leads

---

[1] We must carefully distinguish between the concepts of a metropolitan area and city. In recent years metropolitan areas have registered an increase in population, while even cities like Zürich or Basel show a loss of population.

[2] The same is increasingly true for third world countries.

[3] According to H. P. Städeli, "Die Stadtgebiete der Schweiz," dissertation, Zürich, 1969, p. 108.

Figure 1. Selected Subpopulations of Persons Living in Switzerland 1850 to 1980

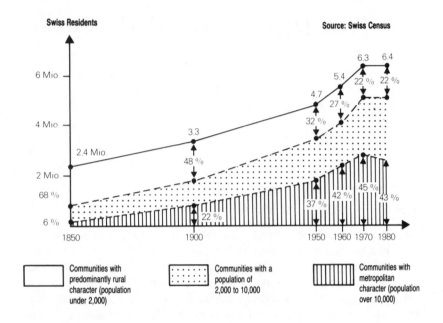

to a higher tax rate, which in turn makes these communities less attractive places to live.

In the realm of job opportunities we encounter the same process of concentration. While more than half of all jobs at the turn of the century were in agriculture and hence in the country, today about 80% of all jobs in Switzerland are found in metropolitan areas. In 1980 scarcely 6% of the workforce was employed in agriculture. Because of disadvantageous geographical factors affecting production technology, remote country areas usually attract little new business investment.[4] Existing production facilities grow old and thus become less competitive. They can only survive with low wage rates; otherwise, they disappear completely. This situation leads to the migration of young people to the more favored central areas with their more attractive job opportunities. The influx of young workers naturally increases the economic strength of these centers and attracts new investments in infrastructure, production facilities, and housing construction. Because living and working conditions continually

---

[4]Excluded are communities with good potential for developing tourism.

improve, the attractiveness of the centers increases. This leads to a vicious circle of continuing loss of population from geographically disadvantaged communities and regions.[5] Figure 2 illustrates the interconnection between population concentration in proximity to urban centers and the decrease in population in peripheral rural areas.

For us in Switzerland, the loss of population from economically poor rural districts weakens the federalistic decision-making structure. The balance between city and country is markedly compromised by the shift of balance in population, as reflected in this comment by three members of the Government of Canton Glarus concerning the contemporary political situation in Switzerland: "Swiss politics are made in the areas of industrial concentration. But we are no longer willing simply to swallow everything that in the eyes of the city folk looks necessary for us in rural communities."[6] You can hear similar statements from other agrarian and mountain areas. People complain about the well-known fact that to the same degree that the population and availability of jobs cluster in the urban centers, the decision-making power in the political and economic spheres is concentrated there, too.[7]

Cultural policy in Switzerland is also experiencing increasing centralization. With growing mobility and increasing influence of mass communications, the rural folk culture of small, local communities gets absorbed in larger catchment areas in the middle of which an urban center usually stands.[8]

Of course, many things have been undertaken to counter this so-called flight from the country. Industrialization, mechanization of agriculture, tourism, and facilitated commuting have improved the prosperity of many rural areas and have given numerous—if not all—villages a new basis for their economic existence. On the one hand, these efforts to increase the prosperity of rural areas have brought about an increasingly efficient and busy life-style. Today people in the country acknowledge the principle that "time is money." On the other hand, virtually unchangeable natural circumstances in these areas are

---

[5]The new results of the 1980 Swiss census confirm this statement for the last ten years: in 1,348 communities (44% of all communities), the population has decreased, and in 133 of these communities by 20% or more.

[6]From U. Kägi's interview of three members of the cantonal government of Glarus; "Weltwoche," no. 18, 29 May 1981.

[7]See, for example, the investigations under the auspices of the Nationalfondprojekt "Regio" by K. Müller, *Räumlicher Wandel wirtschaftlicher Entscheidungsprozesse*, Bern, 1981.

[8]See also Richard Weiss, *Volkskunde in der Schweiz*, Zürich, 1946, e.g., p. 256.

Figure 2. The Feedback Loops of Economic Over- and Underdevelopment

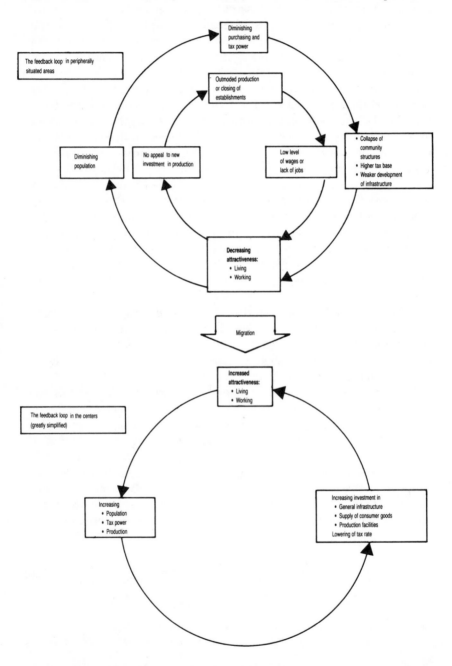

coming increasingly into conflict with the principles of modern thought and action based on reason. External natural circumstances such as topography, distance, and climate do not harmonize easily with economic expediency, productivity, specialization, and yield. Long commuter distances, especially in the winter, can hardly be described as economical. A store or a skilled-trade shop in a village can increase its productivity only to a very limited degree. On the remote small farm, the farmer needs to be very versatile and in the country numerous official tasks and duties for the village community must be fulfilled on an honorary basis without regard for return.

Alongside these external, natural constants, the inner-personal natural constants often play a significantly more important role in rural areas than in an urban life-style. Here it is a matter of the so-called instinctual basis. That is to say, the more the external course of human life is determined by nature and her laws, as in the case of a mountain farmer, so much more must one be guided in one's dealings with nature by the time-honored practical experience passed on from one's ancestors. This *"Erfahrungswissen"* (empirical wisdom or *mémoire collective*) manifests itself in our instinctual basis and enters the field of consciousness in the form of intuitive, motivating impulses. Normally this inner practical knowledge is complemented by knowledge handed down through tradition.

Now as the instinctual basis is truly fundamental to an understanding of the rural way of life, we must define this concept more precisely.[9] What we understand by instinctual basis is the sum of all the drives that form the cause and patterns for definite actions. There is in mankind an inner, fundamental model that makes him lead a specifically human life. Uniformity, regularity, and unconsciousness of motivation characterize reactions based on instinct. However, motivations determined by reason can superimpose themselves on actions triggered by the instincts to the point of making the latter almost unrecognizable. By its nature, instinct is a collective phenomenon, that is, a commonly and uniformly distributed phenomenon. Since they are normally unaltered, our instincts form—in contrast to our adaptable and progress-oriented consciousness—the conservative foundation for our behavior patterns. In summing up we may com-

---

[9]Details on this can be found in H. Heusser (editor), *Instinkte und Archetypen im Verhalten der Tiere und im Erleben des Menschen*, Wissenschaftliche Buchgesellschaft, Darmstadt, 1976, cf. particularly C. G. Jung's essays.

pare our instinctual basis with a network of inner natural constants which influence our ways of behaving in a decisive manner, even if we are often scarcely conscious of it.

Now a way of behaving that is co-determined by instinct is by no means to be dismissed as backward, as people often do who advocate a way of life guided solely by reason and will. On the contrary: so-called instinctual certainty acts as a guide in all those situations and crises that are part and parcel of everyone's lives and which humanity has had to master since time immemorial. Such situations occur wherever someone is confronted directly with the living force of nature, be it internal or external. In the country and especially in the mountain regions, the greater dependence on the external forces of nature causes people living there to conduct their lives largely in accordance with ancestral adaptation schemes. Each individual can thus deal with external nature in an intuitively correct fashion.[10] The well-known, rather conservative stance of the rural and particularly the agricultural population is, therefore, not to be ascribed simply to inadequate enlightenment. Rather, this attitude is in many ways grounded in the understanding by these people that the traditional way of doing things is an appropriate response to natural conditions, even if its applicability is not immediately evident to rational and goal-directed thinking.

Because the rural way of life is naturally attuned to ancestral knowledge, innovations coming into rural and mountainous regions from outside can create apparently crass contrasts to time-honored structures and concepts. This clash of the rural population's practical knowledge with scientific rationality can be seen, for example, in the consolidation of land holdings. The instinctive persistence of land-owners—arising out of long-standing experience with and hence "emotional ties" to a specific piece of ground—often comes into the most severe conflict with a redistribution of the land based on rationality. In a similar manner, too, the generations-old interpersonal relationship structures of rural communities come into conflict with innovations promising progress, be it in a school consolidation within a community, a merger of communities, or the creation of new regional units. Catch words like "church-tower politics" or "local spirit" (Kantönligeist) as expressions for this persistence in this context should not be taken only negatively. True, this conservatism of the instinctual nature renders cooperation with the next-larger and hence less famil-

---

[10]A very beautiful document on this topic is Eduard Renner's *Goldener Ring über Uri*, Zürich, 1941.

iar social unit more difficult; yet on the other hand, this tenacity preserves an inner cohesion of existing communities.

In general we can state that, between the conservative external and internal facts of nature on one hand and progress which brings changes on the other, there exists in rural areas a greater field of tension than in the metropolitan areas. The further people live away from a villagelike environment, structured on a small scale and close to nature, the less they feel bound by external and internal factors. For Zürich urbanites accustomed to mobility, such things as seasons, climate, landscape, community structure, traditions, and also the stages and transitions in their own lives, do not have the same determining power as for, say, a mountain farmer close to the soil in Central Switzerland.

Naturally, people in the country are not blind to the advantages of progress. But on the other hand, they are often "instinctively" against innovations and want to cling to the tried and true. In the more remote rural communities and particularly among the agrarian population, this leads directly to a clash of opposites. For the most part, people are hardly aware of this.

The following example illustrates the point. When asked about the continuing migration from an unspoilt mountain village in the Canton of Wallis, a forty-year-old father of a family answered: "We have to develop tourism in our village. We have to create a tourist resort. We need to have jobs for our kids." Asked a few days later about the quality of the still-intact community life, the same man replied: "We have to preserve our village. Tourism would destroy everything."[11] A fickle man? By no means. I know him, his family, and his outstanding reputation. What emerges from his words is the frequently unconscious dilemma of countless persons in peripheral areas. On one hand is the pressure to rationalize, mechanize, to motorize, and to increase usage of natural resources. On the other hand, people in these regions sense much more acutely than city dwellers that, along with progress and expansion come an attitude and way of life which causes old values to vanish.

We know the generally skeptical stance toward innovations taken by persons in remote areas, as when railroads were being built or when an area is opened up by a new highway or through electrification. Thus in the Lötschen Valley (Canton of Wallis) after the construction of the new highway, people were happy about the conven-

---

[11]I am indebted to Dr. Ch. Darbellay, Charrat (VS), for making me aware of these conversations.

ient link with the outside world thanks to the new bus routes; but they also sensed the shadow sides of this progressive step. "The bus has a black trailer, and the Devil rides in it," people said in the valley.[12] Only recently have we generally begun to notice that there follows upon the heels of progress a sinister, demonic element. The image of progress with darkness in its wake is thus not simply stupid superstition, but rather an intuitive comprehension of the entire situation, whereas modern reasoning often gets carried away by the positive individual aspects of the progress.

For the rural population, the deep dilemma between attachment to tradition and the pressure for—but also the enticement of—progress is often revealed in evening conversations. At first, there are arguments for progress, rationalization, and technology. But after one or two glasses of wine, the values of tradition are suddenly defended. Indeed, even various parliamentarians from country and mountain areas are hardly aware how very much they are inwardly torn by the often insoluble conflict between meaningful old structures and the pressure for adaptation to new circumstances. When the elected representatives in Bern were discussing the first draft of the new federal law dealing with regional planning, there were parliamentarians from rural areas who supported the draft in Bern but who spoke against it once they were back home. As far as could be determined, this could not be attributed simply to opportunism. Rather, this phenomenon seems to be an expression of the dilemma that as we are faced with the pressure for an increase in planned interventions, at the same time we sense that these innovations carry with them the danger of inner alienation from what has long been in existence.

This assumption is well founded. It is common knowledge that relatedness to what is and what has been weakens as rational thought and planning gain the upper hand. The cult of community is gradually replaced by a cult of the individual.[13] People no longer have any appreciation for old customs,[14] and even the beloved moor, for example, with all its childhood memories is drained to increase the arable acreage. Whenever the rational frame of mind predominates, the transpersonal powers are usually no longer heeded.[15] Thus what usually falls victim to progress is the vital feeling of relatedness to the

---

[12]Numerous personal communications in connection with my investigations in the Lötschen Valley in 1972.

[13]On this point see Richard Weiss, *Volkskunde in der Schweiz*, loc. cit.

[14]On this point see, for example, Albert Hauser, *Bauernregeln*, Zürich, 1973.

[15]The increasing secularization in rural areas is associated with the spread of urban ways of thinking.

community, to the traditions bound up with it, to the entire surrounding environment, and—last but not least—to the transpersonal
dimension. This quality of life seems to be irreconcilable with the
principles of progress, so much so that we can compare them to fire
and water: where one dominates, the other must yield.

It is not only the sudden confrontation with a new material reality that
causes a virtual revolution in our rural and mountainous areas; it is also
the change in mentality that nearly always accompanies it. The clash
with a new way of thinking and living is strongest where rural communities are "discovered" by agents or tourists thanks to their attractive
landscape and their good accessibility. Then, in such villages, traditional
cultural values and community relationships are often destroyed entirely
by all too hasty development without being replaced by new values of
equal merit also centering around village life. As various studies in rural
and agricultural sociology have demonstrated, this revolution in ways of
thinking and living leads to uncertainty and to a sense of disorientation
among the indigenous rural population, especially in agrarian circles.[16]
The old values of agricultural-village communal life must yield to modern goal-directed efficiency, yet they have not been replaced by any
effective models capable of giving rural community life a valid orientation. Reason alone is incapable of giving a village community the feeling
of belonging together. Likewise, the new branch bank in the village is
not felt to be a replacement for the focal center of village life found in the
church.

What is obviously lacking is an attitude through which traditional
village life and its nonmaterial values can be reconciled with the
undeniable values of an approach to life based on reason. However,
such an attitude is necessary not just to enable the indigenous rural
population to participate in the development of recent years without
losing their roots. Politicians, officials, consultants, engineers, planners, and scientists, too, who are involved with rural social issues,
need to acknowledge and comprehend this problem of opposites in a
fundamental way. For if seen only from the materialistic viewpoint,

---

[16]See, for example, J. Nussbaumer, "Die Lebensverhältnisse der Bauernfamilien in
Homburgertal," dissertation at the Federal Institute of Technology (ETH), Zürich,
1963, p. 153; U. Jaeggi, *Berggemeinden im Wandel*, Bern, 1965, p. 261; A. Dönz, "Die
Veranderung in der Berglandwirtschaft am Beispiel des Vorderprättigaus," dissertation at the Federal Institute of Technology (ETH), Zürich, 1971; F. Gerber, "Wandel
im ländlichen Leben, eine sozialökonomische und sozialpsychologische Untersuchung fünf Gemeinden des Oberemmentals," dissertation at the Federal Institute
of Technology, Bern, 1974, p. 311, and Th. Locher, "Bindung und Freiheit im bäuer-
lichen Leben," dissertation at the Federal Institute of Technology, Zürich, 1978, p. 62,
156ff, 176.

life will always remain second-rate in remote rural and particularly agricultural communities, despite all the technological improvements and all the measures directed toward rationalization. Since a purely rational and materialistic approach to life is furthered by thinking in statistical comparisons, and since indigenous values of rural life are simultaneously pushed to the side as obstacles to progress, we have little hope of putting a stop to the vicious circle of migration from the country to the urban areas. With such a one-sided attitude we would actually have to set aside the peripheral areas simply for "utilization as recreation areas," as the regional planner characteristically says— recreation areas for the city dweller.

The above is an outline of the major aspects of the rural social problem. Before we go on to define the questions that have emerged, we want to look more closely at that sector which has been most upset by these socioeconomic changes: agriculture. The profound dilemma between traditional and modern forms of life can be shown most clearly in the change in agricultural methods. We shall therefore go into this subject in more detail.

Agriculture under the Pressure of Industrialization

The Farmer between Peasantry and Agribusiness

It is probably the farmers who most intensely experience the tension between tradition and progress. They are under pressure to rationalize, mechanize, and specialize, but they experience daily how nature obeys its own laws. Regardless of technology and mechanization, weather, animals, plants, and soil are changed by forces that are beyond our control. Between the pressure for modernization and the calculations of applied economics on one side and the compelling laws of overpowering nature on the other stands today's farmer.

Generally speaking, it was not primarily love of the new but purely a question of survival that brought the farmer, conservative by nature, to abandon original ways of farming in favor of making a farm an operation, an enterprise, a business. "The heart of a peasant, the head and hands of an entrepreneur"—that would be a way of describing the tension, actually the inner emotional strife for the peasant who reluctantly "internally upgrades" a no-longer profitable small farm with a laying battery for hens.

But how do we understand the term "peasant," or, rather, what are the distinctive characteristics of "being a peasant?" "For thousands of years," Albert Hauser writes, "it was a pious maxim to live in harmony with nature, *'secundum naturam.'* "[17] When Placide Rambaud speaks of the "archetyp paysan,"[18] the *secundum naturam* is doubtless a central characteristic of what originally pertained to the peasant mentality. Schmidt has pertinently delineated the tradition-conscious farmer type "of the old school": "The farmer of earlier times was subject to Nature, bound to the soil. He exhausted his strength in the battle with the obstacles of the earth, with the inclemency of the weather; he was totally taken up by his attempt to ensure that his harvest met the needs of the members of his household. . . ." This original mode of farming, which we could find up until recently in out-of-the-way Alpine valleys, "had strong support in the farmers' respect for tradition."[19] Not that this original peasantry existed in anything we could call an ideal state, as the city dweller fed up with our civilization would like to believe! In tradition-conscious peasant societies, too, there are shadow sides and hence also people who are bound to experience them. Here we find the day laborers, farmhands, maids, children in service, and unmarried mothers. Yet what distinguishes the traditional peasant life from the idealizations is precisely its submission to nature. They were thankful to nature for the food she had produced. For in the experience of primal peoples, food always meant life itself.[20] For this reason the earliest divinities in all human cultures were plant and animal divinities.[21] How easily the entire basis of life could be destroyed by weather, illness, and epidemic.[22] People were totally dependent on plants and animals, and so they did everything necessary for them to thrive. The knowledge for this was handed down from generation to generation, manifesting itself in regional customs and traditions.

The peasant was thus originally bound by tradition, adapting carefully to natural processes and gratefully accepting nature's products. Evidence of this is the well-known harvest festivals in our country; but let us also not forget the rich custom among the Alpine herders of

---

[17]A. Hauser, *Bauernregeln*, loc. cit., p. 61.

[18]P. Rambaud, "Organisation du travail agraire et identities collectives," speech delivered at the XI Congress for Rural Sociology, Helsinki, 1981.

[19]G. C. J. Schmidt, *Der Schweizer Bauer im Zeitalter des Frühkapitalismus*, vol. 1, Bern, 1935, p. 35ff; quoted from Albert Hauser, "Bäuerliche Leitideen im Wandel der Geschichte," reprinted in the *Festschrift for Hans Bach*, Agrarpolitik, Landentwicklung und Umweltschutz, Vienna and New York, 1982, p. 74.

[20]Thus even today in India a bowl of milk means life itself for countless people.

[21]This holds true from the Arctic to Africa and from Central America to East Asia. I am indebted to Dr. Marie-Louise von Franz for this reference.

[22]A document worth reading in this connection is: Jakob Stutz, *Sieben mal sieben Jahre aus meinem Leben*, Winterthur, 1960 (originally 1853).

venerating the basis of their life, the cow.[23] To be perpetually at the
mercy of nature's whims, to feel forever anxious and to worry
whether or not there will be enough food – this awakens the perfectly
understandable longing for deliverance from dependence on nature.

By careful study of nature's hidden laws, humanity is ever more
successful in liberating itself from numerous external natural constraints. Indeed, today humanity appears even to have succeeded in
creating a *"natura secundum hominem."* "Today, mankind can, at will,
melt down and recast Nature right down to her material and vital
core. She is unveiled, deciphered, seen through, and can be formulated and manipulated. We no longer experience her, as did our predecessors, as a majestic system of pre-existing, lawful, and meaningful order. There are no more secrets to make us shudder and fill us
with awe because Nature is no longer experienced as a numinous
secret."[24] Modern mankind is no longer afraid of nature; we believe
we are her master. With this, the general attitude toward tilling the
soil has changed, too. For the modern mentality, the soil, plants, and
animals no longer represent a confrontation for mankind and no
longer inspire reverence. They are now solely raw material. This
modern viewpoint also makes possible agriculture as a "business" –
utilization of the ground through rationally and industrially operated
plant and animal production.

In this general transformation of attitude toward tilling the soil,
Switzerland is not exceptional. In our country the farmers find themselves somewhere between the primordial image of the peasant who
must adapt to nature and the modern image of the enterprising agro-
businessman who has, and must have, an eye toward optimal yield.
Farmers suffer from these tensions, even if in numerous cases they
only vaguely sense them. Yet before we go into this question further,
we must ask how did it reach the point where agriculture faces this
dilemma between traditional farming and industrial agroproduction.

Change in Swiss Agriculture

The necessity for cultivating the soil on an increasingly industrial
basis is closely linked with the drop in agricultural prices. Prices

---

[23]Cow decorations, ritual food for cows, etc.; in his investigation, Paul Hugger writes
that the basis or inner motivation for the festive parades of cattle in the Swiss mountain regions is "the love of the animal, for without them there can be no such
parades." (Paul Hugger, *Hirtenleben und Hirtenkultur im Waadtländer Jura*, SGV, Krebs
Verlag, Basel, 1972, p. 138.)
[24]Quoted from A. Hauser (1982), p. 74.

declined principally with the improvement in transport routes and the concomitant beginnings of competition from cheap imports. Switzerland's agriculture often being disadvantaged by geographical location, corresponding upheavals followed in the wake of the collapse of prices. Migration from the increasingly unprofitable farms to expanding industries offering attractive wages was an important consequence. Next to protectionist and organizational measures for the protection of domestic agricultural production,[25] there was the possibility of countering the collapse of agricultural prices through increasing productivity. People hoped that in this way the farmer could finally develop an income that to some extent corresponded to that of the industrial worker. The means of increasing productivity are well known: ready-made industrial products such as artificial fertilizer, sprays, and machines; structural alterations (such as improvements, extensions and expansions); better breeding techniques for plants and animals; and, of course, improved education and efficiency for the farmer himself.

Where the requisites for these improvements were present, the goals were attained. Thanks to the aids mentioned above, it has been possible to increase agricultural productivity in Switzerland, especially since the Second World War, to an extent never known before.[26] As a consequence, the farmer's standard of living has risen considerably. However, this has effectively reduced the income differential between agricultural and nonagricultural activity only for some farmers.[27] For those whose operations that were not already large enough or whose land was less well suited for mechanization, productivity could be increased correspondingly less well. Consequently, many such small and midsized operations could no longer support their owners and were either given up entirely or carried on only as sidelines. The accelerated decline in the number of agricultural operations since the Second World War reflects this change in Swiss agriculture (see figure 3).

In 1980, there were only half as many farms as at the turn of the century. As many farms were given up, the remaining farms, of course, were able to increase their acreage, which in turn had beneficial effects on their productivity.[28] Yet not all operations had the

---

[25]In this connection see the overview by Robert Jörin, "Parastaatliche Organisationen im Agrarsektor," in: *Zeitschrift der SGA*, 2/80, p. 10ff.

[26]See also the fifth agricultural report, Bern, 1976, p. 22ff.

[27]Op. cit., p. 52.

[28]Especially the number of operations of 20 to 50 hectares has increased greatly since 1955 (1955 to 1965 sS + 24%, 1965 to 1975 SS + 42%SS), cf. loc. cit., p. 10.

Figure 3. Decrease in the Number of Agricultural Operations in Switzerland

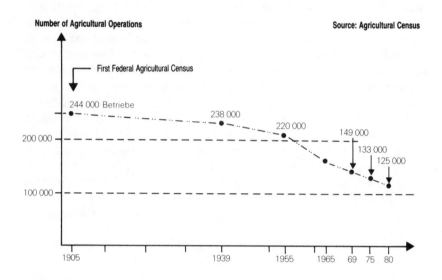

opportunity to increase in size to the extent that introduction of machinery would be profitable. Especially for farms with topographically unfavorable conditions, the income level continued to remain unsatisfactory. Thus in spite of massive rationalization measures in our agriculture, countless small and medium-sized farms can still survive today only because they live off their assets. Their meager earnings do not suffice for the most urgent reinvestments, for example, keeping the buildings in repair! In recent years, constantly increasing federal subsidies to agriculture have had little effect. In Canton Uri alone in 1976, it was ascertained that there was a pressing need for investment in building construction amounting to SF232 million.[29] If one day major investments in buildings must finally be made, the farmer has been compelled to go into debt. "That's why," explained an aide for Paul Hugger during his investigations in Waadtland, "many farmers would rather sell and have done with it

---

[29]See Th. Abt, et al., *Aufrüstungsprogramm für die Urner Landwirtschaft und Forstwirtschaft*, Institut für Agrarwissenschaft, Federal Institute of Technology (ETH) Zürich, 1979, p. 48.

than plague themselves for the rest of their days with the tough questions of investment and repayment of debt."[30]

Where a farm was not sold, people usually have gone into debt in order to carry out modernizations. The consequence of this has been the burden of higher interest rates and hence pressure for greater productivity. These, in turn, were possible only through mechanization. The agrarian life style has thus changed fundamentally. After all, mechanization was usually also an answer to the great decrease in agricultural workers. In many places, as we all know, it was not only the nonfamily workers who left the farm but family members, too. The result of this development is the so-called one-man operation common today, which has brought a new way of working and living for the farmer.

Mechanization has indeed compensated for the decline in the work force. Yet even in structurally healthy operations, the stresses of daily work have often increased rather than decreased in spite of mechanization, especially where the operation is growing.[31] In one-person dairy operations, the predominant sort of operation today in our mountain and hill areas threatened with migration, workdays of 13 to 14 hours are very common. Now, however, it is not solely the long working hours, as A. Dönz determined, that are burdensome, but rather "being tied down, the necessity, the pressure, day-in and day-out, weekdays and Sundays, year-in and year-out, to be on the job. For many it is impossible to get away from the farm for even a short time."[32] In his study of farm work in Appenzell-Innerhoden, F. Fuchs used the expression "torture operation" or *Quälbetrieb*.[33] And on the basis of his investigations in the Bernese Oberland, U. Jaeggi speaks specifically of the small farmer's and mountain farmer's chronic overexertion.[34] This excessive work load stands in direct relation to an equally difficult problem: many farm operators in such small farms cannot find a wife—or find time to look for a wife.[35]

In spite of mechanization, the work load has not really diminished, neither on the dairy farms in the hill and mountain areas, nor on many

---

[30]P. Hugger, "Das Nein zur Scholle," *Regio Basiliensis* XI/1, Basel, 1970, p. 28.

[31]See A. Hauser (1973), p. 52.

[32]See A. Dönz (1972), p. 172ff.

[33]P. Ferdinand Fuchs, *Bauernarbeit im Appenzell-Innerhoden*, Basel, 1977 (*Schriften der SGV*, vol. 61), p. 219; cf. also Priebe, *Landwirtschaft in der Welt von morgen*, Düsseldorf, Vienna, 1970, p. 105.

[34]U. Jaeggi (1965), p. 259.

[35]Information concerning the extent of the high number of single persons in the agricultural population in the chill and mountain regions can be found in Ch. Darbellay's dissertation, Federal Institute of Technology, Zürich, 1980.

farms in the plains. In Hugger's study mentioned above, one farmer characterized the change in the farmer's work methods thus: "The day's work doesn't last longer, but it is more tiring and taxing. . . . The work climate has changed. You used to work quietly, in the peace and quiet of the countryside. Now you continually have the roar of machines around you. People have become nervous."[36] Jakob Nussbaumer describes the work of farmers in his youth as "noiseless working with living things." He continues, "I like to remember the almost contemplative work with axe and saw during winter forest work and compare that with the screaming of the now common chain saw."[37] Today in the mechanized everyday life of the farmer there reigns a widespread "shortness of breath."[38] Even the winter rest period, which once upon a time served for regeneration and reflection, has for the most part melted away in the modern agricultural operation.

However much the change in agriculture just described has brought about advantages from the material standpoint, the consequences of this change for the agrarian life-style or *Läbtig*, as we say in Switzerland, are of just as much concern. For people are perpetually exposed to such excessive work stresses, the recuperation and relaxation necessary for this sort of work is insufficient. A continuously heavy work load ultimately leads to tension, and the fundamental mood of a farmer's daily life is changed. How easily a feeling of dissatisfaction and bitterness can arise when farm folk, returning home exhausted and tired on a summer's evening, see how the non-farmers can take it easy lounging in front of their houses.[39]

Unlike the countless farmers of today, people a few decades ago had time, or they took time. "There are," as A. Hauser writes, "countless direct and indirect pieces of evidence. They took breaks, which people today shorten or forego entirely."[40] Thus an older farm woman in the Appenzell area said, "It used to be when we did the haymaking that we'd eat together in the field, or we'd sit around of an evening with the neighbors. Today you don't have time for that any more."[41] In the same

---

[36]P. Hugger, p. 26.

[37]J. Nussbaumer, "Brennpunkte bäuerlicher Lebensgestaltung," in *Die Grüne*, no. 45, 29 October 1976, p. 17.

[38]See A. Hauser, "Leitideen des Bauerntums im Wandel der Zeit," in *Die Grüne*, no. 45, 29 October 1976, p. 6.

[39]See Hugger, p. 27.

[40]See A. Hauser, *Bauernregeln*, p. 53.

[41]A. Wetter, "Auswirkungen des Strukturwandels in der landwirtschaft auf die Besiedlung der landwirtschaftlichen Räume und die wirtschaftliche Tätigkeit," diploma thesis for the Institut für Agrarwirtschaft, Federal Institute of Technology (ETH), Zürich, 1981, p. 70.

region a farmer stated, "If you have more and more cattle (thanks to the expansion of the operation and mechanization), there's no time left to see the beauty of the farm. You don't find the time to delight in a blossoming tree. There's no time to watch the cattle. . . ."[42]

As Albert Hauser states, "it is above all the customs that have fallen victim to the new concept of time. In a study of the Baselbiet folk life, an old informant said that, of course, there were still families who followed the old ways, sticking a branch on the last load of hay they drove home. " 'They still take it easy.' But otherwise this custom has fallen victim to the pressure of time."[43] As there is less and less time for cultivating "useless" peasant customs, a piece of peasant identity and quality of life is lost, a piece of the life of the soul and of the community. Hence what Hugger, somewhat exaggeratedly, says of peasant culture is true for many areas in Switzerland: "Is there a peasant culture? Was there ever a peasant culture? Say what one will, it existed in the past. . . . It existed in its regional forms and with its strong seasonal variations characterized by a wisdom that generations had gleaned from nature, trusting in fate with a relationship to their own soil bordering on the religious. . . . Today this culture has disintegrated, perished in the noise of mechanization, displaced by modern farming."[44] Even in mountainous regions similar findings have been made. On the basis of his studies in lower Prättigau, A. Dönz speaks of a weakening of the cultural life and of village community. In the wake of the mechanization of the day-to-day work on the farm, the formerly active peasant cultural creativity has, to a large extent, turned into passive consumption.[45] In the early 1960s J. Nussbaumer had the same findings in his studies of the living conditions of rural families in the Homburg valley. "They limit themselves to the materialistic; they now do only what is profitable. Agrarian values have become shallow and hollow, family and village life have atrophied."[46] Increasingly even in agrarian rural communities, the communal village culture has been overlaid with the individualistic culture of industrial society. The social event of the milk payday has fallen by the wayside because the milk bill is paid through the bank.[47] The evenings playing *jass*, a Swiss card game, have been given up

---

[42]loc. cit.
[43]From Eduard Strübin, *Baselbieter Volksleben*, Basel, 1952, p. 61, quoted from Hauser, loc. cit.
[44]Hugger (1970), p. 35f.
[45]A. Dönz (1972), p. 177.
[46]Nussbaumer (1963), p. 167.
[47]A. Wetter (1981).

because today everyone has a TV.[48] Public works fall into disrepair
because more and more people are looking out only for themselves.[49]

Thus in recent years, the agrarian way of life has fundamentally
changed in Switzerland. Agriculture has adapted itself increasingly to
the modern economic order. We appear to be approaching that goal
which progressive agrarian sociologists such as H. Kötter have
demanded we strive toward: "Finally the modern farmer must be led
out of his idealistic attitudes and brought to mechanization and
rationalization, to sober calculation and to thinking in terms of business economics."[50] Agricultural schooling has contributed significantly to the transformation demanded of the agrarian way of thinking. One of Paul Hugger's interviewees describes this influence of
agricultural schooling aptly: "The young peasants have a love for
their soil, their farm; in contrast they are taught at agricultural schools
to consider their soil a utility and their farm a factory." As illustration
of this change in thinking, he refers to the magnificent old trees that
set the character of the landscape and to which the peasants are often
very attached. "Trees that do not produce should be felled, according
to the teachings of the agricultural schools."[51] A judgment based on
feeling is cast aside as outmoded. A modern farmer shouldn't let
himself be guided by sentimental reflections. In order to survive, he
must let himself be guided wholly according to economic viewpoints;
"love for the object has lost all importance."[52]

To cope with the whole transformation, the peasants had to become
entrepreneurs. They had to learn to work with a sharp pencil and be
ready to accept innovations. They often saw themselves forced to
accept modern forms of production that went against the peasant
sensibility. Among these are maintaining large herds of cattle and
intensive orchard cultivation, artificial insemination, the use of poisons and mechanization in general. In order to remain at all competitive, peasants saw themselves forced away from the peasant archetype toward acceptance of the time and work concept of the industrial

---

[48]R. Abt, "Arbeiterbauerntum in Schächental," dissertation, University of Zürich,
1975.

[49]T. Abt, "Was sind die Ueberlebenschancen des kulturellen Erbes im Lötschenthal?,"
thesis, Federal Technical University, Zürich, 1972. E. Messmer comes to similar conclusions in regard to Scharans (Graubünden) in Scharans, eine Gemeindestudie aus der
Gegenwart, Publications of the SGV, vol. 59, Basel, 1976, p. 71.

[50]Quoted from Hauser, "Entmythologisierung der Landwirtschaft," in Agr. pol. Revue,
no. 204, Jan. 1967, p. 186.

[51]Here we are reminded of the agricultural policy of the late sixties intended to remove
solitary old fruit trees by paying farmers a premium for them.

[52]Quoted from Hugger, op. cit., p. 29.

world. All the empirical rationality of their predecessors, the entire *"mémoire collective"* of their particular area, all the wisdom of their ancestors embodied in the rules, usages, and rites, and all the structures of the land developed and cultivated—all that was largely given up or pushed aside, "in many places quite readily," as A. Hauser observed.[53] Thus the old yardsticks and guidelines were exchanged for the widely publicized and clearly convincing increase in productivity. Instead of custom and respect for superior forces, reason and yield became the measure of things. While in earlier times the rule was that "The measure of all things is man, the measure of man is God and nature" (W. Röpke), in contemporary Swiss agriculture the second part of this rule is increasingly absent. The result of a generally increasing secularization is that the measure of a human being has become the person driven by cravings—with boundless, self-willed, utilitarian thinking.

Torn between Tradition and Progress

The peasant has surrendered, forgotten, repressed, or destroyed— or as the case may be—has been forced to surrender and destroy old ways in favor of technological progress. The importance attached to respect for and belief in the knowledge handed down from the ancestors has been replaced by the harsh light of reason, embodied in natural science and engineering. Short-term concern for yield has, to a large extent, replaced thinking in terms of generations. This reorganization of agriculture according to industrial principles has, however, taken its toll. Not only has agrarian life become more hectic in the wake of rationalization and mechanization, but the enormous increase in productivity has also brought the problems of agrochemistry and of overproduction. To this is added the oppressive isolation of those who have remained behind in many rural areas. All this has led to new dependencies: on the world market; on state intervention in the agricultural market; on state regional policy; on natural science, technology, and industry; on subsidies and the associated regulations; and by no means lastly, on one's own powers of decision and adaptation to the often rapidly changing conditions for agricultural production.

More than ten years ago F. T. Wahlen had clearly and explicitly pointed out the dangers of a one-sided focus on yield. He aptly

---

[53]Hauser, "Leitideen des Bauerntums im Wandel der Zeit," in *Die Grüne*, no. 45, Oct. 29, 1976.

described the general goal of increased productivity as a "productivity fetishism."[54] Since then, the justification for this expression has become ever more apparent. In agriculture as in the whole economy, people have let themselves be blinded by this one particular aspect of progress—in point of fact much as a fetish—and today have had a rude awakening. The grave problems that have been caused by increasing agricultural productivity can today no longer be talked out of existence. Catch-words like "poison in our food" appear not only in the tabloids. The strain on the environment due to agrochemistry and monoculture is no longer the concern of just a few environmentalists; and problems like maintaining large herds, overproduction, and the so-called "unhealthy shrinkage" of agriculture have in recent years become topics for highly explosive political debates.[55] That the problems of increased productivity are not only of national but worldwide magnitude must be emphasized.[56]

These problems of increased productivity, which are becoming ever more apparent, have repercussions in agriculture. The consumer who yesterday compelled agriculture into a forced industrialization with his vehement demands for the cheapest possible foods, today demands a form of agriculture sensitive to the environment and foods as free as possible from poisons.[57] This has provoked deep insecurity in the farmer. On the one hand, through his own labors—and that means increased productivity—he is supposed to earn a sufficient income and thus cost the state as little as possible. On the other hand, the form of agriculture forced on him by society brings him the very reproaches mentioned. Until very recently the requirement was that Swiss farmers, like their bigger counterparts in the U.S.A., till their fields in a mechanically optimal way. Hence they removed those living hedges and fruit trees standing in the path of mechanization, drained unproductive wetland meadows and swamps, and channeled brooks. They thus improved the profitability of their farms as had been demanded. But for their labors the farmers suddenly harvested reproach for placing stress on the environment and for the

---

[54]Wahlen, "Stellung und Rolle der Landwirtschaft in der heutigen Gesellschaft," address on the occasion of the centennial of the Department of Agriculture of the Federal Technical University, Zürich, published in the *Bulletin des SVIAL*, no. 160, Zollikofen, 1971.

[55]See also Darbellay, *Agriculture et Societe—un nouveau contrat*, Charrat, 1981, for his statement of the problem.

[56]The European Common Market spends approximately one third of its entire budget for agriculture and most of that for the costs and consequences of overproduction.

[57]The strong growth of an agricultural "submarket" for organic products is one sign of increasing consumer displeasure with the quality of agricultural products.

effects of agrochemistry, as well as for laying waste the landscape.[58] The farmer is supposed to care for an unspoilt, charming environment and produce top quality products. But whenever the price for a staple food is to be raised a few pennies, the consumers' representatives bitterly oppose it.

As we have seen, the work load in agriculture is already significantly greater than in other occupations. In addition, earnings are often very modest in spite of increases in productivity. Now on top of all this comes the insecurity concerning agrochemistry, overproduction, vanishing resistance to diseases in animals, etc., not to mention the high costs of agriculture to the state. The consequence of this insecurity is a deep mistrust on the part of many farmers vis-à-vis all that "comes from above," be it from the state, from scientists, planners and experts, or from engineers. We can recognize this profound malaise in Swiss agrarian circles in various complaints that admittedly are usually concerned with an external problem.[59] The spectrum of complaints extends from parliamentary campaigns to more physical demonstrations with chickens and tractors in front of the House of Parliament.

Despite well-intentioned recognition of agrarian concerns on the part of their fellow citizens, farmers have a growing feeling of being patronized, of being outvoted by the majority. First of all, this feeling is nourished by the perpetual struggle over prices for major agricultural products. Here the farmer, unlike the worker or the employee, is not confronted by an employer but stands, as it were, vis-à-vis the entire remaining population. But even, say, in regional planning, the farmer suddenly sees himself confronted by an overpowering, so-called "public interest." Here, too, he is threatened with being outvoted, which naturally contributes significantly to his insecurity.[60] As illustration, the following comes from a report by Pfenninger, Director of the Agricultural Office of the Canton of Zürich.[61]

> *The preservation of at least some village farmers lies in the interests of every community. They assist in the preservation of the least expensive green areas that today are supposed to be created everywhere. The planning authorities take little thought of these questions. In many of*

---

[58]In the Federal Republic of Germany there is currently the concept of the "green scapegoats."

[59]Concerning the unrest among farmers see the the emotional tract by W. Wütherich, *Vom Land—Berichte*, Zürich, 1979.

[60]See Locher (1977), p. 171.

[61]Pfenninger, "Raumplanung gegen Landwirtschaft," in the *Zürichseezeitung*, no. 288, Dec. 11, 1981, p. 7.

the extensive reports on overall plans, agriculture is not mentioned at all or only peripherally. On the other hand, zone limits, regardless of ownership and the consequences for the farmers affected, are blithely planned and drawn up. Without consulting the owners, broad recreation areas for sports facilities, family gardens, public lands, parks, playing and sports areas, parking lots, fire stations, etc., are designated. The municipalities are instructed to procure these areas for the designated use, and should the land not yet belong to the public domain, they are to obtain it. Nobody appears to be concerned that this partially or totally deprives the farmers tilling this land of the basis for their existence.

Of course, the conditions of land-utilization planning vary from canton to canton. What our example is intended to illustrate is a general tendency of disposing of the farmer more and more at the public will. This becomes particularly evident in certain federal norms, regulations, and directives that are linked to individual government subsidies and felt to irritate and disenfranchise the farmers—for example, the funds for building new stalls in mountain area barns.[62]

In reaction to feeling thus overruled, the view has circulated both within and outside of the agrarian sector that agrarian independence should be strengthened. Yet among farmers themselves there is no agreement on the guidelines to be adopted.[63] On one hand, voices argue for even more scientific and technical progress in agriculture. Thus one French-Swiss farmer stormed, "In the United States . . . the animal breeders go a lot further. There all the data are already stored in a computer program. Even the feeding of herds. Almost everything happens by electronics because that gets better results. . . . Today you can just about plan on paper a cow with such and such characteristics and milk production and ultimately breed her. But the gentlemen in Bern haven't yet understood that here. . . . They don't want any development in our agriculture."[64] Believers in progress like this French-Swiss farmer are convinced that, through more refined techniques, genetic manipulation, and the like, it is possible to improve the prosperity and thereby the image of agriculture. At the same time, they assure themselves that further progress will solve the

---

[62]See Dönz (1972), p. 158.
[63]That a valid guiding image for Swiss agriculture is lacking has been repeatedly stated in various quarters, e.g., at the 1982 conference of the Swiss Society for Agricultural Sciences and Agrarian Sociology in Châteauneuf.
[64]Quoted in Wütherich (1979), p. 94.

Agriculture between peasantry and agribusiness: Does progress have to destroy feeling, *joi d'vivre*, and the relationship to animals and the land?

environmental problems which have been caused by modern methods of farming. "If only they would finally understand. . . ."

Opposed to these extreme beliefs in progress we find equally extreme voices prompted by a "longing for pre-modern structures."[65] These opponents of a further technologizing of agriculture see the right path, the necessary alternative, in a return to small-scale agricultural practices in harmony with nature. Hence the one group advocates continued progress, wanting to get a grip on nature and failing to see that nature is always the stronger and tends to go her own way. In contrast, for the second group "progress" is the root of all troubles;

[65]Dahrendorf, *Lebenschancen, Anläufe zur sozialen und politischen Theorie,* Frankfurt, 1979, p. 143.

they forget that it is due to the progress in natural science and technology that famine, pestilence, poverty of the masses, and wild superstition are no longer a part of everyday life.

These opposing views of agriculture are reflected especially clearly in the question of the size of agricultural operations. While the one group regards a certain operation size as reasonable and accepts expansion as sometimes necessary for optimal utilization of machinery,[66] there are others who are of the opinion that supporting larger operations is wrong.[67] Instead of large-scale farming, the latter group advocates "small is beautiful." That these two tendencies exist together in Switzerland was shown particularly clearly in the founding in 1980 of an Association for the Protection of Small and Medium-sized Agricultural Operations (*Vereinigung zum Schutz der kleinen und mittleren Landwirtschaftsbetriebe = VKMB*). The Association arose outside of the Swiss Farmers' League, and forms a united front opposing an agricultural policy supporting large-scale farming.[68] The Association found a considerable response both within and outside of agri-

---

[66]For example, Jean-Claude Piot, Director of the Federal Agricultural Office, in the volume celebrating the centenary of his Office, "Les limites de l'interventionnisme dan la politique agricole suisse," Berne, 1982.

[67]See Congressman Urs Nussbaumer's worthwhile article, "Bauernstand zwischen Freiheit und Dirigismus," in the *Neue Zürcher Zeitung*, Nov. 6, 1982.

[68]The "list of complaints" of the VKMB is clearly expressed in the goals of the organization (Article 2 of the Statutes, Feb. 21, 1982, revised version). In its activities it pursues the goal of influencing Swiss agricultural policy in the following ways:

a) The number of independently run farms in Switzerland should be stabilized. The continuing decimation should be halted.

b) The families that operate these farms should receive an income from the sale of their products and from direct payments out of public funds, which assures their livelihood and provides them with working and living conditions comparable to those of other groups in the population.

c) Income differences in agriculture should be reduced to the extent that they result from differing conditions of production (e.g., size of operation, elevation, etc.). This should be attained through the utilization and just distribution of public funds strictly on the basis of need. Public funds should be distributed without regard to size of operation.

d) In the distribution of public funds, those who pursue farming as a second occupation should be treated the same as those who pursue farming as a primary occupation.

e) The agriculturally usable areas in Switzerland should be preserved as much as humanly possible. The independent owner-farmer should have precedence in the ownership of agricultural land. Through this an ordered cultivation of our land should be achieved that serves both farmers and the general public.

f) So far as at all possible, domestic agricultural production should be given precedence over imported foods and animal feeds.

In order to achieve these goals, the Association exerts all permissible efforts within the limits of the federal constitution and laws and supports the efforts of other organizations with similar goals.

cultural circles. This fact is viewed as an indication that farmers have lost a degree of confidence in their established, official representatives and in the federal system.[69]

Obviously the same problem emerges in the agriculture that we encountered at the end of our consideration of the vicious circle of migration. What is lacking is a unifying concept and a guiding image through which farmers guided by tradition—in the sense of *hominus secundum naturam*—and modern agricultural science can come together in a fruitful union. In order to strengthen the independence of agriculture (and, of course, of rural areas in general), we must develop a guiding image which has a "unifying effect." However, it must be able to unite not only the opposing standpoints among farmers themselves, but also to reconcile the factors that divide farmers and nonfarmers, indeed, city and country. This brings us to a central question: what is the condition of the relationship between farmers and nonfarmers, and between city and country in general? For the rural population and especially agriculture are increasingly dependent on the nature of the city-country relationship, in the material as well as in the spiritual and cultural realm.

---

[69]In the arguments advanced by the representatives by the VKMB, trade unions and organizations appeared to be relatively out of touch with the farmers. *Neue Zürcher Zeitung*, no. 167, July 22, 1982, p. 33.

Chapter 2

The Disturbed Relationship between the Country and the City[1]

The farmer—"the underdog of society," observed A. Bodenstedt of the Institute for Agrarian Sociology in Giessen (Federal Republic of Germany).[2] Even if not put so bluntly, Swiss studies[3] have nevertheless shown that in various regions there predominates among farmers a feeling that they "have become the pariahs of modern society."[4] In many places the farmer feels at a disadvantage and inferior. This feeling of being second-class is not simply pure imagination, but rather rests on a widespread and deep-rooted point of view according to which farming ranks lowest in the hierarchy of forms of employment.

At the beginning of the last century, even in the country, agricultural work was already felt to be second-rate. "The stronger cottage industry became and the more pay it promised good years, so much the greater was the self-confidence of those engaged in industrial activities. Gradually individuals began to ridicule farmers because of their hard work and exposure to the whims of climate. "They laughed at the farmer and his sweat."[5] "The Zürich Oberland cottage workers," wrote Pastor von Wildberg, "wantonly scorn or despise the

---

[1]The problems in delimiting city from country will be discussed later.
[2]A. Bodenstedt, "Housewives in Rural Households," address delivered at the XI European Congress for Rural Sociology, Helsinki, 1981.
[3]Nussbaumer (1963), Jaeggi (1965), Dönz (1972), Locher (1977), "Establishing an 'ideologically outmoded self-image' as in the instance of numerous Bavarian farmers (Ziche, 1968) can be confirmed only in scattered instances in Switzerland." (Gerber, 1964, p. 215f., and Hugger, 1970).
[4]Hugger (1970), p. 34.
[5]A. Bolliger, "Die zürcherische Landschaft an der Wende des 18. Jahrhunderts," Zürich, 1941, p. 54, cited from A. Hauser, *Feld und Wald in der alten Schweiz*, Zürich, 1972, p. 208.

peasant who bears the day's burden and heat."[6] Only in areas with little industry and relatively little tourism, such as upper Emmental and in certain Alpine valleys, has this devaluation of the agrarian way of life not taken place.[7] In this century the devaluation of farm work has changed little. Up until not too long ago it was customary in many places to pass the parents' homestead on to the dumbest member in the family.[8] In his 1975 studies of choice of agrarian occupation, Th. Locher established that complaints were increasing that those in authority such as teachers and career counselors, were advising against the occupation of farming. "A smart fellow like you should learn a proper trade," said a teacher to a young farmer, for example.[9]

As Hugger has aptly observed, nonfarmers and city dwellers protest against farmers being treated with contempt; they feel this reproach is unjustified. "But nonetheless the farmer is looked down on; he is regarded as lacking in refinement, coarse, certainly cunning, but with limited horizons."[10] Rating agriculture as well as peripherally situated communities as second-rate is particularly obvious whenever the conversation is about those who have remained behind in the country working in agriculture — in contrast to those who have moved away. Just as in school when the "dumb" ones lag behind and must repeat grades, a similar prejudice echoes unconsciously in the expression "those who have remained behind in the country working in agriculture," as though such people were examples of negative selection. The bright ones moved on! The frequency of the expression "those who have remained behind" reveals to us the deeprootedness of this stereotyping of the country and agriculture as second-rate[11] in our society. Even the most recent German-language textbook of rural and agrarian sociology speaks of the regions that "remained behind," designating by this expression those rural areas that have not yet been developed and are economically weak.[12]

What characterizes those people who have intentionally remained in their rural community or in agriculture, especially those who could

---

[6]J. C. Hirzel, synod speech of 1816, Zürich, 1816, p. 12, quoted from Hauser.
[7]Wyder (1971), Hugger (1973), Gerber (1974), R. Abt (1976).
[8]See Brugger, "Die Landflucht der Begabten," *Allgemeine Zeitschrift für Psychiatrie und ihre Grenzgebiete*, 112 (1939), p. 337–348.
[9]Locher (1977), p. 94; Gerber (1964), p. 216, notes similarly: "Still today people speak of farmers who let some or all of their sons learn 'nothing.' They are the ones who then became farmers." (Cf. Albert Ilien and Utz Jeggle, *Leben auf dem Dorf*, 1978, p. 100.)
[10]Hugger (1970), p. 33.
[11]We understand stereotyping to mean firmly established, schematic, verbalized images of other groups and their members not based on personal experience. Definition according to Planck and Ziche (1979), p. 120.
[12]Planck and Ziche (1979), p. 27.

have had opportunities for a more comfortable life? One characteristic of these people certainly must be their attachment to the ancestral environment, an attachment to a place and to the soil. This attachment to a locality contains precisely the element of steadfastness, of holding out, of being undynamic and hence of being backward, or remaining behind.

The view of attachment to the soil and locality as being something backward is comprehensible in terms of social history. Along with certain pains of separation, the separation of individuals from their attachment to the parental home, the clan, and the community always has something liberating about it similar to a child's maturation. For this reason, separation from dependent attachment to a locality has generally been felt as progress. Along with economic issues, the wish for urban anonymity and lack of restraints has also been an important motive in migration from rural areas. Today freedom from any and all attachment to a locality has even become an important requisite if one wants to get ahead, be it in a modern business or in an academic career. Whenever it appears reasonable, one must be able to change one's place of residence and work, according to the modern manager's motto. It is thus apparent why attachment to the soil has been associated with undynamic backwardness. This attachment to a place is of an irrational nature and hence stands in opposition to reason and will.

Attachment to the soil, then, has for most people the strong overtone of backwardness. Yet people are generally happy that there still are Swiss farmers "faithful to the soil" like those praised, for example, in wine-inspired official speeches. Without a doubt, my neighbor, a distinctly open-minded and critical farmer, noted something essential when he declared, "If we farmers were not so attached to the land, there would be only a fraction of the number of present-day farms."[13] In point of fact, the attachment to the land is a highly significant portent for our rural areas. "In spite of all disadvantages, I wouldn't want to leave," said a woman from Sernf Valley adding the explanation, "It is an inner force that holds me to the mountains, to the landscapes, and to the snow in winter."[14] Particularly in mountain areas there are many people "who remain on the land they grew up on because of resignation and lack of decisiveness."[15] Yet in contrast, we also know of countless extremely ill-situated homesteads, ham-

[13]Conversation dating from 1981.

[14]Eva Buff, et al., *Migration der Frau aus Bergregionen*, Zürich, 1978, p. 119.

[15]Richard Weiss, "Alpiner Mensch und alpines Leben in der Krise der Gegenwart," in *Die Alpen*, 33, 1957, p. 215.

lets, and villages that are still inhabited and worked, not because of the yield but primarily because of attachment to the land. Were it not for the love of the parental homestead and the accustomed surroundings, migration from rural areas and out of agriculture would doubtless have taken on entirely different forms, particularly in times of peak economic prosperity.[16]

What does "attachment to the land" actually mean? How is this relationship to the world of physical objects, the environment, expressed? And how can we understand this phenomenon of undoubtable significance for rural and agrarian sociology? I got my first real awareness of what attachment to the world of objects means in the fundamental sense in a carpentry course at the Heimatwerk School in Richterswil. At the end of the three-week course my workbench neighbor, a mountain farmer from Uri, said, "So, now I've said goodbye to the workbench and the tools, I can go now." In the three weeks there an emotional relationship obviously arose between the mountain farmer and his hand tools—a soul connection that he felt at the end of the course, that he took seriously, and that he accepted without question. For him the workbench and the tools were not merely dead matter; but rather, through the daily contact they had become for him almost a person from whom one takes proper leave before one goes.

The relationship to matter expressed in our example is an aspect of attachment to the land. By that expression we understand an encompassing, emotional attachment to all those things with which one lives, to all that which concretely supports and carries the human being on this earth. Attachment to the land or the locality is, then, a spiritual and emotional phenomenon and signifies an inner union of a person with the land on which he lives and to what that land has brought forth.[17] This extends from the forms of the landscape, including vegetation and the animal world, all the way to the folk culture shaped by the locality—the way of eating and drinking, the clothing, the language, the customs, etc.

To feel bonded to something also means to be bound. One must consequently take these ties into account; one can no longer do as one will. Hence such ties can be associated with backwardness. Modern

---

[16] A 1980–81 study concerning part-time farming embracing all Switzerland carried out by the Institute for Agrarian Science of the Federal Institute of Technology, Zürich, confirmed the significance of attachment to or love of the homestead as the reason for the continued operation of numerous "unprofitable" farms.

[17] R. Weiss said, regarding the often-mentioned local loyalty: "It means not only a spacial and economic, but also a spiritual attachment to the land." (1946, p. 77).

man would like to live as free and unfettered as possible—in every relationship. For this reason, material things—plants, animals, even human beings—figure as statistical units in modern economic thought, interchangeable and replaceable. One speaks of material— production material, genetic material, animal material, and poignantly in certain hospitals of patient material.

The following examples from North America, which we often admire so much, may illustrate how this exclusively economic thinking can appear in rural areas. A Swiss farmer who emigrated to Quebec told me that he was doing his utmost to extract the maximum yield from his farm. He intended eventually to buy another farm somewhere else and do the same thing. He was thinking of spending his retirement in Florida in the sun.[18] A farmer in California on whose farm I spent several months in a practicum told me, "I know that my heavy machinery is destroying my soil and that this way wind erosion carries more and more of my earth away. But it brings cash! My son might have to look for another job."[19] That we in Switzerland are also flirting with this line of thought is shown most impressively in P. Hugger's poll of students at the Marcelin-sur-Morges agricultural school. The students generally supported the idea of gearing agricultural work to yield and profit. "The modern farmer works with capital like any other enterprise. He has to make use of it in the most economical fashion in order to get the most out of it."[20] For modern agribusiness, attachment to the land is unvalued[21]; and there is no demand for the thinking in terms of permanence that goes along with it. If, however, we pursue this one-sided yield-orientation to its logical conclusion, we extract the maximum remaining in our planet— and then sell it.

Freed from irrational attachments to localities, modern man believes himself able to master his life solely by reason and will-power, and thus to find contentment. Farmers and people living in the country are, in his eyes, simply not awake to all the present-day possibilities. Yet paradoxically today we experience a countermovement, coming in fact from urban circles and from America—a countermovement that, to some extent, takes an equally extreme a course. In

---

[18]Conversation dating from 1980.
[19]Conversation dating from 1969.
[20]Hugger (1970), p. 30.
[21]For more on the difference between husbanding the land (*bäuerliche Landwirtschaft*) and technologized farming (*Farmerlandwirtschaft*), see Planck and Ziche (1979), p. 246. The ruthless exploitation of the fertility of the soil has, as is well known, led to the destruction of extensive tracts of farmland in the U.S.A.

contrast to the one-sided striving up and away from any attachment to a rustic, peasant, or agrarian past, one sees a sudden reversal. Complete lack of attachment has been unmasked as a deceptive source for happiness, and a re-evaluation of the lowly has begun. Nostalgia as a cultural mood and the entire movement for an alternative life-style (*Alternativbewegung*) are aspects of this. We are thus confronted with a contradictory sociological phenomenon. On the one hand, things rural, peasant, and agrarian are viewed as lowly and second-rate, from which one must get away in order to be urbanely cultivated in clean surroundings. On the other hand, we find an increasing fascination with the natural, agrarian existence. The unattached, rootless modern person feels a loss, yet does not quite know what is lacking. Nevertheless he somehow senses that what he has lost is to be found in "the despised lowly things."

The equivocal, ambivalent stance of many modern persons toward things rural and agrarian is beautifully illustrated by Hugger. "The same (non-rural) person one is talking with who had previously uttered exalted words on the beauty of things rural and agrarian, can break out in ugly tirades; and the previously noble farmer becomes a perfidious, sly knave."[22] The ambivalence vis-à-vis things rural and primal, however, is expressed not only in such paradoxical eulogistic insults. Even the whole manner in which people attempt to embrace this "lowliness" reveals a mixture of fascination and defensiveness. One would like, for example, a second dwelling in a wild and primal mountain valley, tended and maintained by genuine mountain farmers. Yet the primary residence must be an urban fortress. Not too out-of-the-way, it must be a self-contained unit where one need only turn the key in order to be alone. Naturally the second residence in the wilds has central heating, is hygienically perfect, and has the saving grace of a TV in case the quiet of the valley becomes too eerie. "If one specifically examines the effects of the rural environment on a city dweller, one finds that over longer periods of time in the country, the urbanite is acclimated only with great difficulty to the quiet, the solitude, the dirt, the inclemency of the weather, the long distances, personalization of social relationships, gossip, and different manners."[23] What generally evolves in the urbanite's currently popular search for rural relaxation and recuperation—be it in the boom in

---

[22]Hugger (1970), p. 33; also F. Kromka in his essay "Selbstund Frembild der deutschen Landwirte" speaks of an ambivalent relationship of the city dweller to the farmer; in: *Agrarwirtschaft*, 30/8, August 1981, p. 243f.
[23]Quoted from Planck and Ziche (1979), p. 52.

private homes, mechanized recreational tourism, or in the extreme instance of the "super resort" — is an uneasy city-country relationship. The city dweller would like to make use of something in an "intact, rural world" and would like to acquire it without really having to relate to things rural. And in many villages there are people ready to put the natural charms of their surroundings on the market for a good price.[24]

With this last statement we come to the question of what, then, seen from the other side, the relationship of the rural, particularly agrarian, population is to urbanites? As already pointed out, the modern farmer suffers more or less consciously from a tense internal relationship between traditional farming practices and agribusiness. Why a tense relationship? The ancestral relationship to the land and to tilling it, put to the test over generations, cannot simply be laid aside after a few years like a worn-out shirt. This ancestral worldview continues to exist in the emotional background.[25] Even if relegated to the background in favor of yield-oriented agriculture, it nevertheless surfaces again and again whenever the new attitude is no longer effective,[26] just as a crisis has caused many a canny rationalist to utter a sudden prayer.

Depending on the context of departure from traditional values, therefore, we find among farmers — as in the case of city dwellers — an ambivalence. On one side is a turn toward, and often a real fascination with, the worldview of natural science and technology with its rational ideas of yield. On the other side is the Christian worldview of one's ancestors, with its tradition-dictated ways of tilling the land. The coexistence of these two different worldviews in agriculture can be seen in agrarian publications. There we find technical journals that disseminate the newest knowledge, and at the same time, the

---

[24]This doubtful attitude could again be seen in a very extreme form on the issue of forbidding or permitting "heli-skiing." The "economic interests" swayed the decision; heli-skiing is still permitted.

[25]See J. Ziche's empirical-sociological investigation of the public self-image of the agrarian population in Bavaria (1970, p. 240). Ziche writes: "In face, the farmers act faithfully in accordance with the demands of the industrial society; the brisk structural changes prove it. Only intellectually do they appear to be stuck in the preindustrial mentality, as is revealed in their predilection for the motto, 'True to custom, true to the faith of our ancestors, simple and upright, we preserve the land for coming generations.' " (The word "stuck" is, to be sure, not well chosen considering the present-day recognition of the value of agrarian permanence and constancy.)

[26]In instances of the so-called "abaissement du niveau mental" (Jannet).

agrarian-Christian devotional literature, such as "Der katholische Schweizer Bauer." Many farmers subscribe to both kinds of literature simultaneously.[27]

The more intensely these two inner worlds of knowledge and belief stand in opposition to each other, the more insecurity wells up. For whenever two contradictory inner tendencies predominate, one falls subject to inner doubt. Easily thrown back and forth, a person in such conflict no longer really knows where he or she stands. The great inner ambivalence is then mirrored in the relationship to one's existence as a farmer[28] and concurrently in the relationship to things urban, which embodies the new mentality—after all, the new, agribusiness ways of thinking come from the city. Corresponding to the inner disunity regarding the old and the new, an external ambivalence vis-à-vis things urban exists, composed of more or less fascinated affirmation and wholesale rejection.

Consequently, things urban have an uprooting effect insofar as they have power of attraction. People are fascinated by things urban and have a concealed respect for progress, along with the sense that things rural and agrarian are inferior, second-rate. For example, often on a mountain homestead, the practical, old, peasant furniture may suddenly be sold to a passing antique dealer. (This furniture later finds it way to a city apartment or second home.) In place of the "old junk," people in the country—frequently with good reason—like to get modern things of the sort pictured in mail-order catalogues. With the money from the sale of the old peasant furniture, they buy an elegant bedroom suite, although the mirror of the new dressing table is so large that it touches the low ceiling of the peasant bedroom. The indigenous domestic culture is thoughtlessly and carelessly thrown out and replaced with "alien" mass-produced wares.[29] Yet we find, not only in the realm of domestic culture but practically in all areas of life, that among the rural-agrarian population there is a widespread fascination with urban life: in eating and drinking, in clothing and leisure activities, in the choice of names, and especially in mechanization.[30] In recent years television, now quite widespread in the coun-

---

[27]For this reference I am indebted to the Agricultural Director of Canton Uri, Hans Zurfluh, member of the cantonal government.

[28]For more on this, see A. Hauser (1972), p. 60ff.

[29]Concerning these issues, see the chapter "Bäuerliche Wohnkultur" in K. Waldvogel, et al., *Landwirtschaft in Kanton Schaffhausen*, published by the Cantonal Agricultural Directorate, Schaffhausen, 1981, p. 62f. See also Renner, op. cit., p. 66.

[30]Concerning the compulsive "wave of mechanization," see, for example, Gerber (1964); concerning the theme in general, see Weiss (1946), p. 18.

try, has brought new standards of value, which are reinforced by extensive advertising—from mail-order catalogues to advertising by telephone to personal visits.

Along with the overvaluation of urban things, we can often find in the same person a more or less concealed rejection of all that comes from the city. Not infrequently people view the city as the hub of vice and moral deterioration and are happy to be able to live in the country, healthy and far from the hubbub.[31] Toward things urban, alien, and new, as well as toward all that comes "from above," people adopt an attitude that can range from skeptical to reflex rejection.[32] This rejection has been strengthened recently in part by certain new federal laws that curtail freedom,[33] and in part by the generally increasing skepticism vis-à-vis innovations and progress. In particular, it is the engineers, planners, researchers, and experts, all trained in the city, who get a dose of this mistrust whenever they survey, calculate, ask questions, observe, and plan in the country. An incident during a survey for a research project at the Institute for Agricultural Economy of the Federal Institute of Technology, Zürich, offers a crass illustration of this rejection.[34] At the end of an interview in the living room of a French-Swiss farmer, the interviewer asked the farmer what use, in his opinion, this study might have. The answer: "For breeding more parasites like you!"

Thus rejection of what is alien, new, and urban, and at the same time admiration and fascination for this other world—this is the contradictory image of the relation of the agrarian population toward things urban that emerges from empirical social research. The findings are similar for the country-city relationship in general; however, discussion of this aspect would overburden our general survey of the situation.[35]

Just as we have observed a mixed, contradictory attitude in the urbanite's relationship to the country and agriculture, we find among the rural agrarian population similarly mixed feelings of rejection and fascination with respect to things urban.

In summarizing our chapter concerning the relationship between farmers and nonfarmers, as well as that between city and country

---

[31]Locher (1977), p. 138ff. See also Kromka (1981), p. 242, who speaks of an ideologically outmoded self-image of the farmer in Germany; similar views in Ziche (1970).
[32]See, for example, Wüthrich's sometimes exaggerated literary presentation; Wüthrich (1979), p. 12ff.
[33]Concerning water protection and regional planning, among others.
[34]Namely the project entitled "Nebenerwerbslandwirtschaft" ("Farming as a Secondary Occupation").
[35]We will speak of this again later.

populations in general, a specific picture emerges. In many instances, the relationship rests essentially on mutually distorted view – that is to say, on a mixture of defensiveness and fascination, or of over- and undervaluation. Such a state of affairs is an indication of the disturbed condition of a relationship. If one now bears in mind that the numerically small rural and agrarian population is dependent on a real understanding of their problems and concerns,[36] then a disturbed city-country relationship is a problem to be taken seriously. Following acknowledgment of the problem in these terms, suggestions for improving this relationship came from various quarters. They ranged from better information in schoolbooks and encouraging direct contact and promotional work in rural regions, to demonstrations by farmers.[37] The problem, however, goes much deeper. More information and increased contact fall far short of creating real relationships. For, just as we have seen in the instance of the farmer's relationship to his land, the essence of a relationship is spiritual. For this reason the phenomenon eludes the scope of technological terms – unless one can speak of a technician of the soul.

Thus we cannot avoid the question of what lies behind this disturbed relationship. Only when we recognize the partially unconscious roots of these mutually distorted images will it be possible to see ways in which we can understand and then maybe resolve this momentous sociological problem. Before we can fully formulate the problem, however, we must add a final chapter to our description of the starting point. This is a survey of the present-day situation of political efforts directed toward mitigating the rural social problem. Here, too, we will restrict our attention to the Swiss frame of reference.

---

[36]One thinks particularly of regional and agrarian policies.
[37]See, for example, Kromka (1981), p. 244.

Chapter 3

Current Attempts
to Mitigate the Rural
Social Problem

The weakening of the social, economic, and cultural independence of the rural, and particularly the agrarian, population, following recent technological development has led to political reactions. The continuing migration away from rural areas and from agriculture has prompted the need for compensatory interventions by the state in more and more sections of the population. Consequently, the government is now attempting to reduce the appeal differential between urban and rural areas through a comprehensive regional policy and, further, to check the continuing loss of capital from rural districts. The possibility of diminishing regional imbalances was seen in the concentrated effort to advance economic development of rural regions. Public intervention of this sort in the socioeconomic structure of economically weak areas has, in the course of recent years, continually increased in importance and correspondingly influenced the way of life in the country.

This innovation has created new terminology. The expression "rural development"[1] designates the purposeful and wide-ranging alteration of the economic, social, and cultural structures, institutions, relationships, and processes in rural areas.[2] In the wake of

---

[1]This term corresponds to the internationally accepted concept of *Landentwicklung, development rurale* or *desarollo rural*. (Planck and Ziche, 1979, p. 331.)

[2]Expanded from Ph. H. Coombs and M. Ahmed, *Attacking Rural Poverty: How Nonformal Education Can Help*, Baltimore, 1978, p. 13.

these intentional alterations, rural and agrarian sociology have also developed increasingly in the direction of a "sociology of social change."[3]

In Switzerland the first measures aimed at checking migration were expressly for the benefit of agriculture as well as the general improvement of the infrastructure in the mountain regions. Comprehensive regional economic planning[4] for advancing economically weak areas arose as a fundamental instrument out of these individual, often uncoordinated measures. On the basis of a thorough analysis of the situation, all the possibilities for development in a rural area are compiled and ordered according to area. The result of such development planning is a comprehensive system of goals and measures. In this way, it is intended that the material disadvantages of the economically weak regions relative to strong ones be diminished as directly and as quickly as possible. All reasonable possibilities for development in a region are to be optimally exploited; all hindrances to development are to be eliminated, as far as possible, through appropriate measures. A development concept of this sort is intended to make possible the application of state resources for economic advancement and enhancement of residential appeal. At the same time, the potential for development in an entire region is more likely to be realized than would be the case with uncoordinated efforts by individual communities.

In recent years, regional policy as an instrument of development planning has become more prevalent in Switzerland. Based on the 1974 federal law regarding investment assistance for mountain regions, this sort of development concept was worked out in approximately fifty mountain areas. Yet the experience derived from these undertakings showed that even these comprehensive economic development programs are relatively ineffective in creating an effective countercurrent to the autonomous dynamics of the socioeco-

---

[3]See Planck and Ziche, 1979, p. 331; this holds true especially for the countries of the Third World. Approximately one third of the contemporary German-language *Lehrbuch für Land- und Agrarsoziologie* is devoted to the sociology of rural development.

[4]For the sake of conceptual clarity, we distinguish between *Auffangplanung* (aimed at containment) and development planning, in the sense of Keeble Lewis (*Principles and Practice of Town and Country Planning*, London, 1972, p. 3). Taking into account certain contextual conditions, the latter is oriented toward purposive action and is essentially the attempt to unite overall economic and regional planning.

nomic and sociocultural concentration.[5] The gulf between the well-devised and well-intentioned system of planning concepts and the actual forces at work in economics and politics is too great. It seems that people must accept, with a shrug of their shoulders, the autonomous dynamics of geographic and industrial concentration as pressure inherent in the situation—think, for example, of the "pressure to grow" for reasons of competitiveness and efficiency.[6]

In addition to the external obstacles, there are interfering factors arising out of the human emotional background which, usually, are completely unexpected. These psychic influences can interfere markedly with efforts to create a sensible rural development policy. For example, in the course of development planning in a mountain area, a general apathy sets in among the local politicians because of the flood of paperwork concerning analyses of countless factors and the typical mountain of red tape. An overschematized procedure is capable of suddenly smothering every ounce of enthusiasm for a joint project. To mention another example, a development in an economically weak area is often introduced and advocated with much idealism without seeing the shadow side of the idealism. An unrelatedness to the people one is dealing with may occur because, as is well known, the idealist is certain he knows what is good for others. We can recognize the result of such a lack of self-criticism and modesty in the often-criticized "arrogance of development policy." As a consequence of this, we observe an increasing uneasiness, indeed, a downright peevishness on the part of the rural population concerning government policy. Linked to this is a growing mistrust of planners, engineers, government officials, and scientists.

Now, in order to understand this uneasiness better, we must examine more closely the human emotional background—that realm in which these feelings have their roots. Very generally, we understand the term "emotional background," which is ignored in a one-sided perception and ordering of external data, to refer to the sociopsychological realm of the feeling-toned reactions—of valuations and prejudices, of the sympathy-antipathy mechanisms, and the misunderstandings due to divergent models of thought. Particularly in rural

---

[5]G. Häberling and E. A. Brugger, for example, writing in the *Neue Zürcher Zeitung* (13 May 1978): "The real significance of the concept of overall economic development for mountain regions (in accordance with the investment assistance law) is hardly to be found in an actual 'check on migration,' but rather as a signal for future political efforts at regional planning."

[6]In addition we would refer to the collection of nine lectures entitled *Raumplanung im Kreislauf der Schzwänge*, Schriftenreihe des Instituts für Orts-, Regional- und Landesplanung der ETH Zürich, nr. 11, 1972, particularly pp. 6–17.

areas, where the cyclical course of the year and natural life still represents an essential part of human experience, irrational reactions with respect to a linear, goal-directed mentality can easily arise in the form of a resistance that can scarcely be overcome with "reasonable" arguments out of the experts' reference books. Contemporary attempts at developmental policy in rural areas do not appear to be a sufficient match either for these irrational inner-psychic influences or for the external forces of circumstances.

In general, such difficulties in contemporary regional planning policy are attributed to an ignorance of certain causal interconnections. Hence in order to fill these lacunae, the funds for a national research program in Switzerland were approved in 1976.[7] Under the heading "Regional Problems in Switzerland–the Mountain and Border Areas," the basis for an effective, regional adjustment policy by means of an "integral approach"[8] was sought. This research was concerned essentially with a more precise investigation of the causes of undesirable regional imbalances. Based on this, a "comprehensive, consistent, and operationally defined cluster of goals" was to be developed, which could orient regional policy.[9] Finally, concerning the measures to be used, the mechanics of regional policy instruments in particular had to be examined. This integral approach clearly expressed the intention of broadening the perspective to include noneconomic interconnections. But it also presented the problem of diversity in achieving a comprehensive development policy. For the question of an effective development policy in rural areas opens up the entire issue of national economic and cultural policy. With present-day, worldwide interdependencies, however, this leads unavoidably to the question of the international division of labor, indeed ultimately to the question of the shaping of society itself.[10] In short, the more precisely we follow the individual causal chains that lead to contemporary regional problems, the more we must confess our powerlessness to gain an overview of the totality of interweavings.

The breadth of knowledge that one would have to possess to

---

[7]Additionally see *Ausführungsplan des schweizerischen Nationalfonds-Forschungsprogramms Regionalprobleme*, Schweizerischer Nationalfonds; Bern, 1987, p. 11.

[8]Concerning the problems of integrated rural development as a concept, I refer to the article by John M. Cohen, "Integrated Rural Development: Clearing away the Underbrush," *Sociologia Ruralis* (SR), vol. XX, no. 3, 1980, p. 195–212.

[9]*Ausfuhrungsplan des schweizerischen Nationalfonds-Forschungsprogramms Regionalprobleme*, Schweizerischer Nationalfonds, Bern, 1981.

[10]W. A. Jöhr and H. W. Singer, *Die Nationalökonomie im Dienste der Wirtschaftspolitik*, Göttingen, 1969, p. 32.

account for everything essential to a sensible regional policy is still too great, despite technological resources. Even with volumes of compiled research results there will still be a peripheral dark area impervious to rational scrutiny.[11] Associated with this peripheral dark area is the irrational side of mankind, another great obstacle to a rational regional policy. This inner dark realm beyond consciousness is what psychology calls the unconscious.[12] However much we may labor within the confines of scientific research to illuminate interconnections relevant to development, there nevertheless remain areas that we overlook or that exceed the limits of our intellectual capacity. Given the epistemological organ called the psyche, which consists of both a conscious realm and an unconscious, and hence uncontrollable, realm, every insight gained by means of the psyche must be inherently incomplete.[13]

The necessity for a total view and the impossibility of ever attaining that overview is the dilemma of any comprehensive development plan. Just as we can never really grasp the totality of interconnections with our naturally limited consciousness, paradoxically, we should never make regional policy decisions without orienting them to a higher totality. However, the questions of what this higher totality really ought to be in the individual instance, and how the individual or a group can be consciously oriented to the best interests of the whole, appear to be so insolvable that they are generally excluded from the scientific examination of practice-oriented development planning.[14] Consequently, we simply come to terms with the fact that our individually planned interventions, aimed at the restoration of balanced conditions, do not fit together as a whole as well as they might in more natural structures.

The dilemma of rural development policy—of what we should know and what we can know—is obviated by the relevant branch of science thanks to an artificial limitation of scope. More or less complex individual systems, to the extent that they are felt to be impor-

---

[11]On this point see Konrad Lorenz, *Die Rückseite des Spiegels, Versuch einer Naturgeschichte menschlicher Erkenntnis*, Munich, 1973, p. 54, and in general Kant's *Critique of Pure Reason*.

[12]Medical psychology has provided the necessary empirical and experimental proof that consciousness and its contents are always demonstrably influenced by an unconscious psychic reality.

[13]Details on this are given below.

[14]See, for example, B. J. Maurer, *Grundzüge einer Methodik der Raumplanung*, Zürich, 1973, p. 13ff.

tant, are analyzed precisely.[15] Proceeding from that, the politician is then supposed to be able to make the necessary decisions. In other words, our contemporary rural development policy takes scientifically precise knowledge of sections of domains as the focal point of its activity, in the hope that these part-systems can then be meaningfully coordinated, interdisciplinarily or by means of sophisticated simulation and evaluation models.[16]

Especially in the country we notice the gap between individual intervention and everything that existed before. Next to a mountain village that arose organically we find, for example, modern apartment blocks for tourists, set in a meadow but unrelated to the setting. Indeed, the structures correspond to the concepts in the regional tourism development plan, the local zoning, and the building regulations—and yet, "something isn't right." Individual interests and the interests of the whole seem increasingly to diverge despite more and more state intervention, individual measures and overall organization. Viewed from the standpoint of social history, this phenomenon is associated with secularization, which led to a dissolution of collectively binding values.[17] New values of personal freedom and individual self-realization took their place. The other side of this liberation from the bonds of community and religion is a way of thought and action in which decisions can be made entirely according to personal judgment and personal advantage. Because of this change, social life and hence activities relating to the environment can no longer be regulated with the help of inherited, communal limits, according to usage and custom. In the place of (usually) unwritten checks on behavior, which were possible thanks to limited mobility and to a community where everybody knew what was going on, today more and more instruments of state regulation must be created in order to govern the relationship of the individual to society. But somehow or other, in spite of efforts to perfect and coordinate them,

---

[15]So-called piecework technocracy. K. R. Popper has very nicely examined this aspect of science. He writes, "The empirical basis of objective science is, then, nothing absolute (given); science is not built on a rock. The ground on which it is constructed is more like a swamp, its foundation are piles driven into the swamp from above, not down to a natural solid ground, but as deep as needed; driven deep, until one decides that one has gone deep enough so that (according to calculations) the piles will now probably support the building. But if the building gets too heavy, the piles must sometimes be replaced, or often driven deeper." (From Popper, *Die beiden Grundprobleme der Erkenntnistheorie*, Tübingen, 1979, p. 436.)

[16]E.g., those of F. Vester.

[17]By values we mean "a society's collective images of what is good, right, and hence worth striving for." H. de Jagaer and A. L. Moll, *Grundlage der Soziologie*, Köln, 1972, p. 305.

we lack a common denominator, that is to say an effective general attitude by which individual measures and interests are truly reconciled with the structure and interests of the whole.

The fact that the state's individual interventions aimed at the restoration of balanced and settled conditions no longer fit together into a whole (such as we can recognize symbolically, say, from earlier community structures) must be seen in relation to the change in our values. Here the value standing behind or over the values of a society, which therefore represents the highest spiritual value and determines all further social values, is the image of God. By this term we mean the idea or the image of the divine that every person has, insofar as he is convinced of the existence of a transcendent power. If there exists in a society a more or less common idea of God, it impresses itself on all the facets of social life in a transcendent, centering manner. Simultaneously, this idea shapes the understanding of the meaning of the life of the individual. Thus for us, the Christian understanding of God focuses human social life. The concept of an immortal soul gave dignity to the individual. The generally acknowledged meaning of life consisted in the individual's tending to the salvation of the soul through a Christian conduct of life. All our traditional values, norms, laws, customs, and usages have their roots in this overarching idea.

Whenever the common, uniting concepts of God and the meaning of life lose their general persuasive power in a society, all the values, norms, laws, etc., based thereon begin to crumble.[18] A profound lack of orientation and a divergence of individual measures from the whole are part of the phenomenology of this condition. Today, in the age of rationalism, a large part of the world's population finds itself in this sort of phase, in which ideas of the divine have become ineffectual, incomprehensible, lacking in vitality—a phase in which particularly the Christian image of God has lost its spiritual force.[19] The loss of a common, higher concept of value, according to which the individual orients all the areas of his life, has been expressed most clearly for us in Switzerland in the total revision of the federal constitution. There has been some thought of striking the old preamble which reads, "In the Name of God, the Almighty!" The consciousness-transcending power, which gave fundamental order to the social life of our ancestors and which manifested itself externally in the "church in the village," no longer functions everywhere among us, either.

---

[18]One might call to mind the various phases of secularization in the history of the world, say in ancient Rome at the time of Augustus.

[19]See on this the "Epilogue" in Albert Hauser, *Schweizerische Wirtschafts- und Sozialgeschichte*, Zürich, 1961, p. 355.

The problem of secularization is of central significance for rural development policy, for it is precisely in the hill and mountain districts far from urban areas, that the agrarian population is still a long way from an exclusively worldly orientation in their thought and action.[20] Living and working for these people are not purely matters of reason—their life is still more "being" than "business," to use Jakob Burckhardt's dichotomy.[21] However, with contemporary means of communication, their link with the transcendental is vanishing in these areas.[22] "Indeed, often something like the breaking of a dam takes place in that an initially well-defended conservatism is suddenly thrown aside to clear the field for an extremely materialistic attitude."[23] In place of traditional dependence on a metaphysical foundation, thanks to which the problems and sufferings in this world are always viewed in relation to a transcendental world and thereby can be coped with emotionally, material progress emerges in the context of a purely worldly attitude as virtually the sole goal of human existence. Development is seen only in terms of this goal; improvement of living conditions is expressed in per capita income and the trappings of an infrastructure.[24] In the light of material progress, everything immaterial becomes second-rate, even in the most remote mountain valley. "I haven't lived on culture," was the dry remark of a mountain farmer in Th. Locher's poll.[25]

All our objectives in regional planning are, accordingly, geared to greater prosperity; and a convincing role is played by science, which in politics has taken over the function of the church—a politician likes to ask scientific experts what he should do. Material growth initiates a positive feedback loop; material stagnation, on the contrary, soon leads to a vicious circle of shrinkage. Material progress is therefore the highest goal from a rational point of view. The soul and the

---

[20]Thus, for example, in the summer of 1980, during the incessant rains of June and early July, the so-called rogation processions were introduced and well attended in many Catholic communities in the mountains. In general, see the studies of Ziche (1970, p. 43f), Locher (1978, p. 74ff), and Jürg Knoll, *Ländlicher Raum und Kirche im Umbruch*, Hanstein Verlag, Köln, Bonn, p. 75ff.
[21]Jakob Burckhardt, *Gesammelte Werke*, Basel, 1956, vol. 4, p. 48.
[22]On this, see the poll by Locher (1970 and 1977), p. 75.
[23]On this, see Richard Weiss, *Alpiner Mensch und alpines Leben in der Krise der Gegenwart*.
[24]See, for example, *Leitlinien für die Berggebeitsförderung*, Bern, 1973.
[25]Locher, p. 19.

spiritual[26] dimension is generally included only insofar as it yields material advantage (schools, etc.) or has a very concrete form (e.g., cultural institutions).[27]

Whatever goes beyond this or touches on the so-called "transcendent dimension" is, to a great extent, taboo for practical rural development policy. Yet the dimension of relationship, affiliation or belonging that involves the soul as well as the spiritual issue of the meaning of life is doubtless just as important for the happiness and the unhappiness of the individual as are external, material conditions. Specifically, whenever life is experienced as meaningful and humanity feels part of a larger context, material disadvantages appear in quite a different light and are given a different significance. Newer tendencies, say among youth or among organic farmers, confirm more and more that today a meaningful activity in comprehensible relationship structures is valued more highly than maximal yield.[28]

But so long as our materialistic concept of development continues simply to exclude the dimension concerning the well-being of soul and spirit, it will not be surprising if all our efforts toward a sensible regional development consequently fall correspondingly flat. After all, with a one-sided, statistical, and scientific point of view, we are propagating precisely this superficial and materialistic judgment of the condition of the local population. With such a distorted view of the essence of development, a rural region's existing values of spirit and soul are diminished beyond recognition. The entire autochthonous culture—tradition, the introverted body of thought of so-called "folk knowledge," all the understanding of the necessity for careful consideration of the powers of the soul[29]—what does all that count for in an area that in twenty years is supposed to experience an increase in material prosperity of x percent? In contrast, it is scientifically and statistically demonstrable how materially disadvantaged the person living in the country really is. "If these people living in the country really were conscious of how they are missing out on prosperity, they would all be dissatisfied," a woman sociologist recently said. No matter how well-intentioned the assistance to rural areas is, it will, unfortunately, never be possible to eliminate the material provocations of

---

[26]Later we will discuss the concepts of soul and spirit in detail.

[27]See, for example, B. P. von Planta, *Die Förderung wirtschaftlich bedrohter Bergregionen durch eine aktive Entwicklungspolitik*, Winterthur, 1971, p. 220, and the "Richtlinien für die Berggebietsförderung," op. cit.

[28]On this see, for example, the studies in agrarian sociology by Rätus Fischer, *Das Selbstbild von biologisch wirtschaftenden Bauern*, dissertation at the Federal Institute of Technology, Zürich, 1980, p. 176f. (published as a book, Zürich, 1982).

[29]We will have the opportunity to speak of this in detail.

nearby urban centers. Promoting a materialistic way of thought in rural districts by means of scientific, statistical methodology tends, consequently, to be counterproductive in the long run. It impairs precisely those values of spirit and soul that we recognize today increasingly as the rural area's advantage over heavily populated areas—spiritual and cultural identity and continuity, as well as the space to be creative. Precisely these values could possibly, if they were more widely recognized and cultivated, make migration to the city less desirable. Hence our present-day rural development policy based purely on material values, certainly seems far too narrow to provide a sufficiently effective counterforce to growing regional imbalances.

Let us summarize the main points of our overview of the present-day attempt to mitigate rural social problems. Our well-intentioned systems of rational and consistent objectives for promoting economically weak rural areas run into sizable obstacles. On the other hand, there are also certain irrational, intrapsychic factors at work in the decision-makers themselves. One way or another, the direction in which rural development must go is determined by a partial view of life—i.e., either "external forces" or intrapsychic forces, but not always both. This problem obviously arises from the difficulty of adequately allowing for the effects of those domains of life not under conscious control in our decision-making process. Our far-reaching inability to deal appropriately with that realm of reality lying beyond what is clearly comprehensible is related to the limitations of the scientific field of vision focused on objects. The contemporary science of rural development has also been shaped by this viewpoint. With an exclusively intellectual comprehension of external objects—splitting off consideration of that dimension of life having to do with spirit and soul—all questions of development ultimately revolve around external, material things. In this way, a planned development loses its references both to the totality of human experience and to the whole human being.

PART 2

DEFINITION OF THE PROBLEM

Chapter 4

Inadequate Explanations—Inadequate Rural Development Policy

Splitting of the Opposites

If we examine the essential aspects of our initial situation in terms of common elements, one basic feature is striking. In all three realms— first, in the overall rural-agrarian social problem; second, in the disturbed city-country relationship; and third, in the present-day rural development policy—we see a characteristic confrontation of opposites. The essence of our observations concerning the rural social problem lies in the fact that the traditional rural-agrarian way of life appears irreconcilable with the principles of progress. The fundamental life-feeling of union with community, locality, tradition, and the transcendental dimension stands in seemingly unbridgeable opposition to the principles of progress: reason and liberation from bonds of every kind. We can disentangle the problem of opposites with the help of coordinate axes, as follows:

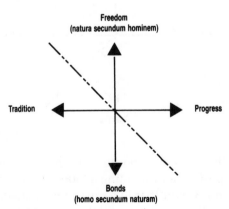

The diagonal designates the "line of demarcation." In the same manner we can represent the disturbed city-country relationship:

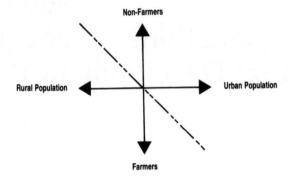

The final theme in our initial situation, present-day rural development policy, has also presented us with a problem of opposites. In the application of development policy to rural areas, material problems seem to bear no tangible relationship to the dimension of life relating to spirit and soul; and the so-called "culture of the individual" (as Richard Weiss calls it) seems increasingly less reconcilable with the interests of the community. Represented graphically, we can sketch this pair of opposites as follows:

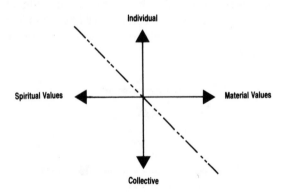

Naturally all the pairs of opposites represented here have always been pairs of opposites; and standing in opposition always means the possibility of conflict. Not that in earlier times harmony had always prevailed between the individual and the community or between city and country. Had that been the case, neither a Stanser Treaty[1] nor laws would have been necessary. However, in contrast to earlier centuries, what is striking as a characteristic of the present age is the growing weakness, indeed to some extent the loss, of any link between these respective opposites. Thus, we can speak of a break between tradition and progress and see the fault line in almost every village where the architecture changes. We find similar ruptures between spirit and matter, individual and community, as well as between city and country.

If opposites no longer have a direct link with each other, the disturbed relationship creates an increasing alienation, comparable that between spouses who have grown apart. Thus, according to a currently widespread view, spirit and matter or freedom and linkage no longer seem to belong inherently together.[2] Since there is a lack of reciprocal regulation in a disturbed relationship between opposites, excesses may arise correspondingly. As illustration, we see increasing materialism and the popularly uncommitted way of life which is indicative of a rapidly pervading suburban culture. The aspects of spirituality and attachment to the environment, when separated from matter and freedom, emerge and survive in compensatory forms, including all sorts of enslaving spiritual phenomena, from various kinds of drug abuse to the manifold "-isms" of our time.

In noting the deficient, disturbed, or nonexistent relationships between these fundamental opposites, we touch, in my opinion, the central problem of the rural area.[3] In order to elucidate this further, we must understand how it is possible that a disturbance of the inner relationship between the opposites could come about in the first place. This is to say, we must deal with the spiritual roots of the problem of opposites.

---

[1]A crucial moment in Swiss history (1481) when the urban cantons almost split from the rural cantons.

[2]That in the traditional way of life, contrasted with present-day freedom, only bondage prevailed is a misperception of historical facts. On this Josef Dünninger writes: "It is surely absolutely wrong to see only social coercion in all traditional behavior; within the traditional domain there are enough possibilities for free choice." Quoted from "Tradition und Geschichte" in *Kontinuität? Geschichtlichkeit und Dauer als volkskundliches Problem*, ed. by H. Bausinger and W. Brückner, Berlin, 1969, p. 62; on this see also Locher (1977) and, among others, A. Hauser (1982), p. 73ff.

[3]Comparable to Toynbee's well-known "schism of the soul."

Social Problems as Mirror of the Predominant Worldview

Every change in consciousness influences social events.[4] For this reason we must assume a connection between the problem of relationship described thus far and the change in our common worldview. To examine this connection we must cast a glance at the evolution of present-day Western consciousness.

Roughly stated, the Christian originally struggled to free himself from the drives of nature and found his goal in spiritual and otherworldly values. Hand in hand with this rejection of sinful matter and instinctive life, ego-consciousness was differentiated from the rest of the psyche. The gradual separation of ego and non-ego that went along with this indicates a clear capacity to differentiate subject and object. This separation of both pairs of opposites ultimately made possible the rise of the exact sciences.

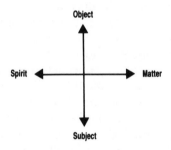

During the Renaissance and especially the Enlightenment, the values of worldly life were rediscovered. Subsequently Christian ideals were replaced more and more by their opposites. Whereas matter and the things of this world had once been scorned, in modern times they evolved more and more as the only valid values. Spirit, or the meaning aspect of life, was shoved into the background in favor of matter — that is to say, in favor of a materialistic viewpoint. Objective, external facts came to be valued increasingly higher at the cost of humanity's subjective, emotional background.

---

[4]See also W. Rüegg, *Bedrohte Lebensordnung, Studien zur humanistischen Soziologie*, Zürich, 1978, and Josef S. Roucek, "Die Entwicklung des Begriffs 'Sozialer Wandel' ", in *Wirtschaftliche Entwicklung und sozialer Wandel*, ed. Harald Winkel, Wege der Forschung, vol. CDXCIII, Wissenschaftliche Buchgesellschaft, Darmstadt, 1981, p. 43.

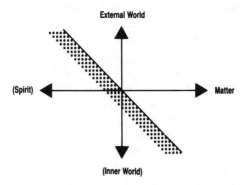

Together these trends led to an extraverted, materialistic attitude. This change in consciousness is helpful in understanding the social change in rural areas. The need to free consciousness from archaic restriction explains the prevailing overvaluation of one pole of the opposites, namely the urban, progress-oriented, materialistic individual culture, in preference to the tradition-oriented, manual labor-agrarian community culture.

Applied to the discussion of fundamentals, this structure of opposites in rural social problems can be represented as follows:

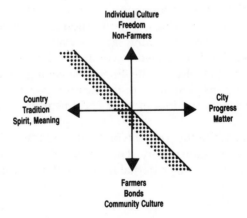

The higher value placed on the upper right half by the currently dominant view indicates the direction of general aspirations and thus of social migrations. As we do not intend to trace the imbalance between city and country back solely to external causes, by careless oversimplification, we cannot avoid treating this question in conjunction with the development of human consciousness. Obviously the inner causes of regional imbalances can be sought in the development of Western culture. Regarded this way, rural social problems can hardly be mitigated only by an expansion of objective knowledge and a policy of adjustment. For if the external imbalances described are to be viewed as a mirror image of a one-sided way of thinking, then it is doubtless advisable to make a point of including that inner domain in treating this group of problems. The fact that external, material motivations play an important role in the rural social problem is not diminished but rather only relativized by the inner, spiritual pole. Yet before we pursue this viewpoint further, we must clarify how present-day scholarship accounts for the rural social problem. We also want to explore the consequences of such explanations for the rural population. The treatment of these questions constitutes the foundation from which we can proceed to the definition of the problem in accordance with the current state of research.

Present-Day Status of Attempts to Explain the Rural Social Problem

Theories of Rural Sociology

Many agree with Pevetz: "Most of the current works on rural and agrarian sociology are predominantly of an exploratory and descriptive nature."[5] What is lacking is a clarification of the obviously deeper interconnections. "The discipline lacks a viable theoretical foundation." This view has been stated by competent persons, and not only in the German- but also in the English-speaking world.[6] Howard Newby describes the symptoms of the current crisis in rural sociology as outwardly a growing loss of trust and inwardly a corresponding uneasiness.[7]

In point of fact, the theoretical work currently found in rural sociological circles is not satisfactory. The various attempts at explanation consistently establish only external factors that are supposed to have

---

[5]Based on W. Pevetz, *Stand und Entwicklung der ländlichen Sozialforschung in Öesterreich, 1960–1072*, Vienna, 1974, and U. Planck and J. Ziche (1979), p. 477.
[6]E.g., Newby, "Die Herausforderung der ländlichen Soziologie heute," transl. by Ulrich Planck, in *Zeitschrift für Agrargeschichte und Agrarsoziologie*, vol. 29, no. 2, 1981, p. 204f and 210, and Planck and Ziche (1979), p. 477.
[7]Ibid., p. 202.

led to the rural social problem, be they the dependency theory,[8] the city-periphery theory,[9] the internal colonialism theory,[10] or the theory of wrong redistribution.[11] In all such observations, the problems of land and agriculture are described as having external causes and having to be treated as such. That such explanations are completely unsatisfactory in elucidating the profound problem of opposites hardly needs to be repeated. Obviously we need a much broader basis for understanding social interconnections, an understanding that, among other things, pays adequate due to ambivalence in the individual human being.

The lacunae in research in rural and agrarian sociology are therefore considered first of all in our review of current basic materials.[12] According to Newby, it is not a further accumulation of individual investigations, nor an easy escape into pseudoscientism via ever more sophisticated statistical methodology and electronic data processing, that could lead the discipline out of the present crisis. Rather, first of all, a reappraisal is needed—an observation (Greek *theorein* = observe!) and interpretation of what is available.[13] This rightly demands a broadening of scope. Rural sociology needs a viable theory of society and social change, within which the "rural" element can be located.[14] In point of fact, the rural social problem is indeed the result of a fundamental social transformation,[15] that is to say, of a profound alteration of our entire social structure. For this reason it seems to me appropriate to search among the theories of social change for a viable theoretical basis in order to lay bare the roots of the rural social problem.

---

[8]E.g., B. A. G. Frank, "Sociology of Development and Underdevelopment of Sociology," in James D. Cockcroft, et al., *Dependence and Underdevelopment: Latin America's Political Economy*, Garden City, N.J., 1972, p. 321–97.

[9]See I. Wallerstein, *The Emerging World System*, Academic Press, New York, 1974, and *The Capitalist World-Economy*, Cambridge University Press, Cambridge, 1978.

[10]See B. M. Hechter, *International Colonialism: The Celtic Fringe in British National Development, 1536–1966*, Routledge & Kegan Paul, London, 1975.

[11]E.g., B. G. Konrad and I. Szelenyi, "Social Conflicts of Underurbanization," in M. Harloe (ed.), *Captive Cities*, London, 1977, p. 157–74.

[12]B. Benvenuti, B. Galjart, and H. Newby, "The Current Status of Rural Sociology," *Sociologia Ruralis*, 15, 3–12, 1975; see also Planck and Ziche (1979), p. 477ff.

[13]Newby (1981), p. 205ff.

[14]Ibid., p. 209.

[15]William Ogburn's book, *Social Change with Respect to Culture and Original Nature* (New York: 1922, revised 1950) made the concept of "social change" well known.

Theories of Social Change—The Problem of the One-Sided Viewpoint

What do theories of social change have to do with the rural population's real problems as described above? Occupying ourselves in detail with these theories could, in this context, give the impression of getting sidetracked. Yet on closer examination we must admit that the effects of these explanatory models on day-to-day political life are of very great significance—for the rural population, too. For it is in accordance with prevailing concepts of fundamental social questions that *guiding images* of regional and agrarian policy are shaped. People may not be aware of this; but the fact remains that rural development policy, which is becoming increasingly subject to planning the world over, rests on certain theories of social change which subliminally or expressly embody the goals of guided social change. The best-known example of such a theory is that of Karl Marx; the living conditions of approximately one-third of humanity carry the imprint of his theory.

The number of attempts made by researchers to uncover the causes, course, and effects of social change is large. The result of these efforts is a confusing multiplicity of theories.[16] They share the goal of delineating the regularity and rules of the social processes of development. In the following we will attempt to outline and comment summarily on the present-day state of the theories of social change. Within the limits we set on this area, we cannot, of course, pursue all the manifold ramifications of this line of research. For this we refer the reader to the extensive specialized literature.[17]

The analysis and interpretation of processes of social change is dependent on the researcher's perspective.[18] Depending on the viewpoint, the economic-technical, the cultural, the social, or the personal structural dimension moves more into the foreground.[19] Since social change is a very complex phenomenon, suitable historical material

---

[16]A good introduction to this is found in Harald Winkel (ed.), *Wirtschaftliche Entwicklung und sozialer Wandel*, Wege der Forschung, vol. CDXCIII, Wissenschaftliche Buchgesellschaft, Darmstadt, 1981.

[17]On this see the bibliography (containing more than five hundred titles) in H. P. Dreitzerl (ed.), *Sozialer Wandel*, second ed., Neuwild, Berlin, 1972, and the very good summary by Günther Wiswede and Thomas Kutsch, *Sozialer Wandel, Erträge der Forschung*, Wissenschaftliche Buchgesellschaft, Darmstadt, 1978, as well as W. Zapf (ed.), *Theorien des sozialen, Wandels*, Köln & Berlin, 1969.

[18]See L. H. Warshay, "Breadth of Perspective in Social Change," in G. K. Zollschau, W. Hirsch (eds.), *Exploring Social Change*, London, 1964.

[19]Wiswede and Kutsch, op. cit., p. 7.

Those who limit themselves to the measurable neglect the immeasurable.

can always be found to substantiate the chosen perspective.[20] Researchers' bias toward a given theory has led to correspondingly distorted depictions of the actual situation. Thus, for example, according to Karl Marx, historical development is a consequence of the changes in the conditions of production. With this approach he falls victim to an explanatory model which takes into consideration only those effects that spread from the economic structure into other subsystems.[21] Conversely, Parsons locates the core of his observations in the overall economic value system, i.e., on the cultural-spiritual structure.[22]

If we examine the scholarly discussion of the theory of social change, a primary criticism of all theories is that they demonstrate a certain one-sidedness.[23] It is as though the founder of each new theory becomes so involved with his ability to offer an explanation that

---

[20]Joseph S. Roucek, "Die Entwicklung des Begriffs 'Sozialer Wandel,' " in H. Winkel, op. cit., p. 51.

[21]See Wiswede, op. cit., p. 6.

[22]Idem.

[23]Discussing theories of social change, H. Winkel (1981) speaks of a "lack of cohesive view" (see op. cit., p. 3).

other viewpoints are overshadowed. As Wiswede and Kutsch correctly state, all theories of social change oriented toward external systems ultimately see the individual human being "only as the one affected, hardly, however, as the one carrying out this change."[24] For this reason they recommend placing the human being in the center of the analysis, explicitly as the one both carrying out and being affected by social change.[25] They depict the relationship between human behavior and the structures surrounding us as follows:

Figure 4. Relationship between Human Behavior and the Structures Surrounding Man (Wiswede and Kutsch, 1978)

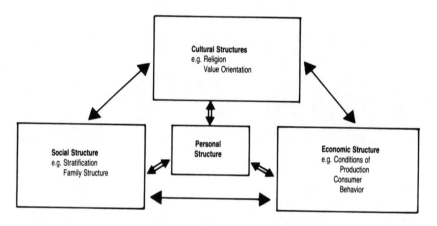

Continuing their discussion, Wiswede and Kutsch recall the pithy fact that "society is made up of people" and that the "alteration of unrelated patterns of behavior and socially regulated patterns of motivation—with which one usually describes change in the social structure—ultimately can be traced back to the specific actions of people and their specific motivations."[26] They reject the reproach that this starting point would reduce the significance of objective givens such as class difference and economic data. They are simply concerned with broadening the field of vision by including change in social behavior along with change in social structure. Proceeding from this, they argue for the continued investigation of theories of social change based on a theory of behavior.[27]

---

[24]Ibid., p. 35.
[25]Ibid, p. vii and p. 27.
[26]Ibid., p. 176.
[27]Ibid., p. 177ff.

This call to view the human being as actor as well as acted upon, and located at the center of analysis and interpretation of social change must be endorsed. It makes sense if we attempt to link the variables of social structure with those of individual action.[28] But as much as this direction of research is fundamentally to be welcomed, it would nevertheless be regrettable if this promising first step toward elucidating social change were to fall victim to a new one-sidedness. This would occur should the human psyche, as bearer of all the complex processes of thought and action, be underestimated. A one-sided picture of the determinants of human behavior naturally results in a correspondingly one-sided conception of social phenomena, even if the human being has been placed at the focus of the observation.

If we examine the known attempts to explain social change that rest on a theory of behavior, we do consistently find inadequate consideration of the state of psychological research.[29] The theoretician relies on, say, Skinner's version of learning theory, to take just one example.[30] As a so-called milieu theoretician, Skinner believes fundamentally in the shapability and reshapability of mankind by external influences. However, the one-sidedness of milieu theory was evidenced most recently in the work of human ethologist Irenaeus Eibl-Eibesfeld. In his work *Der vorprogrammierte Mensch*, (*Preprogrammed Man*) (1973), he was able to demonstrate the significance of inherited behavioral patterns in human behavior.[31] But if the question of what determines human behavior is answered inadequately, the basis for a satisfactory social theory is correspondingly lacking. For this reason, any exploration of the background elements of social change which rests on a theory of behavior demands a reliable foundation in the factors that influence and shape human behavior.[32] Only then can the human being be appropriately placed at the focus of the analysis and the interpretation of social change.

It is not only externally that the human should move more toward the focal point of investigation. The researcher, too, as a human being — and thus as a complex, unique creature — deserves to be

---

[28]See J. H. Kunkel, *Society and Economic Growth. A Behavioral Perspective of Social Change*, New York, 1970.

[29]This holds true both for social theories based on learning theory and on action theory and for those resting on consistency and socialization. Summaries of these positions as well as references to the literature can be found in Wiswede and Kutsch, op. cit., p. 179–195.

[30]Wiswede and Kutsch, op. cit., p. 201.

[31]See the preface to this book.

[32]We will return to this subject later.

included in the observations. Corresponding to the individual structure of consciousness of each individual researcher are different conceptions or even different theories of social change.[33] In discussions of
the various theories, unfortunately, these psychological factors are
usually completely overlooked. Without knowledge of the natural
limitedness and hence one-sidedness of every individual representation of reality, these various theories are defended with just a much
passion as they are attacked in scholarly and political circles, sometimes (as we say in German) to the point of drawing blood. The
inadequacies of all theories of social change and of the newer methodological approaches have their roots precisely in the natural limitedness of the individual's powers of perception. The common element
in all these theories would then be, summarizing Harald Winkel's
discussion, "that they indeed have introduced new facts and have
dissected complex over-all processes, but have offered no comprehensive view, no all-embracing theory."[34]

The net result offers little encouragement. Neither the conditions
nor the meaning of the historic process of change that has led to the
rural social problem can be dealt with satisfactorily by scholarship.[35]
In reaction to this, people have increasingly turned away from the
attempt to understand the fundamental underlying factors of this
process which is so significant for society, and "fled into prophesying
history and predicting the future."[36] "If it is correct that the analysis of
social change is the touchstone of sociology" then, according to
Wiswede and Kutsch, such observations justifiably indicate this discipline's development.[37]

Roots of the One-Sided Viewpoint

One-sidedness is thus a central, common feature of all theories of
social change. There is nothing remarkable about this state of affairs if
we recall the collectively accepted view of life out of which practically
all these attempts at explanation have grown. Proceeding from the
modern, enlightened worldview, the changes in society are analyzed
with a clear intellect and interpreted according to a chosen perspec-

---

[33]On this see the very readable work by Arnold Küenzli, *Karl Marx, eine Psychographie*,
Europa-Verlag, Wien, 1966. Generally concerning theories of social change, see Zapf
(1969).
[34]Winkel (1981), p. 3.
[35]Ibid., p. 5.
[36]Ibid.
[37]Ibid., p. vii.

tive and a specific structure of consciousness. The founder of a theory is reminiscent of reporters who single out an object of interest with their cameras but in doing so necessarily weaken their sensorium for the context in which the object of interest is embedded. The surrounding field is, in the eyes of our reporter, unworthy of interest. Be it the more finalistic theories of Spencer or Marx, or be it the more causal theories of Parsons, Ogburn, Dahrendorf, Rostow, Myrdal, Lenski, McClelland or whatever their names are—they are all characterized by this sort of viewpoint. One takes this or that aspect of social life as the center, thereby seemingly making it into a principle, and about it one arranges the appropriate empirical facts of the case, thus confirming the theory. It is called the "common denominator" of social development, for example, or of differentiation, complexification, secularization, rationalization, or modernization.[38]

What the founders of theories, therefore, normally tend to overlook is that remnant which their chosen conscious viewpoint cannot see. Naturally there is no lack of various attempts to solve the problem of the dark remnant by simply uniting various viewpoints. In the place of so-called monocausal theories there arise polycausal explanations, usually on an interdisciplinary basis. Yet however much the illuminated area is expanded in this manner, there always remains a dark realm beyond the circle of light, the extent of which is unknown. In spite of all scholarly refinement, expansion, and deepening, a remnant always is left, that is, a realm which could be just as important in understanding social change as the domain analyzed.

As a consequence of the rational conscious viewpoint, what is therefore missing from all theories of social change is the conscious reference to the remnant or what is "unworthy of attention." Of course, this omission is understandable; whatever lies beyond the limits of what is worthy of investigation automatically becomes second-rate and thereby becomes the "unimportant remnant." That, however, can lead to an irrational restriction of our capacity for scientific knowledge. We do not want to emulate the man who looked for his lost key under a street lamp because that was where he had the best light! But if we are looking for an immanent explanatory principle of social change, then we are proceeding as that man did: we are looking for the explanatory key only in that area already illuminated by the light of research. Perhaps the key is lying in the dark. Perhaps

---

[38]For details on this, cf. Wiswede and Kutsch, op. cit., p. 15.

in this domain "unworthy of attention" are powers that change social life just as crucially as factors in the dark background of the psyche shape the individual's life.

What do we mean by "immanent explanatory principle" in the context of theories of social change? This term refers to the belief in the possibility of a valid explanation of individual and collective behavior as well as of change in this behavior by means of reason and objective fact. This procedure rests on the assumption that we do not have to refer to that dark domain beyond what can be elucidated. Or in short, this is a worldview that believes it can manage without reference to the world beyond, regardless of what we may call that realm.

The root of the one-sidedness of the various theories of social change (which are usually free of internal contradictions) is obviously found in the structure of human consciousness. Consciousness strives for unambiguousness—away from the paradoxical opposites of unconscious nature. Since, ultimately, humanity is a part of nature, the same thing is true also for society and social change. A social science striving exclusively for unambiguousness would therefore be an inadequate instrument for appropriately comprehending the paradoxical structure of social change.

We can summarize the problem with theories of social change thus: not considering the "remnant" or what is "unworthy of attention," each of these theories splits off the internal opposite of its thesis.[39] Since, however, nature and hence also humanity and society are constituted of opposites—which, if they cooperate, will assure the continued existence of mankind and society—a concept of social change must also take this fact into account. This demand will be fulfilled when social science has found a way to accommodate a relationship to what lies outside of consciousness.

The One-Sidedness of Social Theory: Consequences and Conclusions

Every attempt to explain social change, therefore, has at some point left an area out of consideration. Yet these excluded areas do not differ fundamentally from theory to theory, but rather on closer scrutiny reveal common characteristics. As a rule in sociologic theory, those things downgraded in prevailing opinion lead a shadowy exis-

---

[39]Even the eminent social historian, Arnold Toynbee, must submit to this reproach (see H. E. Barnes, *Historical Sociology: Its Origin and Development*, New York, 1948, p. 109).

tence. Here we want to attempt to sketch this collective shadowy realm and to deduce its effects on the sociological approach.

In contrast to the attitude of our ancestors, who always found their fundamental orientation in the relationship to an otherworldly, spiritual dimension, our orientation is based on an essential belief in the power of human knowledge. Contemporary science cherishes the idea that problems can be solved when they have been clearly elucidated. According to this enlightened view of life, the human being moves to center stage; and there is nothing our intellect is incapable of grasping. Consequently, people are interested in what is intellectually comprehensible and limit their view to that realm. When nothing outside of human consciousness can be experienced in this manner, we then enter into the belief that it is only with the light of consciousness that we can elucidate social change. On the other hand, whatever we cannot grasp—in the literal sense of the word—we devalue. Social science then also restricts itself to the comprehension of the concrete and to interpretation on the basis of causal interconnections. But if the collective dark domain corresponding to this (i.e., its opposite) is systematically excluded from the study of social change, then there is no complement to the concretely comprehensible—namely, the spiritual forces beyond consciousness, which influence consciousness in the form of intuitions, ideas, fantasies, feelings, and moods.

Without reference to this shadowy realm, the interpretation of social change is concentrated wholly on objectively observable interconnections, ranging from economic and fiscal questions to innovation, distribution of goods and power, and increasing secularization and cultural disintegration. Yet this is to misjudge the efficacy of powers from the collective dark realm; for political, religious, and economic changes cannot simply be explained immanently, but are, as B. Roucek says, "the external manifestations . . . of more profound changes."[40] Our century has been forced to experience in an uncanny way the powerful spiritual dimension of ideas and intuitions. The social transformation in the thirties in Germany was brought about, as is well known, not only be external factors but also with the *Blut-und-Boden* myth, the result of spiritual factors emanating from the psychic background of humanity.[41]

The political consequences of underestimating the spiritual counterpole in the predominant theories of social change in East and West are grave. By tracing social change back solely to immanent factors,

---

[40]J. S. Roucek, op. cit., p. 43; R. Dahrendorf has also pointed this out.
[41]See C. G. Jung, *Civilization in Transition*, vol. 10 of *The Collected Works of C. G. Jung*.

social problems also seem, with oppressive clarity, to be solely consequences of such conditions. From this one-sided view people then
believe that humanity is in a position to direct social change toward a
"better world."[42] It is believed that one need only know the visible
interconnections in order to be able to forecast the change and hence
to plan correctly.[43] Whatever is inadequate and evil in social association is expected to be discovered by the light of the scientific intellect;
and, thanks to human reason, it can be made to vanish one day. It is
only a slight exaggeration to characterize the last statement as the
mythology of social-scientific one-sidedness.[44]

The effects of a one-sided theoretical view of rural social problems
correspond to the concept discussed above. Everything is seen,
depicted, and interpreted through concretistic spectacles.[45] In practice
this optical illusion works more or less like this: If one intends to
describe the rural or agrarian social problem in a certain region, everything possible is collected that can be concretely recorded. Using
various socioeconomic indicators, analyses of documents, question-
naires, etc., one forms a picture of the situation, notes any changes in
these individual factors, compares location and development of other
regions, and bases the diagnosis on this "abstract picture of concrete
reality." Normally this goes as follows: compared with population
centers, people in the country earn less, have fewer good educational, work, recreational, and consumer opportunities, have less
attractive living accommodations, and most of all have a smaller share
of general prosperity. All this can be supported with concrete numbers. What could one object to in that? Everything is backed up by
facts.

There is something convincing about this approach. Consequently,
all research is directed toward getting, if possible, an even better X-
ray picture of the specific rural social problem in the various regions,
interpreting it, and recommending the appropriate remedy to the

---

[42]The best-known example and the one having the greatest consequences in the theory
of Karl Marx.

[43]See Wiswede and Kutsch, op. cit., the chapter on the analysis, trends, and planning
of future development (p. 53ff).

[44]The opinion that all the evil in this world can be caught hold of rests on the fact that in
our Christian-colored mentality, evil has been reduced to a psychic fact, but good
remains metaphysical (see C. G. Jung, *Collected Works*, vol. 14).

[45]For the Swiss instance, see the relevant documents of the Federation, as, for example,
the Commission on the Investment Aid Law of 1973 ("Investitionshilfegesetz" =
IHG), the fifth Agricultural Report (1976), and the Bauernverbandes, Bern (1982).

politician.[46] It is believed that the spiritual dimension has also been covered through a procedure involving the intellectual treatment of the numerical data collected. But with a materialistic-statistical image of a given social problem, the connection to the objective spirit gets imperceptibly lost—the connection to the spirit in which the individual, the individual families, villages, valleys, and regions live; to the community spirit; to the sense of responsibility; to the attachment to the land; and to the entire meaning of the cultural heritage.[47] This problem merits comment.

Every statistical abstraction, of course, has its value. It enables a rapid survey of large quantities and of externally complex interconnections. Yet, however innocuous an individual statistic may appear, the consequences of the habit of statistical thinking are far-reaching. One naturally arrives at the position that a human being can be replaced by a number. Then one can add and subtract these numbers and become accustomed to $1 = 1$, that is, that one person is replaceable by another. Only the quantity and not the quality is decisive. Empty theory? By no means. How many normally intelligent persons have apologetically answered my question as to why they are involved in this or that questionable deal by saying: "Others do it too," or "If I don't, somebody else will." But in plain language this means nothing less than: "I hereby declare that I am an interchangeable unit that functions more or less decently according to the social rules of the game. My life takes place in this world, and anything above and beyond this does not interest me." It hardly need be further stated that this is a declaration of spiritual bankruptcy. But it is also a declaration of bankruptcy of the dignity of the individual and at the same time a general absolution for any sort of "dirty trick." After all, somewhere you can always find "somebody else" ready to do whatever lousy deed you want.

What is imperceptibly lost in this materialistic-statistical way of thinking is the reference to the individual meaning of life. It is believed that only the concrete and comprehensible is important for human well-being. The fact is overlooked that since the beginning of time, the life of the spirit has been just as important for humanity as

---

[46]For an extreme example of this, consult Irma Adelmann and Guthia Taft Morris, "An Econometric Model of Socio-Economic and Political Change in Underdeveloped Countries," in *The American Economic Review*, LVIII (1968), p. 1184–1218.

[47]An attempt in this direction was made by Albert Ilien and Utz Jeggle in their book, *Leben auf dem Dorf: zur Socialgeschichte des Dorfes und Sozialpsychologie siener Bewohner*, Opaladen (1978). They attempted to capture the specific spirit of the village (the "Eigensinn"), but in their attempt they got stuck in a concretistic conceptualization of this spiritual dimension.

securing material existence.[48] The expression of this typically human need is the evidence of the sacred found throughout the world in all cultures, including not only edifices, rites, myths, and legends, but also the entire body of custom and habit. A polar structure is thus revealed in mankind.[49] The biological drive structure constitutes the one side, the need for a relationship to something non-material is the other. Today the former aspect is covered by all that we understand as welfare. The latter, on the other hand, leads such a shadowy existence that we can speak of widespread spiritual poverty or lack of orientation. But if a person lacks this dimension, his or her own unique life becomes drab and banal, however great the increase in material well-being.[50] With a one-sided statistical way of thought, which reduces man to an interchangeable unit, the paradoxical truth is lost: On the one hand, $1 = 1$, and on the other hand, $1 \neq 1$. The human being is both a collective creature, like all the others, and simultaneously a unique individual with a unique meaning in the overall structure. If this comprehensive view is lost, and if the materialistic-statistical insistence that $1 = 1$ gains the upper hand, we inevitably fall victim to a myth of equivalence that destroys spirit and meaning.

In sum, we can state that not only the rural social problem but also current attempts to explain it are mirror images of the prevailing *Weltanschauung*. We thus tend to use a one-sided way of observing to diagnose and treat the problem that has arisen thanks to this very viewpoint. Who can be surprised if all promises and hopes "for a better man-made world" based on such theories lead again and again to bitter disappointment? The one-sidedness of sociological theory has its origin in the idea of human existence as limited to the sphere of biological drives, while the general human need for the individual to experience life as meaningful is ignored. The latter concept finds no place in modern sociology's statistical thinking. After all, the meaning of an individual life cannot be abstracted mathematically, and thus it seems to be a phenomenon that cannot be understood scientifically.

The implication for our understanding of social change and rural social problems particularly is that we cannot avoid developing theo-

---

[48]Additionally I refer the reader to the document about Lame Deer, *Seeker of Visions*, by John Fire/Lame Deer and Richard Erdoes, New York (1976), as well as to the work of Sir Laurens van der Post on the African bushman.

[49]In rural sociology circles, Albert Hauser has repeatedly pointed out this fact (see Hauser [1982], p. 89).

[50]On this see Heinrich Pestalozzi, e.g., "Spirit and Heart in Method," 1805.

retical foundations based on an expanded image of humanity. The necessities and needs of spirit and soul must be included with consideration of material needs. Thus the circle closes, returning to the conclusions formulated during our beginning discussion.

Chapter 5

The Goal:
A Model for Regional and Agrarian Policy Including Social Factors

Necessity of a Political Model

The imbalance between city and country, caused by the continuing migration from rural areas and agriculture, calls for man's regulative intervention. But our attempt to explain and reduce this imbalance has shown that this problem cannot be approached with a one-sided viewpoint. The disturbances brought about by rationalization apparently cannot be removed by rational methods alone. On the contrary, the experience in countries where the imbalance is approached with a "thoroughly thought-out," so-called integrated, plan give rise to the suspicion that more planning brings more problems in its wake.[1] In other words, purposive intervention always entails unintended and, above all, undesired side effects.

Of course, the implication drawn from this fact must not be the avoidance of every purposeful intervention and the denial of the entire field of regional and agrarian policy. For the tremendous changes in our times, caused by natural science and technology compel us to carry out well thought-out and purposeful adaptations of those structures and institutions that have come to need renovation. For example, E. Flütsch was able to demonstrate this necessity very convincingly, taking as his paradigm the remote mountain community of St. Antönien.[2] As a consequence of modern mobility, there has been an increase in the number of marriageable persons, who once were restricted to those in the local community. Similarly, the choices

---

[1] On this point, see E. Tuchfeld, *Gefährdete Marktwirtschaft*, Bern, 1977.
[2] E. Flütsch, "St. Antönien, Kulturlandschaftliche Aspekte einer Walsergemeinde," dissertation, Zürich University, 1976.

of residential location have been extended to include areas outside the community. Inheritance rights (*Realteilung*) thereby become meaningless. Emigrant members of the community have remained absentee owners of individual small plots and parts of stalls which has disadvantageous effects on farming operations for those who remain behind. A comprehensive adaptation of these structures to the new conditions is urgently needed, so as to guarantee well-balanced conditions in the community. A well thought-out, appropriate and planned adaptation of existing structures to changed conditions is, therefore, a necessity. Comparable situations can be found everywhere.

An entirely negative attitude toward every sort of conscious effort to regulate a disturbed equilibrium—a *laissez-faire* stance that advocates only the self-regulation offered by nature—overlooks the consequences of a forced regulation by those forces of nature which can be catastrophic under certain conditions. The decline of advanced civilizations adequately illustrates this mechanism. Moreover, in the Swiss frame of reference, a *laissez-faire* policy would stand in contradiction to our basic federalist idea. In order to offset the undermining of the peasantry by modern developments, the Federal Constitution (in Article 31bis, 3b) grants the Federation the authority "to provide for the maintenance of a healthy peasantry and an efficient agriculture" via appropriate measures. In addition to this constitutional basis for the Federation's purposeful agrarian policy, our constitution empowers the Federation to issue regulations "for the protection of economically threatened regions" whenever justified by the interests of the nation as a whole (Article 31bis, 3c). If necessary, the Federation may even deviate from the principle of free trade. Our present-day purposeful regional policy for the benefit of economically weak rural areas rests upon this constitutional foundation.[3] In light of both general considerations, and in reference to the federal agreement, it is thus necessary to approach the general problem of areas threatened with emigration and the particular problem of agriculture with appropriate political measures.

Necessity for a Broader Model

As we can conclude from what has been said, the primary difficulties in contemporary regional and agrarian policy are rooted in the under-

---

[3]See additionally the message of the Federal Council to the Federal Assembly concerning investment aid for mountain regions, dated 16 May 1973, p. 41.

valuation of the active factors in the realm of spirit and soul. One-sided representation of the material disadvantages of rural areas and agriculture especially, without the pertinent inclusion of the spiritual dimension, must necessarily lead to a dead end. In spite of all state subsidy measures, the material disadvantages will continue to exist.[4] Unlike elsewhere, in agriculture one cannot continue to earn one's livelihood ever faster and ever more comfortably. Near to population centers there are always more job openings, educational institutions, and services of all sorts. Viewed through purely materialistic-statistical spectacles, the latitude for decisions within the circumstantial constraints in rural areas seems so limited and insignificant that, of course, no lasting enthusiasm for state development and advancement policies can be generated. In present-day regional and agrarian policy, aimed as it is only at reason and the concrete world of the here and now, the spiritual aspect of life can hardly find expression, say in the form of a renewed feeling of solidarity or meaning.[5] But history teaches well enough what an unexpected transformation of the constraints of circumstance has been effected precisely by people who were inspired to act in concert.

The general overvaluation of the objective versus the subjective realm of man proves likewise to be a troublesome area that must be taken seriously in regional and agrarian policy. That aspect of reality which is not attended to in the one-sided orientation toward the external—namely, the relationship to the inner world—attracts attention when goals are set in the form of a distortion of ideas of reality. With the one-sidedly rational orientation to the object, one does not notice how inner associative and fantasy material intermingles imperceptibly with external reality; that failure of perception can lead to serious false conclusions and one-sided positions. In other words, from this lack of attention to the psychic background, one's own unconscious contents can be carried into external activity. Thus individuals or groups can suddenly deem certain things very important, yet scarcely notice others. In fact, such superimpositions of intrapsychic images onto external reality are continually taking place. We speak of projections where disturbances in human adaptation to the

---

[4]As is well known, the material disparities between city and country, as well as those between agriculture and nonagriculture, have not significantly improved in recent years in Switzerland despite regional and agricultural policies. In part they have even gotten worse!

[5]Actually, the opposite has been brought about by purely economic thinking, as has become evident in recent years in the area of cantonal and regional economic development. Economically weak regions attempted to outdo each other in the attempt to bring in new businesses and hence jobs by offering special services.

outer world arise in this way; in such instances, projections must be differentiated from external objects by reflection.[6] Thus in our context, wherever we determine that there has been a break between advancement measures and the population affected, or between what exists and what is newly planned, we must ask ourselves where and to what extent intrapsychic images have led to a one-sided view of external reality. However, this cannot happen so long as the external pseudo-scientific view predominates, which holds that knowledge about man's intrapsychic world is unimportant compared to the knowledge of the multitude of things of the external world.

Yet it is not only such reflections as these nor the one-sided attempts to explain the social problem of inequalities discussed earlier that make the contemporary procedure in regional and agrarian policy appear in need of fundamental rethinking. On the basis of experiences in other branches of science, the "enlightened," Cartesian worldview which informs present-day science has already been called into question by recent research in physics on the nature of matter and in psychology on the nature of the spirit and soul.

According to the current state of knowledge in physics, the neat division between spirit (energy) and matter appears to be inadmissible at the microphysical level. Likewise, clear distinction between the observer and the object observed in the realm beyond what is directly perceptible—has turned out to be impossible.[7] The popular view fragmenting the world into countless dualities has, consequently, been relativized by modern physics. The world beyond the reach of our sense organs presents itself to the investigator as a unitary reality in which the pairs of opposites cannot be separated. The one-sided overvaluation of the objective material domain of life is also placed in question by the ramifications of subatomic physics. The subjective, the inner side of man as the bearer of judgment, has today become equal in significance to the objective presence of nuclear weapons. Similarly, in the face of the material reality of this potential for destruction, the question of the essence of the creative spirit also has suddenly become acute—the very creativity that has lead to this uncanny possibility. It is the question of the sorcerer's apprentice about how to relate to and deal with this spirit.

Contemporary research results concerning the nature of the human psyche also suggest the need for a fundamental relativization and

---

[6]For details on this, see M.-L. von Franz, *Projection and Recollection*, pp. 1–18.
[7]In Part 3, chapter 7 below, more follows concerning the Heisenberg uncertainty principle and the relationship between matter and energy.

expansion beyond the one-sided materialistic-rationalistic worldview. It is possible for empirical psychology to demonstrate that alongside consciousness there is a second psychic system, unknown to us—one that functions independently of consciousness. The significance of this can hardly be estimated insofar as it means that it transforms our Cartesian worldview. The essential thing about the discovery of the so-called collective unconscious[8] is the empirical demonstration of an objective spirit—that is, of a sphere of action independent of reason and will, which again and again thwarts conscious intention in uncontrollable ways. Moreover, modern psychology can point out ways in which a relationship to this inner, dark reality can be established. By means of what we call *reflection* upon their effects on consciousness, these spiritual forces from the unconscious (dreams, fantasies, complexes, etc.) can be linked constructively with consciousness. Together the conscious and the unconscious psyche form an easily demonstrated self-regulating system, fully analogous to the human body. As we will later see in detail, the unconscious spirit's mode of operation in relationship to consciousness is of a compensatory nature; that is, the manifestations from the unconscious attempt to correct the naturally one-sided viewpoint of consciousness. The discovery of a second psychic system independent of consciousness, as well as the possibility of expanding knowledge thanks to the existence of this realm, thus relativizes the Cartesian view of objective knowledge in a manner completely analogous to modern physics. For the autonomous second system absolutely cannot be separated neatly from the object under investigation, since it (the second system) lies beyond the control of consciousness. As this common human unconscious extends down into the realm of instinct and thereby into the somatic (via the autonomic nervous system as can be demonstrated),[9] the discovery of the unconscious psyche makes the Cartesian separation of spirit-psyche and matter an antiquated idea.

In recent years, numerous additional specialized disciplines have been enriched by this discovery of the relativity of the inner-spiritual and the external-material dimensions. Conversely for their own part, those specialities were able to contribute to a better understanding of this relationship. Examples of this are seen in biology (A. Portman and others), ethology (K. Lorenz, I. Eibl-Eibesfeld and others), and

---

[8]Concerning the discovery of the collective unconscious more is said in Part 3, chapter 7.

[9]All of psychosomatic medicine points to this.

the history of literature (K. Schmid and others). All these research results necessarily raise questions. Do these most recent insights in science have consequences for our viewpoint in the social sciences and particularly for development policy in rural areas? Does our general, scientific view with regard to rural population and rural development, with its tendency toward statistical leveling and its material goals, no longer correspond at all to the modern view of the world?

On the basis of our point of departure and of the description of the problem, it appears necessary to define more comprehensively the concept of "development" which has now become fundamental for the treatment of the rural social problem—that is, no longer only in an external-material sense but also in an inner-spiritual sense. On this expanded basis we will attempt to outline a model for regional and agrarian policy which contributes to an improvement in the relationship between the pairs of opposites described above, by which we intend to demonstrate that rural sociology also has something politically relevant to say.[10]

Structure of the Work

In order to deal with the questions raised, we must cast light from various angles on the themes of social change and development policy in rural areas. As a first step, we will examine the historical context. By investigation the change in relationships between the individual and his environment, as well as his peers, the hitherto undervalued social significance of changes in the collective attitude will become apparent. Then, on the basis of these facts, the model of contemporary, goal-directed regional and agrarian policy will be examined and critically evaluated in comparison with the old and circular folk ways of thinking. In conclusion, we will sketch out the criteria according to which a model for Swiss regional and agrarian policy should be formed, so that, in addition to material needs, human facts and needs in the realm of spirit and soul will be adequately taken into account. Thus in this work we are concerned with a fundamental rethinking of our rural development policy from a sociological and psychological viewpoint.

Treating these problems requires an interdisciplinary approach, a procedure that for questions of this sort is regarded today as generally

---

[10]P. Olson accuses rural sociology of "offering little that is politically significant"— ironically because of its "applied" character. See "Public Policy and the Policies of Agriculture: Organization Inaction," in *Rural Sociology*, 1979, vol. 44, no. 2, p. 266–80. He is not the only one to take this stance (see also Newby, 1981, p. 206).

justified. Starting from practical experience with our regional and agrarian policy, external, material factors will be examined in relation to the inner, spiritual bases. The problem of the one-sided attitude of our predominantly extraverted consciousness will be pointed out, taking the development policy in rural areas as the focus, in order then to look for possibilities as to how the still-undifferentiated relationship to the intrapsychic world of symbols could be united with practical regional and agrarian policy.

PART 3

THE CHANGE IN THE RELATIONSHIP BETWEEN HUMANITY AND THE ENVIRONMENT

Significance and the Overview

The contemporary rural social problem is indeed a result of modern changes, but it is nonetheless rooted in a long past. The background is found not only in acknowledged facts—for example, the cities' continual bloodletting of the country to their own advantage—but can also be explained and better understood[1] in terms of changes in values and beliefs. A retrospective view enables us to investigate social changes against the backdrop of a changing collective consciousness.[2] That possibility is the first reason for choosing the historical viewpoint as the foundation of this study. The second reason has to do with the often ahistorical approach to agrarian development policy.

The sciences of regional and agrarian economics and the political science based on them are young disciplines of the twentieth century. No large background of experience serves them as an aid in orientation; after all, the imbalance between city and country, like that between agriculture and non-agriculture, is to a large extent a phenomenon of our time. Thus to a certain extent this branch of science, aimed at strengthening regional and agrarian self-sufficiency, has no deep roots in history. In view of the newness of the social, economic, technical, and cultural problems in rural areas, it certainly appears correct at first not to seek the tools for dealing with them in the

---

[1] As Planck and Ziche (1979, p. 477) correctly state, research in this direction must be designated a lacuna in the research in rural sociology.
[2] The analysis of social change has, until now, for all practical purposes not made contact with the research in social, i.e., collective, attitudes and their changes. Wiswede and Kutsch are of the opinion that, empirically and theoretically, this is a very well-worked field of research lying fallow.

arsenal of our ancestors. In an age of technology and modern economics, our predecessors' empirical knowledge has, as we know,
generally suffered a profound devaluation. Hence political decisions
for the future are made more and more on the sole basis of considerations of reason, geared to the here and now. Because nearly all
today's social problems are so very new in nature, the more or less
clear conviction has arisen that we simply cannot orient ourselves to
the past and hence no longer need to take the past into account at all.
Seen this way, it seems that the disciplines mentioned would be
compelled to eschew their historical roots, and that research should
therefore concentrate on the horizontal dimension—on interdisciplinary work and a worldwide exchange of experience.[3] Or is there after
all still a vertical, historical dimension out of which the rural social
issues *and* attempts at resolving them have grown? And can we, if we
pay attention to that dimension, find an additional focus of
orientation?

Among the goals established by our development policies for rural
and agricultural areas we can note and summarize the following:
specific interventions aim to improve existing structures and organize
them toward optimal productivity. Through training, consultation,
information, etc., the individual should become able to adapt himself
to these interventions. But this goal-oriented, planned procedure is
only possible because the relationship of individuals to their environment and each other has fundamentally changed in the course of
history. No longer borne along by nature and at her mercy almost
without recourse, the individual can now change natural conditions
to a large degree thanks to science and large-scale technology—often
without knowing or considering the long-term consequences. The
relationship of the individual to the community has changed for us in
the same way. The original condition of being contained and bound
by the community has been replaced by the emancipation of the
individual—with well-known advantages and disadvantages. This
fundamental alteration in the individual's experience with respect to
the earth, plants, animals, and humanity is directly linked to the
problems described and to the attempts to solve them. Hence an
overview of these changed attitudes offers a possible means of linking
the historical context with the modern branch of science concerned
with rural development. Of course, rural development policy must be

---

[3]UNESCO's international research project called "Man and Biosphere" (MAB) has
three characteristics: it is international, interdisciplinary, and related to practical
issues. See Bulletin 2, June 1980, of the association "MAB—Pays d'Enhaut," p. 7ff.

concerned primarily with "today" and "tomorrow." But since the future cannot be built without the rocks of the past, as is well known, an effective rural development policy must pay adequate heed to the historical flow of things. It is precisely history that teaches us that durable things have always been a creative synthesis between what has come into being and the demands of the new.

Since in the case of the rural social problem we are dealing explicitly with a problem related to geography—"rural" is, after all, a spatial, geographic category—every feasible attempt to explain this phenomenon demands an epistemological approach which, according to Newby, "links the spacial and the social."[4] In the instance of rural development, it is largely a case of spatially oriented measures, such as soil enrichment, infrastructure, development utilization of natural resources, zoning, etc. Consequently, in this part of the study we will investigate how man's attitude to his environment has changed. Alterations in the individual's relationship to his fellow man will be discussed later.

---

[4]Newby (1981), p. 204.

Chapter 6

The Archaic Mode
of Experiencing an
Ensouled Milieu

Just as the child develops a secure ego consciousness only over the course of time, so too has individual consciousness gradually crystallized in the course of human history and thereby separated itself from unconscious being.[1] Only over time has humanity learned to differentiate itself from surrounding nature. Originally a human being experienced a great part of what we call today "psychic inner space" as external—outside the body, diffused in the ensouled matter of his environment. This archaic union of human and milieu effects a mode of experiencing that L. Levy-Bruhl designated in his book *La Mentalitè Primitive*[2] as *participation* or also as *participation mystique*.[3] This concept quite aptly describes a non-differentiation between subject and object that brings about a compelling relatedness between them. Just as the territory in which they live belongs to archaic people, they belong to that territory. Should they leave it, they become strangers, either as guests or enemies of the people into whose environs they had traveled.[4] The participation between an archaic person and his land, however, encompasses not only the soil but the entire experienced world. As Levy-Bruhl describes, whenever he leaves it, dangers surround him—it ". . . is no longer *his* fruits that he picks and eats, not *his* mountains that surround him, *his* paths upon which he walks: everything is hostile to him because he lacks the *participation* that he is

---

[1]On this cf. Erich Neumann, *The Origins and History of Consciousness* (Princeton, N.J.: Bollingen Foundation/Princeton University Press, 1954, 1970).
[2]L. Lévy-Bruhl, *La Mentalitè Primitive* (Paris: 1922).
[3]Ibid., p. 243. As Jung remarks, "Lévy-Bruhl later retracted this term under the pressure of adverse criticism, to which he unfortunately succumbed. His critics were wrong inasmuch as unconscious identity is a well-known fact." (*C. W.* 18, 440n.)
[4]Ibid., p. 235.

accustomed to. That feeling is the source of his extraordinary antipathy to leaving his territory, even temporarily."[5]

How can the origin and the effect of a *participation mystique* be understood? This is best clarified through an analogy from an experiential realm. Wherever people encounter something unfamiliar, they imbue it with their own inner images. This takes place involuntarily, hence without conscious contribution. When this happens, one speaks of the projection (literally, a "casting out" or "forth") of a psychic content. Say at night we see a piece of rope lying on the ground and, not knowing what it actually is, see a snake in its place. The unknown substance of the rope fires our imagination (*imago* = picture). Even if our image is erroneous, the psychological effect nevertheless remains real, for it influences our actions. Out of fear we will, if need be, make a detour around this piece of rope. Now, whenever several people have the same image of something external—if in our example several people see the rope as a snake in the half-light—then a "dead" object comes to life by means of and for a collective image. Thus in our analogy we see how lack of knowledge or the unclear perception of a phenomenon leads to the projection of inner images and thereby to a union of subject and object.

Since there are many natural laws unknown to archaic people, the unknown "other" becomes replete with projected fantasy material. Incomprehensible external things are explained with one's own inner material. The history of science offers us a wealth of evidence concerning this process. Inexplicable natural phenomena are caused by gods, demons, spirits, goblins, or witches. Via so-called *magical thinking*, causal connections between events are often seen which for us today are scarcely comprehensible. Just think of the belief in magic and in witches.[6] Naturally, in archaic people's whole environment countless phenomena occur that are frightening or fascinating in their incomprehensibility and that stimulate unconscious fantasy material to explain them. Mountains, gorges, trees, particular stones, springs, rivers, moors, lakes, and other striking or vitally significant things are vivified with fantasy material by the archaic mind.[7] The unknown landscape, both with its beautiful, inviting spots, but also with its

---

[5]Ibid., p. 236, cited (and re-translated) from the German translation *Die geistige Welt der Primitiven* (Düsseldorf: Diederichs Verlag, 1959), p. 193f; in ethnographic works one speaks of "local relationship." A striking document of this is the address of Chief Seattle before the President of the United States in the year 1855, entitled "We are a Part of the Earth."

[6]On this see R. Weiss, *Volkskunde in der Schweiz* (Zürich, 1946), p. 128.

[7]On this, see I. Eibl-Eibesfeld, *Der vorprogrammierte Mensch*, p. 144ff.

dark, obscure places, creates a comprehensive "imaginal world" among its inhabitants. Thus, for example, the dark gorge that is scarcely passable, where the sun never shines in warmly, where many have already plunged to their death—there surely must be the place of the Dark One, the one hostile to life, of the Evil One. In contrast, the sunny hill above the lake corresponds to the image of the place where the light, life-promoting natural powers are at home. Wherever such images are experienced by human groups in a common and similar manner, we have the basis for the local sagas and myths. Structures, figures, or signs are situated at such salient places in nature; and respect surrounds the designated spot. This *participation mystique* of primal people with their milieu means that the land which they inhabit is simultaneously a topography of their unconscious.[8]

The experience of nature as being animated is enhanced by intra-psychic images. These images in turn affect us, influencing and limiting our actions, as in the example of the snake and the rope. Depending on its extent, *participation mystique* constricts one's freedom of movement. In a milieu so animated, an individual may not intervene at will. Precise rules and taboos govern humanity's relationship to its environment. Violation of such limits is seen as *wantonness* with possibly disastrous consequences, not only for the wanton perpetrator but also for the entire collective. The archaic experience of an ensouled milieu is linked with a corresponding angst and lack of freedom, indeed with a state of being delivered up to nature and its effects.

We can identify the collective image of an ensouled nature in practically all cultures from China to South America.[9] Until not so very long ago, even for a large part of the Swiss rural population nature was not simply dead matter but rather a living other. Numerous well-known sagas and legends exist—about animated trees and stones and all the eerie places where unredeemed souls must reside. Countless examples show us how we can ascertain the once ensouled countryside in our rural areas. Recent documents from Swiss regions particularly worth reading are found in the collections and investigations of Josef Müller[10] and Eduard Renner[11] concerning the Canton of Uri; Arnold

---

[8]Jung, *C. W.* 10, par. 44.
[9]On this see Lévy-Bruhl; more recent literature, e.g., in I. Eibl-Eibefeld, op. cit., p. 144–49, and his references.
[10]J. Müller, *Sagen aus Uri*, 32 vols. (Basel, 1926–1945).
[11]E. Renner, *Goldener Ring über Uri* (Zürich, 1976).

Büchli[12] and Christian Caminada[13] on the region in the Canton of Grisons; Alois Senti[14] on the Sarganserland; Melchior Sooder[15] on the Hasli Valley; Elisabeth Pfluger[16] on the Canton of Solothurn; and Josef Guntern[17] on the Oberwallis. The dissolution of these primal conceptions concerning the environment around us occurred, as the study of history and folklore shows us, not in one fell swoop but rather ran a course more or less parallel to the gradual intellectual-historical changes of the West.[18] Thus in order to be better able to understand this development, we shall have to consider these changes.

Desouling Matter

The gradual dissolution of humanity's *participation mystique* with its milieu and the concurrent withdrawal of inner psychic projections on nature are consequences of natural scientific thought. The awakening capacity for distinction made possible a progressively better recognition of objective facts and a critical attitude towards one's own ideas. With increase in exact knowledge of external nature and the concomitant capacity for clear differentiation between subjective fantasy material and objectively given knowledge, matter was desouled. A general enlightenment arose much like that in a child's awakening consciousness.

This separation of spirit and matter has taken place by degrees in the Christian West. In very rough description of the process, out of the original polytheistic, natural religion in which stones, trees, springs, etc., were worshipped, there arose the idea of divine forces in matter—Poseidon is the god of the sea, nymphs are the goddesses of springs. Gods are thus bound up with natural phenomena but no longer identical with them.[19] At a later stage, these gods are gradually fused into one god. In Christianity, finally, this one spiritually animating, divine primal energy is regarded as something different from

---

[12]A. Büchli, *Mythologische Landeskunde von Graubünden*, 2 vols. (Aarau, 1958–1966).
[13]Ch. Caminada, *Die verzauberten Täler, Die urgeschichtlichen Kulte und Braüche im alten Rätien* (Olten and Freiburg i. Br., 1961).
[14]A. Senti, *Sagen aus dem Sarganserland* (Basel, 1974).
[15]M. Sooder, *Zelleni us em Haslital* (Basel, 1943).
[16]E. Pfluger, *Solothurner Sagen* (Solothurn, 1975).
[17]J. Guntern, *Volkserzählungen aus dem Oberwallis* (Basel, 1979).
[18]For a study from this point of view see H. A. Schmidt, *Die Entzauberung der Welt in der Schweizer Landeskunde* (Basel, 1942).
[19]See the comprehensive compilation in Marie-Louise von Franz, *Projection and Recollection*.

nature. With this there has come a further, fundamental separation between spirit and matter. "My kingdom is not of this world," Christ says, thereby emphasizing the distinction between spirit and matter, between the divine and the worldly. In the course of the last two thousand years in the Christian world, this separation has become yet more concrete—the separation into a world of spiritual belief and a world of sober fact. The intermingling of subjective "spirit entities" with objective, concrete things was eventually ended by the critical mode of thought in natural science. The encompassing tapestry of projections onto the material environment was replaced by ever more exact knowledge of the actual constitution of matter.

This process of becoming conscious led to the desouling or, as the German sociologist and historian-economist Max Weber put it, the disenchantment of the world.[20] Critical in this is the mastery of things by means of calculation. Weber writes:

> *Increasing intellectualization and rationalization signifies . . . not an increasing general knowledge of the conditions of life to which man is subject, but rather something else: the knowledge of or belief that, if one* only wanted to, *one* could *experience it any time, hence that in principle there are no mysterious, incalculable powers that play a role, but rather that all things—in principle—can be dominated through calculation. But that signifies disenchantment of the world. One no longer has to resort to magical means in order to rule or entreat the spirits; rather, technical methods and calculation accomplish this. The intellectualization to which we have been subject for millennia and of which scientific progress is only a fraction, albeit the most important, means eavesdropping on the laws of nature in order then to rule her with them.*[21]

Taking Switzerland as an example, H. A. Schmidt has sketched the process of the desouling of our world in his book, *Die Entzauberung der Welt in der Schweizer Landeskunde*. Using the example from M. A. Kappeler of Lucern he demonstrates, among other things, how a collective projection onto a so-called mana center, namely Pilate, began to dissolve:

> *People who had distinguished themselves in science and in religion demonstrated by arguments as well as through experiments that the whole belief (in Pilate's ghost) was futile and untrue. In 1585 Magister*

---

[20]See A. Hauser, *Feld und Hald in der alten Schweiz* (Zürich, 1972), p. 70.
[21]Max Weber, "Wissenschaft als Beruf," in *Gesammelte Aufsätze zur Wissenschaftslehre* (Tübingen, 1922), p. 536.

*Johannes Müller, deacon and pastor of the church in Lucerne, ceremo-
niously climbed the mountain with many people of all classes and
provoked the demon where he was supposed to be hidden in the pool.
They cast into the lake what came into their hands and reviled the spirit
with the words: "Pilate, throw out your shit!" which up until then had
been held a sin. They could do this completely unpunished and without
any bad consequences. One man had to wade back and forth through
the water; that made it clear that the pond was not endlessly deep.*[22]

This example shows very nicely the dissolution of a projection by
means of more precise knowledge of the projection bearer, in this
case of the pond. We can infer a fundamental transformation in
Weltanschauung accompanying this process of disenchantment from
the following Solothurn folk tale about the Water Woman at the Cat
Pond:

*If you walk from the Franciscan house in Dullikon over the wooden
plank to Büchs, you go along a footpath in the wood and across oak
steps, and you come to the so-called "Cat Pond." There you will find a
dark green pond dreaming among the ferns. Thousands of years ago a
silvery spring provided this pond with water. On the clear water there
were water lilies blooming, and in the depths a mermaid lived with her
daughters. The mermaids owned the fountain that shot up into the air
out of the beautiful glass palace. The flowers and herbs, shrubs and
trees that grew all around were her garden. Every day, come rain, come
shine, the mermaids came up into their kingdom on the surface of the
water. When the people in our area embraced the Christian faith, a
chapel was erected to the Virgin Mary on the very spot where the
mermaids used to be worshipped. Especially women and girls came to
pray and ask for advice from Mary and her Son. Later the chapel at the
tranquil pond sank into oblivion. It decayed and finally collapsed. The
pond became murky and ended up as a dirty puddle, for people actually
threw the rubbish from their houses and barns into it.*[23]

We can see quite easily how, in spite of Christianization, the people
in this story held fast to their original veneration of nature, uniting it
with their newly acquired Christianity.[24] Only as the Enlightenment's
progressive development of consciousness caught on in rural areas

---

[22]Hermann Alfred Schmidt, op. cit., p. 165. Here he cites from *Mauricii Antonii Cappel-
lerii Pilato Montis Historia*, 1767.

[23]*Solothurner Sagen*, op. cit., no. 276 (slightly abbreviated).

[24]In many Catholic areas the countryside is so rich in religious shrines and monuments
that one can speak of a "baptized countryside," as a Catholic priest once expressed it.
I am indebted to the Bishop of Chur, Dr. Johannes Vonderach, for this reference.

did the common interest shift more and more away from nature. Discriminating consciousness separated from humanity's dark, instinctive background; and outward veneration and reverence for the natural background of life disappeared. The trees and forests, the springs, rivers and lakes, the mountains, groves and caves — everything lost its numinous or divine depth. Only in recent years do we again observe an increasing turn toward nature, as in Dullikon the Cat Pond was dredged and restored along with its environs to its original condition.

The disenchanting of matter certainly did not come about without friction. On the contrary, it often led to a deep discord in rural communities, as illustrated by the following event, also from the Canton of Solothurn:[25] Derendingen needed new fire-fighting equipment. Since there was great demand for oak at that time, the progressives wanted to fell the great, so-called "Stüdel oak" and sell it. However, it was revered by the village community because "a precious picture hung on it." A dispute arose in the village between those for whom the oak embodied an immaterial, numinous value, and those for whom an oak tree was only merchandise, the progressives. The progressives were victorious in this argument. "But the village war between the supporters of the Stüdel oak and those supporting the new fire-fighting equipment, conservatives and the progressives, continued for a long time." In general, the conflict between these two views of the world or ways of thinking has not ceased, as we will shall yet see in detail.

The advantages of this development toward a realistic, approximately illusionless view and understanding of our external world are obvious. Objective knowledge of nature as the mother of our technological development has redeemed a great part of humanity from their material misery. Simultaneously the dissolution of *participation mystique* with things and creatures of our environment has freed us from a multitude of superstitious compulsions. Seen in the light of these facts, epistemologically critical thinking has led to a certain progress in freeing mankind from nature.

Conversely, the degradation and desouling of nature has placed us in the position of believing we can trust nature just as we see fit.[26] The destruction of our environment is a clearly visible disadvantage of progress. The freedom from nature that mankind has won has like-

---

[25] *Solothurner Sagen*, op. cit., p. 98.
[26] See Genesis, 1:28: "Be masters of the fish of the sea, the birds of heaven and all living animals on the earth."

wise proved to be a mixed blessing. Increasing outward mobility and inward separations from our own natural and instinctual aspect have led not only to feelings of liberation but also estrangement from the space we live in, from other human beings, our work, and the depths of our own souls.

In this context we cannot be concerned with weighing advantages and disadvantages against each other. We are concerned simply with illuminating the intellectual foundations which have given us the possibility of willful intervention in natural structures. Given the historical process of the desouling of matter, moreover, it also becomes possible to understand why theories of social change and rural development policies overall limit themselves essentially to the concretely comprehensible. Matter is disenchanted today; consequently, the spirit-soul element no longer has anything to do with matter, i.e., with the concrete problem.

Chapter 7

Modern Findings

The Limits of "Disenchantment"

Since the Enlightenment, the distinction between concrete matter on the one hand and thoughts about it on the other has been made ever more clear. Practically speaking, only those things we can actually ascertain concretely exist for us in the external world. Such things occupy a certain space, have a certain size, and can be precisely measured on the basis of natural laws governing their changes.[1] Should a phenomenon not be explicable, this is, for the enlightened person, solely because not enough is known about the applicable natural laws. If we can understand everything that causes us anxiety, there is nothing further that is unfathomable, in the true sense of the word. Thus, there can no longer be any higher powers in our milieu, either. Everything numinous, everything daimonic, whatever belongs to the intermediate realm between thought and matter has vanished from the rational view of the world. All overwhelming effects of nature ultimately have explicable causes. This view leads to the conclusion that anything divine simply does not exist.[2]

However, it is precisely on the basis of ever more subtle methods of measurement in natural science that this hybrid worldview must encounter insurmountable limits, limits which suddenly make this causal-mechanistic worldview appear in need of fundamental revision. Specifically, the research findings of modern physics have demonstrated that a neat separation of subject and object simply can not be made. The view of man here, and environment there, separate

---

[1]See Schmidt, op. cit., p. 36.
[2]Laplace, for example.

from him, must be reconsidered as no longer the only valid way of seeing. Starting from a survey of the more recent discoveries in the field of physics, along with a discussion of intrapsychic phenomena in the realm of psychology, the concern of this section will be the formulation of a fundamental interweaving of human and environment as an hypothesis. Further, development of our historical overview will have to show where we must reasonably draw the boundaries of the desouling of our milieu and what sort of conclusions must be reached concerning rural sociology and especially rural development policy.

Digression I: Discoveries of Physics

As C. A. Meyer has already emphasized in his essay "Moderne Physik—Moderne Psychologie," "we have the good fortune of having in physics as in no other discipline a great number of simply splendid examples of the newest developments in this science, and, moreover, from the most competent hands."[3] With this groundwork it is justifiable to summarize those discoveries of modern physics that we must consider in this context.

From Classical to Modern Physics

To outline the development from classical to modern physics we must include the philosophical background of the natural scientists. In classical physics the worldview is grounded in the Enlightenment, which found its fundamental formulation in the work of René Descartes.[4] His view of nature rests on the aforementioned division into two realms, that of spirit and soul on the one hand (*res cogitans*) and the realm of physical objects on the other (*res extensa*). This separation led to the idea of "dead matter" separated from everything spiritual. For the man of the Enlightenment the world was a conglomeration of various objects fitted together into a gigantic machine, held in motion by unchanging natural laws of physics. By the immutability of the Creator, these laws persist in the condition in which they were cre-

---

[3]Meyer, C. A., in *Die kulturelle Bedeutung der komplexen Psychologie* (Berlin: Springer Verlag, 1935), p. 349.

[4]A development came to full fruition in the Enlightenment that had already begun in the early Middle Ages. In the ninth century, Agobard of Lyon fought against his contemporaries' uncritical fascination with miracles and recommended the use of reason in religious matters. From H. Reutter, *Die Geschichte der religiösen Aufklärung im Mittelalter*, (Berlin: 1875), reprinted by Scientia Verlag (Aalen: 1963), p. 8ff.

ated.[5] Consequently, the knowledge of the ultimate, simple laws of motion sufficed to explain all natural phenomena exhaustively. The possibility that the Creator himself could be manifest outside of the strict law of cause and effect is unthinkable in the Cartesian conception. Thus the divine becomes the *causa prima* and its activity is identical with the principle of causality.[6]

In a departure from the natural scientists' original desire to know the divine plan of creation, it was soon accepted that isolation of individual natural processes in order to investigate and calculate the laws of cause and effect would be convincingly successful.[7] Hand in hand with this, specialization was valued ever more highly. The application of exact methods and the general material progress of homo sapiens became the obligatory goal of investigators, rather than increasing the knowledge of a divine unity in creation.[8] The possibility of ruling over nature by means of knowledge of natural law was proven by technical application. It became thus the task of the individual scientist "to calculate the course of the world from given data, and many investigators were convinced that this task could, at least in principle, be solved."[9]

The uncritical acceptance of a generally valid and exclusively causal core of events, as well as of the separate existence of the *res extensa* and the *res cogitans* was fundamental to the progress achieved by materialism.[10] It was only the expansion of the investigation of nature to include the very small dimension—microphysics, and the extremely large dimension—astrophysics, that shook fundamentally our traditional ideas of space, time, matter, object, and causality. The image of the physical world, however, was so radically altered by the results of these investigations that the physicists' statements of shock about their findings are not surprising. Einstein writes in his autobiography: "All my attempts to adapt the theoretical foundations of

---

[5]According to Descartes, God could act otherwise, but did not wish to do so. See also M.-L. von Franz, "The Dream of Descartes," in Jacobsohn, von Franz, Hurwitz (eds.), *Timeless Documents of the Soul* (Evanston: Northwestern University Press, 1968).
[6]See also von Franz, op. cit., p. 73.
[7]See W. Heisenberg, *Wandlung in den Grundlagen der Naturwissenschaft* (Leipzig: S. Hirzel Verlag, 1945) (6th edition), p. 82ff.
[8]We will go into the increasing split between belief and knowledge more fully in Part 4.
[9]Heisenberg, op. cit., p. 80.
[10]Heisenberg, op. cit., p. 28.

physics to this new knowledge failed. It was as if the ground had been pulled from under one's feet and there was no other ground in sight on which one could have built."[11]

The new discoveries in the investigation of matter showed that the idea of reality which underlay Newtonian mechanics was too narrow and had to be extended with something more. The quantum theory of atomic structure and Einstein's theory of relativity have led to a new image of the physical world. Of course, in the realm of the "normal" dimensions—say, for the construction of a machine—the causal-mechanical viewpoint of classical physics is adequate. But as soon as we are up against the complex of questions concerning the relationship of humanity and milieu, or in other words, psyche and matter, this conception no longer seems to suffice. Thus in our context the statements of the modern understanding of nature concerning the essence of matter and the relationship of matter to humanity are of interest.

Concerning the Essence of Matter

Our concept of the essence of matter was fundamentally altered after new procedures had made it possible to investigate the composition of the atom. In classical physics an object always included the idea of ultimately indestructible material substance. Einstein corrected this idea by being able to demonstrate that the mass of a particle as such is a form of energy. The equivalence of energy and mass finds its mathematical expression in the formula $E = mc^2$ (E = energy; m = mass; c = speed of light). According to this equation, energy can appear not only in the forms known to classical physics (potential energy, kinetic energy, etc.), but also be contained in the mass of an object. If we recognize mass as a form of energy, then mass must no longer be indestructible but can be transformed into another form of energy. Extensive experiments with artificially accelerated elementary particles demonstrated how the collision of a greatly accelerated elementary particle with another can disintegrate the first. The original energy of its mass changes into kinetic energy that is distributed to the remaining particles. Conversely, excess energy arising from the collision of two elementary particles can be converted to mass for new particles. On the basis of this discovery the old dualism between energy and matter in the natural science of the

---

[11]Albert Einstein, in P. A. Schlipp (ed), *Philosopher-Scientist* (Evanston, IL: The Library of Living Philosophers, 1949), p. 45.

nineteenth century becomes untenable as the basis for observation.[12] For according to modern physics, effect (*energeia*) belongs to the innermost nature of matter.

High-energy scatter experiments of recent years have been able to show us another essential property of matter, the dynamic and continually changing nature of particles. In these experiments, matter seems to be completely transformable. All particles can be changed into other particles; they can form from energy and decay into energy. In this world, classical concepts such as elementary particles, material substance, or isolated objects have lost their meaning. The entire universe appears as a dynamic web of inseparable energy structures.[13] The experiments show how the properties of one particle can be understood only on the basis of its activity, that is, from its interactions with the environment. The particle is not to be understood as an isolated thing but rather as an integral part of the whole.[14] In summary, microphysics shows us that we must view the universe not as a collection of physical objects but rather as a complicated tapestry of relationships between the various particles of one united whole.[15] By his very nature, this must include the observer—a statement we must now pursue.

The Relationship between the Observer and the Observed

As we have seen earlier, the mechanistic-causal worldview rests on the philosophical basis of a fundamental separation of ego and milieu. "As a consequence of this separation it was believed that the world could be described objectively, that is, without ever mentioning the human observer. This objective description of nature became the ideal of all science."[16] Not until subatomic structures were experimentally investigated was it possible to prove these ideas empirically as fundamentally inaccurate.[17] When observing an elementary particle, one would like, for example, to measure its location and its momentum. Heisenberg was able to demonstrate that these two dimensions can never be precisely measured simultaneously. We can determine precisely either the locus of a particle and find out nothing

---

[12]Heisenberg, op. cit., p. 138.
[13]See Fritjof Capra, *The Tao of Physics* (New York: Bantam Books, 1984, second edition), Ch. 13.
[14]Heisenberg, op. cit., p. 138.
[15]Capra, op. cit., p. 190.
[16]Capra, op. cit., p. 58.
[17]Capra, op. cit., p. 141.

about its momentum (and thus its velocity), or the other way round. The better we determine its position, so much the less precise will be our measurement of its momentum, and vice versa. We can decide to measure precisely one of the two properties but the other will always be unmeasurable. The precise mathematical form of this relationship between the uncertainty of locus and momentum is known to us as Heisenberg's Uncertainty Principle. The limitation on measuring natural phenomena has nothing to do with inadequate measurement techniques that are simply as yet unperfected; but rather it is contained in atomic reality, comparable, say, to the unavoidable blurring of the precise measurement if an observer wants to determine the moment when he falls asleep. Consequently we see how in atomic physics scientists can no longer play the role of neutral observers. Unavoidably they, too, are included in the observed world; and with their choice of what they will observe, they prejudice the properties of the object.

Heisenberg's Uncertainty Principle tells us more than something about the relationship between the scientist and the knowledge gained. It also shows us how there exists a relationship of complementarity between certain pairs of properties (in our example, locus and the momentum). The more importance we assign to one aspect of the object under investigation, the more uncertain the other becomes; and the Uncertainty Principle indicates the precise relationship between the two. We will have to go into this fact in greater detail when we treat the question of the limits of disenchantment of the milieu, for where we encounter the limits of calculability of objects, conscious control comes to an end, and we are prey to the unpredictable. As to how much the view of man and object as neatly separated needs revision, we should examine the research into the essence of the human psyche.

Digression II: Discoveries in Psychology

The Discovery of the Unconscious

The Enlightenment as "the explanation of all things through calculation" psychologically signified an intensive strengthening of human consciousness seeking to assert itself vis-à-vis the indefinition and uncertainty of the original intermingling of subject and object. Through the struggle for the separation of cognizant subject from the external, objective world, the view emerged of the human psyche (*res cogitans*) as that which belonged to the ego. Everything that is united with the ego (I think, I doubt, I see, etc.)—the entire field of consciousness around the ego—belongs to the cognizant subject: "I think, therefore I am." For those of the Enlightenment, the human psyche consists of that which I think or know. This identification of the psychic with consciousness set its stamp on the psychology of the nineteenth century. In general we can call it a psychology of consciousness.

Around the turn of the century, the same period of time in which physics needed a new dimension for the understanding of natural phenomena in the external world, a fundamental upheaval took place in the field of knowledge of the human psyche. Pathological disturbances of human consciousness which could not be related to the influences of the environment or the body forced the assumption of an unknown reality.[18] Sigmund Freud succeeded in proving empirically the existence of an intrapsychic reality which did not belong to consciousness, of which man initially "knows nothing," and which for this reason was called *the unconscious*.[19] Subsequently the effects of the unconscious could be ascertained not only in psychopathology (hysteria, compulsive phenomena, exaggerated fears, etc.) but also in everyday life, as, for example, with significant slips of the tongue.

Freud based his research on the principle of causality or psychic determinism. Charles Brenner writes:

> *The sense of this principle is that in the mind, as in physical nature about us, nothing happens by chance, or in a random way. Each psychic event is determined by the ones which precede it. Events in our mental lives that may seem to be random and unrelated to what went on before are only apparently so. In fact, mental phenomena are no more capable of such a lack of causal connection with what preceded them than are physical ones. Discontinuity in this sense does not exist in mental life.*[20]

In the investigation of unconscious phenomena (e.g., dreams), Freud succeeded in making visible certain invisible causal connections between a psychic disturbance and, say, an earlier experience—a procedure with considerable therapeutic effect on certain illnesses

---

[18]For general background on this, see Ellenberger, *The Discovery of the Unconscious* (New York: Basic Books, 1970).

[19]See S. Freud, "Studies on Hysteria," *Standard Edition of the Complete Works of Sigmund Freud* (London: The Hogarth Press, 1955), vol. 2. As a philosophical postulate, the existence of the unconscious was already suspected in the middle of the nineteenth century by C. G. Carus and E. V. Hartmann.

[20]Cited from Charles Brenner, *An Elementary Textbook of Psychoanalysis* (New York: International Universities Press, 1955).

of the psyche. Freud's investigations led to seeing the unconscious primarily as a domain of stored-up repressions. For him, the unconscious was a secondary phenomenon in relation to consciousness with primarily personal character.[21] For this reason, Freud is seen as the discoverer of the personal unconscious.

A few years later C. G. Jung offered empirical proof of a general human unconscious background of the psyche. He called this realm the *collective unconscious*. This insight into the nature of the psyche came out of observations of phenomena from the unconscious that could not have originated in the realm of personal experience and that were manifested spontaneously, i.e., that could not be explained on the basis of repression. Delusions of the mentally ill and, particularly, early childhood dreams are impressive evidence of a fundamental, collective unconscious layer.[22]

In the phenomena of the psychic background, Jung recognized not only the "effects of causes" but spontaneous new formations from the unconscious—new formations that on closer investigation permitted the inference of a goal-directed tendency of the unconscious psyche. He compared this purposive aspect of the unconscious with developmental impulses in external nature.[23] Consequently the unconscious can no longer be attributed—as Freud assumed—to things repressed from consciousness. Rather than a secondary phenomenon, the unconscious proved to be, on the basis of Jung's research results, the original datum out of which consciousness had arisen.[24] Just as the absolute validity of causality in microphysics had been tempered by the discovery of radioactive decay and led to the concept of "primary probability," so also a dissolution of the purely causal point of view took place with regard to things psychic.[25]

In a Copernican turn, the discovery of the collective unconscious

---

[21]Later Freud partially acknowledged the collective character of the unconscious. He speaks then of "archaic remnants." See Freud, *New Introductory Lectures on Psycho-Analysis, The Standard Edition of the Complete Works of Sigmund Freud* (London: The Hogarth Press, 1964, 1968), vol. XXII.

[22]Early childhood dreams are especially suited as irreproachable proof of motifs that cannot stem from the realm of personal experience. On this, see C. G. Jung's "Children's Dreams Seminar" held at the Federal Institute of Technology, Zürich, 1938–39, and 1939–40 (multigraphed transcript, unpublished) and 1940–41, published in Zürich, 1976.

[23]Phylogenesis and ontogenesis.

[24]See also the comprehensive study by Erich Neumann, *Origins and History of Consciousness*, Bollingen Series XLII (Princeton: Princeton University Press, 1954, 1970).

[25]Alfred Adler worked out the purely finalistic viewpoint in his psychology of the "will to power." See his *The Neurotic Constitution* (New York: Moffat, Yard, & Co., 1917), and *Understanding Human Nature* (London: George Allen & Unwin, 1928).

shifted from a focus on the ego as origin of the psyche to a view of the objective psychic background as the primal ground not only of ego-consciousness but also of creative fantasy and of so-called "chance ideas." If Freud's proof of an unknown reality had constituted a huge step in the direction of recognizing a psychic reality not immediately perceptible "to the naked eye," the results of Jung's investigations signified a fundamental relativization of the ego-centered view of the world.

Concerning the Nature of Psyche and Spirit

Jung's observation of organizing factors which cast our ideas and feelings in a generally human fashion ranks as a fundamental insight into the nature of psyche. He called these basic spiritual structures *archetypes.*[26] The human being has instincts which move him to a typical mode of behavior in certain situations. As the inner aspect of the instincts, the archetypes effect typical modes of understanding[27] in humanity. The presence of such fundamental spiritual structures makes it possible to understand why the same or similar feelings, ideas, symbolic images, judgments, etc., have been manifested throughout humanity in certain common situations (e.g., when encountering the opposite sex or death). "The fact that mythological, religious, and moral ideas or rules appear in similar or the same form among peoples who have had no cultural contact with each other distinctly demonstrates this as does the fact that again and again we can observe the appearance of dream symbols, concepts, etc., of which the bearer has no inkling that they are collective images or ideas already known to mankind at some time and place."[28]

The concept of the archetype is to be strictly distinguished from that of the "archetypal image." The latter designates the result of the ordering effect of the first. Only the archetypes as such are inherited,

---

[26]*Arche* = beginning; *typos* = imprint, form, shape, character. Jung's observation that the contents of the unconscious, as they reach consciousness in fantasies, dreams, and visions, and appear in the products of the psychoses, are not simply chaotic but can be categorized in more or less distinct "types" served as empirical proof of the archetypes. See C. G. Jung and Karl Kerény, *Essays on a Science of Mythology* (Princeton, N.J.: Princeton University Press, 1949, 1959, 1963), and G. Isler, "Archetypus," in *Enzyklopädie des Märchens* (Berlin and New York: vol. 1, 1976).

[27]A good summary is to be found in the book edited by H. Heussler, *Instinkt und Archetypen im Verhalten der Tiere und im Erleben des Menschen* (Darmstadt: Wissenschaftlichebuchgesellschaft, 1976).

[28]M.-L. von Franz, "Zur Psychologie der Gruppe," in *Zeitwende-Kultur, Theologie, Politik,* July 1971. "On Group Psychology," *Quadrant* 13, Winter 1973, p. 4–11.—*Eng. ed.*

common human organizing factors, but as such they are *irrepresent-able*. The visible effects of archetypes in the form of typical images are always the cooperative product of the archetype and the environment at the moment. Thus it is not images that are inherited, for the latter are temporally, locally, and individually determined, but rather only their unconscious organizers, the archetypes per se. The comparison with the formation of a crystal elucidates this difference, for the formation of a crystal from a supersaturated solution is analogously determined in regard to form but not precise shape.[29] An archetype per se would be comparable to the axial system of the crystal, which determines the stereometric structure but not the concrete shape of the individual crystal. As an ordering factor, the axial system becomes visible only in the crystal; prior to the formation of the crystal it was only "in potentia," invisibly immanent in the mother solution. In a very comparable manner, archetypes in the collective unconscious are immanent invisibly and become visible only in the organizing activity which they exert on human ideas and images.

The interaction of common human structural dominants and individual elaboration in the realm of psyche can be similarly observed in the shaping of our bodies. The common human structure of our head or our hand finds concrete manifestation together with the unmistakably individual features of a finger print or physiognomy. Just as our bodies bear characteristics of our ancestors reaching far back into the animal kingdom, so also does our basic psychic structure follow a fundamental phylogenetic law.[30] Stored in the collective unconscious is the experience of our ancestors, which we speak of, depending on the level of depth, as a family unconscious, a regional unconscious, a folk unconscious, a racial unconscious, or ultimately a common human collective unconscious. Visually we can imagine it as in Figure 5.[31]

---

[29]On this see C. G. Jung, "On the Nature of the Psyche," in *C. W.* 8, p. 159ff.

[30]On this see Jung, *Gestaltungen des Unbewussten* (Zürich, Rascher Verlag, 1950), p. 23.

[31]The diagrams come from von Franz, *Projection and Recollection*, p. 80–81, (slightly altered).

Figure 5. The Basic Structure of the Psyche (after von Franz)

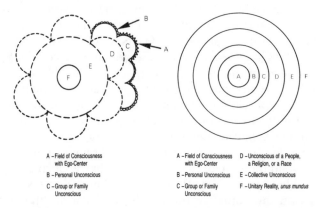

A – Field of Consciousness
with Ego-Center

B – Personal Unconscious

C – Group or Family
Unconscious

A – Field of Consciousness
with Ego-Center

B – Personal Unconscious

C – Group or Family
Unconscious

D – Unconscious of a People,
a Religion, or a Race

E – Collective Unconscious

F – Unitary Reality, *unus mundus*

Following Jung's demonstration of the archetype and of the collective unconscious, his basic structure of the psyche has been corroborated from the vantage point of other sciences, such as psychosomatic medicine, human ethology, comparative history of religions, the study of myth and epic, jurisprudence, economics, and the history of literature.[32] In our context two significant issues have arisen out of the discovery of the archetype as an element of the spirit, and the other concerns relationship of the archetype to matter.

Let us first address the question of what archetypes as such – and consequently the collective unconscious – have in common with the principle of spirit. As we stated initially, the clear separation of spirit and matter was essential to the Enlightenment. An increasing overvaluation of material reality ensued, and simultaneously the spiritual-psychic side became equated with consciousness, the *cogitatio*.[33] Through the identification of the human ego with the principle of spirit (*je pense, donc je suis*), there followed a disastrous inflation of ego consciousness with the spirit of the unconscious. Thus those of the Enlightenment began to believe that the human being was the origin of the spirit. "He had indeed not himself created the spirit, but rather

---

[32]On this see C. G. Jung, "Psychologie vegetativer Neurosen," in *Der Archetyp* (Basel: Karger, 1964); the research results of Eibl-Eibesfeld, G. Isler, *Die Sennenpuppe* (Basel: Krebs, 1971); H. Marti, *Urbild und Berfassung* (Bern: Huber, 1958); as well as the works by Eugen Böhler and Karl Schmid.

[33]Descartes' sentence "je pense, donc je suis" arose from his reflections that all bodily reactions, feelings, and sensory perceptions can be separated from the ego, as happens for example during sleep, but not thought. Consequently, this is par excellence the function of consciousness which is absolutely fused with the ego – and for Descartes the soul consisted only of the thinking ego. See von Franz, "Descartes," op. cit., p. 70.

the latter makes it possible that he creates; spirit gives him the impetus and the chance idea, the endurance, and the inspiration. But it so pervades the human being that man falls into the most serious temptation to believe that he himself is the creator of the spirit and that he possesses it."[34] Only observation of the phenomena coming from the impersonal level of the unconscious made it possible to distinguish between the ego conscious as it receives and executes and the creative spirit of the unconscious.[35] The psychology of the unconscious made it clear that ultimately all our spontaneous ideas—which those of the Enlightenment believed themselves to produce and possess—were really dependent on the whim of the unconscious as to whether it wanted to yield them up or not.[36] This spirit of the unconscious is, as Jung was able to prove, the effect of the archetype. In his theoretical reflections on the nature of the psyche, he writes, "the archetype represents the authentic element of spirit, but a spirit which is not to be identified with the human intellect, since it is the latter's *spiritus rector.*"[37]

We also find a spirit of nature in external manifestations that can constantly amaze us—in a honeycomb, cellular structure, or a living organism. There seems to be inherent in matter the capacity to effect meaningful order. We can conceptualize this impulse toward order and structure as the spiritual side of nature. The exact natural sciences show us, with as much precision as desired, how laws rule our external world—laws which, independent of the existence of man's thought, permit a formulation that corresponds to purposeful action.[38] Archetypes as the spiritual basic elements in nature appear to act in accordance with what physics calls natural laws. "The latter are formulated in strict mathematical expressions, and physical events follow them. A mathematically formulated law is something spiritual. We can call it so, because it is the human spirit that recognizes it . . . Nature follows this abstract spiritual element, the law.

---

[34]C. G. Jung, *Symbolik des Geistes*, p. 11f.

[35]Experiencing the autonomy of the unconscious seems to be an indispensable prerequisite for distinguishing the human ego from the creative spirit, whereby the disastrous hubris of the Enlightenment can be mitigated.

[36]On this see von Franz, "Descartes," op. cit., p. 116.

[37]C. G. Jung, "On the Nature of the Psyche," C. W. 8, par. 406.

[38]Max Planck, *Gigt es eine vernünftige Heltordnung?* (Fähre: Bern, n.d.); for Descartes, the natural laws that structured matter were the work of the Creator. As the Enlightenment progressed, however, the Creator became a "superfluous hypothesis" (Laplace).

Consequently spiritual elements are anchored in nature herself."[39] In the next section the relationship of the spiritual-psychic structural dominants to matter will be traced.

The Relationship between Subject and Object

In the chapter on physics we examined the relationship between the observed external world and the observer, following the modern insights into the nature of matter. Following the overview of the current state of knowledge concerning the nature of the psyche, we shall now discuss the relationship of the psyche to matter or the concrete external.[40]

Probably the most conspicuous relationship of psyche and matter is found in the area of psychosomatic medicine, which is concerned with investigating the effect of unconscious emotional personality factors on physical functioning. The classical example is the stomach ulcer. Experts today generally hold the view that this occurs in those in whom emotional factors create a predisposition to the illness. The relationship of psyche and body is quite evident in, for example, the direct connection between states of anxiety and breaking out in perspiration, or between hearing horrible news and turning pale. On the other hand, material factors influence the psyche. In this connection, the influence of the state of the body on psychic mood is generally known. Obviously psyche and body stand in a relationship of reciprocal effect. We can understand this as a causal nexus; but that does not answer the fundamental question of how the nonmaterial psyche can have an effect on matter and conversely, how physical processes can bring about things psychic. With the assumption of a causal connection, the psyche would either have to be a consequence of matter or else matter would have to be ordered by a pre-existing psyche. For this reason Jung raised the question of whether or not the relationship of psyche to body, or the coordination of psychic and physical processes in an organism, could be understood as an *acausal ordering* instead of a causal relationship.[41] Just as the field of physics no longer

---

[39]Walter Heitler, *Naturwissenschaft ist Geisteswissenschaft* (Zürich: Verlag Die Waage, 1972), p. 14.

[40]Similar to the "problem of observation" in atomic physics, we also have the problem of the reciprocal effect of the observer and the observed in regard to the unconscious. Wolfgang Pauli has discussed this in his essay "Naturwissenschaftliche und erkenntnistheoretische Aspekte der Ideen vom Unbewussten," in *Instinkte und Archetypen*, op. cit., p. 277ff.

[41]See C. G. Jung, "Synchronicity: An Acausal Connecting Principle," *C. W.* 8, par. 816.

makes a distinction between concrete material "building blocks" and the forces operative between them, so, by this hypothesis, the dualism between psyche and body ought to be viewed as a unity at a level transcending consciousness.[42]

In the realm of the psyche, this structural background consists of the nonmaterial archetypes of the collective unconscious which order ideas. But since material effects can also be observed when an archetype has been activated,[43] Jung altered his definition of archetypes in his later works, from the original term "primordial images" to *nonmaterial structural elements of the collective unconscious*.[44] Through his observation that the archetypes possess a psychoid aspect, i.e, that they are demonstrable not only as structural dominants in the psyche but also in matter,[45] he succeeded in defining organizing principles that are neutral in the differentiation between psyche and physics.[46]

The zoologist B. Rentsch advanced the hypothesis that the relationship of psyche and body, or generally of psyche and matter, cannot be understood as a causal nexus but rests rather on a psychophysical unitary reality. Since the human body gradually developed out of inorganic matter, the animated and spiritual aspect, appearing in its most differentiated form in the human being, probably did not come into being suddenly either. Based on the argument of the basic improbability that the parallel connection "suddenly sprang up at some time or other in the course of a gradual and continuous phylo-

---

[42]"We must completely give up the idea of the psyche's being somehow connected with the brain, and remember instead the 'meaningful' or 'intelligent' behavior of the lower organisms, which are without a brain. Here we find ourselves much closer to the formal factor which, as I have said, has nothing to do with brain activity." Jung, op. cit., par. 947. Von Frisch's observations of bees, among others, offer proof of the presence of transcerebral thought and perception.

[43]Note the physiological reactions accompanying a complex reaction in the association experiment, where an activated archetype—as the core of the complex—releases a "material" bodily reaction at the same moment. See C. G. Jung, *Experimental Research*, C. W. 2, and C. A. Meyer, *Die Empirie des Unbewussten* (Zürich: 1968). In the instance of synchronistic events in which intrapsychic and material facts appear united, the psychoid aspect of the archetype is particularly clear. On this see C. G. Jung and Wolfgang Pauli, *Naturerklärung und Psyche*, op. cit., especially p. 90ff. (also in *C. W.* 8, par. 816f).

[44]C. G. Jung, "On the Nature of the Psyche," *C. W.* 8, par. 366–70.

[45]The archetype of the natural number, as M.-L. von Franz has been able to demonstrate, has a special bond with the unitary reality of psyche and matter in that natural numbers both manifest themselves in the realm of psyche as collective structural dominants (number symbolism, etc.) and are also observable in matter as ordering factors (in energy quanta, radioactive decay, etc.). On this see M.-L. von Franz, *Time and Number*. p. 3, p. 35. For secondary literature on this see J. L. de la Cuadra, "Die Proportio sesquitertia in Psychologie und Naturwissenschaft," *Analytische Psychologie*, vol. 8, no. 2, 1977.

[46]W. Pauli, op. cit., p. 238.

genesis," Rentsch points to the basic possibility of "ascribing the most primitive psychic components of exact parallel processes also to life-less and inorganic matter."[47] Accordingly, the primal elements of the psychic would also have to be present in inorganic matter, a thought that no longer seems speculative in the light of contemporary research in nuclear physics and biology which has produced evidence of the dynamic structure and meaningful behavior of matter.[48]

Another reflection confirms this idea of the presence of psychic components in matter, as Walter Heitler has illustrated in the instance of the acorn and the oak tree. The genetic material of the acorn con-tains the entire structural plan for the oak tree that will develop from it. But for this structural plan to be realized, something that can process this stored information is needed. The eventual oak tree is able to accomplish this itself. It is typical of life to take up this infor-mation and to actualize it. The capacity of the oak tree to take in such information and to develop accordingly is what Heitler calls "typical of life."[49] In the processing of the genetic material, we see manifested the *inner essence* of the organism which recognizes this significant content. This inner essence of the organism is what Aristotle called the psyche. In its simplest form it would be revealed in the "meaning-ful" behavior of inorganic matter.[50] But if protopsychic elements[51] must be assumed to exist in inorganic matter, we can no longer speak of "dead" matter.

The direct psychophysical interconnection has become the subject of scientific research, not only from the viewpoint of medicine and psychology but also from that of biology. Since the seventeenth cen-tury, however, this interaction has constituted "a considerable embar-rassment for the world view of 'classical' physics," as Wolfgang Pauli says, "in that precisely here, in addition to the usual causal intercon-

---

[47]B. Rentsch, *Neuere Probleme der Abstammungslehre*, 2nd edition, 1954, quoted by W. Pauli in "Naturwissenschaftliche und erkenntnistheoretische Aspekte der Ideen vom Unbewussten," in *Instinkte und Archetypen im Verhalten der Tiere und im Erleben des Menschen*, op. cit. p. 234, note 11.

[48]For more recent results see W. Boos, *Intelligente Bakterien; Chemotaxis als primitives Modell von Reizlietungssystemen*, (Konstanz: Universitätsverlag Konstanz, 1977).

[49]W. Heitler, op. cit., p. 17 and p. 32f.

[50]Max Planck, op. cit. As an example, Planck offers photons which constitute a ray of light. When such a ray of light comes from a star to earth, it is refracted by the various layers of the atmosphere. In the course of this, the ray of light always selects from all the possible curves that one which most rapidly brings it to its goal.

[51]M.-L. von Franz coined this term.

nection, a different sort of interconnection, the *parallelistic*, had to be postulated."[52] As mentioned above, that interconnection would be through an acausal principle of order.[53]

If the current psychology of the unconscious assumes the presence of certain invisible psychoid structural dominants, it does basically the same thing physics does when constructing a model of the atom.[54] The elementary particles of microphysics are just as invisible as the archetypes. No nuclear physicist has ever seen an electron shoot past but has only been able to view it indirectly through traces on a photographic plate; and on the basis of those effects the existence and nature of the particle are inferred. The structural dominants of the collective unconscious are likewise invisible. Its psychoid nature must be inferred on the basis of its effects in the psychic and material realms. Jung's description of the collective unconscious and its structural dominants, archetypes, provided a foundation for understanding the relationship of psyche and matter in terms of contemporary natural scientific knowledge.[55]

Jung designated the psychophysical unitary aspect of being the *unus mundus*.[56] Ultimately the idea of an *unus mundus* rests, as he says,

> on the assumption that the multiplicity of the empirical world rests on an underlying unity, and that not two or more fundamentally different worlds exist side by side or are mingled with one another. Rather, everything divided and different belongs to one and the same world, which is not the world of sense but a postulate whose probability is vouched for by the fact that until now no one has been able to discover a world in which the known laws of nature are invalid.[57]

---

[52]W. Pauli, "Naturwissenschaftliche und erkenntnistheoretische Aspekte," op. cit., p. 234.

[53]Radioactive decay appears as an effect without a cause and suggests the idea that the ultimate laws of nature may not even be causal.

[54]C. G. Jung, "On the Nature of the Psyche," *C. W.* 8, par. 417.

[55]"Psyche cannot be totally different from matter, for how otherwise could it move matter? And matter cannot be alien to psyche, for how else could matter produce psyche? Psyche and matter exist in one and the same world, and each partakes of the other, otherwise any reciprocal action would be impossible. If research could only advance far enough, therefore, we should arrive at an ultimate agreement between physical and psychological concepts." C. G. Jung, *Aion*, *C. W.*, 9i, par. 413. De la Cuadra, op. cit., convincingly proved this statement for the *proportio sesquitertia* in intellectual history, on the one hand, and in genetics, molecular biology, chemistry, and atomic and nuclear physics, on the other (dissertation for the Medical Faculty, University of Bern, 1977).

[56]The concept *unus mundus* comes from the natural philosopher Gerhard Dorn.

[57]C. G. Jung, *Mysterium Coniunctionis*, par. 767-70, *C. W.* 14, cited by von Franz, *Time and Number*, p. 8.

Even the psychic world is rooted in the same universe. However, Jung goes on to emphasize that there exists little or no hope that that unitary being could ever be visualized, unless perhaps through anti-nomies. Yet we nevertheless know with certainty that the empirical world of appearances rests somewhere against a background tran-scending consciousness.[58]

Consequently we will never be able to say anything definite about the interconnection of psyche and matter.

> Since psyche and matter are contained in one and the same world, and moreover are in continuous contact with one another and ultimately rest on irrepresentable, transcendental factors, it is not only possible but fairly probable, even, that psyche and matter are two different aspects of one and the same thing. The synchronicity phenomena point, it seems to me, in this direction, for they show that the nonpsychic can behave like the psychic and vice versa, without there being any causal connec-tion between them. Our present knowledge does not allow us to do much more than compare the relation of the psychic to the material world with two cones, whose apexes, meeting in a point without extension—a real zero-point—touch and do not touch."[59]

According to present-day knowledge, the relationship of human to the surrounding environment consists not merely in living in it and perceiving it; rather, a direct, parallel relationship must exist.[60] In that the "ultimate" components of matter occur in formations similar to those of the inner world, the collective unconscious, the concept is beginning to be accepted that matter and psyche could be respec-tively the external and the internal faces of one and the same reality transcending consciousness.[61] This unitary reality (*unus mundus*) would ultimately correspond to the idea known in Western intellec-tual history as the animation of matter.[62]

Summary of Discoveries in Psychology

In the last hundred years the development of knowledge concern-ing the human psyche has followed a course from the pure psychol-ogy of consciousness to the discovery of an objective psyche which is

---

[58]von Franz, ibid.
[59]C. G. Jung, "On the Nature of the Psyche," *C. W.* 8, par. 418.
[60]Very fine and convincing examples of this are to be found in Walter Heitler, *Naturwis-senschaft ist Geisteswissenschaft* (Zürich: 1972), p. 9–11 and 19–22.
[61]M.-L. von Franz, *Time and Number*, p. 178 (my italics).
[62]Op. cit., p. 279; see, for example, Hermetic philosophy.

autonomous vis-à-vis the human ego. Viewing the unconscious not as a consequence of consciousness but rather as an irreducible reality representing the matrix of consciousness inevitably led to fundamental revision of our ideas concerning the nature of psyche. The enlightened person of the twentieth century had to give up the belief that the psyche was identical with consciousness. The ego-centered viewpoint had to make way for a more comprehensive conception of the psyche, seeing the ego in a reciprocal relationship with the unconscious background of the soul.

Empirically, contemporary psychology has been able to demonstrate an unconscious psychic reality in humanity that both shows a nonpsychic aspect and touches on the realm of psychic-material unity. Thus, not only the discoveries of physics but also those of psychology lead to abandonment of the Cartesian concept of an objectively existing difference between the *res extensa* and the *res cogitans*. The polar separation of the psychophysical unitary reality into two distinct realms of the spiritual-psychic and the material, or of energy and matter, appears in this light as a means for our consciousness to describe its psychic experiences more precisely.[63] "External-material" and "internal-spiritual" have come to be labels characterizing consciousness. On the basis of current knowledge, however, we must say it is improbable that these two realms are fundamentally different.

---

[63]On this see M.-L. von Franz, *Projection and Recollection*, p. 81ff.

Chapter 8

Reality of the Man-Milieu Relationship

Error of Projection?

Let us now return to the historical consideration of the change in the relationship of human to surroundings. As we have seen, humanity was originally united with the external world via so-called archaic identity. Out of this primordial condition of identity, combined with the often magical compulsion which the external world exerted on the human psyche, differentiation between subject and object, psyche and matter, gradually crystallized. We refer to this process as the withdrawal of a projection. In this context, however, we must ask whether this disenchantment of the milieu was not simply insight into an error. If this is the case, we could limit ourselves to the historical point of view. If not, it is necessary to go deeper into the phenomenon of projection and its withdrawal. To deal with this question, we must elucidate the difference between an error and a projection.

In the example of the snake and the rope, we have illustrated the animation of a "dead" object by means of a human image. It is usually a simple matter to dispose of such an illusion with better information. Without too much resistance we acknowledge the error. The difference between a projection and a common error in judgment or mistake lies in the fact that the latter two can be eliminated without difficulty with better information.[1] In the instance of a projection, on the other hand, the person concerned typically reacts with violent

---

[1] M.-L. von Franz, *Projection and Recollection*, p. 3; see also C. G. Jung, *C. W.* 9(1), pars. 121–123.

affect against every attempt at rectification,[2] for here it is a matter of an unconscious, i.e., of an unperceived and unintentional imposition of a subjective component of the soul onto an external object. One "sees" in this object something of one's own which is unconscious. However, it seldom or perhaps even never occurs that there is nothing at all or only very little of this projected material of one's own in the object. The object needs a "hook" onto which the one projecting can hang the projection like a coat on a clothes peg.[3]

Von Franz illustrates this with the example of the son who experiences his father as a tyrant, and projects the qualities of the tyrant onto authority figures, yet who also comports himself tyrannically, though doing so unconsciously.[4] He will scarcely be able to hang his image of a tyrant on a thoroughly gentle, modest person. Yet when someone exerts even a relatively small degree of self-assertion or power over him (the hook for the projection), the latent image of the tyrant leaps, as it were, onto that person. The projection has taken place and been "hooked"; the person projecting has them the "sacred" conviction that he is dealing with a tyrant. Such an error in judgment can be corrected only with the greatest effort, because it would mean, in this example, an insight into his own desire for power.[5]

The fact that, in the case of animation of the milieu, we are actually dealing with projection and not simply with error is demonstrated by the tenacity with which certain ideas concerning the effect of specific places are sustained, ideas that would not be abandoned simply through more precise knowledge. Historical documents from antiquity to the modern period concerning such resistance against enlightenment offer extensive evidence of this.[6] Consequently a deeper exploration of the phenomenon of projection is called for.

---

[2]"Should he accept the rectification, he experiences depression. He looks reduced and disappointed because the psychic energy that was invested in the projection has not flowed back to him, but rather has been cut off." Quoted from M.-L. von Franz, op. cit., p. 3.

[3]Summarized from von Franz, loc. cit. More precisely, "projection rests on the archaic identity of subject and object. . . ." C. W. 6, def. "Projection," par. 87.).

[4]"How tyrannic and authoritarian are those very people who present themselves as anti-authoritarian." Von Franz, op. cit. p. 63.

[5]Von Franz, op. cit.

[6]From antiquity compare Herodotus' descriptions to those of Plutarch; on the Middle Ages see H. Reuter, Die Geschichte der religiösen Aufklärung im Mittelalter (Berlin, 1975; Aalen: Scientia Verlag, 1963) for the modern period see H. A. Schmidt, Entzauberung (Basel: 1942), and N. Mantl, Nassereith, also our example of the "Stüdelteich."

Projection: Origin and Hook

Since we now must view the "enchanted" landscape as a projection, the question arises as to what it was, then, that led to the projection (*proicere* = to throw forward) of an ensouled milieu in a very specific way? Somewhat more precisely, we must ask ourselves first what the origin of this projected idea was and then what characterized the nature of the hook for the projection in the external environment. We must elucidate these two points if we want to make statements about the limits of disenchantment of the milieu.

The features of a landscape susceptible to projections are found generally in striking places. Because of ignorance of the actual conditions and because of the impression that they make on the human soul, such places are animated with the corresponding inner images. If places are animated by a community in such a manner, they become so-called *mana places*[7] in the landscape; in sagas they are called magical places. But for such collective images to be experienced unanimously, there would have to exist in humanity itself, indeed in the *collective* layer of the unconscious, those sorts of "mana centers," i.e., realms charged with energy. In fact, experimental psychology can, with the help of the association experiment, demonstrate the existence of energy-charged centers in the unconscious of individual persons.[8] With each stimulus word that is called out to the subject, a specific time can be measured until the first association is given (e.g., stimulus word "bottle," association "wine"). A particularly long reaction time to a specific stimulus word points to an intrapsychic disturbance not under the control of consciousness, a disturbance that is associatively related to the stimulus word. A person who, for example, has had decisively negative experiences with people in positions of authority will most probably give a first association to the stimulus word "boss" after a prolonged reaction time. We can envision the prolongation of reaction time as if caused by a magnetic field which attracts an associatively related stimulus word to it. When such a field is highly charged, an association is possible only after a certain lapse of time. In psychology we call such a "magnetic field" a complex. As the association experiment demonstrates, it is not just the psychologically ill person who shows such prolonged reaction times or complex reactions to certain stimulus words; rather, this phenomenon belongs

---

[7]The concept of *mana* comes from the Polynesian and designates a mysterious power or force in persons, animals, and things, that produces extraordinary effects.
[8]On this see C. G. Jung, *C. W.* 2, part 1. A summary can be found in C. A. Meyer, *Die Empirie des Unbewussten* (Zürich: Walter Verlag, 1968).

to the mode of reacting of all persons. The central core of these complexes has proven not to be a personal acquisition, as is evident from the existence of common categories such as inferiority complex, power complex, father complex, mother complex, anxiety complex, etc.[9] "This fact, that there are well-characterized and easily recognizable types of complex, suggests that they rest on equally typical foundations, that is, on emotional aptitudes or *instincts*."[10] Consequently it is the formal, image-forming aspect of the instincts, which we call the archetype, that is at work in the core of the complex.

The mana places in the collective unconscious are, therefore, the archetypes. So long as they are not experienced as working in the intrapsychic realm, an unconscious (i.e., unperceived and unintentional) imposition of this subjective psychic fact onto external objects takes place. The collective nature of archetypes corresponds to the collective nature of the ensouled landscape. Hence the ensoulment of the milieu actually mirrors something collectively, internally psychic. Moreover, this is confirmed when an impersonal, collective layer of the unconscious is experienced and thereby discovered as a consequence of the external disenchantment of the landscape.[11] The origin of the idea of an ensouled milieu, therefore, is found in the "prominent areas" of the collective unconscious, the archetypes; the hook for these projections is found in the "prominent areas" of the external surroundings.

Levels of Experiencing the Milieu

How variously the reality of outside and inside has been experienced right to the present, for example by the mountain folk of Uri, has been impressively described by the Altdorf physician, Eduard Renner, in his book *Goldener Ring über Uri*.[12] In this document we can clearly follow the phenomenon of the gradual insight into a projection[13] and thereby consider how this primordial idea of a unitary spiritual-material realm can be of interest to us today.

In the side valleys of Uri, threatened by natural forces and in part inaccessible until very recently, a primordial view of the world has been preserved. Accordingly, the country surrounding inhabited

---

[9]See Jung's foreword to Jolanda Jacobi's book, *Complex, Archetype, Symbol*, Bollingen Series LVII (Princeton: Princeton University Press, 1959).
[10]Quoted from Jacobi, op. cit.
[11]See C. G. Jung, C. W. 9, i, par. 7, par. 21f.
[12]Renner, E., *Goldener Ring über Uri* (Zürich, 1976), 3rd edition.
[13]See Chapter 3.

areas is generally animated, and the mountain folk of Uri designate it as "It" (*Es*). " 'It' calls; 'It' acts badly; 'It' steals the cattle and brings them back; from the realm of this 'It,' fortune and misfortune befalls man."[14] "This 'It' is no form of thought but rather of experience, itself most intensely alive and active. It explains every situation, even the inexplicable. It lacks the personality to be God or the Devil. It is in itself a sum, the sum of characteristics that do not come to rest around any solid center, moreover a sum of effects and, to make the contradiction complete, simultaneously a place and a time."[15] Renner goes further in his characterization of the "It": "In the 'It' everything uncertain, uncomprehended, and incomprehensible is pent up. . . . Of itself neither good nor evil, it remains uncanny, iridescent, and a domain of the night in broad daylight."[16] It is experienced as an *energy in matter*, to which one must assume a correct relationship and *with which one must be able to deal skillfully.*[17]

> "It often causes objects to lose their solid nature so that they must be held fast in their true nature by means of spells or prayers. In the course of winter the alpine pasture, for example, again falls under the sway of the 'It,' likewise the home that is uninhabited for extended periods of time. Therefore the crystal seeker lays his hat or another object in his possession (of 'his own') beside the crystals so that 'It' cannot take them away again. For example, the people of Uri confront the 'It' with the magic circle of the 'ring' as a spell: In the prayer which is called out in all directions in the alpine meadow, in the circular throwing of the flag, also in such forms of behavior as prayer, cursing, 'Nid-der-glichä-tuä' (continue doing as if nothing has happened whenever 'It' appears), and other customs of self-protection for the soul. The 'ring' is here the symbol of what always remains, the symbol of human consciousness with which man keeps Nature at bay."[18]

---

[14]Renner, op. cit., quoted in von Franz, "Ansicht einer Psychologin," in *Forum Alpinum* (Zürich, 1965), p. 390.

[15]Renner, op. cit., p. 148.

[16]Renner, op. cit., p. 194.

[17]On this see Renner, p. 147 and p. 150, p. 176ff, p. 184, and additionally the collection of sagas by Josef Müller, *Sagen aus Uri* (Basel: Krebs, 1945), 3 vols.

[18]Quoted from von Franz, op. cit., p. 390. Von Franz continues: "According to Renner, the central figure of the ring is man himself. By his mere existence, mankind causes the miracle of the sphere which also lies over his property. And when it is a matter of consequence, his presence alone suffices to hold the 'It' in check; only he must not disturb the balance by any awkward change of his own behavior, for 'uf dä Alpä-n-erlydet's gewiss nit vill' (In the mountains 'It' won't put up with much). Even the minutest neglect of consciousness must meet the disintegrative effect of the 'It' again and again with the 'ring.' "

This description of the 'It' is congruent with what we today call the autonomous character of the collective unconscious. The spirit of the unconscious as *complexio oppositorum* (good and evil!) is exteriorized by the mountain people of Uri and thus experienced as coming from the outside. Now whether or not the autonomy of the collective unconscious is experienced as coming from without or within really makes no difference. What is important is the recognition of these forces of the soul and the insight about the necessity of taking this dimension into account. It is a crime not to understand the utterances of the "It" and interpret them correctly, as the mountain people of Uri say.[19] Today we would describe these overpowering, incalculable effects, which are experienced as coming from outside, in part as eruptions of affect, thoughtlessness, and various other inner impulses. The inherently introverted way of life among the Uri mountain people has enabled preservation of direct experience of the uncertain, uncomprehended, and incomprehensible qualities of inner and outer nature and the experience of living with this dimension. The wealth of this experience can be very helpful in assisting us to deal with our own, more inwardly experienced eruptions of the "It." Later we will speak in detail of this so-called folk knowledge.

The experience of the "It" in the external environment, or in Renner's words this magical worldview, is "rigorously unitary, that is to say, it embraces body and soul as a unity, it knows of no clear distinction between animated and unanimated, between dead and alive, and above all cannot conceive of the soul as having effects outside the body. Clear-cut representations of spirits and demons are lacking."[20] Such is the cast of mind Renner found primarily in the more remote districts of the Canton Uri at higher elevations.

In contrast to the soul's primordial experience of nature as a totality in which the "It" was experienced as an indefinite identity of spirit and matter, Renner found that people in the valley below visualized the same thing in individual embodiments—as souls of the dead, demons, or protective figures. Certain spirit beings animate external nature but are different from it. Renner calls this secondary phenomenon, corresponding to a development of consciousness, animism[21]

---

[19]See Renner, op. cit., p. 150.
[20]Renner, op. cit. Renner borrowed the concepts of magical worldview and, contrastingly, animistic worldview from Herbert Kühn, *Kunst und Kultur der Vorzeit Europas. Das Paläolithikum* (Berlin and Leipzig, 1929).
[21]The contrast between magical and animistic experience is discussed in detail in E. Renner, *Eherne Schalen: über die animistische Denk- und Erlebnisform* (Bern: Haupt Verlag, 1967), p. 17–20.

The Uri bugler sounds his horn as protection against the "It."

(from the Latin word *anima* = soul). "In it the experience of body and soul clearly appears, that duality which, as an intellectual stance, we name with the words dualism. . . . The forces of nature are deified;

even place and time, caught up in this transformation, stalk along as divine figures and demand celebration and sacrifice."[22]

A third step, and a reflection of a further development in consciousness, was the necessity of a moral evaluation of spirit phenomena. In the region Renner studied, this was brought about to a great extent by the Catholic Church through the separation of good and evil, sacred and demonic. In this the Church fundamentally opposed the animistic worldview. But according to Renner, these three levels of consciousness are not clearly separable from each other; rather, "three powers sue for the soul of the mountain people: the magical as experience, the Catholic as religion, and the animistic as temptation. Only in the union of these three does the mountain person's world come into being."[23] Thus alongside the Catholic worldview, the old forms of magic and animism appear as that which they really are—possibilities of experiencing the world.[24]

The Enlightenment resolutely declared war against this world of the magical. In the Enlightenment view, the existence of spirits is categorically denied and the experience of such is dismissed as an illusion.[25] Thus we arrive at the fourth level, that of the disenchanted, de-souled world. But now at a fifth level we really have to ask how such overpowering and extremely intensely felt experiences of the Uri mountain people, known for being extraordinarily thoughtful, could be nothing but self-deception. Perhaps if one assumes that, for example, "It" does not speak in human language and no spirit dwells in trees and rocks, or that objectively there never were spirits at all, "this perception of spirit must still have been a phenomenon emerging from out of the unconscious the psychic existence of which cannot be denied unless one totally denies the reality of the psyche."[26]

To summarize, we have become acquainted, from Renner's description, with the various ways of experiencing the world in a mountain region. The person experiencing them feels them all to be extremely real, and they cannot simply be dissolved by enlightenment. In contrast to the Enlightenment's worldview, the first three levels recognize an objectively present reality of the soul. If today, as a further step in enlightenment, we again experience the reality of autonomous powers in the soul, the circle closes and we have the quintessence of

---

[22]Renner, *Goldener Ring über Uri*, p. 32.
[23]Renner, op. cit., p. 38. In this connection one might call to mind the prayer call (p. 139 and 169).
[24]Renner, op. cit., p. 38ff.
[25]On this see von Franz, *Projection and Recollection*, p. 10.
[26]See C. G. Jung, C. W. 13, par. 248.

the four levels—quintessence because the fifth level signifies the acknowledgment and union of all four views of the world. This step comprises a translation (hermeneutic!) of the accumulated experiences of our ancestors into contemporary forms of experiencing and at the same time satisfies the criteria of the enlightened spirit.

We have now dealt in detail with the origin of the milieu animated via projection and offered step-by-step insight into this phenomenon. But we have left the nature of the projection hook, the milieu itself, completely out of consideration.

Effects Proceeding from the Landscape

The ensoulment of the environment cannot be adequately explained by reducing it to archetypal projection. Phenomena restricted to specific localities—such as the beneficial effect of certain places or the influence of the landscape on the mentality of its inhabitants—are not explicable in this way. How does it come about that at certain places events of a specific quality are observed again and again? How does it happen that even in antiquity numerous people made pilgrimages to a specific place? An explanation of such phenomena referring solely back to the subject—for example, one which traces them back to an inner expectation—is not wholly satisfactory. It offers no answer to the question of how precisely this specific place and not some other became a place of pilgrimage. There are many striking places and impressive things that could justify a pilgrimage. Why precisely Delphi, why precisely Einsiedeln? Mere reference to the subject does not generally explain the specific influence of a milieu on the mind and the mentality of its inhabitants.

What is initially striking is the way in which the milieu to a certain degree forms the mentality of its inhabitants like a mirror image. The ancient Greeks had already noticed a connection between the diversity of individual peoples and differing geographic conditions.[27] Even if the Greek milieu doctrine was taken too absolutely, a *relative* validity must be conceded.[28] In Roman times Cicero made his own observation:

> We see what a great difference exists between the natural constitution of various places: some benefit health, others further diseases; people with excessive phlegm, as it were rheumy people, live in the one; in the

---

[27]See Hippocrates, "The Influences of Air, Water, and Location," Ch. 13 and 24, in *Hippocrates* (Cambridge, Mass: Harvard University Press, 1923), vol. 1.
[28]On this see A. J. Toynbee, "Studie zur Weltgeschichte," Zürich, 1984, p. 74.

other, desiccated and dry people. And there are yet many more features that show great differences from place to place: In Athens the air is delicate, and hence it is believed that the subtlety of mind of the Atticans can be traced to that; in Thebes, on the contrary, it is heavy, and therefore the Thebans are supposed to be ponderous and strong. . . . The geographic conditions have an influence on certain things.[29]

Johann Jakob Bachofen also noticed the influence of locality on certain characteristics of its inhabitants.

From the oldest Argive and Cretian up to the Roman settlements, the most diverse peoples, coming by land or by sea, have established their dwellings in the Lycian mountains (the mountainous country in southern Asia Minor was called Lycia in antiquity). But the folk character has remained the same to the end, what is foreign has always been transformed by the power of assimilation into the native sort. That may be said especially to those who, in their judgement of peoples, view descent through the blood line as the sole determinant. . . . The land, Plato observes in Laws, *rules powerfully over us mortals.*[30]

And with the title *Geopsyche*,[31] W. Hellpach attempted to summarize the direct influences of weather and climate, of soil and locality on human mentality.

A great human experiment that bears out Bachofen's statement is the white man's settlement of the North American continent.[32] Since the living conditions in this region are sufficiently different from those in Europe, we could well expect all sorts of changes in the original racial type.[33] In penetrating studies of immigrants, the anthropologist Boas actually succeeded in demonstrating the now well-known "Indianization." Primarily it is the mass and form of the skull that changes from generation to generation in the direction of the so-called "Indian index."[34] But it was possible to establish an Indianization not only in the physical dimension but also in the realm of the soul.[35] Here we are dealing with the same phenomenon that

---

[29]Cicero, "De Fato," IV, 5–12.

[30]J. J. Bachofen, *Das lykische Volk und seine Bedeutung für die Entwicklung des Altertums*, 1862; cited in E. Egli, *Natur in Not* (Berne and Stuttgart: Hallwag, 1970), p. 132.

[31]W. Hellpach, *Geopsyche, Menschenseele unter dem Einfluss von Hetter und Klima, Boden und Landschaft*, (Leipzig, 1935).

[32]See C. G. Jung, C. W. 10, par. 93 cited from E. Egli, op. cit., p. 133.

[33]See C. G. Jung, loc. cit.

[34]The mingling with Indian blood is totally insignificant so that it plays no role. Cf. C. G. Jung, loc. cit.

[35]C. G. Jung, op. cit., par. 95; also C. G. Jung, *Letters*, vol. I, 26 September 1945, p. 380ff.

the English, at the time of colonization, had designated as "going native." "The foreign land assimilates the conqueror"[36]—from below, we might perhaps have to add.

In order to illustrate adequately the significance of a specific influence of a locality on its inhabitants, let us conclude by quoting from Jung's convincing example "Switzerland":[37]

> *Switzerland consists of numerous valleys, depressions in the earth's crust, in which the settlements of man are embedded. Nowhere are there measureless plains, where it is a matter of indifference where a man lives; nowhere is there a coast against which the ocean beats with its lore of distant lands. Buried deep in the backbone of the continent, sunk in the earth, the Alpine dweller lives like a troglodyte, surrounded by more powerful nations that are linked with the wide world, that expand into colonies or can grow rich on the treasures of their soil. The Swiss cling to what they have, for the others, the more powerful ones, have grabbed everything else. . . . From the earth-boundedness of the Swiss come all their bad as well as their good qualities: their down-to-earthness, their limited outlook, their non-spirituality, their parsimony, stolidity, stubbornness, dislike of foreigners, mistrustfulness, as well as that awful* Schwizerdütsch *and their refusal to be bothered, or to put it in political terms, their neutrality.*[38]

With these examples and documents, to which we could add at will, we must assume a twofold influence of the landscape on the human being. On the one hand there appears to be in humans, just as in plants and animals, a locally specific physical shape. On the other hand, the manner of behaving, the mentality of the population, obviously stands in direct relation to the landscape. On this point Jung once said, "I am deeply convinced of the—unfortunately—still very mysterious relation between man and landscape, but I hesitate to say anything about it because I could not substantiate it rationally. But I am fully persuaded that if you settled a Siberian tribe for a few hun-

---

[36]C. G. Jung, op. cit., par. 102; "Certain Australian primitives maintain that one could not make foreign ground one's own for foreign ancestral spirits dwell in foreign soil, and thus the new born would incarnate foreign ancestral spirits."

[37]C. G. Jung, "The Significance of Switzerland in the European Spectrum," *C. W.* 10; par. 914; see also Hermann Keyserling, *Das Spektrum Europas* (Heidelberg 1928).

[38]C. G. Jung, op. cit., par. 914; "And just as the difference in mentality of the Alpine dweller and the North German can be associated with the landscape, so too can this be observed within the Alpine region. The steep mountain valleys of Uri have formed a different sort of people than the heavily forested, hilly Zürich uplands." (From Theodor Abt, *Entwicklungsplanung ohne Seele?* [Bern and Frankfurt am Main: Peter Lang, 1978], p. 98.)

dred years in Switzerland, regular Appenzellers would come out in the end. It is probably a matter of something like psychic mimicry."[39]

On the basis of current knowledge concerning the nature of matter, we can take a closer look at Jung's hunch concerning the influence of the landscape on its inhabitants. As we have seen, according to present-day knowledge our inorganic environment is not built up simply of "dead" matter that we can perceive with our sensory organs. In the subatomic realm modern physics has recognized the perpetual process of creation and destruction of elementary particles in seemingly inert substance; and physics shows us further that mass is a form of energy (*energeia* = effect). The perpetual transformation of mass and energy within so-called dead matter compels us today to test the hypothesis of an effect proceeding from the environment in which one lives. Let us now pursue further the qualitative side of the material basis of the environment so that we can better judge how far we must relativize the concept of a nature without soul.

Qualitative Aspects of Place

In the book on the Lycian people mentioned above, J. J. Bachofen speaks of a puzzling power of locality.[40]

> In Lycia the decline of a people is thrice repeated. Thrice a new racial stock moves in, an entirely new population which is connected by no bond of blood with the previous people; each time a newly settled citizenry composed of the most diverse elements. But every time the same ethnic image takes shape. Such an agreement cannot possibly be due to chance. So what influences have brought this about? Certainly a major influence is that invisible, mysterious power which defies every attempt at more precise analysis and which links certain fates to a certain piece of ground.

This qualitative aspect of a place compels us to go into the question of the spirit of a locality.

The inhabitants of ancient Italy designated the specific quality of a place, for example of a grove, as the *genius loci* which, as it were, guaranteed the existential continuity of the locality. "Used in this way the word *genius* referred more to the psychic atmosphere or to the

---

[39]C. G. Jung, *Letters* (Princeton: Princeton University Press, 1973), vol. 1, 15 September 1943 (to Dr. Emil Egli).

[40]J. J. Bachofen, *Das lykische Volk und seine Bedeutung*, loc. cit., quoted by E. Egli, op. cit., p. 132.

mood that such a place can evoke."[41] Until now we have understood this animation of nature wholly as a projection from the collective unconscious, and, accordingly, the disenchantment of the milieu as withdrawal of projection. By including the discovery that supposedly dead inorganic matter is actually in perpetual pulsating transformation and bears within something like a "germ" of life,[42] it is fully possible that the effect a place has on us corresponds to a certain degree to an objective reality.[43] The dynamism inherent in matter, as well as the possibility of arranging itself in meaningful structures, completely corresponds in a protopsychic way to an aspect of spirit, a spirit in matter. The Western history of the spirit knows this universal spirit by such names as *spiritus mundi* or *anima telluris*.[44]

In the twentieth century we cannot use a concept like *genius loci* to express the influence of a locality without a certain hesitation. In our minds there is an archaic identity of the experiencer with nature which we have, to a certain extent, animated ourselves. To satisfy the criteria of the natural sciences and at the same time express the identifiable qualitative aspect of a place, we must operate with the concept of *quality of space*. Space as such admittedly consists of nothing and is nothing but a modus for circumscribing a body. Insofar as space is always "qualified" exclusively by the extension of bodies, the concept of quality of space is a tautology.[45] Nevertheless the concept serves to clarify the assumption that matter can qualify or impress the space surrounding it in a specific manner, as, say, a person can alter the atmosphere in his milieu in a certain way by his presence.

Modern physics provides us with evidence of the existence of a quality of space in that it radically revises the classical concept of emptiness. Capra writes:

> *This transformation took place in the so-called field theories. It began with Einstein's idea of associating the gravitational field with the geometry of space and became even more pronounced when quantum theory and relativity theory were combined to describe the force fields of sub-*

[41]See M.-L. von Franz, *Projection and Re-Collection*, p. 146.

[42]On this see also Teilhard de Chardin's studies.

[43]W. Heitler writes in *Der Mensch und die naturwissenschaftliche Erkenntnis* (Braunschweig 1961): "Somehow or other we will not be able to avoid the conclusion that something spiritual exists outside of us, a spiritual principle that has to do both with the laws and events of the material world and with our spirituality."

[44]Thus, for example, Keppler suspected that the secret of wondrous correspondence was based in the earth, for the latter was ensouled by an *anima telluris*. J. Keppler, *Opera Omnia*, quoted by C. G. Jung, *C. W.* 8, par. 816.

[45]On this see the explanation of the tautology of the concept "qualitative time" in Jung, *Letters*, vol. II, 26 May 1954.

atomic particles. In these "quantum field theories," the distinction between particles and the space surrounding them loses its original sharpness, and the void is recognized as a dynamic quantity of paramount importance.[46]

Proceeding from recognition of the electromagnetic field and especially the gravitational field, the general theory of relativity was able to demonstrate that the space around an object is "conditioned"; that is, another object in the vicinity "feels" a force.[47]

Continuing, Capra writes that:

Matter and empty space—the full and the void—were the two fundamentally distinct concepts on which the atomism of Democritus and of Newton was based. In general relativity, these two concepts can no longer be separated. Wherever there is a massive body, there will also be a gravitational field, and this field will manifest itself as the curvature of the space surrounding that body. We must not think, however, that the field fills the space and "curves" it. The two cannot be distinguished; the field is the curved space! In general relativity, the gravitational field and the structure—or geometry—of space are identical. . . .

In Einstein's theory, then, matter cannot be separated from its field of gravity, and the field of gravity cannot be separated from the curved space. Matter and space are thus seen to be inseparable and interdependent parts of a single whole.[48]

Summarizing, Capra says, "Thus modern physics shows us once again—and this time at the macroscopic level—that material objects are not distinct entities, but are inseparably linked to their environment; that their properties can only be understood in terms of their interaction with the rest of the world."[49]

Even if modern physics can supply us with proof that the matter present influences the space we live in, it nevertheless remains unclear *how* a specific, qualitative expression comes about. The hypothesis of the psychoid aspect of archetypes is probably the one that can help us most. "It is conceivable that matter, as Jung supposed, might be the concrete aspect of psyche, yet not the individual psyche but rather of the collective unconscious, and that the archetypes in this case might be not only structural dominants of the latter

---

[46]Capra, *The Tao of Physics*, p. 193.
[47]Summary of Capra, op. cit., p. 194.
[48]Capra, loc. cit.
[49]Capra, op. cit., p. 195.

but rather a world-shaping factor in general."[50] Just as we can recognize certain energetically charged focal points in the collective psyche, it would be quite conceivable that we could likewise find certain areas particularly charged with energy in the material realm, too. As change can be observed in fundamental archetypal structures over the course of the centuries (certain archetypes are suddenly activated and others fade away, for example, in the change in collective values), it is predictable that particular places have been felt to be mana places during particular periods of time—that is, that they exert beneficial or unfortunate effects.[51]

For the time being we will let it rest at this rather speculative point, noting that on the basis of present-day knowledge in physics, the existence and effect of a quality of space and therefore the effect of nonmaterial components in matter must be assumed.[52] But the existence and the effect of so-called mana centers and the like—in short, the ensouled landscape—cannot be understood exclusively as the projection of archetypal images from the collective unconscious. Generally we find ourselves obliged to take into account that there is a spirit in what has been assumed to be dead matter.

Human and Landscape in Interaction

In bringing the archetype into this discussion of the quality of space, we have left an important viewpoint unmentioned. Humanity lives in a landscape developed and cultivated by itself, and so this landscape is the result of the interaction of human and nature. The primordial landscape experiences a very definite transformation: "Through our activity we have imparted something to the earth that arises not from the earth's grace alone but just as much from what we ourselves have done. From the earth we receive form, but it has also received form

---

[50]Foreword (for the editors) by M.-L. von Franz to the German edition of C. G. Jung, *Mysterium Coniunctionis*; ". . . the synchronicity phenomena point in this direction."
[51]Think of the Asklepien of antiquity (Kos, Ephesus, etc.) or of places of pilgrimage. See Kerényi, *Der Göttliche Arzt* (Basel: 1948); English translation by Ralph Manheim, *Asklepios: Archetypal Image of the Physician's Existence*, Bollingen Series LXV, no. 3 (New York: Pantheon Books, 1959).
[52]So-called Kirlian photographs also point to this. The spatial qualities of the Cheops pyramid, described by Ostander and Schröder, *Psi* (Bern, Munich, Vienna, 1975), . 308ff, as well as the attention paid to the quality of place in various cultures would be additional viewpoints on the theme of the quality of space. (See, for example, Mircea Eliade, *Patterns in Comparative Religion* [New York: New American Library, 1963], Chapter 10, "Sacred Places.") It is also well known that building materials impart certain qualities to a space.

from us. And what it offers us is a mirror image of our uniqueness."[53]
Martin Schwind amplified this idea beautifully:

> The landscape developed and cultivated by man is fraught with mean-
> ing, it is the work of man in the framework of that which nature allows.
> It is the mightiest objectification of spirit and for this reason also reveals
> the spiritual form of its creator. It is comparable to every other work of
> man, yet much more complex. A painter created the picture, a poet the
> poem. An entire people created the landscape—not at any one given
> period of time, but over long periods of time and it is still going on
> today. . . . As is the case with every creation produced by mankind, the
> landscape too, has a structure of meaning and an expressive value.[54]

The *Kulturlandschaft*—the landscape developed and cultivated by
man—is thus actually a self-representation of the people who dwell in
it.[55] Now since our form-giving interventions arise from our ideas,
and since these ideas, as we have seen, are conditioned by archetypal
structures, it follows that a *Kulturlandschaft* (for example, in the structure of its settlements and manner of construction) mirrors the collective psyche[56] of its population. Thus we can understand the human-
landscape relationship as something like a relationship of reciprocal
reflection. As the character of people becomes a copy of the space
they live in, in the sense of a "psychic mimicry," the collective psyche
reflects matter. If, on the other hand, we note how the structured
living space reveals the mentality of those who live there, it seems
that matter also mirrors the collective psyche.

If, however, psyche and matter can reflect each other, as M.-L. von
Franz demonstrated in her book, *Projection and Recollection*,[57] then
there must be a similarity in the fundamental structure of psyche and
matter. Here only the archetypes of the collective unconscious come
into question, since they order the psychic realm and, in their psychoid aspect, extend into the material domain. We find these psychophysical structural dominants in all given facts and circumstances

---

[53]Hans Freyer, *Der Staat* (Lepizig 1962) quoted in Martin Schwind, "Sinn und Ausdruck
der Landschaft," *Studium Generale*, vol. 3, 1950, p. 196-201.
[54]M. Schwind, loc. cit.; this article is also reprinted in *Das Hesen der Landschaft*, Wege
der Forschung vol. XXXIX (Darmstadt: Wissenschaftlichebuchgesellschaft, 1973),
p. 353ff.
[55]On this see also A. Reinle's definition of architecture in *Zeichensprache der Architektur*
(Zürich 1976), and especially Richard Weiss, *Häuser und Landschaften der Schweiz*
(Erlenbach-Zürich 1959).
[56]The collective psyche of a population embraces the collective consciousness and the
collective unconscious of this population.
[57]M.-L. von Franz, op. cit., p. xx.

that do not show causal order, such as radioactive decay in the physical realm or the "just-so" properties of natural numbers in the psychic realm. These causeless arrangements in psyche and matter are, with respect to their arithmetical structure, alike; and consequently they mirror each other constantly.[58] The most profound and most clearly distinguished archetypal factors underlying the similarity of psyche and physis are the archetypal "patterns" of the natural number.[59]

Von Franz quotes Jung's remark that number "is the predestined instrument for creating order, or for apprehending an already existing, but still unknown, regular arrangement or 'orderedness.' It may well be "the most primitive element of order in the human mind. It is, she continues, the most primitive manifestation of the spontaneous dynamics of the unconscious psyche."[60] In her book *Number and Time* von Franz pursued this question further and was able to show "that probably at the deepest level of the objective psyche there exists *an acausal orderedness of numerical structure which is equally valid for psyche and for matter. . . .*"[61]

As we have already seen in the instance of the psychoid aspect of the archetypes, transpsychic and transphysical reality seem to touch each other somewhere.[62] On the basis of this relationship a psychic element must be inherent in matter, just as the constants at the deepest level of the objective psyche reveal a material aspect. That seems to be the reason why, on the one hand, a geographical place—inorganic matter—possesses something like a protopsychic quality, and why, on the other hand, humanity, to a certain degree, is linked via the collective unconscious with material surroundings. By this reasoning it would no longer be erroneous to speak of the soul of a place, of a landscape, or of a country, instead of quality of space—just as we speak of the "soul of Africa" or the "soul of Asia" without reflecting too much about what we say.

The idea of a connection consciousness between such apparently separate realms as psyche and matter (or of man and environment) is just as difficult to accept as the concept of the unification of mass and energy in a realm beyond the three dimensions of consciousness— that is, in relativity's four-dimensional space-time continuum. But we

---

[58]C. G. Jung, C. W. 8, par. 816.
[59]See M.-L. von Franz, *Number and Time*, p. 35.
[60]M. L. von Franz, *Projection and Re-collection*, p. 195, citing C. G. Jung, "Synchronicity," C. W. 8, par. 870.
[61]M.-L. von Franz, loc. cit. (von Franz's italics).
[62]See also Jung's appendix to his essay, "On the Nature of the Psyche," C. W. 8, par. 434ff.

can certainly imagine this step toward the uniting of opposites in an expanded dimension if we repeat the transition from two to three dimensions. The following analogy comes from F. Capra.[63] It shows a "doughnut" ring that is bisected horizontally by a plane. In the two-dimensional plane the sections appear as completely independent disks, but in three dimensions we recognize them as parts of one and the same object.

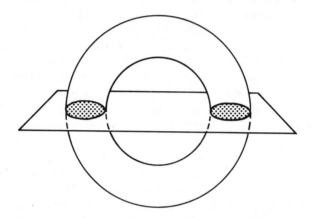

A comparable union of seemingly irreconcilable psyche and matter can be achieved with introduction of the new dimension of the unconscious—that is, through the transition from the three-dimensional space of consciousness to the four dimensions of the "conscious-unconscious continuum." In a comprehensive view of the world of consciousness and the unconscious, psyche and matter—and by extension man and milieu—no longer appear fundamentally separated.

The objection will be raised that I have no feeling of "being separated" if I move away from a region. On the conscious level that may be true. However, with the inclusion of the unconscious, emotional background—a reality to which we can no longer close our eyes—a totally different picture presents itself. We will illustrate this with the familiar phenomenon of "homesickness" and thus at the same time further elucidate the paradoxical facts of the man-milieu relationship.

<hr>

[63]Capra, op. cit., p. 135.

Chapter 9

Homesickness as an Expression of the Human-Milieu Relationship

The sense of total security contained in the term "home" includes a sense of community and tradition as well as the spatial attachment that constitutes an ecological niche—as a protective barrier against everything foreign, as a familiarity factor, and as space or place in which the attachments to community and tradition are actually experienced.[1] Only within the context of a milieu can social life become what we call home.[2] Today we understand the term "home" less as a "thing" than as a relationship.[3] Home is the place to which the human being has "an inner relationship transcending sober, objective judgment, a relationship determined by mood and feeling, and proven by ties of affection. We speak of a feeling of attachment to one's native place (*Heimatgefühl*), of love for it (*Heimatliebe*), and of loyalty to it (*Heimattreue*), all of which find their strongest emotional expression in homesickness (*Heimweh*)."[4] Consequently, homesickness denotes a person's longing for a specific existential place or space which for him bears the stamp of home (*Heimat*). To get our bearings in this question concerning the inner relationship of man to his milieu, let us first familiarize ourselves with the broad chronological sequence of the discussion of homesickness. Here we rely primarily on the works of Fritz Ernst[5] and Ina-Maria Greverus.[6]

Johannes Hofer's doctoral thesis in medicine appeared in 1688 in

---

[1]On this see Ina-Maria Greverus, "Heimweh und Tradition," p. 7–31.
[2]Wilhelm Brepohl, "Die Heimat als Beziehungsfeld," p. 21.
[3]Ina-Maria Greverus, *Der territoriale Mensch*, p. 27ff.
[4]*Hörterbuch der Soziologie*, see the entry under "Heimat."
[5]Fritz Ernst, *Vom Heimweh*.
[6]Ina-Maria Greverus, *Der territoriale Mensch*, and *Auf der Suche nach Heimat*.

Basel under the title *Dissertatio medica de nostalgia oder Heimweh*. In it he describes, for the first time from a scientific point of view, a painful, often fatal, illness that is caused "because the sick person is not in his fatherland, or fears he may never see it again. Because of the Swiss who suffered from it in France, the French named this illness *maladie du Pays*. Since it has no Latin name, Hofer called it *nostalgia* from *nos* or *nostos*—the return to the fatherland—and *algos*—pain or affliction."[7] Hofer describes the syndrome in detail (depression, fever, etc.) and then shows examples of how the best and surest cure is the return of the sick person to his fatherland. When this could be done, miracles happened. "A youth from Bern studying in Basel was cured when only halfway home. A farm woman from Basel who had been hospitalized because of a serious fall got well, not through treatment, but by being released. Indeed, a manservant in Paris, consumed by longing for his province, regained his equilibrium merely by receiving his master's permission to return home, even though it turned out never to be necessary for him to make use of the permission."[8]

Until near the end of the eighteenth century, a distinct symptomatology was ascribed to nostalgia; and in many cases, narrowing down Hofer's thoughts, it was viewed as a purely physiological illness.[9] Only at the end of the eighteenth century was it determined that homesickness could be traced back specifically to the isolation from family and native surroundings. Time and time again, it was impressions of the landscape, customs, and habits that were emphasized.[10] In other words, the causes of homesickness were sought in attachments of the soul.[11]

In the literature of the nineteenth century, interest in homesickness focused more on the psychiatric-forensic area.[12] In our century it shifted clearly to the social-psychological area, and this is where the expression "nostalgic reaction" was coined. Charles Zwingmann understands this to mean "a symbolic return to, or calling to mind of, such events (objects) of the experiential space which offered the greatest sense of satisfaction."[13] The threat or experience of separation from a place or condition providing that satisfaction is seen as the

---

[7]Johannes Hofer's *Dissertatio medica* of 1688 in the 1779 German summary by D. Lorenz Crell, par. 2.
[8]Summarized from Friz Ernst, *Vom Heimweh*, p. 15ff.
[9]E.g., Johann Jakob Scheuchzer's treatise, "Von dem Heimwehe"; see also Greverus, "Heimweh als medizinisch-psychologische Katagorie," p. 106–111.
[10]E.g., Haller, Rousseau, and Schlegel; cf. J. J. Scheuchzer, op. cit., p. 109.
[11]Ernst, *Vom Heimweh*, p. 45ff. (on this see also E. Egli, *Erlebte Landschaft*, p. 313).
[12]Greverus, *Der territoriale Mensch*, p. 108.
[13]Charles Zwingmann, "Das nostalgische Phänomen," p. 308ff.

cause of the nostalgic reaction. The normal ego-satisfaction, which stresses the present or the future, shifts to a focus on the past. Accordingly, 'homesickness' is a *failure to organize the world from a new centre of one's own.*[14] The increasing popularity of the nostalgic reaction, especially among young people, has occupied numerous authors in recent years. We even speak now of a *nostalgic cultural mood.*[15]

In her work on "territorial man," I.-M. Greverus demonstrated how the longing for one's homeland (*Heimat*) from the anthropological viewpoint corresponds to an *instinctive need.* Accordingly, humanity remains a territorial creature in spite of all reeducation and reconditioning; that is, we need a territory or district that affords us identity, stimulation or activity, and security lest the opposite states—anonymity, boredom (or inactivity), and anxiety—take effect.[16] Greverus emphasizes that "the nature of the territory—as a 'possession' to be striven for and defended—is dependent on the value orientations established by norms. These norms can be modified, whereas the 'territorial imperative' as such, insofar as it has to do with a natural potential, *cannot be altered.*"[17] If, then, the feeling for one's home area (*Heimatgefühl*) rests on an instinctual human basis, then homesickness is a primary instinctive reaction, completely in accord with the *participation mystique* of the archaic person.[18] In accordance with primal feelings, human beings naturally feel inwardly united not merely with the territory in which they grew up; for the feeling for one's home area (*Heimatgefühl*) includes attachment to nature and to the cultivation of the soil, along with the attachment to the local community and its traditions, its manner of speaking and thinking, its customs, games, work, food, dress, and way of life.[19] Consequently homesickness reveals that, for someone of the classic peasant mentality, a separation from one's native place really is experienced as a separation. However, the more consciousness distances itself from the instinctual foundations, the less such feelings are registered

---

[14]Greverus, *Auf der Suche nach Heimat*, p. 173ff.

[15]See Greverus' essay, "Zur Kulturstimmung der Nostalgie," and the literature cited there as well as Albert Hauser, "Nostalagie—Krankheit der Wohlstandsgesellschaft" and "Nostalgie—Sehnsucht nach einer besseren Welt."

[16]Robert Andrey, *Adam und sein Revier, Der Mensch im Zwang seines Territoriums*, p. 15, cited in Greverus, *Auf der Suche nach Heimat*, p. 61.

[17]Greverus, *Auf der Suche nach Heimat*, p. 52.

[18]The connection between the archaic mode of thinking and the greatest vulnerability to homesickness had already caught the attention of A. Haller: "The more solitary the village, the more the Swiss is subject to nostalgia." (Abbreviated from the *Yverdoner Enzyklopädie*, vol. XIII, 1773, *vide* Hemvé.)

[19]R. Weiss, *Volkskunde der Schewiz*, p. 30.

According to an ancient idea held in Canton Uri, newborn infants came from the narrow, wooded Rieder Valley. To the right of the Rieder Chapel is the "Tittikasten." The children were told that this was from where the newborn babies came.

in consciousness. "The spiritually independent, individualistic man without presuppositions is at home everywhere."[20] Only in the deeply unconscious vegetative and autonomic realm does our nature become like animals and plants, and at this level we also experience things as they do. A young man from the Lötschen Valley once replied to my question about what kept him in that valley by saying, "Its beauty and my love for the valley and for my native community, for who likes to leave the place where he first saw the light of day and where he spent his beautiful childhood years. . . . A tree reaches its branches out everywhere, but the root stays in the same place. That's the way I am; however far away I roam, my roots will always be in the Lötschen Valley."[21] In his eloquent answer ethnic attachment to the soil and openness to the world are not irreconcilable opposites.

The deep-seated bond between human and milieu, "his piece of God's earth," is revealed particularly well in the widely held view of humanity as *born of the earth*. The French religious historian Mircea Eliade writes:

> *In many languages mankind is said to be "born of earth" (in Russian songs, in myths of the Lapps and Estonians, etc.). It is believed that children "come" from the depths of the earth, from caves, grottos or crevasses, but also from swamps, springs and rivers. In the form of legends and superstitions or simply as turns of phrases, ideas of this sort are still alive in Europe today. In every region, indeed in almost every city and village, there is a cliff or a spring that "brings forth" children: these are the "child wells," "child ponds," "baby springs." We should not assume that these superstitious ideas or picturesque expressions are only intended for children. The truth of the matter is by far not so simple. Right down to our day, Europeans still have a dark feeling of a mysterious connection with the soil of their home locality. It is not a question of a profane feeling of love of fatherland or of one's province, nor of the joy one finds in a familiar landscape, nor of reverence for one's ancestors, generations of whom lie buried in the shadow of the village church. There is something more: the mystical experience of autochthony, the profound feeling that one has arisen from the ground, that one was born of the earth, just as the earth brings forth cliffs and rivers, trees and flowers in inexhaustible fecundity. We must under-*

---

[20]Idem.
[21]Th. Abt, *Helches sind die überlebenschancen des kulturellen Erbes im Lötschental?*, p. 116.

stand autochthony in this sense: one feels indigenous, and this is a
feeling of cosmic order that transcends all bonds to one's family and
ancestors.[22]

Eliade reports further how, according to numerous beliefs in diverse
cultures, women can become pregnant if they go to certain places—
e.g., cliffs, caves, trees, or rivers. In Switzerland, too, such places are
by no means unknown.[23]

According to other ideas still flourishing in nineteenth century
Europe, certain animals—fishes, frogs, swans, and, or course, the
stork—bring children from somewhere out of clefts, furrows,
swamps, or forests. The archaic idea of an existence prior to birth in
the womb of the earth "creates in mankind the feeling of a cosmic
relatedness with his environment; indeed, one could say that in those
times mankind had less a consciousness of belonging to the human
race than the feeling of a cosmic-biological participation in the life of
the world about him."[24] "A secret solidarity with place which, because
of its intensity, lives on yet today in sagas and in folk traditions" is,
according to Eliade, based on this idea of birth from the earth.[25]
According to this archaic concept, "Mother Earth" is the real mother
of humanity, while the bodily mother is only the one who completes
the work of mother earth. Consequently there was, according to the
primordial way of thinking, "a great longing, in the urge to return to
mother earth, to be buried in the soil of one's homeland—this 'home
soil' whose deeper meaning we now surmise."[26]

The fact that people always want to remain in the area they come
from reveals the significance and the intensity of the folk notion of
man's bond to his native heath. This holds true even for those regions
threatened by nature (such as areas threatened by avalanches, volca-
noes, or flooding). The following illustration shows how solidarity
with the milieu is directly associated in folk sensibility with the *joie de*
vivre, the *"élan vital,"* or, as we would say today, with the quality of
life:

---

[22]Mircea Eliade, *Mythen, Träume und Mysterien.*
[23]E.g., the Riedertal Chapel in Canton Uri, the Kühmad Chapel in the Lötschen Valley,
as well as many other places.
[24]Eliade, loc. cit., p. 233; "Certainly he knew that he had an "real mother" whom he
always saw before him, but he knew just as well that he came from far away, that he
was brought here by swans or frogs, that he had lived in caves and rivers. All this has
left traces in language: the Romans called the bastard *terrae filius*; today the Ruma-
nians still call him the *child of the flower.*"
[25]Idem.
[26]Eliade, op. cit., p. 234; hence, for example, the frequent inscription on Roman
graves: *Hic natus hic situs est.*

Off the coast of Schleswig-Holstein lie the Hallig Islands, all that remains of what used to be part of the mainland. Stormy seas gnaw at them. A hurricane in 1825 ripped out wharfs and destroyed houses, so that often only the roofs remained standing on pilings. Many people drowned, and some of the herd was lost. The king—at that time the islands were still Danish—visited the disaster area and resolved to evacuate the islands and move the people to behind the protective dikes. The Hallig farmers, however, wrote a petition asking to be left on their islands "since the Hallig people cleave to their land with such great love that the current generation's joy of life probably would be gone forever if they were to leave their home land; it is to be feared that if this happened they would lead a bleak, joyless existence and would not feel content and at home anywhere."[27]

The Eskimos explain the deeply felt loss when someone leaves their home territory by saying that those who go forth leave a piece of their soul in the place of origin.[28] On the basis of current knowledge concerning the structure of the soul, we can fully understand this idea of a part-soul as the archaic-autonomic side of the human psyche. It would be that aspect of the collective unconscious that extends into the somatic realm and in each case "entwines roots and tendrils about all things like a spiritual plant."[29] This brings us to the main point of our observations, namely to the question of whether or not homesickness and thus a person's relation to a specific territory is solely a projection, or whether the homesickness syndrome actually can provide us with clues concerning the extent to which an inner relation of human to milieu objectively exists.

If we speak today of a person's nostalgic reaction, we understand that to mean, from a psychological point of view, a problem of adaptation. The yearning for a lost paradise finds expression in the homesickness "for a rose garden of the past" (or, as a counterpart to this, in the longing for a future ideal state). Because of a poor attitude, usually revealing infantile characteristics, the life of the modern sufferer of homesickness is somehow provisional. In the absence of an inner "footing" that would enable emotional mastery of the influences from the outer and inner worlds, there arises a feeling of restlessness. Consequently we may first of all understand the nostalgic reaction as

---

[27]Quoted from E. Egli, *Geborgenheit im Raum*, p. 4.
[28]E. Egli, op. cit.; according to Chinese ideas this part-soul would correspond to the gen-soul (i.e., to the soul turned toward the earth) in contrast to the shen-soul that belongs to heaven (see C. G. Jung, "Soul and Earth," *C. W.* 10).
[29]J. H. G. Schlegel, *Das Heimweh und der Selbstmord*, p. 123ff, quoted in Greverus, *Auf der Suche nach Heimat*, p. 109.

projection, not only in archaic but also in modern humanity. The person who thinks in primordial folk terms transfers a piece of the soul out into the milieu via projection. When this object is lost, there is a corresponding loss of soul; the person loses, as the Eskimos say, a part-soul. In the case of the modern person, on the other hand, the phenomenon of projection no longer rests on an archaic identity but rather on a splitting off of consciousness from its origin or "home ground," that is to say, from the unconscious. Thus as a collective phenomenon, the modern homesickness syndrome is related to the rootless consciousness of modern man, a phenomenon which, with Richard Weiss, we can define as the homelessness of the soul.[30] Wherever too rationalistic a *Weltanschauung* has alienated humanity from the existential foundation within the soul and the inner ground that can support it in joy and in sorrow, the inner homeland that has become unconscious or an inner centering factor is projected out— into the past, the future, or the distance.[31] Consequently, for modern humanity, no longer living in archaic identity, the nostalgic reaction has as its aim not a concrete search for a specific external "ideal place of security"; but rather it signifies, in the symbolism of the search for home, as inner discovery of a foundation for life. The sought-for ability to participate, which would enable even modern nostalgics to feel at home wherever fate took them lies in the experience of the foundation of consciousness, namely the impersonal unconscious. In the relation to the unconscious, humanity can order the world from our own center, out of our conscious-unconscious wholeness.

On the basis of these psychological reflections one could now conclude that homesickness is exclusively a projection of intrapsychic contents. If, however, we include the results of ethology in our discussion of homesickness, our conclusion has to be more differentiated.

In the instance of animals, Alverdes speaks of an "archetype of home" and intends this term to mean animals' instinctive relatedness to place which, for example, extends from the minute nest locality to home in the broadest sense. "The archetype of home brings migratory birds back to their native land and to their previous brooding site."[32] Fully aware of possible erroneous conclusions that could arise from an uncritical fusion of animal and human psychology, we nevertheless do not want to exclude cross-reference between these two areas

---

[30]Richard Weiss, "Heimat und Humanität," p. 7.
[31]On this see also Jung's letter to Sandor Török, Budapest, *Letters*, vol. 2, 29 May 1959.
[32]Friedrich Alverdes, "Die Wirksamkeit von Archetypen in den Instinkthandlungen der Tiere," p. 235.

of research, in the sense of comparative anatomy, as Heini Hediger, among others, demanded as early as 1946.[33] If we think of the little redstart bird outside the window born near this house, that migrates to Africa in winter and—if all goes well—returns next spring to this same spot to nest, we really must ask ourselves what kind of orientation and adaptation system is present in this little bird.[34] A typical and adaptable system of preparedness must be at the animal's disposal in its drive to return to the ancestral locale, which enables the individual bird in its specific circumstances to find its way back. This aspect of the animal's adaptation system which enables an extremely accurate return to its locale is exactly what Alverdes called the "archetype of home."

Before we investigate this noteworthy bond of the animal to its territory more closely, we must clarify Alverdes' concept of the "archetype of home." Alverdes transferred Jung's concept of the archetype to ethology.[35] It therefore seems correct to apply Jung's distinction between the abstract archetype per se and the archetypal image here, too. By this differentiation, we must speak of the archetypal image of the home locale and simultaneously ask ourselves what archetype orders these typical images of the home area, what imbues them with energy and thereby situates and centers an individual in this world. Superficially one might believe that, behind the archetypal image of the home locale, it is only the mother archetype at work, in the sense of such typical ideas as security and protection, nest warmth and food base, which, of course, all belong to the maternal principle. However, a very specific localization, division, and boundary—manifestations all clearly belonging to the father archetype[36]—also belong to the essence of the home locale. That archetype embracing and uniting both the feminine and masculine principles is the archetype of ordered wholeness. It is the images and ideas brought forth by this archetype of order which make the birth-

---

[33]Heine Hediger, "Zum Raum-Zeit-System der Tiere," p. 260–63.

[34](*Phoenicurus ochrurus*: "A common European singing-bird . . . , so named from its red tail, which it has a habit of moving quickly from side to side." [*The Shorter Oxford Dictionary*—Translator.]) Of course we also know of similar examples of astonishing feats of homing with other animals, e.g., the cat or certain fish.

[35]Adolf Portmann wrote in the *Eranos-Jahrbuch 1950* on the problem of the primordial images from the biological viewpoint. This article is also found in A. Portmann, *Biologie und Geist*, p. 133–149. See further the literature in the anthology *Instinkte und Archetypen im Verhalten der Tiere und im Erleben des Menschen*, where the article quoted here also appears.

[36]On this see C. G. Jung, "Soul and Earth," *C. W.* 10, par. 641.

place the navel of the world. That place becomes, for the human being, the image of an order similar to a center whereby an animal feels concretely bonded to its locale.

We observe comparable archetypal images of the home locale in the human being that suggest the workings of a centering archetype of order.[37] Depending on circumstances, this central archetype of who-listic order—called the self—is symbolized by a *center* situated both in the narrow and in the more extended home locale, be it the central pole in a wigwam, the house altar, the village church, or a very concrete "navel stone." The more instinct determines a person's behavior, the stronger seem the workings of a direct, animal connection to the *materia* of the environment, although in archaic homesickness projection is also operative. Since modern humanity can never escape its animal and drive nature, despite differentiated cultural consciousness, we must assume homesickness to be an animal drive that confers a concrete bond to a specific space. The interconnection of organism and habitat suggested by locally specific physiological evolution seems somehow to come about via the archetype of the self, and this by way of its chthonic aspect.[38] As central archetype, the self embodies the spirit of the unconscious, which regulates the psyche and which, given its relation to the domain of the body, can also come into concrete union with the *materia* of the environment.

By juxtaposition, we can understand the homesickness syndrome both as projection and as concrete attachment depending entirely on standpoint and level of consciousness. In the archaic identity home-sickness is to be understood as concrete, while at a more highly developed level of consciousness homesickness should be interpreted more symbolically. At this level, nostalgia signifies a tendency toward reuniting discriminative consciousness with the inner archaic person capable of *participation mystique* and rooted in one's space. Hence the nostalgia fantasy works *compensatorily* on the rootless consciousness of modern humanity, with our one-sided drive for progress and mobility. Even as a collective symptom of a cultural mood, nostalgia can scarcely be cured primarily by an external change. First an inner remedy must be found in the individual through which the external

---

[37]Here we tacitly assume that the centering archetype of order is not of a fundamentally different nature in animal and in man; for epistemological reasons we cannot prove this.

[38]Through the development of Christian consciousness, the earthy-feminine aspect of the Self fell to the lot of the dark side to a great extent (on this see C. G. Jung, *Aion*, C. W. 9i, and "Answer to Job," C. W. 11, par. 553). The discussion of this aspect of nostalgia as a cultural mood, especially in connection with the "Heimatbewegung" and the blood and soil myth would, however, divert us from our theme.

concepts such as relationship, community, freedom of expression and home locale can be renewed over the course of time. It would be false to conclude that the nostalgic mood is not bound to influence our external, individual and collective plans and decisions! Today the widespread longing for a home locale—that is, the search for a network of relationships and for a creative space—must be acknowledged so that the floodgates are not opened yet further to increasing mobility.[39] To the archaic person in us, every change of domicile means the *painful necessity of separation from attachments*—the soul's and the heart's nourishment. However, where a person feels, *"Here I can take root,"* the territorial instinct comes to rest. That person feels again in a space belonging to him or her, which eventually and imperceptibly, the archaic soul animates. Wherever the archaic or chthonic soul's[40] reciprocal interaction between inner and outer is taken sufficiently into account—which means a corresponding transformation of the general attitude—a new home locale can arise over time even for a modern, homesick person.[41] Exactly what this means in the individual case, however, can never be stated in general terms but must be experienced individually in dialogue with the archaic soul.[42]

From our overview of the most important treatises on homesickness—the literature fills shelves—we may proceed to summarizing conclusions. Through our archaic-animal or ethnic origins human beings are, on the one hand, directly bound to the space in which we live. However, on the other hand, thanks to liberation from our instincts and to the freedom gained through mobility, modern humanity no longer feels bound to the space in which we live, and that is all the more true with estrangement from our instinctual foundations. Only by expressing the facts of the case as a "not only but also" situation can justice be done to the real nature of this consciousness-transcending relation between humanity and milieu. Humanity has differentiated itself away from nature, from the space where one lives, and in this sense has become separated and freed from nature, just as consciousness has detached itself from the unconscious. Yet it is likewise a fact that with every fiber of being humanity consists of exactly that maternal substance from which it

---

[39]In Switzerland, for example, by means of agreement between two Cantons in regard to schools, and similar things.

[40]Jung's concept in "Soul and Earth," *C. W.* 10, par. 53.

[41]In addition, the impressive document by H. Jakobsohn, "The Dialogue of a World-Weary Man with His Ba."

[42]See also C. G. Jung, "The Relations between the Ego and the Unconscious," *C. W.* 7, par. 202.

has detached itself, and consequently the human being always remains bound both to original, earthy nature, i.e., the collective unconscious itself, and at the same time to inorganic *materia* – a logical contradiction into which we must yet delve.

To overcome the dualism between wave and particle, Niels Bohr set forth the concept of *complementarity*, which has gained general acceptance. He regarded the particle and the wave as two complementary descriptions of the same reality, each in its own way correct but inadequate. Both ideas together are necessary for a complete description of nature, and both aspects are applied within the limitations of the uncertainty principle. The law of complementarity (*Contraria sunt complementa*) has become an essential part of the way modern physics views nature.[43] Yet not only physics but psychology, too, has found itself compelled to express facts that transcend consciousness in complementary statements that, in themselves, are logically irreconcilable.[44]

The physicist has had to assume both the particle nature and the wave nature of elementary particles, although logically they are mutually exclusive. Similarly, we cannot ultimately avoid designating the relation of human and environment or of psyche and matter as nonexistent from one viewpoint and yet *existing* from another. Denial of one aspect in favor of the absolute validity of the other is either an adherence to a Cartesian mode of thought refusing to integrate contemporary knowledge into its image of the world, or else a regression to *participation mystique* sacrificing a certain level of human freedom from pure nature. Each viewpoint is one-sided; only the acceptance of both allows a perception in which the relativity of the notions of animated and inanimate nature becomes visible.

Stefan Sonderegger expresses himself in this sense when he speaks of the Alpstein, the mysterious mountain range in Canton Appenzell. "The actual heart and the secrecy of the Alpstein, however, is found in the Altmann (literally, Old Man); its very name is indicative of the depth of its spiritual significance. It could not be named more fittingly. It is the mountain that holds the entire range together, the towering center above the rock fields and boulders, the real father of

---

[43]This passage comes from Capra, op. cit., p. 145.

[44]From the store of introverted ideas of various cultures we are familiar with the paradox as the possibility of expressing the unity of things that appear to consciousness as irreconcilable opposites. A famous example is the Zen koan, such as the following: "We were parted many thousands of kaplas ago, yet we have not been separated ever for a moment. We are facing each other all day long, yet we have never met." (D. T. Suzuki, *The Essence of Buddhism*, p. 26).

the Alpstein range. Its name expresses awe as well as the beseeching
and timid attempt at intimacy—a touch of numinosity in the midst of
a dead and yet so very much ensouled craggy landscape."[45] With
respect to practical rural development policy, this way of looking at
things—which includes the experience of an ensouled landscape and
thereby an understanding of the archaic person—contrasts sharply
with the "enlightened" viewpoint in which landscape is dead matter
and represents solely a source of revenue. An article in the September
5, 1980, edition of the *Neue Zürcher Zeitung* entitled "Natives against
Mining Interests in Australia" demonstrates this attitude in everyday
life.

> *Petroleum is thought to exist in Noonkanbah, approximately 2,000 km
> north of the West Australian state capital of Perth. The American firm
> Amax Petroleum obtained the exploration license but soon encountered
> the resistance of the Yungngora tribe, with its approximately 200 mem-
> bers, who were joined by labor unions, ministers, and academics from
> all over Australia. They argued that the sacred dwellings of the primor-
> dial inhabitants lay where the large drills were supposed to bore into the
> ground; there, according to ancient myths, was the home of the Spirit
> of the Goanna, a gigantic lizard that, for the Blacks, represents a
> traditional and important source of nutrition and protein.*
>
> *The West Australian state government and especially Premier Sir
> Charles Court hold the contrary opinion that indeed the farm was
> deeded over to the Blacks some years ago in the course of white "restitu-
> tion," but that no special rights are to be inferred from that. Rather, the
> principle holds for them as for all Australians that natural resources
> lying beneath the ground belong to the nation and the owners simply
> cannot prevent exploration.*
>
> *. . . The labor unions have more or less unanimously taken the side of
> the natives; they are discussing possible strikes, and the leading anthro-
> pologist of the fifth continent, Professor R. M. Berndt, has concluded
> that the myths of the "aboriginals" should not be brushed aside so
> lightly as Sir Charles Court has done. In fact the drilling sites lie in a
> region that is very important in the rites of the natives and directly
> within the range of influence of the "Great Goanna of Pea Hill."*
>
> *If one accepts the idea of such ranges or realms of influence, if one
> assumes that sacred places are not simply isolated points but belong to
> an entire network of relics from the dream-time ("The Age")—and not*

---

[45]Stefan Sonderegger, *Appenzeller, Sein und Bleiben,* p. 32.

only the Blacks but also a growing white minority appear inclined toward this view—then this is bound to affect future mining contracts.

This report gives us some idea of how very topical the question is concerning the relative validity of the phenomenon of an ensouled landscape. In Canada an investigative commission, the so-called "Berge Royal Commission," was established for the purpose of resolving possible conflicts between the Eskimos' "soul geography" and the utilization of mineral wealth. Not only in Australia and Canada, but in Switzerland, too, we find a "network of relics from the dream-time," from that time when our ancestors as the "primordial inhabitants" lived in archaic identity with the landscape. Sonderegger's apt designation of a "dead and yet so very animated landscape" is, and yet cannot simply remain a matter of theoretical reflection, if this broader view is to affect our decisions in practice. If this "not only but also" situation is actually to become an experienceable reality, a view that can embrace these opposites is needed. The knowledge of discriminative consciousness that established separation from the world around us must, moreover, combine with experience of the unconscious, capable of *participation mystique*, from which the notion of an ensouled landscape arose in the first place. To the extent that the unconscious background of the soul is acknowledged and experienced as belonging to us and as influencing our consciousness, it becomes possible for us at a more comprehensive level of consciousness to enter again into a real relationship with the world around us, even in a disenchanted world. Such an experience is not, of course, without fundamental consequences for a rural sociology and rural development policy that seeks to take the whole person into account.

Chapter 10

Milieu as Symbol

We have discerned the origin of the ensouled landscape in the spiritual effect of the archetypes in the collective unconscious.[1] Archetypes, whose content is undetermined, actualize in consciousness in the form of archetypal images or symbols. Those symbols can either manifest themselves as inner images in dreams or fantasies, or work their effects on us outwardly, in the experiences of magical places, for example. In the form of symbols, therefore, the meaning or the spiritual effect of the archetypal background reveals itself. For individual people, however, an image becomes a symbol only when the meaning of this image works on them and touches their feelings.[2]

For present-day humanity this spiritual world of the archetype can usually be experienced only to a very limited extent in the external world. We hardly live with living symbols at all; everything is unenchanted and clearly ordered. This gives rise to a feeling of the meaninglessness in human existence, because, in a rational categorization of all domains of life, the symbolic unity of inner and outer, as well as of meaning and matter, has been lost. Our surroundings thus became devoid of meaning, without symbolic value. For modern humanity the space in which one lives consists of virtually nothing but dead matter and had primarily a utilitarian function. With this attitude we speak, for example, of utilization plans, exploitation figures, and regional exploitation potential.

If, however, we recognize the unconscious background of our soul,

---

[1] As we recall, the fifth level of withdrawal of projection consists in exploring the question of what it really was that led to the idea of an "It" or of individual spirits in the landscape.

[2] C. G. Jung, *Man and His Symbols*.

there appears an entirely different reality even for the dyed-in-the-wool rationalist. In a dream the inner landscape is still experienced as ensouled. There the stones and plants speak; there small pieces of wood suddenly dance about in a circle; all sorts of objects turn into living beings; uncanny demons dwell at fords or other dangerous transit points; devilish creatures come together on a lonely Alpine meadow or in a dark corner of a modern metropolis; wind and clouds are alive. In short, all those fabulous things that archaic man experiences in the outer world come to life in the soul's microcosm as *inner reality*. Given approximately one hundred years' empirical research into the nature of dreams, we can no longer be of the opinion that dreams are meaningless froth, and given that the phenomenon of the dream also belongs to our psyche, we must conclude that in the modern human unconscious system an archaic manner of experiencing still exists.

Now to the extent that we take pains to establish a relationship with this other, unconscious mode of experiencing that has become a stranger to us, the paradox of the split unitary reality can become an experiencable reality for us. For both modes of experiencing belong to us—the archaic-participative and the enlightened discriminative. The compelling, unconscious *participation mystique* of modern humanity with our automobiles and our possessions illustrates this fact for us. The goal would have to be that of consciously establishing a connection between the level of consciousness where matter is experienced as soulless and that level of the unconscious which can be characterized as archaic identity. A new attitude[3] can arise when we succeed in bringing the two worlds in ourselves, the conscious and the unconscious, into relationship.

The symbol is the bridge that can create this connection between the "night landscape" and the "day landscape." A relationship arises between these two worlds when the spirit of the unconscious, manifesting itself in symbols, is able to unite itself with consciousness through its efforts to understand meaning. As the sense of this spiritual dimension rewakens, even external things are suddenly seen in a different light. External, dead matter—and consequently the so-called force of circumstance—can quickly become symbolic thanks to openness to meaning; that is, they can convey a meaning. The following example will illustrate this.

A youngish woman whose image of the world was informed by

---

[3]Attitude means expectation, and expectation always works to select and direct. (See C. G. Jung, *C. W.* 6, definition of "Attitude.")

natural-scientific, statistical thought had the following dream during a serious life crisis that gave her the feeling of not being at home anywhere:

> *I am in the countryside where I live, but I feel isolated and like a foreigner there. I get to the top of a mountain in a hot-air balloon. From there I see the same countryside in a new light; now it begins to live for me. Completely satisfied, I now would like to return to the same countryside.*

This dream shows clearly how, from the vantage point of a higher elevation, that is, from a higher level of consciousness, the momentary situation in life can be seen entirely differently. The life crisis, previously felt to be foreign and unpleasant, or just her estranged countryside, when seen from a higher level is suddenly felt as belonging to her and meaningful. The symbolic aspect of a crisis or suffering usually becomes visible only from a superordinated standpoint and has, then, a redeeming effect for the person involved. It is common knowledge that the human being can bear the most incredible suffering if convinced that it has meaning.[4] This is true also for the situation out of which the woman's dream arose. To see what is significant or symbolic in a crisis one needs a fundamental alteration of viewpoint, that is, a different attitude that can conceive a given phenomenon as symbolic.[5] Such a symbolic attitude takes into account the material phenomenon *and* the spiritual effect. It attaches meaning to what happens on both large and small scales, whether coming from within or without, and "places a greater value on this meaning than on mere factuality."[6]

This symbolic attitude permits the joining of the enlightened view of the world with the archaic mode of experiencing. In the experience of a symbol, dead matter comes to life without the emergence of a compelling archaic identity. In our day, however, it is not always easy to champion this symbolic attitude toward things. In the first place we consider everything from the viewpoint, what does it do for me? Because the symbolic quality of an object cannot be grasped by reason alone, we can never say straight out why something becomes a symbol. The essence of a symbol depends precisely on this fact. It is the bridge to that domain beyond reason to the deeper levels of the soul by which we can sense a vital meaning. Through it we *feel* good,

---

[4]C. G. Jung, *Man and His Symbols.*
[5]The symbol of the hot air balloon is to be understood as determined by the situation.
[6]See C. G. Jung, *C. W.* 6, "Definitions" vs. "Symbol," par. 894ff.

which, as the word expresses, has nothing to do with thinking and reasoning. Nobody says, "I think good."[7] Given the nature of a symbol, it is not at all simple to champion a symbolic attitude in the face of utilitarian thinking. A young mother and housewife experienced that very problem, when, with much love and joy, she made apricot jam one afternoon. That evening she had a row with her husband. He held the view that you could buy jam more cheaply at the store. His wife, in contrast, saw something more in her work than the material product. But, as she said, she could not quite put it into words. She was not able to defend her standpoint against her husband's utilitarian arguments, which grieved her very much. That night she dreamed that a piece of apricot was afraid and desperately sought refuge somewhere and finally hid under her blouse. Her dream attempted to compensate for her own uncertainty at the conscious level and to show her that the matter which she had worked with the preceding day was not simply dead and meaningless but rather alive and ensouled through and through.[8] In the symbol of the living apricot this image of living matter sought protection with her, protection from the clutches of rationalistic, utilitarian thinking. If things and activities are judged only according to use and profitability, how, for example, can we find meaning in the mysterious transformation of a "perishable" apricot into a lasting one? From the purely utilitarian-materialistic viewpoint the young wife's jam-making, indeed that sort of work in general, must appear as senseless and accordingly would lead to dissatisfaction.

Is this step toward a symbolic attitude not a utopian one, especially if it involved not just the attitude of a few but rather a *general shift in* our general attitude toward the material world? Where is the reference to reality? We want to begin the answer to this with an example. On the 14th of December 1978 the following news item appeared in the *Neue Zürcher Zeitung*:

> *A fir tree has become the major subject of discussion in the town meeting in Bubikon. In a petition 172 residents advocated preserving a tree planted in 1907 in the Kramen Meadow in Wolfhausen; the area where the tree stands is now quite built-up. Although the purchase of this fir (costing 10,000 Swiss Francs) as well as the 150 square meters of surrounding land had lain within the authority of the community council, the council submitted a funding application to the town meet-*

---

[7]M.-L. von Franz drew my attention to this.
[8]Dreams as instinctive reactions exert a regulating effect vis-à-vis the attitude of consciousness, i.e., they compensate for the one-sidedness of consciousness.

ing. For reasons of cost the Office of Budget Control petitioned for denial; yet after one rejection of the petition, the funding application was approved by a large majority in a secret ballot of the 164 persons at the town meeting.

Such a report must take one aback. There we have thrifty Swiss citizens paying out 10,000 Swiss Francs for *one* tree! Neither as producer of oxygen nor as lumber does this one fir tree even remotely represent a value equivalent to that sum of money. Consequently, the tree had an nonmaterial value for those advocating its purchase. To them it seemed meaningful to preserve the fir tree; for them the one tree became a living symbol of something. The episode from Bubikon is reminiscent of what happened in Derendingen when the great Stüdel Oak, revered by the village community, was felled in order to purchase new fire-fighting equipment from the proceeds of the sale of the wood.[9] The victory of the progressives over the conservatives in that instance was a step in the direction of general disenchantment of the space in which we live. That viewpoint won out which saw only the material advantage of the value of the wood in the oak tree. In Bubikon the progressives were again victorious over the conservatives, but this time the progressives were the ones who recognized that matter is not only a dead object to be used but also embodies a certain objective meaning. The symbolic attitude recognizing both the spiritual dimension and material reality is therefore progressive because it is based on a broader *Weltanschauung* in which body and spirit are experienced as aspects of reality that are independent and of equal value *and* that are unseparated from each other—this in contrast to archaic *participation*.

The campaign to relocate the so-called Teufelsstein ("Devil's Rock") in Canton Uri offers another fitting illustration of the symbolic attitude. The mighty granite chunk[10] which had fallen to the valley and ended up standing on end like an egg, was in the path of construction of the Gotthard highway. But this rock was more than an ordinary boulder. As a prominent monolith it had made an impression on the hearts of generations of people who lived there or passed through, and it had stimulated their imagination. The saga of the Devil's Bridge and the Devil's Rock, in which the Devil intends to use the rock to

---

[9]Cf. chapter 6 in Part 3 of this work. The story of the fir tree in Wolfhausen-Bubikon later came to a sad end. In 1980 when lightning struck the fir tree, the community council failed to repair the damage to the tree. Later the fir tree had to be cut down. The land surrounding it was sold to an adjoining landowner.

[10]Approximately 500 cubic meters.

destroy the bridge he had built but can not because of a grandmother's protective sign, is among Switzerland's best-known legends.[11] The Devil's Rock must have made a lasting impression even on Goethe, since he immortalized it in no less a work than *Faust*.[12] E. Muheim, the former chief physician of the cantonal hospital in Altdorf, aptly elucidated the symbolic quality of this mighty rock in his article, "On the Spiritual Value of the Devil's Rock."[13]

Because the Devil's Rock obstructed the construction of the highway, the Federal authorities wanted to simply blow it up, which would have been the least expensive solution. But thanks to intervention by the Uri government, the Rock was saved. With an expenditure of about 300,000 Swiss Francs, part of which the Canton Uri had to shoulder, the boulder was pushed to one side.[14] Thus an unmistakable landmark of the upper Reuss Valley was preserved for posterity. The Devil's Rock will continue to stand as a symbol of the successful banishment of the soul-robbing side of progress-bringing Lucifer, along with all the other associations belonging with this legendary incident. Perhaps the Rock stands for even more if we consider that it was little more than fifty years ago that the same rock was painted a chocolate brown from top to bottom as an advertisement for Maestrani chocolates.[15] In the light of these changes, the Devil's Rock could certainly be regarded as a hopeful symbol of a transformation in our collective attitude towards matter, a transformation which is gradually appearing. It is precisely that symbolic attitude which grants due attention to the spiritual dimension of life in addition to material reality. The guiding principle for this sort of attention is no longer found solely in usefulness but also in meaning.

---

[11]A detailed interpretation of this saga is to be found in my work, *Entwicklungsplanung ohne Seele?*, p. 216–19.

[12]J. W. von Goethe, *Faust*, Part II, Act 4, lines 10, 120ff.

[13]E. Muheim, "Vom geistigen Wert des Teufelssteins," *Gotthardpost*, no. 1, 1973.

[14]The decision of the government of Uri did not meet with understanding in all quarters. There were vehement opponents who called the relocation of the Rock a waste of money. In an interpellation in the Cantonal Assembly of Uri on 30 July 1972, the question was posed, "Is the Devil's Rock really a natural monument or rather a huge boulder standing in the way of the constructing of the federal highway?" In its argument the Government Council stated its point for preserving the Devil's Rock, "Just as this block of granite is unique in its form and size, so, too, the saga associated with it is also our cultural heritage and consequently a possession of outstanding national significance belonging to the people and handed down to posterity." (From the answer to the interpellation, p. 10.) A poll in Göschenen showed that a significant majority would miss the Devil's Rock if it should be destroyed (see the special edition of the school paper of the Oberschule in Göschenen; "Der Teufelsstein").

[15]Maestrani AG gave the Rock to the Commission for Protection of Nature of the Canton Uri in 1925.

The spirit that lets something become a symbol or carrier of meaning is, as we have seen, the manifestation of the unconscious archetypal background. Fundamentally, therefore, a symbolic attitude simply means a careful consideration of the spirit of the unconscious. To the extent that we mean simply whatever is at hand by the term "nature," which also applies to archtypes, we can speak of the *spirit of nature* instead of the spirit of the unconscious. By acknowledging and taking into consideration a spirit of nature, a spirit which can manifest itself as meaning in matter, the symbolic concept meets the original idea of an *anima mundi* or *spiritus mundi*, the all-ensouling spirit in matter.[16] It is related to the sense that the psyche is as if disseminated throughout the world and is personified in its totality as the world soul. There appears to be an archetypal, that is, typically human, experience underlying this conception. Whenever consciousness, experiencing its limitations, feels joined directly with the collective psyche, this condition is described as a union with the matter surrounding the individual concerned.[17] We read the following in Jung's memoirs about his vacation house: "In Bollingen I am my truest self, in that which corresponds to me. . . . At times I am as though spread out into the landscape and into things and I live in every tree, in the lapping of the waves, in the clouds, the animals that come and go, and in things."[18] This feeling of an inner unity of man and milieu finds clear expression in a song from the modern "hippie" world:

> Sometimes when I am feeling
> as big as the land with the velvet hills
> in the small of my back
> and my hands are playing the sand.
> And my feet are swimming
> in all of the waters. . . .
>
> Sometimes when I am feeling so glad
> and I become a world
> and the world becomes a man
> and my song becomes part of the river. . . .

---

[16]We find this idea in various cultures, for example, in the texts of late Sankhya philosophy in India, where the Purusha (the original man) is designated as the soul of matter. (See M.-L. von Franz, *Creation Myths*, p. 97ff.)

[17]As we have seen, the collective soul stands somehow in direct connection with matter, for reasons of plausibility in regard to evolution!

[18]C. G. Jung, *Memories, Dreams, Reflections*.

Experiences of this kind as well as various *creation myths* in which the world rises out of one human being,[19] point to a certain structural kinship between the collective human soul and the substance of the world. This inner kinship might well be the reason why we feel comfortable in structures that grew somehow organically; in products of the drawing board, by contrast, we do not feel so immediately at home.

Testimonies about personal experiences of feeling inner union of human and landscape, experiences that are by no means rare curiosities, lead to the question of the extent of the soul. What spatial size does the soul have? "The psyche could be regarded of as a mathematical point and at the same time as a universe of fixed stars," Jung once said.[20] He pointed out, among other things, that the collective unconscious "contains subliminal perceptions whose scope is nothing less than astounding."[21] From this we can gather that, where the unconscious is experienced as a living, acting other, that is, where it becomes an objective reality, the physical-spatial limitation of the ego is also removed. The surrounding space we inhabit is thereby experienced as ensouled, ensouled by the spirit of the objective psyche whose extent is, of course, not bounded by the human body.[22] But whenever the spiritual dimension becomes thus experienceable in the material environment, indeed, whenever the landscape really embodies a symbol of the collective psyche, this materia also becomes empirically more than a mere object. Regrettable relapses into an archaic identity? No, for the symbolic attitude sees the concrete facts *and* pays attention to the meaning aspect of a phenomenon. This way,

---

[19]In German mythology the world arose from the body of a dismembered anthropomorphic being, the giant Ymir. The earth arose from his flesh, the sea from his blood, the cliffs from his bones, the trees from his hair, the vault of heaven from his skull, and the clouds from his brain. The cosmology based on the death and dismemberment of an anthropomorphic being has parallels in the myths of Tiamat (Mesopotamia), Purusha (India), and P'an Ku (China). For details see Mircea Eliade, *Patterns in Comparative Religion*, sections 21, 73, 129, 172; also Mircea Eliade, *Creation Myths*, and M.-L. von Franz, *Creation Myths*, especially p. xxff.

[20]C. G. Jung, "Basic Postulates of Analytical Psychology," in *The Structure and Dynamics of the Psyche*, C. W. 8, par. 671.

[21]Op. cit., par. 672.

[22]Jung already sounded this note in his work, "The Spirit Mercurius," C. W. 13, par. 249: The fifth level assumes that the unconscious exists and has a reality just like any other existent. However odious it may be, this means that the "spirit" is also a reality, and the "evil" spirit at that. What is even worse, the distinction between "good" and "evil" is suddenly no longer obsolete, but highly topical and necessary. The crucial point is that so long as the evil spirit cannot be proved to be a subjective psychic experience, then even trees and other suitable objects would have, once again, to be seriously considered as its lodging places.

neither the discriminative, masculine principle nor the participatory-uniting feminine principle become absolute factors but rather are related to each other, that is, *relativized*. Without lapsing into a regressive-concretistic participation, the symbolic understanding makes possible a coming together of both ways of experiencing the world, the archaic-participatory and the enlightened-discriminative.

In an unsurpassable manner the Czech immigrant Johannes Urzidil depicts how such an attitude in one's relationship to matter can convey meaning for a person even in the thoroughly rationalized world of New York. He writes of his relationship to leather, thanks to which he built a new life for himself in New York. "For me in the midst of the city of skyscrapers, craft was a true return to nature. I was like a farmer or fisherman or wood cutter who comprehends the mutual terms of employment between man and the elements. . . . True craft is never exploitation but service to the material that never gives more than it itself receives."[23] With this sort of attitude, human work leads to a relationship to the matter with which we are involved and with which we live. But wherever things become our counterpart and hence no longer "dead matter," matter can no longer be simply something to be used, that I can throw away when it is no longer of use to me. Whenever matter of any kind becomes thus a carrier of meaning, that is, becomes an embodiment of a spirit which also works its effects on us, we can no longer interfere arbitrarily in externals according to what we deem useful for the moment.

At a very practical level the experience of the collective soul, which somehow extends into the external-physical, material basis of things, signifies an act of becoming conscious that we also touch something within the soul at the place where we interfere with external structures. Every interference with the organically developed structures of our landscape affects us via the participating collective soul and inflicts a certain damage on it depending on the extent of the interference. The village linden tree that must make way for a street to be rebuilt, the course of a river or a moor that must be changed for soil improvement, the lights of an express highway through the country that shine half the night—all these external interventions or interferences also mean interventions or interferences in the domain of our soul. To the extent, however, that we have lost contact with our participating collective soul, we apparently do not recognize this

---

[23]Johannes Urzidil, *Väterliches aus Prag und Handwerkliches aus New York*, p. 53.

damage to the soul.[24] It manifests itself in creeping symptoms of dissatisfaction, restlessness, and dissonance. Only when we return to the participating side in us and experience it as belonging to us do we feel the damage that our soul has suffered whenever familiar natural structures are destroyed. For this reason we must demand that reconstruction and soil improvement projects, as well as development projects, no longer be carried out simply according to what is technically possible, but rather that *these intentions be restricted to absolutely necessary interventions in existing structures.* A development policy with the fundamental stance "here we destroy a landscape in favor of industry and the like, there we 'create' in its place a compensatory space" becomes very questionable in light of these insights.[25]

In his book on the strategy of progress, the engineer Ernst Basler writes: "If humanity survives a few hundred years more on this planet, the turning point at the year 2000 A.D. will doubtless be designated by future historians as the turning point in the relationship between man and nature. . . . The turning point will be characterized by mankind learning anew to live, build, plant, and shape *with* nature and not *against* nature."[26] Following this undoubtedly correct statement, Basler sketches out the movement away from a purely extraverted and all too optimistic standpoint. He believes that we now must magnanimously spare the nature we have tamed. "Man is the stronger one. He can thrust nature aside, change her, manipulate her, dominate her whenever that is his intention."[27] However, obviously correct and necessary it may be to respect nature unconditionally, it is a most serious sort of hubris to believe that humanity has tamed nature. After all, we know we cannot even ward off a bad mood. Yet what is a mood but nature? And where is our superiority over nature if the "earth animal" upon which we live really shakes itself vigorously? And where is our superiority over nature when people form mobs and, seized by wild emotions, pay homage to certain "ideals" or "-isms"? Events of our century hardly illustrate the superiority of humanity over its own nature.

Basler is, of course, not alone in his optimism that humanity has tamed nature. The belief in the power of clever Homo sapiens is still widespread, especially among scientists and planners. Hence we

---

[24]In his book *Die friedliche Zerstörung einer Landschaft und Ansätze zu ihrer Rettung in der Schweiz*, Weiss speaks of a "lack of awareness of the landscape."

[25]On this see Klaus C. Ewald's measures for protecting the landscape in *Der Landschaftswandel: Zur veränderung schweizerischer Kulturlandschaften im 20. Jahrhundert.*

[26]Ernst Basler, *Strategie des Fortschritts*, p. 112.

[27]Ibid, p. 113.

always find, as the conclusion of analyses of current problems, some sort of well-intentioned challenges to politicians or to humanity in general that they should do this or that to set the world in order. Yet a glance at history shows us that humanity always begins to change its ways of thinking and acting only when forced to by some crisis or other. This holds true for the new relationship of human to nature or matter that Basler appropriately demands. Only through suffering from the split between humanity and nature or between consciousness and the unconscious—through suffering that presents itself in the form of some sort of symptom (nostalgia, depressions, obsessive fantasies, compulsions, etc.)—does there arise a real interest in the other side, called nature. Only then is the unconscious experienced as autonomous reality, and only then does the search begin for the meaning of the symptoms. Here we must not overlook the fact that these symptoms are of both individual and collective nature. Among the latter are all our external imbalances, not least of all, the regional ones. Whenever we begin to inquire about the meaning of a symptom, we confess our intellectual ignorance. At that moment the spirit of the unconscious can manifest itself and the symbolic stirrings can be perceived.[28]

The link between consciousness and the unconscious domain which is made visible by symptoms is, to emphasize it once again, the symbol. Externally most things have forfeited their symbolic content in the course of disenchantment. This loss, however, is compensated for in the symbols of our dreams.[29] But since this language of nature has become, to a large extent, alien and incomprehensible to us, these symbols must be translated through interpretation into our rational mode of thinking. If the unconscious world of archetypes, which manifests itself in images of meaning, can be united with the world of consciousness through an understanding of their meaning, then a relationship arises between these worlds. Where the sense of the dimension reawakens, thanks to experiencing the reality of the unconscious's autonomous spirit, this spirit, coming from outside, can speak to humanity once again. External things, of whatever nature, can suddenly become vehicles of meaning, i.e., living symbols, be they apricots or an entire landscape. Thus the necessary turnabout in the relationship between human and nature takes place, the turnabout from a utilitarian relationship to one aware of its

---

[28]Additional details regarding rural planning and development are to be found in my *Entwicklungsplanung ohne Seele?*, especially the chapter on the speaking stone, p. 58ff.
[29]See C. G. Jung, *Man and His Symbols*.

responsibility. Wherever a person begins again to live with living symbols, the needs of the deeper levels of the soul—the archaic in us—become a factor to be respected. The spirit of the unconscious manifesting itself in the symbol becomes a counterweight to, and a measure of, modern consciousness driven by a boundless delusion of omnipotence. At the same time, the individual feels again at home in that place where one can live with a sense of one's own meaning, felt in the effect of the symbol.[30] Seen from this vantage point, a cultural mode of nostalgia can be understood fundamentally as the expression of modern humanity's search for a spiritual life, a life with meaning, a life with living symbols.

---

[30]"Cultural identity is objectified in symbols which depict the value orientation and simultaneously patterns or models of behavior in [a people's] space, their territory or their home area." I. Greverus, *Versuch zum Heimatphänomen*, p. 57.

Chapter 11

Conclusions for Rural Sociology and Rural Development Policy

Rural and Agrarian Sociology on the Basis of a Complementarity Viewpoint

We recall the problem with most theories of social change— somewhere they are all burdened with one-sidedness. In our investigation of the change in the relationship between humanity and the space it inhabits, we have been able, using the hypothesis of the collective unconscious, to sketch a passable way in which a significant phenomenon in rural sociology can be adequately explained from a *viewpoint of complementarity*. Only in the composite view, in the paradoxical "not only but also" view demanded by the symbolic viewpoint just described, is it possible to gain a real understanding of the complex interaction between a population and the space in which it lives.

By including the hypothesis of the collective unconscious, we base our investigation of sociologic issues on the *expanded image of humanity* called for in Part 2. Thus, next to the conscious need for lack of restraint, the unconscious need for containedness in a supraordinated whole is also recognized and included, although these two viewpoints regarded logically are mutually exclusive. With this composite view it becomes possible to bring the spiritual background of man into relationship with practical development policy in rural areas.

What Grows and What Is Planned

The gradual process of disenchantment of the space in which we live came about in remote rural regions much later than in urban areas. Archaic images of an ensouled landscape have been able to survive in these areas up until recent times. Although enlightened thinking is making more and more headway in rural areas in the wake of improved mass communication, the traditional view of the world is nevertheless retained subliminally. A population's specific, traditional picture of their area is an expression of an entire dimension of local history and only a thin veneer of modern rationally purposeful concepts lies superimposed upon this feeling-toned realm. Failure to take this dimension into account when making planned interventions in a rural area can therefore work out very detrimentally. This holds true particularly for regional economic planning, but also for soil improvement projects and merging of land holdings. If the collective emotional background of a rural population is ignored, either a diffuse discontent arises against any and all "interventions from above," or else the procedure awakens absolutely no commitment and feeling of involvement in the common interest. Both eventualities make such a one-sidedly rational methodology appear unfruitful or at least inadequate. For this reason researchers and practitioners active in rural areas must become conscious of the manner of experiencing the world. We must take note that another mode of experiencing can be operative among natives in rural areas and also in modern persons and hence is a living reality of the deeper levels of experiencing in us, too. Only through this sort of consciousness can real connection between modern, goal-directed thinking and the tradition-bound world of ideas come about.

Current rural development policy attempts to utilize space optimally. Given the limited availability of land and the need for relatively intact landscapes, regional planning in rural areas is supposed to strive for an equilibrium between various forms of utilization (agriculture, industry, recreation, etc.). Moreover, it seeks to fulfill the regional potential as comprehensively as possible by means of a goal-directed rural development policy. In dealing with these landscapes and structures that have evolved organically, we follow our momentary inclinations, as if this materia were not our partner; for, after all, matter is a dead mass for the enlightened person. If a landscape or an organically evolved settlement is to be fundamentally changed by extravagant intervention, it is seen as part of the price of progress; "nobody will complain anyway." Dead matter seemingly accepts everything. In the light of modern insights, this conclusion must be questioned. Since the deeper layers of our psyche stand in some relation to the matter in our environment, we must formulate the hypothesis that external alterations of the space in which we live will have repercussions on the person and influence the disposition of the soul, just as a change in the body influences the psychic state. The validity of this hypothesis would have profound consequences for all development policy. No longer limited to the material realm, we would not restrict our investigations to ascertaining the extent to which nature can be burdened with interventions or interferences, and where, if need be, one could still exploit a regional resource. Rather we would also have to take into account the effects *on the soul* associated with all external interventions. Thus the division into zones for exploitation and for recreation would have to be examined anew in the light of this hypothesis. A recreation zone *there* cannot really recompense us emotionally for the destruction of our immediate home space *here*.

The validity of our hypothesis would have, in general, an effect on the normative decrees in our rural development policy. If the psyche indeed should be united with matter—and the probability of this borders on certainty—then that would necessarily cause a fundamental change in the relation of expert to subject. If a psychic component dwells in matter, a component that somehow stands in relation to the collective unconscious, the possibility of a fundamental relationship between human and matter exists and *via the collective unconscious*. The spirit of matter which somehow has something to do with the holistic order of nature would also have to be consulted in the event of any interventions in organically evolved structures. This can happen through our efforts to include in our work those expressions of nature which relate to the *materia* we shape.[1] A dialogue or a coming to terms with the materia can only come about if we renounce all claims of power—namely the claims that, if we wanted to, we could define limits and the uses of the world about us. The consequence of such a change in attitude would be that such things as the earth, minerals, etc., would no longer be appreciated only for their exploitation potential and function but rather for their inner value or spirit as well—which would then have relevance to the questions of limits and exploitation. In practice this means that we may no longer hold only to the guidelines and norms of reason when intervening in the world around us; rather we must set limits *in each case* that we can meaningfully defend according to our best knowledge and conscience. Here knowledge represents the area of the problem we can elucidate; conscience, on the other hand, refers to the spiritual dimension of meaning. Responsible and courageous authorities with so-called healthy common sense have, as we know, never acted otherwise.

Where we can free ourselves from an all too rigid network of guide-

---

[1] An investigation of this closely connected with practice can be found in my work, *Entwicklungsplanung ohne Seele?*

lines and norms and approach development or planning with an unbiased approach of asking questions, a relation to matter can come into being. The dimension of soul can manifest itself again when, for example, a region's development problem suddenly gets "under our skin," in other words, touches our soul. The *materia* to be worked on is no longer dead but rather a living, independent counterpart that affects our soul. Thus it has a kind of soul that can freely realize effects—in the sense of reality. Our ancestors in the Middle Ages would have called this inner step of development liberation of the *anima mundi*. The quintessence of our historical observations concerning the relation between humanity and landscape lies in the postulate that, in future treatises concerning the relation between humanity and the space in which we live, as well as the consequences of that relationship for sociology and politics, the reality of the soul must receive unconditional consideration.

Summary

In the West the relation of human being to milieu has changed over the course of history. Parallel with the development of human consciousness, humanity separated itself from archaic identity with its surroundings. Nature was de-souled, the idea of an *anima mundi* was abandoned, and thus the existence of an objective psyche given up. With this change in the manner of experiencing the world, a separation of spirit and matter came about. De-souled matter became dead matter, and the dimension of the spirit was identified with the intellect and seen as wholly separated from matter. Moreover, in this *Weltanschauung* humanity felt a fundamental differentness from the objective external world, corresponding to a separation of subject and object. This image of the world found its ultimate expression in the Cartesian thinking of the Enlightenment and forms the philosophical foundation of contemporary rural sociology and development policy.

The results of contemporary research in physics and in psychology, however, put the validity of this *Weltanschauung* in question. They are able to demonstrate the probability of a fundamental, unitary reality in which the psyche and matter appear as inseparable in a domain transcending consciousness. The Theory of Relativity and the proof of a psychoid aspect of archetypes point in this direction. In addition to this, the findings of these sciences reveal a certain perpetual, unavoidable relation between subject and object. The Uncertainty Principle and the existence of a qualitative aspect of matter support this concept. Thus we have now enough empirical material to demonstrate that the separation into outer-material and inner-spiritual is a model of the world, but not reality itself. "The polarization of the psychic middle range between the two consciousness-transcending poles of matter and psyche is only a means for our consciousness to describe its psychic experiences a little more exactly; 'outward-material' and 'inner-spiritual' are only characteristic labels that tell us nothing about the real nature of what we describe as 'matter' or about what we call 'spirit,' except that both move and affect us psychologically."[2] The separation into opposites for purposes of identification appears a worthwhile aid in mastering everyday reality; but according to recent research findings, it is no longer an essential feature of reality. On the contrary, reality is characterized by the unity of things. In this new yet ancient view of the world, the separation of psyche and matter and of ego and world is abolished, even if, for purposes of identification, consciousness must discriminate time and again.

On the basis of these discoveries we have shown how the disenchantment of the space in which we live can claim only a relative validity, in that our environment must not be regarded as consisting simply of dead matter but rather as having a certain direct connection with the human psyche. By the hypothesis formulated in conjunction with this, interventions and changes in our milieu have a more or less perceptible influence on humanity. What until now was viewed as two completely different realms exerting no influence on each other is, given the current state of our knowledge, seen as a unity. For this reason, consciousness of the relation of psyche and matter must be sought and maintained when working on development problems in rural areas, if human being and milieu are not to fall into yet deeper polarization.

---

[2]M.-L. von Franz, *Projection and Recollection*, p. 91.

PART 4

CHANGE IN INTERPERSONAL RELATIONSHIPS

Overview and Significance

Having observed the fundamental change in the relationship of humanity to the space in which it lives, we now want to investigate the extent of comparable alterations in the relationship of human beings to each other. Again we limit ourselves to the attempt at understanding this change in rural areas. Actually, the alteration in humanity's attitude to plants and animals could also be investigated in detail—especially for agrarian sociology—but that would unduly expand the scope of the present work. Besides, this change can be inferred from what has already been said and from what is to follow.

Social life in the country and especially in agriculture has changed in every respect in recent decades. Catchwords and phrases such as money economy, competitive education, mobility, and dissolution of village or clan solidarity through supracommunal organizational and care-provision systems may suffice to outline typical manifestations of a change in interpersonal relations. As we saw in the section entitled "Theories of Social Change," this process of change in society has been explored, described, and interpreted from various viewpoints. These attempts at explanation usually proceed from a so-called dichotomous or two-part schema, by which we understand a juxtaposition of earlier human forms of living together and our modern way of life. Examples of such juxtapositions or dichotomies are, for instance, F. Tönnies' *Gemeinschaft* and *Gesellschaft*,[1] M. Weber's traditional and rational action,[2] R. Redfield's folk society and urban soci-

---

[1]Tönnies, *Gemeinschaft und Gesellschaft*.
[2]Weber, *The Theory of Social and Economic Organization*, p. 115ff.

159

ety,[3] H. Becker's sacred society and secular society,[4] H. Freyer's primary and secondary systems,[5] T. Parsons' five "pattern variables" for distinguishing preindustrial and industrial societies,[6] the *culture nongrammaticalisé* and *culture grammaticalisé* of M. Pop,[7] or *société archaïque* and *société industrielle* in the work of A. J. Greimas.[8]

Instead of this dichotomy, numerous authors prefer a threefold classification in which the third level often represents a new form of human social life to be striven for or even immanent. Karl Marx points out the dichotomy of communal property (in primordial society) vs. private property (in slaveholding, feudal, and capitalistic societies). The third and last level would, according to Marx, be socialism with socialist ownership.[9] Other gradations, for example, are D. Bell's "pre–industrial–industrial–post–industrial"[10] or J. Fourastié's *civilisation primaire–secondaire–tertiaire*.[11] Now whether one proceeds from a dichotomy or a trichotomy, what is common to both is the observation throughout the world of a process of change away from a way of life oriented to tradition and the collective and toward a more ego-oriented[12] way of life that neglects tradition.[13]

We will proceed just as in part 3 of this work: we will investigate this social change in connection with the origin of an ego-consciousness separated from the unconscious. Thereby we hope to be able to elucidate this process of change that is so significant for rural life.

---

[3]Redfield, "The Folk Society," p. 293–308.
[4]Becker, "A Sacred-Secular Evaluation Continuum of Social Change," *Transactions of the Third World Congress of Sociology*, ISA, 1956, vol. 6, p. 19ff.
[5]Freyer, *Theorie des gegenwärtigen Zeitalters*.
[6]Parsons, *Societies: Evolutionary and Comparative Perspectives*. The "pattern variables" are: affectivity vs. affective neutrality, collective-orientation vs. self-orientation, universalism vs. particularism, ascription vs. achievement, diffusivity vs. specificity.
[7]Pop, "Problèmes généraux de l'éthnologie européene," *Actes du Premier Congrès International d'Ethologie Européenne*, Paris, 1971 (Paris: Editions G.-P. Maisonneuve et Larose, 1973).
[8]Greimas, "Rèflexions sur les objects ethno-sämiotique," *Actes du Premier Congrès International d'Ethologie Europèenne*, Paris 1971 (Paris: Editions G.-P. Maisonneuve et Larose, 1973).
[9]Marx, *Zur Kritik der politischen Ökonomie*.
[10]Bell, *The Coming of Post-Industrial Society*.
[11]Fourastié, *Le grand espoir du XXe siècle*; additional examples in Wiswede and Kutsch, *Sozialer Wandel*, p. 20f.
[12]This word stands in conscious opposition to Parsons' concept "self-oriented," because of the psychological differentiation of ego and self (about which more later).
[13]This holds true also for nations that call themselves "peoples' republics" or something similar.

Chapter 12

Primordial-Participatory Social Relationship

We recall how originally the world was experienced as ensouled. The archaic person experiences a great part of what we today assign to psychic inner space as external, outside the body, extended in the ensouled matter of his environment, and effecting an archaic identity or *participation mystique* between human and milieu.[1] Just as archaic man finds psychic contents superimposed on the landscape and thereby lives in "his" landscape, so, too, interpersonal relations at this level rest on primordial *participation mystique*. To understand the essence of this social context, we must first of all elucidate two things: the size of archaic societies and the nature of *participation mystique* between people in general.

As Arnold Toynbee has written, "Since our ancestors became human, mankind has lived, during all but the last fraction—perhaps the last sixteenth part—of its time-span to date, in the Lower Paleolithic way. A band of Lower Palaeolithic food-gatherers and hunters had to be small in numbers and to give a wide berth to other bands. At this stage of technology and economy, a concentration of population would have spelled starvation. . . . each band was small enough for all its members to be acquainted with each other personally."[2] Ethnological and human ethological research on archaic societies of

---

[1]See Part 3, chapter 6, above.

[2]Arnold Toynbee, *Mankind and Mother Earth*, p. 588 (Engied). On p. 23, Toynbee writes, "We may guess, as an inference from our ancestors' survival after descending from the shelter of the trees to the comparatively dangerous ground-level that, by then, they were already social animals or that at least they had become such in the act of shifting their habitat. At ground-level, solitary hominids would have been an easy prey for non-hominid predators for whom, at that stage, our ancestors would have been no match if they had not banded together."

modern times also consistently shows us a form of life in relatively small, closed groups.[3] These original societies were usually rigidly isolated and their members were in some way related to one another. The small group held together by relationship bonds is thus doubtlessly the primal form of human society.

In the context of social relations at this primordial level we spoke of *participation mystique*, that is to say, an archaic identity of the individual with the tribe. Now how is this to be understood? In explaining this phenomenon, let us begin with the very first social relationship in the life of an individual human being, normally the mother-child relationship. In the first place, this relationship rests on the maternal instinct. It awakens in full force during pregnancy and creates something like a magical bond between mother and child, so that a mother immediately hears her child's cry from among all possible distractions and reacts instinctively. Conversely, the child learns very quickly to distinguish the familiar nurturant quality of the mother or other accustomed person from any stranger: "It reacts to strangers," as they say. In this manner mother and child are during the initial phase indeed two separate beings, but they still live psychically as if coalesced, that is, in archaic identity. Only in the course of all sorts of separation-individuation phases does the child gradually differentiate out of this primordial relatedness in order to become an independent being psychically, too.[4] Ontogenesis corresponds to phylogenesis in the social dimension as well as the physical development of the body; that is, the primordial relatedness of archaic human with tribe is based on the same pattern as the mother-child relationship. The tribe vouchsafes the individual maternal protection for survival—for archaic man could never have survived alone—and vice versa, as the individual is integrated into and bonded to the sheltering tribe.[5]

The characteristic social behavior belonging to this primordial stage thus involves no behavior "in the interest of the individual" but only "in the interest of the many."[6] At this level of consciousness, the individual human being plays only a meager role. He is essentially a part of his clan or tribe. John Layard expressed this aptly: "A really primitive community resembles an individual person in the sense

---

[3]See also Eibl-Eibesfeldt, *Menschenforschung auf neuen Wegen*, Vienna, 1976.
[4]Excluding, of course, neurotic, faulty development.
[5]See also the valuable document on early man by Bleek and Lloyd, *Bushman Folklore* London, 1911; regarding archaic identity, the section on "Bushman Presentiments," pp. 330–339 is especially worth reading.
[6]The concepts in quotes come from Redfield, "The Folk Society."

that its members are all one."[7] Concerning the unconditional interdependency of all members of such an archaic society, Layard continues, "They are in the first place all closely related to one another, so that the action of one has immediate repercussions for all the others; and in the second place the solidarity of these tiny groups in the face of natural forces as well as enemy tribes is of such overriding importance that any major departure from the accepted order is highly dangerous to the delicate balance on which the whole tiny structure depends."[8]

Now this does not mean that people in the archaic tribe all behaved the same way. On the contrary, just as distinctly individual expressions can be seen in the infant who has not yet developed separate ego-consciousness, the archaic person also reveals individuality.[9] But what has not yet crystallized is a separate ego-consciousness that would enable deviation from the "group consciousness" or the "we-consciousness."[10] Therefore, we must distinguish clearly between individuality and ego-consciousness, since the former signifies the entire personality whereas the latter designates only consciousness.[11]

The fact, therefore, that the individual does not yet experience himself as psychically separated from the tribe is a feature of primordial social life. The person feels an archaic identity with the community or emotionally bound to it. This means that a part of the soul lies outside the body. Since these externalized psychic components are likely to be collective contents analogous to the above-mentioned "geography of the soul" in the landscape, a collectively valid, psychically conditioned social order arises within an archaic, closed tribe. To each member of the group belongs an "aura of images," which we call the person's reputation. The person is composed of empirically evident characteristics and collective expectations which we would label in contemporary terms as projections from the collective unconscious. Parallel to the concept of "geography of the soul," one could, in the

---

[7]Layard, *Stone Men of Malekula*, London, 1942, pp. 102, 115ff., 593. Sigmund Freud's theory of the primal horde (developed in *Totem and Taboo*) in which promiscuity ruled corresponds to no form of society known to anthropological research. (Layard in *Institutionen in primitiven Gesellschaften*, p. 59; see also Birket-Smith, *Geschichte der Kultur*, Zürich, 1946, p. 271. Frankfurt: Suhrkamp, 1967)

[8]Layard, "The Incest Taboo and the Virgin Archetype," in *Eranus Jahrbuch*, p. 267. vol. 12, Zürich, 1945.

[9]The Danish ethnologist Kaj Birket-Smith, among others, referred to this and criticized the one-sided view of the sociologist E. Durkheim, who speaks of the "collective thought" of primordial peoples (in *Geschichte der Kultur*, p. 34ff).

[10]See Battagay, *Der Mensch in der Gruppe*, Berne, 1967–1972, vol. 1, pp. 10–16.

[11]See the introduction to von Franz, "Zur Psychologie der Gruppe." ("On Group Psychology," *Quadrant*, no. 13, Winter 1973).

case of the primordial, closed tribe, speak of a typical geography of reputation. Individual ones are never alike; but all have their definite place in the social body, a prominent phenomenon we can observe in rural village communities insofar as people there still know each other personally.[12] And just as there are mana centers in the local geography of the soul, there are also, in the "geography of reputation" of the primordial tribe, persons with "positive mana," such as the opinion leaders, and persons with "negative mana," i.e., witches, scapegoats, and so forth.

Unconditional relatedness to the closed tribe and to its members, consequently, characterizes the primordial social relationship. Even among us, many features of that sort of inner kinship of the individual with a tribe have been able to survive, since individual villages in the country and especially in mountainous areas were more or less closed social organisms right up into recent times. How isolated our village communities were is attested to by the strictly respected marriage circles, whose boundaries normally coincided with those of the villages or parishes. The marriage circle was kept under surveillance by the "unmarried fellows or 'Knaben,'" as we called the single young men. Formed into "Knabenschaften" and similar units resembling men's associations, they kept a sharp eye on the eligible women of their village. "Girls belong in their own village."[13] Woe to the fellow from outside who dared to invade this marriage circle. Rough punishment awaited him on his dark path home.[14] In 1980 I got a detailed report from an informant about one of the last punishments of this sort in the Schächen Valley (Canton Uri). In many places such things have obviously gone on until quite recently, and presumably they have not entirely vanished even today. Outside the alpine regions, too, the marriage circle was often identical with the boundary of the village parish. "Up until twenty years ago 'everybody intermarried' in Oltingen (Canton Basel-Land), and the physician from Gelterkinden often said we really should bring in new blood from outside, otherwise it was pure inbreeding." An informant from Strübin made this statement in 1951.[15] Yet not only in regard to marriage, but in quite general terms, the village community appears from outside as a unit.

---

[12]Concerning the phenomenon of village reputation, the reader is referred to the significant references in Illien and Jeggle in *Leben auf dem Dorf*.

[13]On this see Strübin's discussions in *Baselbieter Volksleben*, Reihe der SGV., vol. 8, Basel, 1952, p. 141ff.

[14]Details in Wackernagel, *Altes Volkstum der Schweiz*, Schriflen der SGV., vol. 38, Basel, 1959, p. 22; a general discussion of Swiss boys' nocturnal visits to their girls (Swiss: *Kiltgang*) is to be found in Windmann, *Die Einleitung der Ehe*, Aho, 1937.

[15]Strübin, *Baselbieter Volksleben*, p. 141.

The circle of intimacy is close, and foreign territory that is felt to be hostile begins at one's very doorstep.[16] "Foreign territory is embodied most palpably in the neighboring villages that one quarrels with."[17] Testimony to this is the still widespread and well-known baiting between villages, involving antagonism toward strangers and those who are different.[18] Thus self-containment is the outstanding feature of earlier village communities and to this naturally belongs the inner and outer kinship of all with all.

Similarly, the individual in such a primordial-closed village unit was, as in archaic communities, like a part of a living organism.[19] In saying this, perhaps it should be emphasized again that, of course, this primordial form of life is nothing romantic but rather was just as bright and just as dark, just as good and just as cruel as things close to nature actually are.[20]

For such a social organism to function, correct behavior of the individual was of decisive importance.[21] Taking the mountain people of Uri as an example, Eduard Renner has shown how significant this correct behavior was in our primordial-closed societies. In Uri "Yserte einä sy" means being a part of the local community.[22] If such a member of the community "doesn't do things like folks do them"–"nit tuet wiä d'Lyt"–that is, as Renner emphasizes, "the basis of every sacrilege."[23] Here it must be noted that "the sacrilege in its pure form has nothing to do with transgressing the commandments of God and the Church. Rather, it is linked to the concept of the magical efficacy of usage and tradition."[24] As Renner points out elsewhere, "the one committing the sacrilege rends, as it were, that magical bond that binds him with all others."[25] Therefore "Nit tuet wiä d'Lyt" is a threat to the functioning of the entire organism, comparable to a malignantly proliferating cell in the body. It is for this reason that in the

---

[16]On this see Strübin, *Grundfragen des Volkslebens bei Jeremias Gotthelf*, Basel, 1959, p. 24ff. Concerning the traditional closedness of our parishes and communities, see also Hauser, *Schweizerische Hirtschafts- und Sozialgeschichte*, Zürich, 1961, p. 130.

[17]Strübin, op. cit., p. 25; on this Eibl-Eibesfeldt writes in *Der vor-programmierte Mensch*, p. 109: "This schema of the enemy, 'foreign = enemy,' is obviously inherent. Cultural comparison confirms that xenophobia is a universal phenomenon."

[18]More on this in Hauser, "Heimatbegriff," p. 34; in Wackernagel, *Altes Volkstum der Schweiz*, p. 41; and in Weiss, *Volkskunde der Schweiz*, p. 31.

[19]Weiss, *Volkskunde der Schweiz*, p. 333f.; see also Tönnies, *Gemeinschaft und Gesellschaft*, p. 7ff.

[20]See also the description in Stutz, *Sieben mal sieben Jahre* (1853).

[21]Analogous to the earlier-mentioned quote from Layard.

[22]Renner, *Goldener Ring über Uri*, p. 227.

[23]Ibid., p. 254.

[24]Idem.

[25]Ibid., p. 227.

writings of Jeremias Gotthelf "the people" are a great power, whom one avoids offending if at all possible.[26] An offense against usage and custom is also "an outrage or a sacrilegium" against traditional life in the Emmen Valley—just as in Canton Uri.[27]

So that the correct functioning of the social organism will be guaranteed, the entire productive activity at this primordial level is never directed solely to economic goals but rather is always permeated with ritual elements that express and secure the social unanimity of the tribe.[28] This feeling of unity finds its high point and its ever-recurring renewal in the calendar of religious holidays, with the various rituals including everyone, anchoring and bonding them in something transworldly.[29]

An important point must not go unmentioned in this connection: the structures of the original social organism are not, as often thought, the ingenious inventions of individual persons who wanted thereby to assume power and privilege. Investigations of the primordial forms of human social life reveal that the archaic social structures have gradually crystallized in a process of maturation. As in the process of cell division, the first essential event is a division of the tribe into two parts, out of which then further differentiation comes about over time.[30] This archaic division, as Richard Weiss has observed, can be seen also in villages where "the original and confessional unanimity of the village community has still been retained."[31]

---

[26]Strübin, *Grundfragen des Volkslebens bei Jeremias Gotthelf*. [Jeremias Gotthelf was the pen name of the Swiss pastor Albert Bitzius, 1797–1854, who wrote realistically and with elemental force about his life and times. Titles of some of his works give a sense of his areas of focus: *The Peasant's Mirror, or The Life of Jeremias Gotthelf*, 1837, *Sorrows and Joys of a Schoolmaster*, 1838–39, *Ulrich the Farm Servant*, 1841, and the continuation, *Ulrich the Tenant Farmer*, 1847.—Trans.]

[27]Strübin, op. cit., p. 43.

[28]In addition to this, think of the ritual assignment of responsibilities "in turn" for the village oven, the water supply, the use of commonly held land, wood lots, etc., (see additionally Bachmann, *Daheim im Lötschental*, Habilitationsschrift an der Universität, Zürich, 1972. Cf. also Hoselitz, "Main Concepts in the Analysis of the Social Implications of the Technological Change," p. 198.

[29]Thus Escher shows how in St. Antönien (Canton Graubünden) individualization is a young phenomenon in religious usage. Celebration of Christmas was transformed into a family Christmas only at the turn of the century! (From Escher, *Dorfgemeinschaft und Silvestersingen in St. Antönien*, Basel, 1947, p. 47. See also Neumann, *Kulturentwicklung und Religion*, Zürich, 1953, p. 19.

[30]On this see Birket-Smith, *Geschichte der Kultur*, p. 228f. Details on these archaic "moieties" ("halves") are in Hocart, *Kings and Councillors*, Cairo, 1936, as well as in Frazer, *Totem and Exogamy*, London, 1910, vol. 1; concerning further differentiations, see Birket-Smith, op. cit., p. 289, and Layard, "The Incest Taboo and the Virgin Archetype." p. 272–281.

[31]See Weiss, *Volkskunde der Schweiz*, p. 339.

But it was not only a separation that takes place. In the primordial social unit these two halves are always bound together by multifarious rituals. In this connection A. M. Hocart speaks of "ritual interdependence of the two sides" and of "mutual ministration."[32] In New Guinea one half of the village breeds and raises pigs and dogs, not for themselves but rather for the other half, and vice versa. Whenever there is a death in a village and a funeral feast is prepared, it is the other side that eats it. Further, the division is revealed in "dual kingship."[33]

In our originally closed village communities we also find, with the division into two, numerous ritual actions which guarantee the fruitful cooperation of both halves of the village. Thus village elections, governed by custom, have deeper meaning in a ritualization of humanity's inborn aggressive drive. The ritual transfer of power in the village from the one half to the other can be compared with the periodic shift of weight from one leg to the other. Along with the emphasis placed on unity by numerous rituals and symbols (religious feast days, village coats of arms, community efforts, etc.), ritualized conflict affords a fruitful, self-regulating cooperation of the "antagonists," the two halves of the village—just as can be observed everywhere in nature. But it was not only election campaigns that involved such a ritual. Widespread ritual contests and games, and folk dances, too, again and again represent intravillage cohesion.[34] In Blatten in the Lötschen Valley the two halves of the village held ritual games up into this century. On certain Sundays in summer they bowled against each other or a sort of "hornet contest" was held.[35] After the contest, the losers had to bring nidla (cream) and the winners, bread. "Und dänn hät me sich im Burgerhuis zusammengetan." ("And then we got together in the village hall.") There the cream was whipped in a large bowl and the bread was added to it. Similarly to the sharing of "milk soup" in Kappel (when Catholic and Protestant adversaries during

---

[32]Weiss, op. cit., p. 265.

[33]Weiss, op. cit., p. 157, p. 193; the summary was taken from Jung, "Psychology of the Transference," *C. W.* 16, par. 435.

[34]See Weiss, op. cit., p. 138ff.; doubtless the creation of mandala-shaped (circular) designs in folk dances is a central aspect of meaning in this custom. (Concerning the mandala as a symbol of the union of opposites see Jung, "The Secret of the Golden Flower," *C. W.* 11.)

[35]Here we are dealing with the so-called *Tschärrättä*. The *Tschärrä* is a wooden sphere, identical with the Bernese "hornet." See also Stebler, *Am Lötschenberg, Land und Volk vom Lötschen*, 1907/1981, p. 127, and Weiss, *Volkskunde der Schweiz*, p. 194.

the religious wars ended up sharing milk and bread instead of fighting), the participants then took their common meal from the bowl.[36]

The obligatory game of *jass* following a session of the community council, the citizens' assembly or any other local "squabble" has been a ritual common among the Swiss in many places until recently.[37] It often happens that in drawing lots village political opponents become partners in the game of *jass*, and they must adapt as best they can to each other's wavelength to play together successfully. If someone makes a mistake, the other can nonchalantly say to him, on another level as it were, "Du chunsch halt ebe doch nit drüss,"—you really just don't understand. However, the beer or the wine generates humor and good feeling so that nobody gets hurt at this *gemütliche* part of the meeting. Only when such recurring rituals are dropped has it been possible for the two halves to split into hostile village partisans with vendettalike, never-ending antagonisms.[38] But we do not want to get ahead of ourselves here: we are, after all, not yet dealing with the dissolution of *participation mystique*.

Let us now return to consideration of social structures, keeping clearly in mind that the primordial social structures gradually become differentiated in a manner quite comparable to the development of a "social structure" of a colony of bees or ants, which likewise arises without conscious intention. As emphasized earlier, we must exercise the utmost caution when making comparisons between animal and human behavior. For this reason we want the comparison to be taken solely as a bridge to understanding. The following reflections are to be understood in this sense, too, for we now intend to follow up the question of how the individual can align his actions correctly with the entire social organism. To elucidate this spiritual problem of "correct orientation," we will again take a look at the animal world.

As zoological studies have shown, the actions of an individual termite, for instance, are oriented in all respects to the entire termite colony. If one thrusts a long sheet of lead vertically down through the initial mound during the first phase of termite hill construction,

---

[36]Personal communication from the former Senior Counsellor and President of the Community, Paul Bellwald, 1982; in Anneler, *Lötschen*, Berne, 1917, p. 237, this custom is mentioned only briefly.

[37]Individual governments of small places still cultivate this meaningful custom up to the present, too, for example the government of the Canton Uri. Concerning other games, see Weiss, *Volkskunde der Schweiz*, p. 196.

[38]Also see Weiss, op. cit., p. 339; in addition one might call to mind the numerous villages in our mountain areas that today are regularly split into two parts: two pubs, two general stores, etc.—a situation in which one goes strictly to only "our" pub or "our" store!

thereby dividing the colony into two, the structure is nevertheless completed flawlessly on both sides. When the hill is finished, one can remove the lead plate and the individual tunnels of the two halves of the hill match each other perfectly. Since the insects in the separated halves obviously cannot orient themselves externally to each other but are nevertheless capable of relating to the whole, this holistic pattern must somehow also be present in the individual insects. Because our termites can rely on the inner instinctual pattern that enables them to relate correctly to the entire colony in their "social action," we can speak here of a "pre-existing relation to life."[39] This relation signifies an inherently conditioned "adaptation to each other."

How close primordial human societies are to such a "naturally regulated" order is shown, for example, by the construction of a new temple in Bali. Although it is the joint undertaking of the whole village, there is neither architect nor master-builder nor plan for the structure. Yet everybody knows what they have to do, and in the end everything in the structure fits.[40] In the structure of our primordial settlements we get something of the same feeling of an organic whole. The individual buildings fit correctly into the whole, albeit without previous village planning. This is only possible if the individual stands in direct inner connection with the whole. If this is unconscious, as in the instance of primordial man, we then speak of *participation mystique*.

Studies of the renewal mechanisms of these wholly archaic societies show how decisively significant the integration of the individual into the overall structure of the tribe has always been. Normally the individual did not have the freedom to marry just any woman in the tribe. According to division into the so-called marriage classes, each man was confined to looking for a bride only in the marriage classes open to him.[41] In this kind of marriage system, documented throughout the world,[42] it is not a question of some "barbaric" coercion but rather of an astonishingly sensible institution for the perpetual renewal of social unity by means of a kind of "rotation mechanism." Here we must emphasize once more that these marriage class systems in

[39]Portmann, "Das Lebendige als vorbereitete Beziehung." This example is found in von Franz, "Die Erlösung des Weiblichen im Manne." A. Portmann, "Das Lebendige als vorbereitete Beziehung," Eranos Jahrbuch, vol. 24, Zürich, 1956. I am indebted to M.-L. von Franz for the example.
[40]I am indebted to M.-L. von Franz for this example.
[41]Details in Layard, "The Incest Taboo and the Virgin Archetype."
[42]The well-known system of "cross-cousin marriage"; see Layard, op. cit., p. 266–281.

archaic societies are not conscious constructs but rather copies of preconscious drive regulation. "The world of instinct, simple as it seems to the rationalist, reveals itself on the primitive level as a complicated interplay of physiological facts, taboos, rites, class systems, and tribal lore, which preconsciously impose a restrictive form on the instinct from the beginning and make it serve a higher purpose."[43] This higher purpose, as Layard has shown, is to make possible the close social cohesion of larger tribes.[44]

Likewise in our village and particularly in our farming societies we know of comparable "mechanisms of renewal," which often severely restrict individual freedom for the benefit of the viability of the organism.[45] For example, countless persons took it upon themselves to remain single in order to guarantee the continued existence of the peasant society.[46] For not everyone could marry and have children; the food supply was simply too meager. From the perspective of today's cherished individual freedom, such limitations appear inhuman. In Gotthelf's works those single persons who would have loved to marry are not drawn without tragic features.[47] Yet on the other hand, we find an *amor fati* at this level of primordial identity with the tribe: "In the name of God, it had to be that way; someone else commands; it does no good to resist; what's not supposed to be won't be—'One has one's place.' " With these words from Gotthelf, Strübin outlined man's original acceptance of fate.[48]

We can perhaps best empathize with the fate of a person who remained single out of consideration for the peasant society if we observe the growing child. In a child, of course, as already discussed, *participation mystique* with his milieu and with those close to him is likewise the initial mode of experience. The "I will" as the expression of individual consciousness crystallizes only in the course of time. But now to the comparison: At the level of *participation mystique* it never occurs to the younger sister to quarrel with her fate and to complain because she has to make do with a smaller and darker room than her older sister for reasons of space. And just as the little person grows into a narrow room, at peace with her fate, so does the primordial

---

[43]Jung, *Mysterium Coniunctionis*, C. W. 14, par. 602.

[44]Layard, op. cit., p. 269.

[45]Concerning the functionality of the closed marriage circles, see Flutsch, *Kulturlandschaftliche Aspekte einer Halsergemeinde*, 1976.

[46]A farming society is in miniature the same as a village society: "It is the model of a close, well-ordered living community, a small cosmos sufficient unto itself." (Strübin, *Grundfragen des Volkslebens bei Jeremias Gotthelf*, p. 18.)

[47]Quoted from Strübin, op. cit., p. 13.

[48]Summarized quote from Strübin, op. cit., p. 33.

human fit unreservedly into the meaningful role necessary for the entire tribe, even if this role signifies, according to modern-day notions, a so-called shadow existence. Feelings of social coercion by the tribe arise only when *participation mystique* with the tribe dissolves.[49]

At the level of primordial *participation mystique*, the individual not only fits unreservedly into the tribe; the reverse is also valid: *The individual's fate always was also a concern of the collective*. There are countless examples of this from our previously closed village communities. Thus in Swiss mountain villages up to our times it has been the widespread custom to pause momentarily in one's activity whenever the knell resounded from the church tower. Days later the funeral procession was made up of the entire village. The individual experiences similar interest on the part of the community in all of life's typical transition phases, the so-called *rites de passage*, such as the transition into adulthood or into marriage.[50] Community work, previously common, is also an expression of the community's support of the individual whenever a necessary task exceeded individual strength.[51] The Swiss federal principle, "One for all, all for one," is the essence of this primordial, unreflecting, unsentimental social relation within a closed tribe.

In a manner thoroughly comparable to that which we noted in the disenchantment of matter, the dissolution of the individual's *participation mystique* with his tribe occurred not at one blow, but rather step by step. We now intend to investigate this development.

---

[49]On this see the fate of Marie Mérailler from Evolène, Canton Wallis in Marie Métrailler and Marie-Magdeleine Brumage, editors, *La Poudre de Sourire*, Lausanne, 1980.
[50]We will speak of this later in detail.
[51]On this see Niederer's beautiful work, *Gemeinwerk im Wallis*, Schriflen der SGV, vol. 37, Basel, 1965. See also Strübin, op. cit., p. 23.

Chapter 13

Dissolution of *Participation Mystique*

Preliminary Remarks

As already alluded to, worldwide social change is a mirror image of the crystallizing of individual ego-consciousness out of the archaic identity with the social group and the space in which one lives. We now want to attempt to work out the different steps in this process of change with regard to interpersonal relations.

It must be emphasized in advance that this process of development has moved not simply in a unilinear way but rather in numerous cycles, in full analogy to the de-souling of space that we have already mentioned. Moreover, we must be clear that *participation mystique* as an interpersonal bond is never completely dissolved in spite of all "disenchantment"; it can suddenly reappear on the surface. Modern individualistic culture notwithstanding, it spontaneously arises again and again; and it imparts to those involved a feeling of primordial containedness and security. Thus a demonstration or a rock festival can, for a short period of time, impart to the participants a feeling of being "one." In an interest group or a travel group such unconscious unity through *participation mystique* can arise and be experienced as enlivening. Even the majorities in modern nations can suddenly feel themselves as "one heart and one soul" and rally round a Führer or Duce. To be sure, between these new feelings of oneness and those of a village community, there exists an essential difference. The modern, spontaneously arising phenomenon of *participation mystique* lacks rootedness in tradition and stability.[1]

---

[1]On the difference between community and mob, see Weiss, *Volkskunde der Schweiz*, p. 12ff.

Stages in the Dissolution of *Participation Mystique*

At the outset let us again remember that the primordial social relationship of humanity rests on the immediate sense of unity and solidarity with one's tribe. In mirror image to this, an analogous connection exists between inner nature and the ego, in that the ego is wholly imbedded in the naturally given system of drives and their regulation. By "drive regulation" we understand all those vivid triggering and inhibiting mechanisms that make peaceful social life possible in groups of the species.[2] The rites, taboos, and symbols of archaic societies are to be understood as the system of psychic regulation that is part and parcel of the dynamics of drive.[3]

In his book the *Origins and History of Consciousness*, Erich Neumann demonstrated how human consciousness arose in the course of a process of development.[4] This process is characterized by the gradual differentiation of ego-consciousness out of its amalgamation or *participation mystique* with the drives toward a relative freedom through distance. We also find this process of creating distance between the ego and pure nature, between above and below, in the history of the development of social structures. Hence wholly primordial societies, such as, say, that of the Bushmen of the Kalahari, are not yet subordinated in any way to a leader or king.[5] The latter are formations of a central organ of regulation within a social body. To a certain extent they are the differentiated cortex in the tribe that feels itself to be "one individual." The word "headman" points directly to this interrelationship. Just as differentiation of ego-consciousness in the individual brought about culture (we remember the accompanying differentiation in the use of the hands, thanks to which craft arose), the crystallization of a social structure with a headman or king made possible a differentiation of the tribe that brought culture in general. Associated with that there was usually the formation of smaller social units under a "superior authority." This developmental step is one foundation of the so-called advanced civilizations. Consider the epoch of peace and order in ancient Egypt under the leadership of the pharaohs that lasted more than three thousand years, as well as the cultural development thus made possible. Only occasionally was this

---

[2]Thus the aggression drive is held in check among many species of animal by the weaker one's so-called posture of submission.
[3]See C. G. Jung, *C. W.* 14, par. 602, and Eibl-Eibesfeldt, *Der vorprogrammierte Mensch*.
[4]Neumann, *The Origins and History of Consciousness*.
[5]The Bushmen visited by Eibl-Eibesfeldt know, as he writes, no form of leader or headman (in Eibl-Eibesfeldt, *Menschenforschung auf neuen Hegen*, p. 28.)

extended period of peace interrupted by brief periods in which the normal condition of inner peace was shaken.[6]

To the extent that sociological structures became differentiated, religious ideas also developed, their function being to bind together the individual and society.[7] We can observe this process in the development of the image of god particularly clearly in Mediterranean antiquity, where the development toward a hierarchy of gods and monotheism—that is, toward an all-embracing god—depicts the archetypal background leading to the crystallization of the institution of a societal leader and ultimately to development of the individual ego. In each case, the ruler was the representative of the divine will on earth and hence infallible as god-man.

As we can read in various sources, the chieftain or king was always the outstanding personality.[8] His correct behavior guaranteed the growth and prosperity of land and people.[9] However, ritual regicide, which has been extensively documented,[10] indicates that such rulership cannot have arisen out of a hunger for power and privilege but rather is a reflection of a collective structural differentiation of the soul. That is to say, the regent takes it upon himself to be killed when his time is fulfilled. The external sign of this was the waning of his procreative power. Only in the course of time did regicide as a ritual of renewal become symbolic. The king then was not literally killed; instead, his power was regularly regenerated by means of ritual. Consequently the power of the ruler was no longer identical with his procreative power. However, through these rites the regal mode of acting was always continually being adapted to the changing needs of the entire people. Thus the ruler remained bound to the people.

Hence, it was at first only outstanding individual people who embodied the ego-consciousness of the guiding social organism that, outwardly and inwardly, was responsible for the correct functioning of the entire tribe. Such people had to develop their own special adaptation in order to be equal to this task: namely, a stable ego-consciousness that made possible a certain control of affects and drives. A consciousness not held together by an adequately strong

---

[6]Quoted from Toynbee, *Menschheit und Mutter Erde*, p. 64.
[7]See Layard, *Institutions in Primitive Societies*, p. 63 [German edition].
[8]E.g., Hocart, *Kings and Councillors*, p. 61, and Frazer, *The Golden Bough*, vol. IV; see also Jung, *Mysterium Coniunctionis*, C. W. 14, §270.
[9]Hocart, loc. cit.
[10]Frazer, op. cit., p. 331ff.

ego is perpetually threatened with fragmentation into individual affective processes,[11] as can be easily observed in the growing child.

Since the sign of a consolidated ego-consciousness is differentiation and distance "from everything else," there is always the danger of a rigidification of the ego. The ego as organ of control comes into conflict with the psyche as a whole, and the external connection "with everything else," i.e., the tribe, is lost. When a person with this sort of rigid ego happens to be the ruler, we speak of a willful regime. The ritual of renewal of the king was therefore always of central significance, since the ritual's meaning lay in constantly melting down the "royal ego-consciousness" so that it could enter into a new union with its primordial matrix. This effects a reconnection of ego-consciousness to its origin, whence the ego draws its strength and in whose service the ego ultimately stands. Since this relation of ego-consciousness to the supraordinate totality or, as its reflection, the relation of the ruler to the totality of the people was so central to the people's well-being, this matter was always carried out with religious scrupulousness.[12]

One might believe that this discussion digresses from the theme. But as we shall see later, it is precisely these observations that lead to central, sociological insights that are particularly relevant for problems in rural areas.

At first, then, it was outstanding individuals who were able to develop an individual ego-consciousness. In the course of time this process also extended to the whole upper stratum,[13] and here what was said about the renewal ritual also applies. When the upper stratum ruled in harmony with the totality, an inner solidarity between upper and lower obtained. As we know well enough from history, however, a strengthened ego-consciousness has again and again seduced humanity into ego rigidity. In spite of all rituals of renewal,

---

[11]As an illustration of this, think of the well-known destructiveness under the power of affect among primal peoples. A bushman slew his small son in an eruption of affect, only to rue it bitterly later. Also the condition of "running amok," corresponding to the Germanic "going berserk," is an example of this.

[12]On this ritual see also Frazer, *The Golden Bough*, vol. IV, and Jung's psychological commentary in *Mysterium Coniunctionis*, par. 271; see also Wilhelm, *The I Ching*, hexagrams no. 45 and 59; also the worldwide occurrence of the motif of the renewal of the king in fairy tales should be mentioned.

[13]Due to limitations of space, it is not possible to illustrate this process of differentiation with examples, especially since the line of development, as mentioned, reveals not only a linear but also a cyclical course. Also the differentiation between a spiritual and a temporal chieftain, which appears in tribal cultures, cannot be further discussed. Likewise the connection between ego-development and private property can only be alluded to.

rulers have arisen who have been able to turn against the whole, against those below, against the people. Instead of service to the whole, there arose the familiar exploitation of the lowly.

We come then to the third stage. After a distinct head has emerged out of the original social body (in the second stage), there follows a further separation of the ruler or rulers from their accompanying social body. As a mirror image of this, a further separation of ego-consciousness takes place at the same time, internally vis-à-vis the matrix of origin and externally vis-à-vis the social unit. Every rigidification of the ego vis-à-vis psychic wholeness signifies a "refusal of recognition" of the real ego function, which is service to the whole or the supraordinate meaning. Instead of continual readiness on the part of the leader or the king to serve something supraordinate, this level of ego rigidification typifies a ruler who rules "as he sees fit," as it is so aptly put. Doing so demands a capacity for moral valuation, one's own ability to discriminate between good and evil, which reflects a Luciferian doubt about the absolute validity of the supraordinate facts of nature. Indeed, while the realm beyond is acknowledged, a certain willfulness takes firm root alongside it. As soon as the ruler or rulers no longer feel they are the executive organ of a supraordinated wholistic purpose, questions arise about the proper nature of rulership. In this regard, consider Plato's, Aristotle's or Confucius' early reflections on social philosophy. We come eventually to a moral evaluation of the ruler or rulers and thus in educated circles to a gradual withdrawal of the projection of the god-man onto external leaders.

We thus arrive at the fourth stage, the actual disenchantment or de-souling of interpersonal *participation mystique*, fully analogous to the gradual de-souling of the relation between humanity and the space in which it lives. This developmental step is first taken by individual personalities having particular ego-strength. Among the sophists in ancient Greece we find the rationalistic view of human relationship, in which all social action is directed only by self-interest; religion and belief in a hereafter are nothing but illusions good enough to mystify the people so that they are more easily ruled. At the time of the decline of the Roman empire, too, this cynicism was common.[14] With

---

[14]Beginning with the cult of personality of the Caesars and extending to the cynical inscriptions on gravestones of Roman citizens. I am indebted to Dr. M.-L. von Franz for this reference.

such absolute limitation of human existence to ego-consciousness one still speaks, if the occasion arises, of religion, but it is at most lip service.

Again and again in the history of the world, we can find this process, most clearly in the Renaissance, a period of particularly strong ego-consciousness. The change in worldview of that era on the threshold of the modern age is clearly characterized by the rise of the Central Perspective. "This is how *I* see the world" was the new viewpoint. The ego of the Renaissance man is in the midpoint, the center. In startlingly clear language the Florentine Niccolò Machiavelli (1469–1527) outlined the ego-centered manner of the ruler and thus impressively documented the complete willfulness of an ego-consciousness separated from the whole. Karl Meyer summarized it this way: "Political success is the new god justifying the means: breaking one's word, lies, cruelty. For Machiavelli, even religion, morality, and law descend to the level of a means that may be employed without hesitation in the interests of the state. One does not need to be good, just, and pious; one must only seem to be."[15] The best-known historical example of royal willfulness may well be the French Sun King. "L'Etat c'est moi" ("The state is me") is the expression of complete identification of the ego with the whole, which, viewed psychologically, always signifies a dangerous identification of ego-consciousness with the creative principle. It was in that vein that Louis XIV called himself "Le Roi-Soleil."

By the late Middle Ages the general dissolution of *participation mystique* had begun to set in. If Machiavelli's theories had remained merely the affair of a limited upper class, no fundamental social revolution could have taken place in the Renaissance. The "horizontal discovery of the world" by the Renaissance, as well as its fundamental strengthening of the ego found increasing appeal in the lay education developing in the cities. This very broad effect of the Renaissance—which began very slowly and which was made possible above all by the invention of printing—exerted a powerful influence on humanity's communal life. However, this trend became decisive only in the eighteenth century when the Renaissance's secularization became a concern of the masses as part of the Enlightenment.[16] With the enthronement of the "déesse raison" (goddess Reason) individual ego-consciousness, which could arbitrarily turn against internal and

---

[15]Quoted from Meyer, *Heltgeschichte im Überblick*, Zürich, 1965, p. 268.
[16]In comparable periods of secularization of an upper class, lower classes were never affected so powerfully, owing to lack of education (e.g., in ancient Greece or Rome).

external nature, became the generally acknowledged social lode-star.[17] In contrast, any relationship to the irrational, the past, the whole became superfluous.

Dissolution of *Participation Mystique* in Rural Areas

We want now to pursue the question of how this process of enlight-enment or disenchantment developed in Switzerland, since that will elucidate some aspects of the dilemma of the rural population.

In the course of the past few generations, enlightenment has also spread into our rural communities. This development began with a "progressive and rational attitude of an upper class that, depending on the times and the conditions, penetrated the broad range of the people and fundamentally transformed them, now more rapidly, now less."[18] In our most remote mountain valleys, this dissemination of the Enlightenment, with its principles of a rationally guided life and individual freedom, finally led to a pervasive dissolution of the primordial social solidarity based on *participation mystique*. Even if a large segment of the populace in many mountain villages today still have one of only two family names,[19] "everyone looks out for him-self" more and more, as I was assured repeatedly. How did things get to this point? To answer this question we want to investigate what led to the dissolution of *participation mystique* in the individual. To forces of change belong, probably first of all, the change in the nature of education and communication, as well as in the legal and economic systems. When we investigate the loosening effect on community solidarity in these areas, we must not forget the positive effects of this development. A one-sided condemnation of progress would, as already emphasized, ignore the conditions out of which the need for change arose: mass poverty, hunger, superstition, and often suffocat-ing traditionalism. Also, the sequence and extent of treatments of the individual factors has nothing to do with their relative significance in dissolving *participation mystique*, since their efficacy lies in their mutual interaction.

Doubtless the school has had a decisive part in the dissolution of the village sense of community. The beginnings of public schooling reach back to the time of the Reformation; and school instruction in the seventeenth and eighteenth centuries still followed the same pat-

---

[17]We can only note in passing the existence of countercurrents to the Enlightenment in Germany, such as Romanticism and other movements.
[18]Quoted from Wackernagel, *Altes Volkstum in der Schweiz*, p. 68.
[19]See aditionally Weiss, *Volkskunde der Schweiz*, p. 339.

tern, without significant innovation. The school did not aim to pre-
pare the child for practical life but simply sought to rear the child to
lead a life pleasing to God. Therefore the pedagogic goal consisted
solely in learning religious texts by heart, the more the better.[20]

Only at the beginning of the nineteenth century did the goal of
learning change radically. With downright religious fervor the men of
the Enlightenment set about creating better schooling for the people.
"To educate the people is to liberate the people" was the slogan of the
proponents of basic public education.[21] The idea was to overcome
popular traditionalism "by means of systematic individual education."[22] The result of this Enlightenment movement was the cantonal
school laws, newly enacted in the middle of the last century.[23] Fundamental improvement in teacher training also came at that time.[24] The
school gave each village, no matter how out-of-the-way, a center from
which scientific knowledge and rational thinking and living could
gradually be disseminated.[25]

But how did the school have the effect of dissolving the sense of
community? Certainly in part by undermining traditional folk knowledge. The life wisdom of generations that had crystallized out of
countless events over time in the local, customary rhythm of life was
abruptly replaced by a "better, school education." Whatever was
newly discovered and taught at the universities was supposed to
become common property.[26] As Strübin writes, "the new public
school was, to a certain extent, built from the top down."[27] This liberation from tradition signified a powerful devaluation and disenfranch-
isement of custom—the local ways of living, talking, farming, building, dressing, and eating. The model offered to the school youth

---

[20]See also the discussion by Kunz and Lerch, *Geschichte der Landschaft Oberhasli
Meiringen, 1979*, p. 523–43, especially p. 528, and Braun, *Industrialisierung und Volksleben*, Zürich, 1960, p. 135ff.

[21]On this see Strübin, *Baselbieter Volksleben*, p. 248, and Braun, *Sozialer und kultureller
Handel in einem ländlichen Industriegebiet im 19, und 20, Jahrhundert*, Zürich, 1965,
p. 298–300.

[22]Strübin, op. cit., p. 249.

[23]In the Federal Constitution of 1848, obligatory elementary school instruction was
anchored at the federal level (Article 27).

[24]The teachers' college of the Canton of Zürich was founded in 1832 on the occasion of
the new school law, which governed the organization of public schooling.

[25]In his *Gespräch über Volksaufklärung und Volksbildung* (1806), Heinrich Pestalozzi gives
us a pithy and very readable insight into this period of popular enlightenment and
into the meaning of popular enlightenment.

[26]See Strübin, op. cit., p. 256.

[27]Strübin, loc. cit. As we know from numerous documents, the school emphatically
dissuaded the youth from carrying on the old customs (from Wackernagel, *Altes
Volkstum der Schweiz*, p. 69).

became that of knowledge handed down from above, knowledge that was bound by no tradition and always better than yesterday's knowledge. Those of the Enlightenment went to work on liberating the people, drawing an active energy from their conviction "that the past had rested on nothing but error, and that in reason they had found the key to a natural, absolutely correct, and consequently happier world order."[28] This spirit imparted the feeling of "always knowing better" to young people, thus dissolving the bond between generations. As Gotthelf observed about the divisive effect of school knowledge, "The school boys come prancing in as if they were princes and despise the old people as if they were Hottentots or half-wits."[29] Since science had not managed to bring the values of homegrown folk wisdom into a fruitful union with scientific knowledge, the old and the young in the village could not agree either. The public school sowed the seeds of dissension in the villages, and the growth of those seeds was aided by numerous other factors.

Before we look into more of the bond-breaking aspects of the school, we must acknowledge how frequently the school has worked and continues to work to form bonds, especially in recent years. In urban settings school is often the sole element building bridges between families; and studies[30] have shown that village school teachers in the country often contribute significantly to local community life, say by leading choirs, or theater or sports groups, or as moving forces in conserving festivals and old customs.[31] In the discussion that follows we should not lose sight of this.

But let us return to the school's effect in dissolving bonds. Above all the school promoted this by teaching reading and writing through which abstraction and conceptual thought were encouraged, in contrast to the imagistic-associative thought of preliterate indigenous culture. An intentional advancement of abstraction and detachment is also evident in the replacement in the schools of the native dialect—an expression of the people's spirit—by a standard spoken and written language (in the case of Germanic Switzerland, by "High Ger-

---

[28] Quoted from Meyer, *Weltgeschichte im Überblick*, p. 417.

[29] Gotthelf, *Jakobs Wanderungen*.

[30] From the Bureau d'économie régionale of the Federal Institute of Technology of Zürich in Charrat (Canton Wallis).

[31] Of course we can always read (e.g. in Bonderer, *Bildungsprobleme der Bergbevölkerung*, Berne, 1964, p. 64ff.) how teachers again and again have no capacity to perceive in this regard.

man").[32] In Lower Wallis, people went even further; the patois was banished from the school area under threat of punishment.[33] This ability to abstract continues to be ever more significant in modern professional training. "In the contemporary work world, sensory experience is increasingly replaced by calculation, formulas, and tables. Thus "feeling" is no longer as important as the capacity to think logically and to make decisions on the basis of measurable values."[34] Those elements in the public school which promote detachment thus cannot simply be condemned wholesale. On the other hand, it would be foolishly one-sided to devalue what is known in German as "Gespür," which means "having a feeling for something."

The artificial, rational idea of scheduling has specifically contributed to the training of the individual's will, thus promoting individual ego-strength. This development of individual ego-consciousness has been enhanced by an emerging principle of competition under which the individual learns to distinguish himself from others. As a consequence, communal effort took a back seat to individual accomplishment. Thus the purposeful detachment of individual effort gradually dissolved communal bonds both vertically and horizontally; and there arose, as Gotthelf pointedly expressed it, "a society composed of nothing but stiff and starchy egos."[35]

An additional important aspect must be mentioned, that is, the secularization of the schools. While in the beginning the often slavish, meaningless memorization of religious texts was held to be the most important task of the school, in the first half of the last century the need arose for a clear-cut separation of church and school. This was accomplished in the young canton of Basel-Land with the public school law of 1835.[36] In Catholic areas the association between church and school was maintained significantly longer, aided by the extensive teaching activity of the clergy. In Uri, for instance, the college in Altdorf staffed by priests was converted to a cantonal middle school

---

[32]The local dialect now finds application only to "less important things," things that have generally become second nature. When a farmer from the Schächen Valley fell into the water while boarding a steamer in Flüelen, Canton Uri, he shouted—in accordance with the seriousness of the situation—in High German: "Help, this is Peter Brücker speaking!"

[33]Later we will have occasion to speak of the present-day tendency toward a turnabout (analogously to what already took place in the Romantic period).

[34]E. Wettstein's report, "Signale für die Berufsausbildung von Morgen," given at the annual meeting of the German-Swiss Office for Professional Education in Basel, 1982.

[35]Gotthelf, *Zeitgeist und Bernergeist*, p. 140.

[36]See Strübin, *Baselbieter Volksleben*, p. 250.

only a few years ago. With an almost complete secularization of the school, the general interest in knowledge turned from transcendental things entirely to things of this world. Science and scholarship became the uncontested prime powers in education. Science and scholarship "celebrated palpable successes in all areas of life, dethroned belief, and set itself in its place."[37]

The most important consequence of the increasing orientation of school knowledge toward the earthly is the almost exclusive limitation of the image of human existence to this life. The connection backward in time to ancestors was broken by rejection of their empirical knowledge. The forward connection with the life in the beyond was jeopardized by rationalism and completely rationalized away. Thus, more and more, only the individual sphere of life constitutes reality. Optimally living a life limited to the worldly becomes the single goal and content of existence. This restriction of the image of the world to the level of consciousness, cut off from the empirical background that unifies the species in being common to all humans, had as its ultimate consequences a dissolution of the feeling of an inner connectedness with the tribe, for nothing bonds the individual, isolated ego-consciousness effectively—in the sense of having an effect—unless it is personal advantage.

Another institution that dissolved *participation mystique* in the wake of the general literacy was the newspaper. At the beginning of the last century in many places there was only one newspaper subscription per community. By the turn of our century in the Canton of Basel-Land, for example, "everywhere even the poorest house had its own newspaper."[38] As Eduard Strübin continues, the power of the press is today incalculable: "For many, reading the newspaper has become a downright compulsive act."[39] With the newspaper, and later with radio and television especially, the range of information available to the village opened up. This weakened the village habit of conversation and hence also of oral transmission of folk wisdom.[40] The concern for passing on the wealth of local experience declined. In exchange for this, today everybody, even in the most remote village, knows, that President A shook hands with President B, and that Prince C married Lady D, thanks to the mass media. Via the international news services people living in Kuwait and people living in

---

[37]Ibid.
[38]Strübin, op. cit., p. 270.
[39]Strübin op. cit., p. 271; today this compulsive information hunger has probably shifted in favor of T.V.
[40]As illustration of this, see Bonderer, *Bildungsprobleme der Bergbevölkerung*, p. 27ff.

Greenland have the same sensationalistic informational stew set before them. This sort of daily "information" about all possible things has led, especially since the rise of television, to people's being over- whelmed with stimuli, even in the country. Village "grapevines" are replaced by impersonal organs of information, and "what is of world interest" more and more takes the place of nearby events that could be experienced empathically. The increasingly popular tabloid press adroitly meets the need for personal gossip that people naturally continue to have, even in the country.

Because the mass media are children of the urban world, it is predominantly the urban way of thinking and living that finds expression through them.[41] People in the country learn how people in the city live and can make comparisons. Thus, imperceptibly, the feeling arises that folks in the provinces are missing something. "Nothing's going on in the village" becomes the complaint of young people in the country. No wonder village conviviality—the evenings playing *jass*, the festivals, customs, the choir, or the folk theater—is neglected: people spend their leisure time privately in their mute family half-circle before the tube. "You can't get people together any more," a woman from Geissholz in the Hasli Valley complained to me, "because one day this one and tomorrow somebody else wants to see a T.V. program instead of getting together like we used to, to sing or put on a play."[42] Even in mountainous areas fewer and fewer houses can be found without a TV antenna; and wherever the set stands, it is usually used. Consequently, in addition to the school system, the mass media have an undoubtedly important part in the disintegration of the sense of village community.

The change in the legal system has likewise contributed significantly to the dissolution of community bonds. "The tendency in the development of modern law away from irrational traditionalism toward rationality, away from the bonds to family, brotherhood, and community toward individualism"[43] goes hand in hand with the rise of the modern, centralized state. The indigenous sense of justice and injustice has been increasingly replaced in the course of the past few generations by general, rational laws which, in certain spheres, have led to differences in the sense of justice between local inhabitants and

---

[41]From this follows the justified feeling among the rural and particularly the agrarian population of being outvoted by the mass media. This problem is incomparably stranger in Third World countries.

[42]Conversation dating from 1982.

[43]On this see Huber, *Schweizerisches Privatrecht*, vol. 4, p. 281ff., cited in Weiss, *Volkskunde der Schweiz*, p. 345.

the "authorities in Berne." Consider, for instance, the Federal hunting and forestry laws and particularly the question concerning to whom the game belongs. "De Wild gheert den Lyten und nid dem Staat" ("Game belongs to the people and not the state") is the judgment of people living in the Hasli Valley.[44] Game wardens in the entire Alpine region can tell tales about the persistence with which hunting laws are given a "local interpretation."

Equality before the law is also a new achievement whose value is certainly uncontested. Yet the original sense of justice was different. In Renner we read, for example, of the following incident in Uri: "A man born in Brunnen (a neighboring community in the neighboring canton of Schwyz) who had long lived in Erstfeld (Uri) was reprimanded and fined by the local community council for some infringement of the forestry laws. The man pleaded that many others had been guilty of the same transgression without anyone's making a great fuss about it. 'They're our people,' the local authorities thundered at him, 'but you're a foreigner!' "[45] In the distinction between community of residence and community of citizenship[46] that often occurs in Switzerland, differing interpretations of justice are often held by the old established families and newcomers, as, for instance, in the recent legal battle between the municipality and the citizenship community of Zermatt over the question of authority over the Matterhorn.[47]

Let us now turn to the community-destroying effect of the modern constitutional state. One example from the recent past can best illustrate this. Let us consider modern legislation concerning building codes and zoning. The village community, guided by tradition, needed no written building codes and no zoning; as a matter of course, one built as was locally customary. But with increasing mobility, freedom to establish residence, and especially the disappearance of a sense of respect for local building styles and traditions,[48] a legal limit had to be set to arbitrary individual action. Therefore new, standardized building codes, zoning plans, and utilization rates were created. But as something "coming down from above" these new regulations could not take into account local conditions to the same

---

[44]Quoted from Weiss, op. cit., p. 349.
[45]Renner, *Goldener Ring über Uri*, p. 53 and p. 245.
[46]Today the citizenship communities ("Burgergemeinden"), as the original village communities, often represent within the political communities a significant power, having large land holdings.
[47]See the *Neue Zürcher Zeitung* of 6 November 1982; the case was taken to the Federal Supreme Court.
[48]Weiss, *Volkskunde der Schweiz*, p. 97.

extent as had been the case with custom and usage. Moreover, the guidelines in these new laws were created for areas with a building boom but were eventually applied to the most remote mountain village, like a net cast out over the entire country. The consequences of the planners' intrusions into the sense of village solidarity were extraordinarily far-reaching. On any given day, one person's land might be turned into building lots with values of perhaps one hundred Franks per square meter. Another's land lying immediately adjacent might not be included in the same zoning, and its value might be far less than ten Franks per square meter. This creates a lot of bad feeling especially when—justifiably or unjustifiably—it is rumored that the land had been included in the zoning because the owner is a friend of the community president! The owner may then sell his building lots and become a millionaire overnight. Modern condominiums can be built on that land, beside the heart of the old village. And once again we see the now familiar accelerated rate of change in the village after the forces of individualism have become dominant.

Of course, our modern planning laws were not the first to have a destructive effect of this sort. The constitutional article enacting freedom to establish residence[49] stimulated greater mobility and ultimately such overdevelopment that zoning became necessary. As with the educational system and the media, one could ascribe many things to the legal system that had a disintegrative effect on village solidarity. In this connection, however, it must be mentioned that our lawmakers were farsighted in recognizing local common law as supplementing standard law, and thereby making extensive concessions to local usage.[50]

The fourth significant factor in the dissolution of social solidarity arising out of *participation mystique* is the new economic order. As we have already described with regard to schooling, the Enlightenment emphasized personal freedom and pleaded the cause of individual and earthly well-being over the transcendental solace of the life to come.[51] A consequence of directing interest toward the individual human being on the basis of equality was the postulate of the "natu-

---

[49]In Article 45 of the Swiss Federal Constitution we read: "Every Swiss has the right to establish residence in any locality within Swiss territory."

[50]Weiss, op. cit., p. 346f. To be mentioned in this connection is the judicious retention of cantonal militia (in Article 19a of the Federal Constitution).

[51]See also the very fine synopsis of the Enlightenment in Meyer, *Heltgeschichte im überblick*, especially pp. 342–51.

ral, i.e., liberal economic order."[52] With the schools' liberation of the common person, people began to value economic freedom within the nation and among nations.

With the dismantling of tariffs and the freedom to establish residence and take up a trade, as well as the accelerated construction of trade routes, the original, locally contained economic sphere was gradually destroyed. Industrialization, as well as the developing import and export trade, made a money economy dominant in the country, too, and led to increasing specialization, commuting, and a gradual separation of various areas of life.[53] Especially with industrialization and tourism, the awareness grew of what an hour was worth in money, for cash money originally came predominantly from hourly work. With the "industrialization of life"—*industria* from the Latin, literally "diligence"—a busy-ness invaded rural areas which by its nature is detrimental to the cultivation of local interpersonal relations.[54] People in the country today follow a schedule more and more; and thanks to the moped or the automobile, the possibility of full use of leisure time exists. Of course, with social mobility the feeling of village unity perceptibly weakened. Communal support has been replaced by centralized insurance companies or by the state.[55] Even in the last century Gotthelf wrote of this fundamental change. "The village community forgets its responsibility toward its neighbor; the state plugs the gap with its facts and figures,"[56] or, as we might say today, with its abstract statistical thinking.

The result of this cultural development toward individual freedom and mobility is so-called *individual culture*. The manner of living, dwelling, eating, and dressing is informed less and less by local tradition and more and more by the influence of style trends adopted by the masses. The original unconscious solidarity of relatives and village community has been dissolved or "lost its magic spell" thanks to this development. Hence relationships in the country have become more matter-of-fact and businesslike. As a result of this development, the individual has been increasingly free from the bonds of the social unit or—not to forget the other side of the coin—has become isolated.

---

[52]Ibid., p. 351; hence the "natural economy" of the French physiocrats and the "natural freedom" of the English philosopher of economics, Adam Smith (1723–1790).

[53]Details in Hauser, *Schweizerische Wirtschafts- und Sozialgeschichte*, p. 178ff.

[54]Likewise to be considered in this connection, however, is the fact that, with industrialization of the life of the common man, folk culture in many places "has not been broken down or destroyed but rather given a new shape." (Braun, *Industrialisierung und Volksleben*, p. 255.)

[55]In this connection, note also among other things the provision of medical care.

[56]Strübin, *Grundfragen des Volkslebens bei Jeremias Gotthelf*, p. 81.

At this stage of consciousness, social relations become predominantly ego-referenced, yet the need for social *participation mystique* at this level of consciousness has not disappeared. On the contrary, "being able to participate" has today become a central need.[57] The reason for this will be dealt with next. It has to do with the nature of real social relationship following the dissolution of "participation."

---

[57]On this see Peccei, *Das menschliche Dilemma*.

Chapter 14

Modern Findings

Limits to Dissolving Participation

The dissolution of the archaic identification with the environment and the community also signified a change in the general way of thinking. With the possibility of knowledge based on reason, incomprehensible things were explained less and less in terms of magical causality. To understand the magical manner of thinking, one should recall, for instance, that when it was newly introduced from America, the potato was believed to cause plague. Where did this idea come from? In form, the potato tubers resemble the buboes of bubonic plague. The consequence of this association was the prohibition against planting these "devil's roots." Today we see that this primitive attitude arose generally on the basis of similarities and temporal coincidences. Thus myths, magic, witchcraft, and belief in spirits also belong to the realm of magical causality. They served as explanations of incomprehensible or unexpected events, e.g., atmospheric phenomena, epidemics, insect plagues, floods, accidents, illnesses, and death.[1] Magical practices, such as spells, exorcisms, divinations, and astrology, as well as all the codes of behavior contained in folktales, enabled archaic people to cope emotionally with what was inexplicable and hence threatening in this world. Yet with knowledge acquired in schools and the other innovations that dissolved participation, "magical folk knowledge" as a whole was revealed as wild superstition and dispatched to the museum of historical curiosities.

Magical thinking was supplanted by rational thinking in the areas

---

[1]Probably one of the best anthologies on this topic is Müller's *Sagen aus Uri*, e.g., vol. 1, no.114–364.

of quantifiable interrelationships of cause and effect. This new view of the world brought about a dissolution of the psychic veil spread out over the world and humanity. The external dissolution of the projection of the soul's contents and the corresponding transfer of interest from the communal-instinct-bound way of life toward an ego-referenced style of life led, however, not to liberation from archaic restriction but rather to intensification of a grave social problem, namely modern man's aloneness in a cold world devoid of soul.

The United States, where individual freedom has been promoted most intensely, has probably also most clearly encountered the limits of this movement, which is destructive to the community and behind which reigns a destructive egoism. Isolated individualism has already become so commonplace there that hardly anyone reacts to a call for help on the street. "I don't want to get involved," was what I often heard as the explanatory excuse for this social behavior that certainly cannot any longer be called human.[2] Externally and internally people dwell in "little boxes" and are generally intent on living as free of obligation as possible.[3] Yet at the same time an increasing longing for real human relationships can be observed, that is, relationships that hold, since a life without the sense of belonging feels like a string without a soundbox. We the Lonely People is the title of a book by Ralph Keyes, in which he names three major reasons for the destruction of community life in the U.S.A.: mobility, secrecy, and reluctance to be inconvenienced.[4]

We recognize the characteristics of callous, isolated ego-consciousness in these three factors. Thus mobility embraces the external liberation from local, social, and spiritual constraint and hence the separation from the past. Internally, on the other hand, it signifies a dissociation from connection with instinct. The term secrecy aptly grasps this mental attitude, which no longer can or will stand by the past. As an isolated ego, one is internally split off from one's emotional background, no longer feeling quite "like oneself"; but one cannot admit that and consequently must repress it or keep it secret from oneself and others. In the figure of Peter Schlemihl in the story of the same name, Chamisso etched in stone this sort of person who sells his shadow to the Devil for material advantage, and in exchange spends his whole life trying to conceal this deficiency in restless mobility. Reluctance to be inconvenienced, as the third major motiva-

---

[2]This attitude is, moreover, increasingly common in Switzerland.
[3]According to Linda Dégh, the "little boxes" characterize the American way of life much better than skyscrapers. (Dégh, "Stadt-Land-Unterschiede in den USA.")
[4]Keyes, We the Lonely People.

tion, actually outlines the "final condition" of the calloused ego. In this stage, one is much too greatly infatuated with oneself and one's cherished prejudices to submit to asking about the reasons for the "splendid isolation."

In reaction to this isolated individualism there have arisen in America and Switzerland, too, all sorts of attempts to resuscitate the community as a form of life, above all in the formation of communes and the hippie movement. The appearance of countless new religious communities and group therapies of all sorts reveals a growing need for the dismantling of ego barriers. This contemporary reaction to individual culture is admittedly not new. Movements like "Sturm und Drang" ("Storm and Stress") and Romanticism were earlier attempts to let the irrational powers of the soul flow forth against the rationalism of the Enlightenment that disenchanted everything. The opposition of community and society finally led to the formation of political ideologies in Germany. "The reaction against abstract order and mechanical civilization has made the return to community its slogan."[5] What finds clear expression in all these efforts toward renewal of community is a nostalgia for *participation mystique* with the tribe.

Obvious limits are set on the liberation of humanity from the primordial inner bond with a tradition-directed community and in general on a rational mastery of life. Precious as rational knowledge doubtless is, it is one-sided to assume that rootless intellectualism alone can do justice to the whole person. Just as homesickness is the expression of a primordial human need for rootedness in a place, the longing for security within an intimate community is the expression of the yearning of the archaic level of the human soul.[6] For the archaic person everything foreign is at first hostile, which is why increasing mobility constantly creates uneasiness in the primordial realm of the soul. More and more strange, new faces—in the department store, in the train, in the elevator, etc. In human ethology these inner burdens, normally not registered consciously, are rightfully called "alienation stress factors." Thus the limits of dissolution of *participation mystique* are made visible in the discovery of these usually unconscious aspects of human nature. These are the needs and demands of the archaic

---

[5]Quoted from Aron, *Deutsche Soziologie der Gegenwart*, p. 20; also the end condition of the classless society in Karl Marx's theory seeks to free man from alienation from his fellow man.

[6]Reference was made earlier to the empirical evidence of this collective dimension of the soul as well as to the history of its discovery.

person in us and, in spite of all reeducation and enlightenment, they cannot be wished away, since they are ultimately anchored in humanity's instinctual nature.

Roots of the Dichotomy

When we contemplate the developmental history of humanity, the emergence and separation of ego-consciousness from unconscious identity with the totality of the psyche appears to correspond to an inner finality of nature. We can compare this collective process with the development of a young person. In order to develop an independent personality, the child must first of all be able to break completely away from home. The well-known years of adolescence, bonding with single members of the same sex, military school, and not least the years of apprenticeship and moving about enable or support this transition from childhood to adulthood. Seen collectively, we appear today to be in this stage of transition. We have defiantly broken away from Mother Earth and from the community, as well as from the paternal spirit of traditional knowledge of how to behave, in order to plan our future according to our own judgment. Probably the most precious fruit of humanity's search for conscious independence is the independent attitude of empirical science toward authority.

Yet we succeed in breaking away from our predecessors collectively no more than the individual human being ever succeeds in dismissing his ancestors—after all, we carry the lot of them in our unconscious psyche, as Leopold Szondi has certainly demonstrated. Therefore, whether we will it or not, the manner of experiencing the world known as *participation mystique* that we get from our ancestors always remains a part of us. Admittedly, modern humanity is not conscious of this in most instances, and the danger arises that the needs of this archaic side are not granted the necessary attention.

Body organs react to neglect with illness; neglected, instinct-bound demands of the psyche respond similarly. They have their way compulsively, which leads to a so-called pathological psychic condition. There is the famous example of that respectable gentleman who, while experiencing an "abaissement du niveau mental" [lowering of the threshold of consciousness] suddenly goes to pieces and, to everybody's amazement, behaves in a pathologically primitive manner. The embarrassing attack of impulse is later totally forgotten—just as the sinister compulsiveness of the archaic-Wotanic "blond beast" during the Third Reich in Germany is supposed to be as much forgotten as possible. In psychological jargon one speaks in both instances of "repression." Yet such ongoing repression of the needs of the archaic side, coupled with the periodic, compulsive eruption of the emotional background into the ordered world of consciousness, is not a healthy condition. Thus there must be a further development of consciousness in the sense of a "linking back."

In order to discuss this question let us turn again to our analogy. Following the process of separation, the young person must also recognize in his soul his dependence on the eternal forces of fate, side by side with the newly gained individuality and freedom. In the eternally unchanging manner, like all his ancestors right back to the animals, he too will mate, build a "nest," care for his progeny, defend his territory, etc. Mastering such typical life situations has called for a certain sureness of instinct since times immemorial. For the individual this signifies nothing other than a "linking back" to the most conservative strata of all, namely the empirical knowledge of one's ancestors, which is anchored in the instinctual core and has proven to be true for thousands of generations. The externally visible expressions of the life of instinct are traditional customs and practices,[7] the way of life, "how people have always lived." Inwardly this ancestral knowledge appears in the form of sudden helpful ideas, stirrings, hunches, fantasies, dreams, etc. Consequently the ability of consciousness to relate to the unconscious, instinctual core in order to receive fundamental help in orientation is part of the next developmental stage in strengthening the ego and educating the will. By analogy this holds true for the collective, too.

A further development of collective consciousness must take place, such as we have already observed in the change in the relationship between humanity and its environment. With liberation from the maternal ground humanity has been robbed of its roots. Now, in the realm of interpersonal relationships an additional step must obviously follow the four steps of general disenchantment of all bonds between the individual subject and the objective world. The fifth step would be a newly gained individuality that could be united anew with the generally human, instinctual core. The collective consciousness would be brought into lasting relationship with the unconscious empirical knowledge of our ancestors. In the rupture between progress and tradition we have already recognized the central problem in rural areas from various vantage points—be it the lack of relationship between school knowledge and homegrown empirical knowledge,

---

[7]On this see Lorenz, *Die acht Todsünden der zivilisierten Menschheit*, chapter 7: "Abreissen der Tradition," p. 84–105, and especially Jung, "Medicine and Psychotherapy," *C. W.* 16, par. 198ff.

the entire ambivalence in the city-country relationship, or the irreconcilability of the opposites of connectedness and freedom. But if the
entire dichotomy of primordial and modern social life has its roots in
a process of psychic differentiation, we cannot ever hope to be able to
solve the problem of opposites externally if the two worlds of consciousness and the archaic background of the soul have not been first
reconciled in the psyche of the individual. Only through the individual's repeated recognition that one carries the outer problem of opposites within oneself and must reconcile it within oneself can this gap-
ing wound between yesterday and today be cured externally over the
course of time.

This demand could at first seem unfulfillable. For modern, rational
people, the *Weltanschauung* of our predecessors is so remote and
strikes us as so superstitious that it seems absolutely pointless to look
for any meaning whatsoever in our predecessors' manner of thinking
and living. "What's the point of all those old legends and customs?
That's fine for an idle conversation beside a cosy fire or for the tourist
trade." Such are the comments of the modern average person. There
seems to be no bridge between our world and that of our ancestors—
tertium non datur. Or is there?

One accessible route is to proceed analogously with the human-
environment relationship. If we observe the background of our own
soul, which spontaneously expresses itself in dreams and fantasies,
we notice that images and series of images take shape that, with the
help of some specialized knowledge, can easily be brought into relation with our predecessors' view of the world. There is scarcely anyone who has never in his life dreamed fabulous things, either by day
or by night. In a dream, animals suddenly change magically into
humans and vice versa; witchlike and demonic figures appear; and
even long deceased persons are alive again and on occasion appeal to
the dream ego. In the unconscious world of dreams and fantasies,
then, the world of our ancestors lives; and from that world intima-
tions arise that this inner world also has needs that must be heeded.
But for the most part, we have lost that primordial-naive sight capable
of understanding the sense of these emerging images; and consequently our relation to the inner realm of the ancestors has been lost.
We can no longer grasp the meaning of images directly and intuitively, and hence we no longer understand symbols in folk culture
such as legends, customs, etc. Therefore this world of our predecessors appears to us as devoid of meaning, just as we all too frequently
dismiss our dreams and fantasies as senseless, convinced that dreams
are nothing but froth anyway.

One way of drawing the "upper world" of reason with its logical-conceptual manner of thought closer to the world of our ancestors, and hence to the imagistic utterances of our instinctual core, would first be not to dismiss our predecessors' magical attitude of thought and behavior a priori as complete nonsense. The next step lies in exerting the effort to grasp the sense of the archaic manner of thought and life without falling back into the magical-participatory view of the world. Before we tackle this central theme, we want to illustrate with a third observation how timely it has become for us today to reconnect modern collective consciousness with our instinctual core. It is not only the limits of the dissolution of *participation mystique* and the recognition of the now clearly visible roots of the social dichotomy that make it necessary to ponder the roots of consciousness, but also the fact of external control (i.e., one's life being controlled by external forces) as a problem of the spirit.

External Control as a Problem of the Spirit

With the dissolution of the way of life grounded in *participation mystique*, the spiritual-emotional bridge between human and the external world, between subject and object, vanished. As a consequence, spirit was identified completely with intellect, and the realm of the soul was reduced to that domain which is, or was, connected to the ego. For the enlightened person an objective realm of soul and spirit no longer exists. Exercising scrupulous respect for an ensouled environment is just as incomprehensible to the modern mind as the idea that the individual and the collective should maintain an inner connection with each other. While for archaic people the direct relation—that is, correct behavior—vis-à-vis nature and the tribe was often a question of survival, modern people seem able to do as they like without special regard for nature and society, provided, of course, they observe the laws of the state.

A Swiss immigrant to Canada summarized this view of the world most clearly for me. "America is a great land—all you need is dollars." A context of enduring relationship, borne in joy and sorrow, no longer is the source of satisfaction, but rather money and its potential for buying and consuming things, that is, of using the world instead of relating to it. Only in recent decades have doubts arisen as to whether the primordial consideration of society and nature is really antiquated. Today selfishness and destruction of the environment have assumed such forms and proportions that rethinking the relation between man and his entire surroundings has become a recognized necessity. In this light the effort of the archaic person to maintain a carefully respected condition of equilibrium with environment and other human beings suddenly appears decidedly modern and relevant.

This concern for equilibrium—or more precisely the concern for restoration of the lost intra- and inter-regional equilibrium at the human and the economic level—is now also the preoccupation of regional and agrarian policy. The autonomous dynamics of increasing concentrations of population and jobs, with the attendant weakening of agrarian areas, supposedly can be slowed through a goal-oriented rural development policy. But as we discovered at the beginning, both the so-called external "force of circumstances" (*Sachzwang*) and the irrational side of human beings behave in a downright autonomous manner despite our policies of control; that is to say, they escape our conscious manipulation. If in the case of our irrational side it is unequivocally a phenomenon of spirit and soul, one might think, when it comes to the "force of circumstances," that it was primarily a material problem. Things, concrete things of whatever sort, force us to certain actions. The phenomenon of the "force of circumstances," however, has a significant spiritual aspect that we now intend to investigate more closely.

The expression *Sachzwang* ("force of circumstances") is a neologism of recent years. What is meant is action constrained by certain external, concrete parameters that are or appear to be unalterable. Hence rationalization, concentration, mobility, and growth have become powerful "forces of circumstance." Strictly speaking, we understand "force of circumstances" to mean the constraint to act in a certain way arising from technological progress and the modern economic order. When the occasion arises, natural catastrophes and the like can force us to adopt certain courses of action. However, we do not regard naturally determined constraints as "forces of circumstance"; were that so, our ancestors would certainly have coined the expression long ago.

Today there is probably no politician, entrepreneur, adviser, or engineer who is not familiar with the problem of the force of circumstance. Again and again decisions must be made according to the dictates of technological machinery of our civilization rather than according to the human scale, as we would like. If we do not build a new alpine tunnel, our neighbor certainly will. If we do not expand and improve, our rivals will. If we do not develop and form a larger operation, we will be left behind and lose jobs. Thus one thing forces us to another, one thing calls forth the next. It is not any particular solid material that exerts this sort of force on us as "acting subjects," but it is rather the images and ideas about the structure we have created that have this autonomous dynamic within them. It is they that perpetually drive us. From these reflections we see that *Sach-zwang* should be called, first and foremost, a problem of the spirit. In other words external conditions behave *as if* they could autonomously constrain us because they force us to certain decisions and actions.[8]

Growth, concentration, organization, mobility, innovation and the like can force us, for competitive and other reasons, into a certain course of action because our enlightened view of the world is restricted to concrete reality. If only the physical world of earthly life is significant for the happiness or unhappiness of humanity, then it follows that material goods, health, and the longest life possible are also decisive. Whether or not a healthy, long life in the midst of an abundance of material goods is then experienced as meaningful is, however, not relevant from this viewpoint. In this respect material well-being has become the highest value and highest goal of human existence all over the world. Here we recognize the spiritual power that we call the "force of circumstances," which, despite our most carefully thought-out plans, we cannot get a grip on: the compelling attractiveness of matter. As is well known, attractiveness is not determined by the object but rather by the subjective experience of satisfaction or gratification. Consequently we must seek the origin of our contemporary collective illness—which we might term "determination by the force of circumstances"—in our intrapsychic realm. We will elucidate these thoughts by considering a regional problem.

We speak aptly today of the external control of a region and mean the "force of circumstances" exerted by external parameters imposed by, say, large industrial concerns or the state. Yet there are equally compelling forces of circumstance for these seemingly all-powerful decision makers, too, such as rationalization, concentration, and economically appropriate deployment of financial resources. The image of a vicious circle arises. In fact, viewed from a purely materialistic standpoint, we have to accept an increasing degree of external-directedness in economically weak regions as an established fact. Every analysis of the *causa prima* of an external control ends up somewhere far past the possibility of any effective intervention. Viewing the force of circumstances or external control as a problem of spirit could however, lead us to a more profound confrontation with the fundamental problem. For we thereby expand our scope to include the compelling and decisive spiritual-emotional forces in the human psyche. Confrontation with facts that humanity has created but cannot command no longer lies primarily outside in the battle with the

---

[8] I am indebted to Dr. Marie-Louise von Franz for pointing this out to me.

"windmills" of the force of circumstances. The heart of the problem then shifts from external things to the settling of accounts with the premises of our thinking. We have already discussed these roots of our consciousness under the concept of archetypes. An essential feature of the archetype (as the contents of the collective unconscious) is, as we have seen, its high degree of autonomy. As long as these factors are unconscious, they meet us externally in projected form and lead to misperception that the external things we create are capable of exerting a compelling force *by themselves*. Fundamentally we are still in the same plight as the archaic person, who is surrounded by overpowering, demonic forces with which one has to live somehow or other.[9] We have purged the world of all traces of the objective spirit and are convinced we live in a "palpable" world, only to awaken horrified to the fact that the demonic and the intangible simply approach us in a different form. Overly programmed life-styles, mobility, superabundance of innovations, floods of information and laws—today these are the names for the autonomous forces that rob the individual of certainty and threaten our life as social creatures. Ever more clearly we see ourselves forced to learn to deal correctly with these overpowering spiritual forces, for they have attained a terrifying autonomy or dynamic of their own. Indeed, we are frightened all the more as no means are yet in sight by which we can master this development.[10]

As the worldwide "spiritual urbanization" grows, life becomes more and more restless and unintelligible. Since we know that humanity itself has created these developments, we live, as Jung says, "under the illusion that [we] could and should control them—like Goethe's sorcerer's apprentice, who uttered his master's magic spell, brought his broom to life, and could not stop it. This prejudice increases the difficulty, of course. In a way it would be a much more manageable situation if man could understand his unruly monsters in the primitive way, as autonomous demons."[11]

Let us take up this thought and attempt to understand the spiritual problem of development and progress as humanity's confrontation with demonic powers—not as demons in the objective sense, but rather as rational images that, in some inexplicable manner, escape our control.[12] Understood in this sense, the archaic person's knowledge of the right or wrong way to deal with autonomous spiritual

[9] Cited from Jung, *Letters* [German edition, vol III, p. 357].
[10] Loc. cit.
[11] Loc. cit.
[12] Loc. cit.

factors—demons, in his language—must be of definite interest to us. For this reason we want to explore the main features of the archaic spiritual-emotional stance vis-à-vis these uncontrollable phenomena. To lay the groundwork for our observations, we must, of course, expand the framework in a manner alluded to earlier. We must familiarize ourselves with the fundamentals of the primordial way of thinking and behaving.

Chapter 15

Fundamental Characteristics of the Primordial Manner of Thought and Behavior

Geographic Limits of the Investigation

The archaic or magical manner of thinking and acting is not restricted to certain groups of people but can be found, as we have repeatedly seen, in the deeper levels of every civilized human being's experience. This original manner of acting is basically the answer of the human soul to incalculable, threatening nature.[1] Therefore above all it is difficulty and danger that actively preserve or renew the inner archaic instinctive reactions.

The predisposition toward this sort of behavior is particularly conspicuous among the mountain folk in our steep Swiss alpine valleys; and this is "purely due to their occupation and their homeland, which again and again threaten these people's life and possessions in the snow storms and avalanches of winter, in the mud slides of summer thunderstorms, in the torrents of wild brooks and falling rock."[2] Especially in the Alps, "mag's nyt vill lyde" ("It doesn't take much"), as the mountain folk of Uri say. In such an environment it is of decisive importance to be in harmony with oneself, that is, connected to one's inner instinctual core. He who does not act with the sureness of instinct can easily fall prey to all sorts of accidents.[3] In his distraction he easily knocks his head with a resounding blow on the devilishly low lintel of his Alpine hut; he stumbles, drops something, or forgets to extinguish the fire on the open hearth in the evening. Under such conditions, these are no small matters. Stumbling at the edge of a

---

[1]Renner, *Eherne Schalen*, p. 22.
[2]Op. cit., p. 23.
[3]More extensive treatment is to be found in Jung, "Archaic Man," C. W. 10.

precipice, careless behavior in the path of an avalanche, or an unattended fire when the Föhn (strong south wind) moves in can easily mean disaster and death. One false step while coming down the mountain with a sled loaded, say, with a massive tree trunk and the man is trapped and killed by the powerful load. Once when I was in the Schöchen Valley I witnessed a breathtaking trip like that. When I later asked the farmer who drove the sled what he would do in those circumstances if he missed his footing, his laconic answer was, "Dä mües i vorezüe lüegä" ("I just have to keep my eyes open"). Only the proven "gut" reaction makes possible the correct, instantaneous, reflexlike behavior. Rules of action learned or derived rationally are of little use. Because the forces of nature in our Swiss alpine valleys demand this sort of instinctual sureness again and again, we continue to find primordial ways of experiencing and behaving in the Alpine regions up to the present day. We can thus restrict our investigations to these regions.

Documentary Delimitation

Numerous documents show the archaic-magical form of thought and behavior. Among these sources we find myths, folk legends, spells, rules, songs, jokes and games as well as customs, the older forms of justice, and the entire realm of artifacts. In our context, we can restrict ourselves to the investigation of folk legends and customs, since we are sketching only the fundamental features of folk thinking.[4] The inclusion of other sources would indeed further illuminate this overview of the characteristics, but it would hardly expand it in any fundamental way. For all documents of primordial folk culture are forms that express the same folk thought. Eduard Renner's studies may be mentioned as evidence of this. He was able to demonstrate how the mentality expressed in folk legends from Uri is also recognizable in the old laws and statutes from the so-called *Urher Landbuch* (the *Land Register of Uri*).[5]

---

[4]We take "folk thinking" to mean the manner of thinking appropriate and peculiar to the people (in the sense that Richard Weiss defines "folk").

[5]Additionally see Renner, *Goldener Ring über Uri*. The reference to this interrelationship is to be found in Hauser, *Waldgeister und Holzfäller*, p. 126; on the internal relationship between legend and custom see Wackernagel, "Altes Volkstum der Schweiz," p. 28.

On the Nature and Meaning of the Folk Legend

What Are Legends?

By legends we understand what the people, the "folk," recounted about encounters and experiences with things otherwise not obvious or evident in the everyday course of events,[6] like meetings with poor souls and witches, benevolent or dangerous spirits, hobgoblins, part-animal, part-human creatures, or even the Devil himself. Tales in which fantasy plays a large role can be considered folk legends, in addition to reports of actual supernatural experiences.[7] Research into legends shows that at the beginning of all legends there is the actual experience of a spirit or ghost.[8] "A person casts a glance into another world and is shaken by what he sees: this indeed is the essence of all legends."[9] Legends not only recount the experience but also show precisely the correct way to behave toward these phenomena. "A complex of legends of some size embodies, to a certain extent, the knowledge [folklore, lore-knowledge] of a given population of those powers from the beyond and additionally contains the rules for scrupulously taking those powers into account."[10]

Folk Legends and Folk Thought

Legends used to be told in the evening at social gatherings "until the younger listeners had such gooseflesh that you could have grated cheese on it and had pulled their feet up on the benches and didn't even dare to go out to the potty."[11] Today even in remote areas there is hardly any spontaneous storytelling left. According to Max Lüthi, recounting legends and legendlike stories among Western adults has disappeared for both external and internal reasons. "Sitting about in the evening at a shared task and with shared conversation no longer

---

[6]On this see Medweth, *Die Kärtner Sage*, p. 33.
[7]This simple grouping by Isler is adequate for our perspective. It comes from Isler's talk at the Basel Psychology Society in 1977 entitled "Zur Erlösung des Weiblichen in den Alpensagen." Concerning other groups of legends see Weiss, *Volkskunde der Schweiz*, p. 289ff.; and Bausinger, *Formen der Volkspoesie*, p. 177; generally concerning definitions and terminology of the saga see Röhrich, *Sage*, p. 1ff.
[8]Isler, *Die Sennenpuppe*, p. 2.
[9]Lüthi, "Märchen und Sagen," p. 29.
[10]Isler, *Die Sennenpuppe*; the reader is referred to this work for extensive documentary evidence.
[11]Müller, *Sagen aus Uri*, vol. 2, p. 28.

has the significance it used to have, and the effects of the Enlightenment, which are only now really being felt in remote regions, have undermined the legend from within."[12]

The origin of legend narrators reveals to us that, in the case of legends as a whole, we are not dealing with stories of a specific stratum but with a possession common to all folk, with folk legends. As we can deduce from various anthologies of legends, narrators come from all classes and walks of life.[13] For example, among A. Büchli's informants we find "the farmer as well as the goatherd, the alpine cattle herder as well as the tinsmith and the umbrella maker, the civil servant and the manual laborer, the school teacher and the college professor, as well as the jurist and the cleric, the business man and the innkeeper as well as the day laborer, the farm wife as well as the peddler woman, the well-to-do city matron and the washerwoman, and all generations, from the ninety-year-old granny to the shepherd boy."[14] Even if a saga does not tell of the narrator's own experiences, it is always associated with specific persons and conditions, places, and times. This gives these stories the distinct flavor of their environment, a local character.[15]

As Albert Hauser states, the informant for most of our larger collections of legends (Büchli, Müller, Sooder, etc.) lived, almost without exception, in a preindustrial world of peasants and craftsmen. "Consequently the wealth of legends comes from an agricultural world that was close to the earth and to nature. Even the cities at that time still had a small-town, agrarian character."[16] Consequently, what was commonly shared by all the people in those circumstances, independent of their social status, was their *volkstümliche* behavior and attitude, i.e., thinking and acting according to their local sense of common tradition.[17] Therefore folk legends show us "the living expression of the '*volkstümliche*' frame of mind."[18] Moreover, because legends preserve facts and experiences that do not harmonize with the modern view of the world held by natural science or the church,

---

[12]Lüthi, *Es war Einmal*, particularly the chapter on legend and folk or fairy-tale, p. 55.
[13]For example, Senti, *Sagen aus dem Sarganserland*, p. 452; Sooder, *Zelleni us em Haslital*, p. 14ff.; Pfluger, *Solothurner Sagen* (third edition), "Introduction."
[14]Büchli, *Mythologische Landeskunde von Graubünden*, vol. 1, p. viii; cited in Hauser, *Waldgeister und Holzfäller*, p. 13.
[15]Weiss, *Volkskunde der Schweiz*, p. 288.
[16]Quoted from Hauser, *Waldgeister und Holzfäller*, p. 122.
[17]Hauser, op, cit., p. 123.
[18]Beth, "Sagen" in *Handwörterbuch des deutschen Aberglautens*, VII, p. 872; also ibid., p. 874f.

they provide us with a comprehensive view of the primordial way of thinking characteristic of the common people.[19]

Legends as Archetypal Configurations

We saw the origin of legends as mixture of spiritual, otherworldly or fantasy elements with the more or less locally and temporally determined earthly elements. On the one hand, the legend claims to be true,[20] but on the other hand, the things of which the legend reports are, objectively viewed, not present. We must therefore assume a cooperation of objective-material and subjective-psychic realities in legends. In the experience of a spirit or ghost or in a "fantastic" legend, intrapsychic contents must therefore become mingled with the external world. In order to examine this process more closely, we must briefly review the phenomenon of projection.

As we have already seen, the ability to differentiate is—in contrast to the enlightened way of life—less pronounced in the archaic person, who cannot determine so precisely whether an effect comes from outside or inside, and so psychic things are projected. Consequently, not only do external objects appear as bewitched or animated, but inner experiences such as strong fantasies or dreams appear to be objectively real events. Especially those legends reporting experiences of an encounter with a different world are mingled with what we today recognize as products of the unconscious.[21] Now, part of the essence of the legend is that it is a story told over and over again.[22] These stories were not preserved primarily in written form but rather handed down from generation to generation in so-called "storytelling circles" (*Erzählgemeinschaften*). Even if there is a personal experience at the beginning of a legend, it nevertheless cannot be solely a matter of statements from the personal level of the unconscious. For only such stories that by their very nature have a generally human character arouse general interest; "experiences that leave others 'cold' yield no legends."[23] Hence it is especially the nature and effects of contents from the collective unconscious that legends tell us about.

On the basis of these considerations, we shall proceed on the

---

[19]Weiss, *Volkskunde der Schweiz*, p. 8 and p. 371; see also Renner, op. cit.
[20]On this see W.-E. Peukert, *Sagen*, p. 79 and p. 126.
[21]As an illustration of this see the informative article by Dëgh, "Stadt-Land-Unterschiede in den U.S.A., dargestellt am Beispiel moderner Sagenbildung," pp. 93–107.
[22]In contrast to the legend (Lat. *legenda* = something to be read); see Lüthi, *Es war Einmal*, p. 20.
[23]Isler, *Die Sennenpuppe*, p. 33.

assumption that in the folk legend, particularly that recounting personal experiences, we are dealing with configurations that have been essentially shaped by a deeper and hence more generally human level of the psyche. It is striking that we meet very similar legends in all times and all places. Only to a limited extent can these parallel manifestations be attributed to the effects of migration. Where no historical bridges can be proven unequivocally, we must assume the effects of commonly human, intrapsychic structural dominants (i.e., the archetypes of the collective unconscious). The hypothesis, consequently, that legends are fundamentally configurations or formulations of an archetypal nature has proven extraordinarily fruitful for the understanding of legends.[24]

Concerning the Contemporary Understanding of Sagas

The form of folk legends is more or less shaped by the structural dominants of the collective unconscious. Consequently, the spiritual or fantasy component of legends derives from the same psychic background as archetypal dreams. Numerous legends that recount experiences even permit the conclusion that, in part, legends have their origin in precisely those sorts of dream experiences.[25] For example, in a legend about a young girl that had an experience with a dwarf, it is said that "it seemed to the girl that she had dreamed him."[26] Various "Venice Sagas" very clearly must have something to do with a dream experience.[27] In Canton Uri people tell how, following experiences in Venice, one of their compatriots had to take three drinks of a liquid from a small bottle, "lie down and calmly wait to fall asleep. He did this and awoke at home next to his wife in bed."[28]

I can illustrate the close interweaving of dream, vision, and legend with something I chanced to hear the very day I was writing these lines, on the first of August, 1979, in the Bernese Oberland. The man who told me the following is the owner of a firm, hence he certainly has his feet on the hard ground of business reality. Some time earlier he had had three brain embolisms a few days apart, during which he was unconscious. During his unconsciousness each time he had a dreamlike vision that occupied him so much that, after he recovered

---

[24]On this see the discussion in Hauser, *Waldgeister und Holzfäller*, p. 24f., and in Isler, *Die Sennenpuppe*, p. 22, p. 27, and p. 31ff., as well as Jaffe, *Apparitions*.
[25]See Isler, "Zur Erlösung des Weiblichen in den Alpensagen," p. 23.
[26]Pfluger, *Solothurner Sagen*, p. 239.
[27]See, for example, Müller, *Sagen aus Uri*, no. 296 a–e.
[28]Op. cit., no. 296e.

from the third embolism (to everybody's amazement), he discussed his experience with his pastor. The pastor's minimization of the vision, saying "dreams are like bubbles," did not satisfy him. Since he knew that I was concerned professionally with such things, he paid me a visit and told me three sequences of images that I will briefly relate here.

While he was hovering between heaven and earth during the first embolism, he saw himself on a highway. Many people were walking in front of him, but those he recognized were dead. Suddenly this procession of the dead accelerated and left him behind; and he awoke in his hospital bed, to his and his physician's amazement. During the next embolism he ascended a beautiful, natural stone staircase to a portal. To the left and to the right there stood a deceased person from his village. Through the portal he saw a very large, unembellished hall with countless people. Among them he recognized his departed father, his grandfather, and even his great-grandfather whom he knew only from a photograph. He wanted to cross the threshold to join them, but the two men at the portal slammed the doors in his face; and he again gained consciousness. During the third embolism he was again on a highway, and again the procession of the dead was ahead of him, which he was following. Then the last one in the procession (a deceased woman from his village) turned around and called to him, "You don't belong with us yet, go back." Thereupon he awoke, and since then he has been in very satisfactory health.

He described these three scenes movingly and asked me what they meant. When I asked him if he knew of the horde of the dead or of the "night folk" of local legends, he replied with an astonished "no." He was unfamiliar with Melchior Sooder's *Zelleni us em Haslital*[29] with its numerous tales about the horde of the dead. His experience seemed to make him aware of something that had been neglected in his industrious life—the direct relation to the world on the other side of consciousness, to the world of the ancestors and the dead, in short, to our world of legends as an expression of the unconscious or of what transcends consciousness. In this sense, these legendlike images compensated for the one-sided, worldly orientation of his consciousness and showed him in a drastic way the reality of another world. This initial explanation of his dream experiences made sense to him.

From this example we see how many legends concerning experi-

---

[29]Sooder, *Zelleni us em Haslital*, p. 24–26. Whether or not the narrator had really not heard of the army of the dead in his youth could not be checked.

ence arise directly from dream experiences. When I told these stories to a circle of friends sitting around the fire in the evening, it provoked a very animated discussion of this world and the next. The legendary quality of this experience left none of us unaffected; sooner or later each of us also faces death. We can imagine easily how such archetypal dreams turn into legends. "My grandfather saw the people of the dead himself . . ." might be the sort of experience passed on by grandchildren because they could not have known that their grandfather, who told them the story, was having a brain embolism during his experience. Therefore, insofar as they have a numinous, archetypal content, dreams, visions, or dreamlike irruptions from the unconscious into waking consciousness are adopted by people in the folk community and told over and over again. Such legends are accepted as true and valid. Wherever the dreamlike experience predominates, we can designate such legends as folk dreams on the basis of the collective validity of this psychic reality.[30]

In extrasensory experiences or fantasy elements in legends, we are similarly confronted with contents from the unconscious. We can therefore apply the same method to analysis of legends that has proven its value in the interpretation of dreams. The *amplification method* developed by C. G. Jung is suited to understanding all contents arising from the unconscious. The language of the unconscious is a picture language; it is pictures, images, that speak or seek to impart a piece of information or a meaning. In our language these are images of meaning (German: *Sinnbilder*) or symbols. Often we can understand such images of meaning immediately; but in many cases we must first circle around, elucidate and clarify the meaning of such a picture or image, using the same or similar motifs. Thus we amplify (Latin: *amplificatio* = an extension, enlargement) individual dream or legend motifs with parallel symbols or sequences of symbols from the history of religions, mythology, fairy-tales, legends, etc., until we have grasped their meaning.[31] An interpretation of this sort does not explain a legend but must rather be understood as a new reading of the legend, a reading in which the conscious, with its conceptual language and way of thought, approaches the archetypal world of image. With this method, the symbolically expressed facts of the

---

[30]As a parallel to this, it should be mentioned that among primitive peoples so-called "big dreams" were told to the entire tribe.

[31]On this see Jung, "On the Nature of the Psyche," C. W. 8, par. 403, and Isler, *Die Sennenpuppe*, p. 21ff.

unconscious psyche can be understood by modern consciousness, thus making it possible for the compensatory efforts of the unconscious to become more effective.

Since in folk legends no personal associations to specific motifs can be obtained, only an objective amplification using parallel archetypal motifs is possible. In our legendlike dream example, this sort of amplification would be indicated for the symbol of the procession of the dead and for the visit to the hall of the dead, along with their attendant symbolic details. We would have to seek an initial amplification of this motif among the local legends of the dead. Should that not suffice, we would draw on the testimonies and statements about the world of the dead found in legends, fairy-tales, and myths of other religions. This does not "explain" such a dream experience. What amplification does is to connect our conscious world to our unconscious, ancestors' world. Understanding of the symbolic expression of the unconscious makes possible a connection between the progressive, enlightened attitude of consciousness and the naturally conservative ancestral world of the collective unconscious. The procession of the dead that marches over our paths and roads, and is yet separated from our world by a portal, is a symbolic expression of a paradoxical fact. On the one hand, the procession of the dead indicates the omnipresence of deceased souls. They are among us, even if not visible. On the other hand, the isolating portal to the world of the dead shows that this world of the beyond really is separated from ours.[32] The world of spirits is immanent and transcendent in relation to our concrete here and now, fully corresponding to the qualities of the unconscious. "Originally, however, people expected blessings, prosperity and well-being from the dead," Sooder says in his collection of legends from the Hasli Valley.[33] Thanks to the exploration of the unconscious, we know today that our own ancestors actually are powerful factors in our fate.[34] In general the world of the spirits in the beyond is not to be overlooked as a power, as is impressively demonstrated in this dream experience.

---

[32]Jung reported a similar experience of a woman patient. On the brink of death she had the following vision while unconscious: "Behind me lay a park-like landscape. . . . I knew that here was the entrance to another world and that, if I should turn around in order to see the image directly, I would feel tempted to step through that gate and thus out of this life." (Jung, *C. W.* 8, par. 940.)

[33]Sooder, *Zelleni us em Haslital*.

[34]On this see for example Szondi, *Schicksalsanalyse*, as well as his subsequent works.

Collectively Compensatory Sagas

Surely the most important principle concerning the relation between the unconscious and consciousness is the compensatory relationship. Just as the law of self-regulation holds true in the body — think of the activity of the muscles or of the relation between waking and sleeping — we also find the self-regulating activity of the unconscious vis-à-vis consciousness in the psychic realm. (For example, an approach to life that is too one-sidedly dependent on thinking is compensated initially by feeling-toned dreams and fantasies and, if continued, eventually by uncontrolled moods and affects.) Since conscious ideas, proven rules of life, are voluntarily altered only infrequently, there is always the danger that such attitudes will harden in the course of time. Everything new becomes a threat to that hardened consciousness that can very easily assume an antilife stance. Today we know that the contents from the unconscious attempt to compensate for one-sided attitudes on the part of consciousness. The compensatory contents from the more collective layers of the unconscious relate in a compensatory manner to the collective level of consciousness of a more or less large collective. The collective-compensatory effect of folk legends can be understood if we call to mind that "they treat of incredibly fascinating, and in part terrifying, accounts that have lastingly influenced and determined the state of mind from early youth onward. Whoever heard such things had to come to terms with them again and again, frequently for an entire lifetime. 'That is the purpose of the old legends: to make you think about them,' a storyteller from the Grisons said."[35] With regard to the regulative-compensatory function of the legend, Walter Medweth has correctly spoken of "our ancestors' naturally wise therapy for the soul."[36] When we undertake detailed investigations of individual legends in the following pages, we must keep in mind this compensatory relationship of the folk legend with respect to the prevailing consciousness of the story's audience.

---

[35] Quoted from Isler, "Zur Erlösung des Weiblichen," p. 3; the statement mentioned in the quote comes from Büchli, *Mythologische Landeskunde von Graubünden*, vol. 2, p. 751.
[36] Quoted from Isler, *Die Sennenpuppe*, p. 256.

Characteristics of Folk Thought in the Saga

Nature and Spirit

Right down to inorganic matter, nature in legend is spiritual and by no means dead. In the folk imagination that recounted legends, the spiritual element in nature was capable of confronting anyone at any time, and legends attempt to show how humans must deal with this spiritual dimension of nature. Nature communicates with humanity as an indefinite "It"[37] or as a quite specific manifestation of spirit. The spirit aspect of matter is depicted in the legend as an autonomous counterpart that demands to be taken seriously and be scrupulously respected. In the following legend from Uri this comes in its most direct form.

> *At Rinderbüel in the Maderaner Valley an entire Alpine dairy farm lies buried under a huge layer of loose stone. One evening, as the herdsman was milking the cows, a voice shouted down from the steep face of rock that hung above the hut threateningly, "I'm gonna let it go!" The herdsman cupped his hands around his mouth and shouted back, "Just hang on to it!" The next evening the voice resounded again, "I've gotta let it go!" And again the fearless farmer replied, "Hang on a bit longer!" The third evening fell over the quiet meadow, the last cow was just being milked, and the entire herd was still standing together chewing their cud, when the terrifying, threatening, and yet almost pleading voice again screamed down from the overhanging rock face, "Quick! I've got to let go!" The herdsman was just pulling his one-legged milking stool out from under the last cow. He stood up, the full milk pail in his hand, and shouted up at the cliff, "So let it go then!" And in that instant the cliff exploded with a roar, fell thundering down throwing sparks everywhere, and buried the entire magnificent herd, along with the herdsman and the hired hands, under huge piles of debris and boulders. Only the herdsman's boy and a little red Trychel cow, the only cow of a poor widow, survived. The cow just happened to be down the meadow at the brook.*[38]

The idea expressed here is that the rock mass of the cliff obeys natural laws not only in a purely mechanical fashion but is permeated by something spiritual that announces its presence to people and can be registered by them. If we do not want to set the entire legend aside

---

[37]See Chapter 8 in Part 3.
[38]Müller, *Sagen aus Uri*, vol. 1, no. 70.

as nonsense because we "know" that inorganic matter cannot speak, we must ask ourselves what is being expressed in the legend in symbolic form.

In the speaking cliff, an unknown counterpart attempts to communicate with the alpine dwellers, that is, with human consciousness. And obviously this unknown counterpart, this spirit of matter, knows more than the human does. But the herdsman fails to recognize the warning in this voice of nature nor does he take it seriously, which leads to the destruction of the herdsman's Alp. Today we could understand the voice of the cliff as an exteriorized expression of the impersonal unconscious. It is well known that our instinctual core has more comprehensive knowledge. In especially threatening situations the manifestations of the unconscious can have such a high energy charge[39] that in some instances they can even be perceived externally.[40]

But that would not be sufficient to understand of our legend. Some sort of effect must have proceeded from the cliff, from matter itself, for after all there is a dialogue between man and material. The intrapsychic capacity for perception that can register effects of matter rests on the psychoid nature of archetypes. As we have already seen (Part 3, chapter 8), archetypes, as contents of the collective unconscious, are the bridge between the realm of the psyche and that of matter. This archaic or animal side in us still has the sensorium for perceiving things in the environment that are no longer accessible to the perceptual faculties of consciousness. Unfortunately we still know far too little about the exact course of these processes. For the time being, the available empirical information will have to suffice, but it has already adequately revealed that the spirit of the unconscious actually does have vitally important things to impart, that is, information that was unknown to consciousness[41] in exactly the same way that "unknown" nature knew about the impending avalanche. Here old folk wisdom and the most recent research findings come together.

Before the Enlightenment, people paid much more attention to such expressions of the spirit of nature. Today we are again learning to see that important knowledge is indeed revealed in the imaginal expression of our own nature or of our instinctual core, knowledge

---

[39]For example, intense dreams in the middle of the night. A classic example is Xenophon's dream in the middle of the night when the Greek army in Persia was threatened. The dream ushered in the decisive turning point (*Anabasis*, III/1).

[40]See Jung and Pauli, *Naturerklärung und Psyche*, and Jung, "Flying Saucers: A Modern Myth," *C. W.* 10, par. 589–824.

[41]In this regard, see the broad field of dream research.

that it is important to register consciously.[42] Although there used to
be a readiness to take this spirit of nature into account, there was still
need of "warning or guiding legends"[43] showing the significance of
the instinctual or animal side.[44] This is especially clearly expressed in
the following variant of the same legend:

> *One evening a white bird was flying over the mountain pasture, cry-*
> *ing, "Go 'way! Go 'way!" The Alpine swine pricked up their ears,*
> *listened attentively, and raced off at a wild gallop down the valley. But*
> *the other animals and the people did not; they stayed. The same call*
> *resounded on the second evening. The Alpine herdsman at one of the*
> *dairies thought they ought to heed the warning and leave the meadow,*
> *but he was only laughed at. The third evening—it was the evening*
> *before St. Jacob's Day—there were black clouds that settled threaten-*
> *ingly over the meadow, and again the white, winged messenger*
> *appeared over the meadow and cried with a ghastly voice, "Go 'way! Go*
> *'way!" The one herdsman gathered his cattle together and with his*
> *hired hands left the sinister meadow. A terrifying thunderstorm*
> *erupted. When they reached Heitersbüel and looked back, the face of the*
> *cliff directly above the meadow burst and plunged with a roar down*
> *upon the meadow and into Jakob's Lake that lay just behind it, burying*
> *the pasture along with the remaining people and cattle under rubble as*
> *high as a house.*

In another account, the voice was that of a Little Wild Man or of a
spook or ghost. In this variant it is the swine that immediately understand the signs of nature or the nature spirit and act in accordance
with the warning.[45] Like rats abandoning ship, they leave their
endangered environment. According to the legend, it is important for
humans to pay attention to this instinctual side of human nature
when it manifests itself in us as hunch, inspiration, sudden idea, etc.
All too often our consciousness is too far removed from our instinctual core, and we obligate ourselves to do some project or undertake
some development scheme in spite of the so-called "bad vibes" we
sense. With excessive detachment we lose the self-regulating or com-

---

[42]Previously these things were perceived more as exteriorized; today these instinctive
reactions are registered primarily as inner sequences of images (e.g., in dreams); see
also the passage quoted earlier from Blaek and Lloyd's *Bushman Folklore*, p. 330ff.
[43]Lüthi, "Warn-oder Leitbildsagen," p. 38.
[44]Compensatory to Christianity's contempt for man's animal nature.
[45]That it is precisely swine that race off is not a matter of chance; the sensitivity of
swine is well known not only from numerous legends (e.g., bell legends) but also
empirically. The legend mentioned is found in Müller, *Sagen aus Uri*, vol. I, no. 69.

pensatory effect of the instinctual basis that ultimately, as the legend attempts to show, can turn against life or even destroy it.

We can clearly recognize the spirit of nature in fantasies and dreams that can often appear to us as "warning birds." The reaction of the swine would then correspond to the spontaneous reaction we feel following an impressive dream—a reaction that we enlightened Westerners all too often and all too easily dismiss as irrational. According to the legend, the one herdsman who did heed the bird, who took the sign in nature seriously, was laughed at by the others. "He's got a bee in his bonnet" is a phrase still used when speaking of a person who seriously attempts to behave according to the voice of nature.

Of course, many who have had dealings with the spirit of the unconscious have gotten "a bee in their bonnet" in the negative sense, and then we say they have "bats in the belfry" because they have misunderstood the expressions of the unconscious or have even been inundated by the unconscious. Psychopathology provides copious illustrations of this. Consequently the problem is that of correctly understanding nature's "bee" or "bat." It was only after the swine had rushed off, in an immediately comprehensible confirmation of the phenomenon of the bird, that the herdsman seriously urged departure. In any case, we may assume this although the legend reports nothing concrete on this point. It restricts itself to the warning that we pay attention to the voice of nature and take it seriously. In our terms, the legend's "news flash" is that it is important to include the spiritual-psychic dimension in our conduct: "Nature knows more than you do." In other words, the voice making itself known through an unknown counterpart is not simply an illusion. Thus fantasies and wisps of dreams, woven by an unknown spirit from out of the depths of nature, really want to be taken seriously as our autonomous counterparts. Otherwise, the beneficent, compensatory effect of our instinctual foundation, as the legend shows, cannot develop. Neither legend gives us information on the right way or wrong way to understand the spirit from the unconscious. To elucidate this consideration we must draw upon a larger circle of Alpine legends, that of legends about dwarfs.

Dwarfs as Manifestations of the Spirit of Nature

In our Alpine valleys the names of dwarfs or creatures who, according to legend, enter into relations with humans are legion. In central Switzerland they are called *Berglütli* ("little mountain people"), *Herd-*

mannli[46] ("little hearth men") or *Heidenlütli*[47] ("little heathen people"). In Upper Wallis they are called *Gotwärgini*,[48] and in Tirol they are called *Holzleutchen* or *Erdleutchen*[49] ("little wood people" or "little earth people"). Equally numerous are the various spirit groups that appear in the shape of dwarfs, one of several forms of manifestation such as the "Fänggen," water spirits, kobolds, and numerous ghosts and spooks.[50] We will limit our observations primarily to the dwarf sagas and draw extensively on the scholarship in that area.

Dwarf legends belong for the most part to the so-called legends of experience. According to storytellers, dwarfs were still revealing themselves to humans until the beginning of our century (!), and "still today there are old people alive who saw and had dealings with them. . . . In 1875 in the Upper Simmen Valley (Bernese Oberland), it was said that the dwarfs had been alive up until recently."[51] According to legend, it was curiosity, ridicule, or very specific historical events or persons (such as, the railroad or the French) that drove the dwarfs away.[52] According to Müller-Bergström, dwarfs disappeared at about the turn of the nineteenth century – that is, the period when the Enlightenment penetrated rural areas.[53] This correlates with our earlier observations about the disenchantment of nature. This concurrence is one reason that the investigation of dwarf legends is particularly suited for our analysis, especially because the depiction of the spirit of nature or of the unconscious itself as a dwarf is an archetypal motif.[54] In the most diverse cultures and eras, the spirit of nature (or the spirit of the unconscious itself) is initially experienced as something quite insignificant. Only upon "closer acquaintance" with the dwarfs was their other side revealed, their power. The dwarfs are like the cabiri in *Faust* II: "klein von Gestalt, gross von Gewalt" ("small in size, great in power"). Consequently dwarf legends give us compre-

---

[46]Cysat, *Collectanea pro chronica lucernensi et Helvetiae*, vol. 1, part 2, folio 247.

[47]In remembrance of the original inhabitants of the area; see Niderberger, *Sagen aus Unterwalden*, vol. 1, p. 42ff.

[48]See Guntern, *Volkserzählungen aus dem Oberwallis*, p. 743ff.

[49]Vernaleken, *Alpensagen*, p. 188.

[50]*Handwörterbuch des deutschen Aberglanben*, XII, p. 1015ff.

[51] *Handwörterbuch des deutschen Aberglautens*, XII, p. 1104; see also for the sources of this information.

[52]Op. cit., pp. 1090–1101; note also the comprehensive anthology of reasons given there for the dwarfs' disappearance.

[53]Op. cit., p. 1105; in contrast to the disappearance of the dwarfs, the folk have regarded the giants – personified forces of nature (storm giants, etc.) – as long since extinct (*Handwörterbuch*, XII, p. 1136). It is the Devil that assumed the characteristics of almost all the giants (p. 1137).

[54]On this see also Kerényi, *Mythologie der Griechen*, p. 86, and Isler, *Die Sennenpuppe*, p. 143.

hensive information about the archaic view of the characteristics of the spirit of nature, how it exerts its effects, and what the proper attitude should be toward this phenomenon.

Helpful and Creative Function

Individually or in bands, the dwarfs enter into relations with mortals; and, depending on the behavior of the humans, these relations are a blessing or a curse. Let us begin with the positive effects of these little people. Known to us as brownies or little people, dwarfs help, for example, to do work "in the twinkling of an eye"; they bake and cook delicious things, or make themselves useful in other ways in the house or barn.[55] When humans accept dwarfs with goodwill—giving them food, lending them dishes, or midwifing for them—the reward is often a "mysterious, marvelous gift subject to the one condition that maintains its inexhaustibility."[56] Humans must keep the secret of the wine barrel that never runs dry,[57] or that of the yarn that never ends.[58] Likewise, inexhaustible food is among the dwarfs' gifts.[59] Also very common is the motif of the inconspicuous gift that—for the person who does not despise it or throw it away or lose it along the way—turns into pure gold when the owner returns home.[60] Usually what is originally given is foliage, chaff, or horse manure. Of course the recipient is almost always very disappointed and ignores the dwarfs' warning "je meer düü zätsch, je minder düü hätsch!"[61] ("The more you throw away, the less you'll have!"), throwing all but a meager remnant, say one leaf, away. Once home, however, this remnant is revealed to be pure gold. But the search for what was lost very seldom helps the owner get more.

As a projection of unconscious contents, the dwarfs represent something on the order of life spirits. They correspond to that inconspicuous intrapsychic force that suddenly gives us the necessary courage and impetus to master a large task and bring it to a satisfying conclusion. How the dwarfs like to sing, make music, and dance is

---

[55]*Handwörterbuch des deutschen Aberglaubens*, XII, p. 1083f.
[56]Op. cit., p. 1080.
[57]Vernaleken, *Alpensagen*, p. 180.
[58]*Handwörterbuch des deutschen Aberglaubens*, XII, and Vernaleken, *Alpensagen*, p. 181 and 188.
[59]Jegerlehner, p. 145; Zingerle, *Sagen aus Tirol*, p. 88.
[60]*Handwörterbuch des deutschen Aberglaubens*, XII, p. 1080; the following three sentences summarize p. 1081 of the *Handwörterbuch des deutschen Aberglaubens*, XII; only seldom do dwarfs give gold directly.
[61]Sooder, *Zelleni us em Haslital*, p. 105.

also often mentioned.[62] Enlivening spirits and joie de vivre simply belong together, and the dwarfs' gift of inexhaustible food symbolizes the unconscious source "of lasting animation for the soul."[63] That gift of inexhaustible food (or something similar) shows that we are dealing with divine powers that are close to the Christian deity in their significance; we need only recall Jesus feeding the five thousand. But in contrast to the celestial, bright, Christian god-image, the dwarf figures are divine chthonic powers belonging to dark Mother Earth. Significantly, by far the most frequent animal form in which dwarfs appear is that of the toad.[64] In folk belief, the toad is a common symbol for fertility,[65] and consequently dwarfs are, in the imagination of the legend-telling folk, clearly spiritual aspects of the lower, feminine-natural forces and of the dark.[66] This means nothing less than that, according to these legends, all good and divine things derive not only from above, from the heavenly father, but also from the nether realm, the realm of the mothers. The insignificant gifts of the dwarfs, which are revealed as of great value only at home, show clearly how the legend-telling folk know that in the interior of the earth—that is, intrapsychically, within the soul[67]—the highest values lie hidden.[68] These gifts from the depths of the soul (dreams or fantasies) are in fact thrown away in the true sense of the word, in most instances as horse manure. Only after the gift of the nature spirit has been carefully carried home—when consciousness has retained and integrated the inconspicuous product of the unconscious—only then does the gift become valuable. The conscious view is then complemented by hints from the spirit of the unconscious. In this way the inconspicuous images of fantasy or dream are transformed into gold; that is to say, only then do they reveal themselves as something of great value, a fact that has long been known to psychotherapy.

In our context, an additional helpful characteristic of dwarfs is of particular interest, namely their capacity to teach people new things.

---

[62]*Handwörterbuch des deutschen Aberglaubens*, XII, p. 1045ff.

[63]Von Beit and von Franz, *Symbolik des Märchens*, vol. 2, p. 84.

[64]*Handwörterbuch des deutschen Aberglaubens*, XII, p. 1033; a particularly fine example is to be found in Pfluger's *Solothurner Sagen* (no. 194) where a large toad that was not killed turns out to be a brownie.

[65]Hence, for example, the uterus was usually depicted as a toad on ex-voto images to express thanks for the curing of uterine ailments.

[66]Concerning dwarfs as belonging to the realm of the Great Mother, see Kerényi, *The Gods of the Greeks* (New York: Thames and Hudson, 1951), p. 80ff.

[67]For as we have already discussed, archaic people project their unconscious on the landscape; in the landscape they then find entrances into the deeper levels of the soul; we have already spoken of the phenomenon of the so-called *genius loci*.

[68]The numerous treasure legends belong here also.

In the region of Vättis in the Sarganserland, people tell the following story: "Folks used to go into the woods only with an ax. They didn't know any different 'till one day two dwarf men showed how you work with a saw."[69] In the folk mind in general, dwarfs are the mediators of new methods. According to legend, they not only taught the use of the saw, but also invented cheese making.[70] Among other things, they also taught humans baking, smithery, shoemaking, tailoring, and even singing.[71] In general dwarfs know more than humans;[72] this is why they can also see the future and prophesy.[73] They give all sorts of good advice. Indeed, they want to be asked for advice; otherwise their anger brings misfortune.[74]

The folk legend thus conveys an additional important feature of the spirit of the unconscious, since creative inspirations and humanity's creative imagination are rooted in this deeper layer of the soul. Just as the stirrings of the unconscious are small and insignificant like dwarfs, the consequences of such creative inspirations can be of great power.[75] In the atomic age we hardly need mention additional examples to demonstrate this.

Today we know from research on creativity that creative impulses in fact are rooted in the unconscious background of the human psyche. Human creativity does not therefore arise from the realm of consciousness at all.[76] And just as, according to legend, it has never been possible to capture the dwarfs and forcibly make them serve humans,[77] human creativity cannot be manipulated either. Creativity is and remains, in spite of all progress, a divine spark from the beyond; the relation to the domain of the dwarfs, that is, to the unconscious, remains critical for creative work.

So long as the "innovative activity" of the unconscious was seen in projected form in the dwarfs, there was no danger that humans would identify with the spirit of the unconscious. In the Enlightenment, all external images of spirit were dissolved. Their largely intrapsychic origin, however, was not recognized; and thus arose a new

---

[69]Senti, *Sagen aus dem Sarganserland*, p. 177.
[70]*Handwörterbuch des deutschen Aberglaubens*, XII, p. 1053.
[71]Op. cit., p. 1048.
[72]Op. cit., p. 1058.
[73]Op. cit., p. 1059.
[74]Loc. cit.
[75]In this sense dwarfs correspond to the Greek *daktyls*, the inventive gods, who—as the *megaloi theoi*, the "great gods"—were revered although they were only as large as fingers (see Kerényi, *The Gods of the Greeks*, p. 83ff).
[76]A compilation on this topic is to be found in Kast, *Kreativität*.
[77]*Handwörterbuch des deutschen Aberglaubens*, XII, p. 1094.

illusion that consciousness was the sole source of knowledge. Consequently, humanity identified with the spirit of nature, which is equivalent to a huge inflation.[78] Because of this identification with the spirit of the unconscious, the recognition that humanity must adjust the impulses from the unconscious to human size has faded away. In particular, politicians, development experts, engineers, and planners—who are involved directly with the creation of new things, promoting progress and growth—are particularly susceptible to identification with the creative spirit and the attendant overvaluation of their own powers. For the spirit of the unconscious is not always helpful, which brings us to the consideration of the negative aspects of these little people.

Negative Function

Spontaneously—but especially when humans behave improperly—dwarfs can become roguish, malicious, and even deadly when angry. Renward Cysat (1545-1614), the Lucerne chronicler and "father of Swiss ethnology," reports the following example:

> *People believed the dwarfs on Mt. Pilatus to be not only good-natured and helpful but also demonic beings delighting in others' misfortune. If the Alpine dairymen failed to proclaim the Alpine blessing and the Ave Maria in the evening, a ghost later appeared that looked like a long-bearded dwarf carrying a stick in his hand and a salt bag over his shoulder. People claimed to have seen him driving the cattle away through the sky at the moment they arose. Only on the third day did the cattle return—lean, miserable, and unable to give milk, a great loss for the Alpine people.[79]*

Here the sin of not proclaiming the Alpine blessing or the call to prayer moves the old dwarf to intrude into the Alpine people's territory and do damage. This image of the single dwarf as humanity's experienceable counterpart comes very close to the magical idea of the "It" against which the mountain folk of Uri protect themselves by confronting the "It" with the golden ring. We have already discussed the archaic worldview of the Uri folk in detail (see Part 3, chapter 8, above) and recognized in the "It" the collective unconscious, while the golden ring corresponds to the closed arena of consciousness. The

---

[78]Cf. Jung, "Symbolik des Geistes."
[79]Cysat, *Collectanea pro chronica lucernensi et Helvetiae*, fol. 220; textual adaptation by Lütolf, *Sagen, Bräuche und Legenden aus den fünf Orten Luzern, Uri, Schwyz, Unterwalden und Zug.*

wrong way of behaving toward the "It"—that is, not heeding the relationship between the ring and the "It," or between human consciousness and the unconscious—is regarded by the mountain folk of Uri as wantonness. Where the unconscious reveals itself in folk thinking in personified form—as here in the dwarf—this relationship is fully maintained. Hence analogously, wanton behavior toward the dwarfs brings misfortune, illness, or death to the offender.[80]

Dwarfs, as creatures belonging to the "Great Mother," were regarded as the actual protectors of nature,[81] especially animals. Whoever offended these higher powers faced punishment, which was often death. As an illustration of this, let us listen to the story of a person from central Switzerland that Cysat heard firsthand:

> I myself, in my younger days, heard about an old man named Heinrich Omlin, who was the governor of Underwalden. In his youth he was very keen on hunting. He told me that he met a little hearth dwarf as he was hunting chamois in the mountains. The dwarf admonished and abjured Omlin not to continue; but when the latter replied scornfully and did not heed the little fellow, half his size, he cursed Omlin, a strong man, and threw him down over a cliff where Omlin lay half dead for several hours until his folks found him, revived him, and carried him home. They [the dwarfs] are also supposed to have lain in wait for young children and also sometimes to have kidnapped them.[82]

Many examples of this sort could be cited, but in the legends, a transgression does not always end so mildly. According to the original folk belief, nature not only constitutes a living counterpart but commands respectful acknowledgment of certain limits.[83] There is no legend in which a human being has come to rule over the dwarfs; the dwarfs have always been stronger.[84] The very fact that disdaining or ignoring the laws of these nature spirits is viewed among the folk as wantonness (which means, of course, an offense against sacred powers) confirms the idea that for the folk lowly things or matter itself was of a divine nature.

As spirits of matter, the dwarf spirits can also spontaneously appear as veritable spirits of roguery and torment, whose entire endeavor

---

[80]*Handwörterbuch des deutschen Aberglaubens*, IX, p. 1041.
[81]On this see Lütolf, *Sagen, Bräuche, Legenden aus den fünf Orten Luzern, Uri, Schwyz, Unternwalden und Zug*, p. 48f., and Hauser, *Waldgeister und Holzfäller*, p. 101–108.
[82]Cysat, op. cit.
[83]Examples of this are also to be found in Jegerlehner, *Walliser Sagen*, p. 144f.
[84]*Handwörterbuch des deutschen Aberglaubens*, IX, p. 1092; at most only an occasional apparent mastery.

and life seem directed toward practical jokes and malice. "They teased and annoyed people in the house, the barn, and the shed wherever they could. Thus for example they would snatch away the milk stool during the milking so that the Alpine herdsman would fall backward into the manure; again and again they would topple the carefully erected haystacks and laugh when the farm hands got irritated."[85] Here the dwarfs clearly produced effects that today we would like to ascribe to the "malevolence of the object."[86] In these activities they really do appear as the active side of matter and consequently represent something of its psychic dimension.[87]

In conclusion we can formulate the following insights. In folk thought, nature is not merely a living counterpart to humanity. Rather, according to the folk worldview, the task of humans has always been to respect the obvious natural limits, lest the spirit or the meaning of nature—symbolized in the form of dwarfs—turn against humanity. In its own right, the spiritual aspect of nature in folk thought is not exclusively constructive and helpful but—as is all of creation—simultaneously light and dark, constructive and destructive.

The Need for Redemption

It is striking and paradoxical that dwarfs, in spite of their reputed power, also long for redemption.[88] For example, dwarfs guarding treasures want to be redeemed;[89] in other legends they go to humans and want to be spoken to in order to find redemption.[90] On the Untersberg, dwarfs look for a "dwarf stone" that is supposed to transform them back into human beings.[91] In the dwarfs' need for redemption we touch on an extraordinarily complex and central problem that

---

[85]Holzman, *Wipptaler Heimatsagen*, vol. 2, p. 99, quoted by Isler, *Die Sennenpuppe*, p. 141f.

[86]Isler, op. cit., p. 142; also the hobgoblins are regarded as personifications of the malevolence of the object (*Handwörterbuch des deutschen Aberglaubens*, V, p. 31).

[87]This finds expression also in the great age of dwarfs. Although they are as small as children, they are primeval and have watched the mountains grow. They, together with the material of the world, were, so to speak, present when the world was created. (On this see Holzmann, "Indogermanische Motive der Zwergsage im Tirol," and Isler, op. cit., p. 145.)

[88]*Handwörterbuch des deutsche Aberglaubens*, IX, p. 1111.

[89]Op. cit., p. 1112; also see Müller, *Sagen aus Uri*, no. 387. We have already referred to the symbolic association of toad and dwarf.

[90]*Handwörterbuch des deutsche Aberglaubens*, IX, loc. cit.

[91]Vernaleken, *Alpensagen*, p. 63 and p. 65.

is broached in many other redemption legends. What does it mean if something in a legend seeks redemption and needs human help to attain it?

Redemption means becoming more free. Within creation, greater degrees of freedom are a fundamental property of what is more highly developed. Thanks to our erect posture, we human beings have a greater range of action than does the animal; the animal has more freedom of movement than does the plant; and so on. In the spiritual realm, consciousness is the carrier of what enables humanity to enjoy a certain freedom concerning our instinctual drives. Consequently, the redemption of a spiritual phenomenon in legend signifies a transformation of something "involuntarily unconscious" toward the lighter and freer realm of human consciousness. If the dwarfs of legend want to assume human form or be asked for advice, and if the experiences of spirits in legends are projections from the collective unconscious, then the dwarfs' need for deliverance means that something spiritual from the unconscious wants to be integrated into the realm of human consciousness. What is also worth mentioning is the widespread designation of dwarfs as heathen folk; and especially in Switzerland this is clearly a reference to the original inhabitants who remained heathen.[92] In the Tirol dwarfs are regarded as unbaptized children, thus associating these little people with the spirits of souls or of the dead.[93] As non-Christian spiritual beings of nature, they are close to the realm of Lucifer, the lightbringer from below.[94] Thus the dwarf people, as symbolic expression of the spirit of nature, belong to the realm that Christianity could not assimilate. Attention to and correct relationship with the lower, natural, heathen spirit is, according to the reports in legend, the task of humanity. Through accomplishment of this task, the ambivalent nature spirit can be redeemed, that is, be brought closer to that level of our consciousness which has been informed by Christianity. The lack of connection between the innovative, chthonic nature spirit and our Christian level of consciousness may well be the primary reason why development and progress can behave with such an autonomous energy. Consequently, the problem of *Sachzwang* (force of circum-

---

[92]*Handwörterbuch des deutschen Aberglaubens*, IX, p. 1111.

[93]On dwarfs as spirits of the dead see *Handwörterbuch des deutschen Aberglaubens*, IX, p. 1112–1119.

[94]In the Middle Ages dwarfs were regarded as, among other things, fallen angels (*Handwörterbuch des deutschen Aberglaubens*, IX, p. 1036); in certain legends, dwarfs complained about the construction of churches and the ringing of bells. (For a detailed discussion of this see Sparks, *The Wounded Finger; Anchorage for Soul and Sense in Technology*, p. 58ff.)

stances) that arose with progress must be seen in connection with the natural "spirit of development" not integrated by our Western cultural consciousness. Dwarfs are, as we have seen, bringers of innovation. As *lumen naturae* (the term comes from Paracelsus) they are a symbol for the spirit of the unconscious.

The dwarfs' need for redemption described in various legends shows us how this spiritual element in nature must exert its effects in an involuntary and hence compulsive manner. In its expressions, this spirit of nature, or spirit of the unconscious, attempts to regulate one-sided developments of consciousness that are adverse to life. However, every natural self-regulative tendency has its way compulsively if consciousness does not pay attention, just as our body reacts with illness to a prolongedly imbalanced way of life. If, then, this spirit of the unconscious is not redeemed—that is, if it is not voluntarily integrated into consciousness—the self-regulating spirit simply must manifest itself in a compulsive or unredeemed fashion. As a consequence, compulsive ideas and compulsive actions of all sorts can appear in individuals as well as in the collective. In the instance of the collective, we generally speak of ideologies and "force of circumstances." The demonic quality of progress, clearly visible in today's *Sachzwang*, which we have recognized as a problem of spirit and soul—is obviously associated with the chthonic spirit of the unconscious that remains unintegrated in our cultural consciousness.

The Meaning of Wantonness

Rather than investigating additional legends with an eye to the fundamental features of folk thought, we want now to inquire into a concept that turns up again and again at decisive points in folk legends: the concept of wantonness. Eduard Renner even speaks of actual "wantonness legends."[95] For example, an Alpine dairyman who squandered food and drink was so high-spirited that he made a staircase of cheese.[96] Another farmer boldly moved his fence a hand's width each year into public property.[97] Yet even the destruction of swallows' nests,[98] skinning the bark off a tree still standing,[99] and—as we saw at the beginning—generally disregarding the voices of nature is regarded in legends as wantonness. And again and again we hear

---

[95]Renner, *Goldener Ring über Uri*, p. 247.
[96]Jegerlehner, *Walliser Sagen*, p. 143.
[97]Renner, op. cit., p. 250 and p. 288 (cited in Müller, *Sagen aus Uri*).
[98]*Handwörterbuch des deutschen Aberglaubens*, VII, p. 891f.
[99]*Handwörterbuch des deutschen Aberglaubens*, III, p. 79.

what heavy penalties await those who have not behaved correctly. In general we understand the term "wantonness" to mean underestimating or offending higher, sacred powers.[100] Now what folk legend calls wantonness is not offense against Christian values but rather contempt for the rules of behavior toward nature.[101]

As we have already seen in Part Three, Eduard Renner encountered the significance of the relation between man and nature in his work on the archaic-magical thinking of the mountain folk of Uri. Incomprehensible nature surrounding humanity on all sides is what the people of Uri call the "It." They confront it with the golden ring that would be understood today as a psychological symbol. In folk belief, gold is the solar metal, the metal of daylight, and it therefore represents the light of consciousness that brings renewed awakening each day. Beyond protection, the ring also symbolizes comprehensive relatedness to something, a meaning that we also recognize in the wedding ring. Consequently, the golden ring symbolizes the comprehensive protection against overpowering nature, thanks to a conscious relatedness with this very same unknown nature. As we have seen, the contemporary concept corresponding to the "It" is the collective unconscious. In addition to the "ring" and the "It," the third central concept in this magical worldview is that of wantonness. This term designates improper human behavior toward the "It" or the unknown nature. Actually, wantonness consists in "nothing other than ignoring old judgments and rules, or not taking them into account."[102] For according to the ancient idea, one human being alone is no match for the malice of the "It."[103] "The individual needs the experience of generations to correctly carry on the battle in which form is always the issue. These experiences are embodied in usage and order."[104] Not only the legends and usages but also the old sets of laws (such as the ancient "Landbook" of Uri) contain the rules and knowledge "that our ancestors established in their daily battle and that were bequeathed from generation to generation." This folk wisdom thus becomes "a powerful support for the ring" or for what we

---

[100]The *Handwörterbuch des deutschen Aberglaubens*, III, p. 79, defines wantonness as knowingly and willfully—and often petulantly—transgressing against cosmic laws or supernatural personalities or powers (transgression against a taboo); see also *Handwörterbuch des deutschen Aberglaubens*, VII, p. 890; additional examples in Isler, *Die Sennenpuppe*, p. 196ff., especially p. 157f.

[101]This statement also holds true for the wantonness of baptizing animals or dolls. Details on this can be found in Isler, *Die Sennenpuppe*, p. 101–109, especially p. 106.

[102]Renner, *Goldener Ring über Uri*, p. 253.

[103]See Renner, op. cit., p. 252.

[104]Ibid.

would call collective conscious life, "for it contains advice and information from all those who for centuries have been gathered to their fathers."[105] Hence it is understandable why wantonness, according to Renner, really is a transgression against the community, against the realm of culture scrupulously defended by the community against threatening nature. A wanton act on a Alpine meadow has the consequence that "It" gains power over that meadow. Therefore every wanton act fundamentally signifies a frivolous violation of the tried and tested relation between man and nature.

We may assume that in rural areas much resistance to modern procedures in agrarian, regional, and especially land use policies has arisen because a one-sidedly rational procedure takes this relationship of man and nature too little into account. Excessively one-sided, rational, utilitarian thought can easily awaken a bad feeling in the folk mind, a feeling that asks something on the order of, "isn't that rather wanton?" To a large degree we have indeed banished the external dangers of nature today. But our *inner* nature—which, thanks to its "innovative activity," has brought about both development and environmental problems—is now the danger. Our threatening rational constructs have indeed, on closer inspection, arisen out of nature, out of the cell structure of Homo sapiens. The archaic concept of wantonness as violation of the relationship between man and nature is consequently still relevant but must be modified to correspond to our present circumstances.

Lost Unitary Reality?

Separating "dead" matter from its psychic dimension is foreign to the legend-telling folk. The reality of the objective psyche is bound up with the here and now of daily life in folk thought and experience. In the wake of the Enlightenment the unitary reality of the traditional worldview was split. Supernatural phenomena no longer exist "naturally" for rational people, and with their demise the spiritual dimension vanished from the world about us. Owing to this separation, much superstition has indeed been banished from the world; but knowledge of the reality of the psychic dimension and the proper way of behaving toward those powers has likewise been lost.

Thanks to the discoveries of modern psychology, we recognize today the collective unconscious as the source where legends origi-

---

[105]Renner, op. cit. p. 253.

The Devil's Rock in Göschenen, Canton Uri. What legends report as external experience is often a symbolic expression of a psychic reality.

nate.[106] Viewed in this light, the empirical materials in legends show us by example the right or the wrong behavior toward the archetypal contents of the unconscious that confront archaic man only externally, in projected form. In the inner experience of the objective psyche, the primordial connection via *participation mystique* between individual and collective or human and world is experienced anew as reality without, however, having to surrender the achievements of discriminating consciousness. Whenever someone experiences

---

[106]On the basis of the psychoid nature of archetypes, this statement does not exclude the phenomenon of the *genius loci*.

events and a world in a dream similar to the external world of legends, it is possible to unite our split-off archaic experience of the unitary reality of the world with the consciousness level of the age in which we live. In order to achieve this understanding of legend, however, we must attempt to understand the legend's report of external experience as a symbolic expression of a psychic reality. As various authors have demonstrated,[107] symbolic understanding is the only possibility of doing justice to these old stories and of preserving their truths.[108] With the experience of the objective psyche's reality, modern humanity becomes conscious that the spiritual aspect of nature is also capable of exerting effects. It is an autonomous counterpart, a dark, overwhelming force that can permanently affect our thought and feeling.[109] As the folk mind knew, these nature spirits are *factors* (*facere* = to do, to produce effects) that must be taken scrupulously into account, and the individual's or the community's prosperity or ruin can depend on them. A scrupulous and respectful regard for these powers of unknown nature is not only advisable but critical.

Conclusion

It is impossible within the confines of this study even to sketch all the important legend cycles to cover all the individual features of folk thought. Consequently the following conclusions summarizing this chapter on the folk legend make no claim to completeness but simply enumerate fundamental features of this worldview.

The legend-telling folk live simultaneously in two worlds. Beside the concrete here and now, there is also present a spiritual here and

---

[107]E.g., Emma Jung, "The Anima as an Elemental Being"; Ammann, *Tannhäuser im Venusberg*; Isler, *Die Sennenpuppe*.

[108]See Isler, *Die Sennenpuppe*, p. 38. Isler continues: "But this is in no way intended to create the impression that the legend-tellers understood their stories symbolically. The narrators understand their stories just as they tell them: as concrete actuality. A witch is a witch, a poor soul is in fact a deceased person who has not yet found peace, etc. The sense of the events is given in and with the story; nobody would think of seeking another meaning 'behind' the story. Nor, at this level, do legends have need of any other explanation than the continual discussion, commentary, and elaboration through additional stories, as happens when stories are told at social gatherings. But as soon as rational criticism is leveled at the legend, it is immediately rejected as untrue. The enlightened person believes he can prove his spiritual independence most readily by renouncing all that old rubbish with its obvious impossibilities as quickly as possible. But then everything that constituted the truth of his soul is lost, and the traditional folk knowledge concerning this truth is also lost."

[109]For additional information on this, the reader is referred to the broad field of psychopathology.

now that the primordial sensibility can always experience. In folk thought and feeling, as we can gather from legends, life is not restricted to what we can factually comprehend with our sense organs. Embedded in the past in the presence of the ancestors, and oriented toward the future in the belief in life after death, material existence in this world is relativized in folk thinking by a continual relationship to a dimension of spirit and soul. In this worldview the spirit-matter pair of opposites, just like the individual-environment pair are relative, that is, related to each other and forming a whole only when taken together. *Materia*, the space in which one lives, has a spiritual component and also carries connection to the ancestors. Conversely, spirits can leave "concrete impressions" in their wake according to folk belief. Likewise the life of the individual is always bound up with the experienced world and community, not only in the economic sense but also spiritually and emotionally; if the individual behaves wantonly toward the transpersonal powers, it makes a difference. For according to legend, wantonness exerts its effects to the disadvantage of the entire community under certain circumstances (for example in a legend of the Blüemlisalp in which an entire alp is destroyed by an "It" because of the wantonness of one individual). By the same token, the individual is not alone when suddenly face to face with an experience of something overwhelming. On the one hand this is due to empirical folk wisdom concerning these things—as is passed on in legends and customs—and on the other, it is thanks to the support offered by Christian faith.

In legend, we find things of the world *beyond* and things of *this* world linked and experienceable, albeit only occasionally or at certain times or in certain places. In legend, the spiritual element is described as immanent in matter and yet exerting its effects outside of matter. Powers of the beyond are helpful and destructive, depending on the attitude with which humanity approaches them. The highest and deepest, good and evil, the spiritual and the concrete, meaning and nonsense, belief and knowledge—in short, the world of opposites is paradoxically united in legend. We can see then that the legend-telling folk live with paradox in all dimensions, indeed that the folk view of the world—to use Max Lüthi's expression—rested on a foundation of paradox. According to this archaic folk concept, the world is both an animate counterpart compelling reverence, and a practical foundation of life from which humanity must wrest food and shelter with toil. The protection of Christianity is a reality, but the individual must also be able to deal with the powers beyond *totally alone* and even to redeem spiritual beings of the world beyond. This tension of opposites, incomprehensible in any rational way, can be expressed as paradox—a state of affairs that modern natural science can help us to understand.

According to this primordial view of the world, what forges the bond between the opposites of spirit and matter, as well as between ego and external world, is the experienced totality of the so-called processes of the soul or in other words, the experienced *reality of the soul*. As the Enlightenment dissolved the dimension known as the soul, the pairs of opposites fell asunder. Only in our century do we see the relation between these opposites on a new level, thanks to discoveries in physics, biology, and psychology. The Copernican transformation in our general *Weltanschauung* is not intended to devalue our natural scientific-mechanistic view of the world. On the other hand, what the contemporary increase in knowledge allows us to find our way into again is the worldview of our ancestors; and consequently their knowledge concerning the conduct of life in this world increases in value. Despite Copernicus, for us the sun still rises in the East—that is to say, in our daily lives the sun turns about the earth, regardless of the knowledge that we, along with the earth, actually revolve about the sun. But where it is a question of larger-scale or fundamental interconnections, we base our understanding on a more objective worldview and orient our research toward contemporary knowledge of those interconnections. Similarly, when we are faced with fundamental decisions about humanity and environment, and especially in the context of regional and agrarian policy, we can hardly avoid utilizing the more objective surveyor's tools, which are more accepted today and which compel us to keep the relativity of the opposites in view as we acknowledge the reality of the psyche.

In complementarity to the Christian concept of faith, we discover humanity in legend face to face with a chthonic *fascinosum, numinosum*, and *tremendum*: supreme values originate out of the darkness of the earth. Where legends are told, people are still firmly anchored in Christian faith. But in addition to reverence of the Christian Trinity with its masculine character, a central feature of folk thinking appears in reverence and respect for the divine in creation, in *mater materia*. Reverence for nature is a central feature of folk piety that complements the view promulgated by the church in a compensatory fashion.[110] Consequently the folk mind, being close to instinct, is charac-

---

[110]In the area of folk piety, Protestant and Catholic have always been much closer than current labels would lead one to believe. (On this see Scharfe, Schenda, and Schwant, *Volksfrömmigkeit, Bildzeugnisse aus Vergengenheit und Gegenwart*, p. 7; also p. 13.)

terized not by the will to rule over nature or to subdue it, but rather to fit into nature in the best way possible.

We can conclude from the legends that the folk mentality is aware of a spirituality in nature that can be helpful or destructive depending on the attitude humanity assumes toward it. This spiritual aspect in nature is, according to folk thinking, also a source of knowledge. Without exception, the legendary descriptions of this nature spirit match what modern psychology says of the spirit of the unconscious. This spirit of nature reveals itself, for example, in the unexpectedly meaningful structure of a dream that can give life totally new (i.e., creative) impulses and insights. To the extent that the unconscious has really revealed itself as a source of creative impulses, rural development policy—which also hopes to promote innovation—must actively turn to this realm, without, however, wanting to capture the "creative dwarfs."

In countless folk legends that have been handed down, the living, experienced world of our archetypal background arises before our eyes. It is the background out of which the conscious world arises, which informs it, and into which it sinks back in the evening. Legends therefore tell of the existence of a collective dimension of spirit and psyche and the correct relations with this world of the archetypes, which can be humanity's blessing or curse. In this sense we can understand legends as pointing to the correct way to include the dimension of spirit and soul in our concrete here and now. Legends are signposts that, over the course of generations, have crystallized out of the experience of the people as folk wisdom. Only when the reality and extensive autonomy of the spiritual-emotional dimension was lost as a consequence of the Enlightenment, did knowledge about how to take this reality into account seem to become superfluous. Today, however, we realize more and more that we lack something in our one-sided objectivity and rationality; when we ignore the autonomy of the archetypal world, it presents a threat to our planned world. In its dealings with autonomous, demonic powers, which we experience today in altered shape as the autonomous dynamics of ideology and the force of circumstances, the folk mind has something to offer because of its intuitively grasped, more comprehensive view of the world.

Our examination of the folk legend concludes our investigation of the primary features of folk thinking. But we would be ignoring a most essential side of this primordial view of life is we did not include the folk manner of acting and living in our observations. Hence in the sections below we shall turn our attention to folk usage and custom.

Lourds Grotto in Unterschächen, Canton Uri. Reverence for nature is a central feature of folk piety.

Expressions of the Folk Mind in Custom and Usage

Introductory Comments

The spiritual attitude of the people finds concrete expression in the daily cycle lived in accordance with custom.[111] Consequently we can understand each type of folk activity as usage or practice. "Since the essence of the people is determined by community and tradition, usage or practice can be defined as a way of acting handed down through a community of people that is felt to be correct or binding."[112] In the following we will abide by this definition of usage. For the sake of order we want to clarify three additional concepts at the outset. If we understand *usage* or practice to mean a way and manner of acting that is prescribed but not necessarily imperative, we use the term *custom* to designate fundamental rules of social behavior the nonob-

---

[111]Weiss, *Volkskunde der Schweiz*, p. 155.
[112]This definition is based that of P. Geiger quoted in Weiss, loc. cit.

servance of which is, if necessary, punishable by sanctions.[113] We designate the individual forms of a usage—for example, noise, water, or fire—as *elements of usage*. If an action in accordance with usage is a symbolic expression for a deeper meaning, then we speak of a *rite*.[114] Consequently we distinguish rites from the mere behaviors of human and animal that imply no deeper significance. Ethologists are concerned with the latter. Now if in the context of the present work we pursue the expressions of folk thinking in usage, we can hardly even begin to shed light on the extremely broad range of practices. This is a task reserved for the specialist. Here we can be concerned only with roughly sketching the shape and color of certain features of folk thinking from the vantage point of the folk way of acting.

According to their function in folk life, practices or usages are usually grouped into so-called usage cycles that intersect:[115]

   a) *the usages of a sacred and a profane nature pertaining to the daily cycle;*

   b) *the annual usages in regard to work and the church pertaining to the course of the year;*

   c) *the usages belonging to the course of life, the so-called* rites de passage; *and*

   d) *the usages not restricted to a certain time, such as church practices, forms of social intercourse, legal usages, and work methods.*

In the following discussion we will limit ourselves to examining individual aspects of the first three usage cycles. They elucidate the primordial, folk feeling for life as cyclical repetition: the endless chain of waxing and waning, of day and night, summer and winter, life and death. The individual who thinks along folk lines experiences his life embedded in this cyclicality.

Concerning Time-Bound Usages

If we visualize the three cycles of the day, the year, and the individual life, which fundamentally inform folk usage, we are struck in each instance by the appearance of four cardinal or turning points:

---

[113] After Planck and Ziche, *Agrarsoziologie*, p. 121.

[114] Weiss defines "rite" as the expression of beliefs. However, that seems to me too narrowly conceived, especially in light of Adolf Portmann's investigations into the "rites of animals" (Portmann, "Riten der Tiere," p. 357–401).

[115] Details on this can be found in Weiss, *Volkskunde der Schweiz*, p. 162f; the usages pertaining to the daily round, however, are absent from Weiss's overview.

Figure 6. The Prominent Transitions in the Course of a Day, a Year, and a Lifetime.

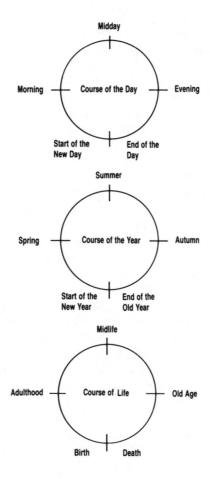

These four points are distinct times of transition that are characterized in folk life by very specific modes of behavior determined by usage.

Concerning Usages in the Course of the Day

In folk life the course of the day is characterized by a special regard for the time frames of morning, midday, and evening. If sunrise and sunset are the natural boundaries of day and night,[116] the middle of the day is the zenith and also a turning point, in many ways analogous to midnight.[117] For the primordial sensibility, morning signifies the end of sinister darkness; the evening, by contrast, is the beginning of the time of nocturnal ghostly beings. At the midday hour we are familiar with the folk idea of the *daemon meridianus*, the incubus that can send fatigue, hallucination, and sunstroke,[118] whereas at the midnight hour the spirits of the dead and similar beings, as is well known, come to life.[119]

For archaic man, every time of transition is fateful, be it in the course of a day, a year, or a life. What does the new day bring? The new year? Will the psychically important transition from childhood mentality to the adult consciousness of responsibility succeed? These are questions that reflect one of humanity's uncertainties, for at times of such transitions into the "no-man's-land" between the old and the new, archaic man feels especially exposed to evil forces and dependent on helpful spirits.[120] Since such feelings are generally human or archetypal, we also find universal agreement in the form of usages that have grown out of them. Countless protective and defensive practices aid in the emotional mastery of these fateful transition times.[121]

In Switzerland church bells originally had such a protective function. At least three times a day they have a longer chime, namely at the transition times: morning, midday, and evening. This practice reaches back into the early Middle Ages. "After the Ave Maria and the extended veneration of Mary gained equal footing with the Lord's Prayer and had become generally popular, beginning in the eleventh century, all churches, from about the middle of the thirteenth century, introduced the ringing of the Angelus or the Ave Maria in the mornings and evenings at first, and then also at midday. Pope John XXII expressly decreed in 1326 that the Ave Maria be said three times daily (morning, noon, and evening), and that each time the call to say the Ave Maria should be given by ringing the bell."[122] Today to grasp

---

[116]On this see the *Handwörterbuch des deutschen Aberglaubens*, vol. VI, p. 576f, especially also concerning the differences between twilight and sunrise or sunset.

[117]Ibid., p. 398.

[118]Ibid., p. 399 and p. 414. According to the antique idea, the goat-footed Pan appeared to the Greek shepherds at midday and aroused *panic*.

[119]Ibid., p. 419f, ff.

[120]See Weiss, *Volkskunde der Schweiz*, p. 175.

[121]Weiss, loc. cit.; the first thorough discussion was that of Arnold van Gennep, *Le rites de passage* (Paris, 1909).

[122]*Handwörterbuch des deutschen Aberglaubens*, vol. I, p. 36f.

the meaning of the bell-ringing, we must recall that bells were not used in earlier times to sound the hour. This task was added to the sexton's list of duties only in the course of the Enlightenment, at the time when people began to plan time rationally. The original function of the bell was that of warding off demons, a function in which there was no difference between the heathen and the Christian view; for according to church teachings, the Devil and his minions are demons.[123] We can compare this protective effect of the ringing bell with the Alpine herdsman's verbal call to prayer and thus better understand it. Only in the Alpine meadows, beyond the range of the protective ringing of the bell, does the Alpine dweller have to use the golden ring to draw the protective circle against the "It." In contrast, where there is a chapel, on the Urnerboden Alp, one hears no call to prayer. There the chapel bell assumes this function.[124]

Thus the sound of the bell protects humans from unfavorable influences at the precarious times of transition during the day, as well as the year and the individual life. But the bell also mediates the relationship to the numinous, spiritual world of the beyond. It rings at all important or decisive moments of common human experience.[125] Normally at these times, the people are accustomed to pausing a few moments and reflecting. In this manner the folk consciousness is reminded by the familiar bell sound (*vox dei*) at least three times a day about the reality of a transcendent dimension, a realm that reaches beyond the daily cycle. Thus harsh, material reality is continually and repeatedly *relativized* by reminders of the existence of the immaterial world beyond.

Concerning the Usages in the Course of the Year

Let us now consider in more detail the practices having to do with the course of the year. Like the course of the day, the course of the year has special transition times in folk life. In considering them, we must imagine these two cycles as bound to one another as inseparably as the rotation of the earth on its own axis is bound to its orbit about the sun.

In agrarian communities, summer and winter are distinct opposites

---

[123]Op. cit., vol. III, p. 86f.

[124]This was the subject of a discussion among Alpine herdsmen in 1980: It was not the question of retaining or abolishing the call to prayer that occupied the dairymen, but rather that the call to prayer was not being practiced on the Alp. For knowledge of this discussion I am indebted to Uri Council member and J. Brücker.

[125]Details on the bell and its function can be found in the beautiful book by Paul Satori, *Des Buch von den Glocken* (Berlin and Leipzig, 1932).

determined by the natural rhythms of the year. Especially in mountainous areas of Switzerland, summer is the period of hard work; winter, in contrast, is the time of necessary rest and preparation, and consequently the time for reflection, rite and festival.[126] For us in Switzerland, wintertime was originally something on the order of "quitting time" and "night's rest" in the annual cycle. For the primordial mind in our northern latitudes, winter has a sinister, menacing quality hostile to life. It is the period in which humans are quite intensely reminded of illness and death, these great, dark dominants of life that again and again disrupt the clear, rational image of the world. In the dark time of winter when the nights grow longer and longer, the inner, unconscious realm of darkness evolves and develops similarly. The unconscious, as the precipitate of our ancestors' hoard of experience, is actually our ancestral realm. It is these ancestors who come to life on winter evenings when the light is dim. Hence this time is not only the time of communal storytelling but also of the cult of the dead.

Death is doubtless the most powerful event in human life. At no other point is a human so inescapably confronted with a dark, destructive superior power. For this reason the cult of the dead and belief in the dead are justly regarded as the oldest form of religion.[127] According to the Basel classical philologist and folklorist Karl Meuli, we can distinguish the following three characteristics in the archaic image of the dead:

 a) *the idea that the deceased person lives on;*

 b) *the conviction that the deceased is powerful; and*

 c) *the belief that the deceased is simultaneously good and evil.*[128]

These three basic features of the belief in the dead are for the folk mind realities to be taken very seriously. In revering the dead according to traditional usage, these three ideas find visible, external expression. This happens especially in winter when the powers of darkness come alive, "when the dead arise." Everywhere in folk life at this time we find complex practices intended to ward off and recall the dead.

---

[126]On this see Weiss, *Volkskunde der Schweiz*, p. 164.

[127]The belief in immortality as one of mankind's oldest common beliefs can be shown incontestably to have existed as early as the Neolithic Age, and this on the basis of articles interred with the dead. (See, for example, Meyer, *Heltgeschichte im überblick*, p. 38ff., and Eliade, *Der religiösen Ideen*, p. 20ff.) See also Meuli, *Gesammelte Schriften*, vol. I, p. 310ff., as well as his bibliography.

[128]Meuli, "Die Grundzüge des Totenglaubens," *Gesammelte Schriften*, vol. 1, p. 303.

The most important elements of this usage are light, noise, and masks. While the use of lights and noise generally tends to strengthen consciousness of the sinister underworld, darkness, and the stillness of death, using masks (according to Karl Meuli) grants the ancestral spirits a very concrete possibility of expression.[129]

"Masks are the dead returned; they have a claim to sacrifice and give gifts that bring good fortune."[130] Therefore the ancestral spirits are permitted to enter into relationship and make exchanges with the living in very specific ways. In the Lötschen Valley, for example, the inhabitants of the valley were haunted in a terrifying way by the *Roitschäggätä*, that is, by bands of masked youths. "They stole grain and other things and spread terror among those dwelling in the valley."[131] The disguised and masked monsters are called *Roitschäggätä*, that is, *Rauchgescheckte* (smoke-stained), because they come out of the smoke (*Rauch*) from the smokehouse chimney.[132] But according to folk belief that is where the souls of the dead members of the household live.[133] "The demons of the dead, therefore, are embodied and depicted in masked form, and the mask-wearers have the same rights and tasks as the feared and revered dead: They reprove and punish."[134] The expression "legal anarchy" has been coined for this primordial law of masks.[135] In our century we are still aware of the ancient belief that "in midwinter the underworld opens up and releases the dead for a brief time so that they can pay a visit to their living progeny."[136] We are familiar with the practice of the feast of the

---

[129]Meuli, "Schweizer Masken und Maskenbräuche," *Gesammelte Schriften*, vol. 1, p. 177–250; general discussion of masks, op. cit., p. 33–299. Animal-headed masks ("beaked goat," etc.) represent our animal ancestors (see op. cit., p. 236). Processions with candle-lit hats, originally were probably lighted heads (op. cit., p. 234), are an especially impressive image for the "night people"! Even if today this view of Meuli's is no longer generally accepted, we must still recognize in it one important source for the use of masks.

[130]Meuli, op. cit., p. 240; the immutability of the mask is a symbol for the eternally valid element of the archetype that has come alive in it.

[131]Meuli, "Lebender Brauch im Lötschental," op. cit., p. 179; additional possibilities for explaining the use of masks are to be found in Chappaz, "Les maskes du Lötschental." In the present context we refer only to Meuli's doubtless most ingenious interpretation. For this reference I am indebted to Prof. Paul Hugger, Zürich.

[132]Meuli, op. cit., p. 181, note a. According to an ancient view, the spirits and souls of the dead are constituted of a subtle substance like a breath of air or smoke.

[133]Meuli, op. cit., p. 182.

[134]From Weiss, *Volkskunde der Schweiz*, p. 166.

[135]In the case of recent youth unrest in Swiss cities, one often got the impression of seeing something of this element of usage flaring up in perverted form, especially thanks to the passivity of the bystanders who, in a way, thereby legitimized the young people's anarchy.

[136]Meuli, op. cit., p. 520.

ancestors' visit, for example in the Hasli Valley. "At night the night people come. What is still on the table is for them," an old grandmother told one of Booder's informants following a meal of milk and bread on Christmas Eve.[137] But these powers from the beyond demand not only food, sacrifices, and attention; they also bring mysterious gifts. This element of usage was preserved as one of the roots of our giving of Christmas gifts when the pagan midwinter festivals were replaced by the Christian celebration of Christmas.[138] "The practice of children's hanging up their stockings or placing their shoes outside the door or by the open hearth (or today next to the heating vent) is preserved primarily in western Switzerland and derives from the demons' mysterious distribution of gifts."[139] Spirits—especially the spirits of the dead—like to enter houses via the chimney or dwell there, as already mentioned.

Before we concern ourselves with the timing of this practice at the winter transition, we must recall one other aspect of traditional winter actions, namely the entire cult of fertility. As the mythology of the Great Mother reveals, the cult of the dead and the fertility cult are closely interconnected in their origin.[140] "The veneration of the powerful spirits of the dead in part served the purpose of assuring their blessing for the fertility of the fields."[141] Thus we find both for the celebrations honoring the dead and for the cult festivals intended to assure the fertility of the new year, a protracted period of rites and celebrations extending from the fateful time of the winter solstice up into spring itself.[142]

To better understand the fundamental features of this entire complex of practices and usages that grew up around the fertility cult and the cult of the dead, we must once again recall how very sinister the winter transition is. Obviously the year comes to an end after the harvest in autumn with the now-dormant vegetation.[143] For plant life, the new year with its fateful uncertainties has not yet arrived; for humanity, it commences only in spring. Until then one must wait.

---

[137]Sooder, *Zelleni us em Haslital*, p. 24f, cited in Meuli, loc.cit.

[138]Geiger, "Weinachtsfest und Weinachtsbaum," p. 229ff.

[139]Weiss, *Volkskunde der Schweiz*, p. 171.

[140]Think, for example, of the Demeter-Persephone myth. The Great Mother Hecate is, on the one hand, she who grants life and, on the other hand, the sinister mistress of all ghosts and demons of the dead.

[141]Weiss, *Volkskunde der Schweiz*, p. 165.

[142]See Weiss, op. cit., p. 164.

[143]Concerning harvest practices and usages, the reader is referred to Weber-Kellermann, *Erntebrauch in der ländlichen Arbeitswelt des 19. Jahrhunderts aufgrund der Mannherdtbefragung in Deutschland von 1865.*

Open chimney, once typical in most peasant houses in the northern Alpine region. According to folk belief, the souls of the dead members of the household lived in or entered the house by way of the chimney.

Like the practices and usages pertaining to the course of a day, the practices concerning the dead and fertility also have a protective function, now for the entire duration of the uncertain transition period from the cold to the botanical new year. The following diagram shows the interconnectedness of the "reawakening practices and usages" in the cycles of a year, of a day, and a human life:

Figure 7. The Interconnection among Reawakening Cults as Seen in the Cycles of the Day, the Year, and Human Life.

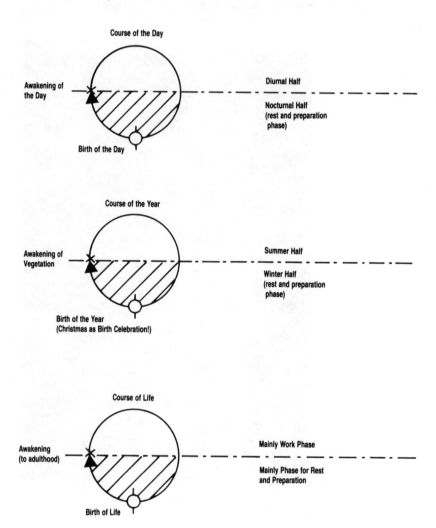

The period following new birth is especially vulnerable and dangerous. What is newly created evokes destructive, dangerous powers. During pregnancy[144] as well as during and following the birth of a child, the evil spirits are exorcised through complicated practices.[145]

---

[144]See the *Handwörterbuch des deutschen Aberglaubens*, vol. VII, p. 1414f.
[145]Ibid., vol. III, p. 415ff.

The twelve days following Christmas are the sinister days of the Army of the Dead.[146] And the hour after midnight is generally the ghost hour, the hour belonging to the dead.[147] Here we must of course add the proviso that for the archaic sensibility, the course of the day begins not at midnight but at evening[148] or at sunrise. In this sense, our diagram is only an aid to clarify the inner coherence of meaning among the three cycles. An additional critical transition is the awakening of the day, the year, or adulthood. Practices having to do with a blessed start of the day or of work are well known.[149] The beginning of spring is still ceremoniously observed at Easter with fertility symbols, rabbits and easter eggs. And we are even familiar with the original rite of initiation into adulthood, now in the modified forms of religious confirmation and military service.[150]

To illustrate, let us mention a transition and renewal practice pertaining to the annual cycle that, besides having significance as a *rite de passage*, reveals the profound, invisible bonds between a person and nature. A common practice in the Salzburg area and the Tirol is known as the *Bachlkoch*. In his article on the Christmas guest and the sacred meal,[151] Richard Wolfram discusses this festival, which is still celebrated in this century. In describing this practice, we will follow Wolfram's account, but in greatly condensed form.

> *The main dish at the midday meal on December twenty-fourth in the mountain regions around Salzburg is the* Bachlkoch, *a flour porridge with honey, butter, and caraway or anise. It is often eaten directly out of the pan, which is not the usual practice. This meal, taken at 11 A.M., marks a distinctive turning point and is a year-counter: "Well, I've got my forty* Bachlkoch," *a person says when he wants to express that he is forty years old. A particular power and efficacy is ascribed to the* Bachlkoch. *It is said over and over that the* Bachlkoch *grants "strength*

---

[146]The Twelve Days of Christmas are, in terms of the calendar, the twelve additional days needed to make up the difference between the lunar and the solar years. These are the twelve days between December 25 and January 6. For more detail on this, see the *Handwörterbuch des deutschen Aberglaubens*, vol. XII, p. 979–992.

[147]Often it is also the hour before midnight, for example in the Hasli Valley (Sooder, *Zelleni us em Haslital*, p. 24f.)

[148]Especially in prehistoric Indogermanic times. See the entry under "Abend" (evening) in the *Handwörterbuch des deutschen Aberglaubens*.

[149]Countless rites among primal peoples take place at sunrise.

[150]In earlier times, the youth received his first watch and his first long trousers on this occasion—entry into consciousness of time and into the man's "shell." See von Franz, "On the Religious Background of the Puer Aeternus Problem," p. 142.

[151]Wolfram, "Weinachtsgast und Heiliges Mahl." I am indebted to Prof. Paul Hugger for knowledge of this article. We also find elements analogous to this practice in Swiss Alpine areas.

that lasts for the entire year." In eating this food, then, we perform an "efficacious act" that determines whether things will thrive for the entire coming year. But this applies not only to humans; people share this food with the natural powers, too. Again and again it is told how, before eating, the farmer spoons four servings of Bachlkoch *onto a wooden plate, sets it on the roof of the house, and leaves it there 'till only a little remains on the plate. This is thought of as a sacrifice to the four elements. In various places, a few spoonfuls of* Bachlkoch *are buried in the orchard, the fields, and the meadow. The benefits of the* Bachlkoch *are intended especially for the fruit trees, hence the words: "Tree, eat! Then next year you'll bear well, too."*[152]

Along with the elements and plants, animals are included in this practice. The following is reported by Wolfram: "Before eating the *Bachlkoch*, the father takes the pan with the porridge and stands in front of the house. All the children go with him. He turns around three times holding the pan and silently invites all the animals and plants to join in the meal. Afterward he again goes into the kitchen and sets the pan on the table. The *Bachlkoch* is then eaten."[153] "This ritual act," as Wolfram aptly expresses it, "bespeaks a downright mystical feeling for the unity and solidarity of all life in a peasant homestead; a veritable community of life, expressed in the symbolism of a community of food!"[154] It embraces not only people, but also the elements, meadows, fields, and animals.[155] "One would hardly suppose that people would have the strength for such thoughts and feelings in our century."[156] One might describe this annual ritual of transition into the new cycle of plant life as humanity's reconnecting with all of nature. In a primordial, magical manner, the special food grants a renewal of humanity's relatedness to the realm of creation entrusted to us. This imparts to the individual the feeling of containedness: one experiences oneself again within a larger context. An inner security evolves, allowing confidence in looking toward the new, unknown year. This, indeed, is the deeper meaning of this New Year's practice.

Of course, much more could be said about the rich practices involved in the annual cycle of folk life. But as was emphasized at the beginning of our discussion, we want to restrict ourselves to a few

---

[152]Wolfram, op, cit., p. 2 and p. 3 (abbreviated).
[153]Ibid., p. 7.
[154]Ibid., p. 9.
[155]In part after Wolfram, loc. cit.
[156]Wolfram, loc. cit.

major points. Only one additional aspect should be mentioned, which is the specific rhythmical order of time observed in actions following usage and custom. Just as the hours of the day are not all the same in intensity and mood as they are experienced by the people,[157] so the days of the calendar year are not simply dates, "but individuals, named after the saints who are their patrons," as Karl Meuli observed in his discussion of peasant customs and usages. Continuing, Meuli says: "Up into our times, the calendar, the *Brattig* (from the Latin *Praktica*), played an important role. Whether a day was favorable or unfavorable for a certain undertaking was often decided according to interrelationships that became meaningful only at that deepest level of thought, the magical or superstitious: whether one would shear sheep in Aries, plant beans (in German: *Bohner*) on St. Boniface, or sow flax seed during Passion Week because the Savior was wrapped in a linen cloth."[158]

How seriously people in Catholic areas take the relationship of the days to the history of the saints can still be seen today in the partially successful retention of the numerous feast days in the ecclesiastical calendar. In Canton Schwyz, for example, the parliament and the government wanted to abolish St. Joseph's Day as a holiday. But a referendum was held and the popular majority defeated the proposal, even though such feast days are not among the usual federal holidays and undesirable from the standpoint of rational scheduling of work.[159] In Canton Graubünden (which is both Catholic and Protestant), some Catholic holidays that could fall on a work day were generally postponed to the following Sunday for just such reasons. A laborer who was also involved in farming in the predominantly Catholic community of Brigels assured me that shifting the feast days to accommodate factory work was good. "But," he added somewhat lowering his voice, "I wonder whether they [the Patron Saints] will put up with it?"[160] In this answer the coexistence of the two forms of thought is clearly expressed. As a factory worker he has one foot in the rational world where there are no factors other than reason to be taken into account. But as a parttime farmer, he is, with the other foot, still in close touch with the soil, tradition, and the way of

---

[157]"It used to be taken as a solid truth among the folk that there are lucky and unlucky hours for being born and for dying as well as for man's entire doing and creating." (Müller, *Sagen aus Uri*, vol. 3, p. 307.)

[158]Meuli, *Gesammelte Schriften*, vol. 1, p. 254.

[159]I am indebted to Klaus Korner, Einsiedeln, for information concerning this referendum.

[160]Survey in connection with a research project on agriculture as part-time source of income, August, 1980.

thought associated with that—namely, folk thought. To that way of thinking belongs the reality of the protective spirit of each and every Patron Saint, whom one is well advised to keep in a beneficent mood.

Concerning Traditional Practices in the Life of the Individual

Like the course of the day and the course of the year, which are communally structured by usage rules, the course of the individual's life is also marked by well-defined stages.[161] Every transition into a new phase of life is eased and made safe by specific rites of transition.[162] In all the important events or changes in life—birth, puberty, marriage, birth of a child, or death—the individual is not alone but can feel safely held and contained in the community. The individual is thereby relieved in part from the burden of mastering a transition phase alone, since the entire community takes part in it through *participation mystique*. If, from our contemporary point of view, we observe this enigmatic folk practice that regulates all essential aspects of life—even marriage and burial—in a communal manner, we soon must question the meaning of the whole. Today we consider individual freedom the highest good. We can, for instance, undertake something instead of observing an obligatory Sunday rest at home. We have the freedom to spend Christmas at home, in the mountains, or in the Canary Islands; and in many places marriage has become a completely individual event involving only the two people. Is this precious individual freedom a reaction to earlier coercion stemming from old-fashioned superstition? In order to answer this question we must examine the origin and meaning of usages and practices more closely.

Meaningful and Meaningless Practices

Just as folk legends are often dismissed today as old wives' tales, people often rashly condemn or condescendingly dismiss traditional practices as superstition—incomprehensible, senseless relicts from dark, ancient times. And at first glance this judgment seems to be borne out. First of all, practices that have lost their meaning are a well-known phenomenon. Among them we number traditional practices or usages that are cultivated only for external reasons, be they social pressure, the inertia of habit, or for prestige or the tourist trade.

---

[161]On this see Weiss, *Volkskunde der Schweiz*, table 2 and p. 143ff., as well as p. 173ff.
[162]See van Gennep, *Les rites de passage*.

Practices and usages of this sort leave the celebrant cold; the only thing still of importance is the form, not the content and attitude toward it. Thus the practice of saying grace can become a mere formula, and wearing traditional dress can turn into a masquerade. As Richard Weiss has demonstrated, it is an essential feature of the folk attitude that precise observance of the form of a practice is often considered more important than its meaning.[163] Doubtless that is why a traditional practice or usage can become "old hat," devoid of meaning and therefore ready for discard.

We must not, however, brand all old practices as devoid of meaning. For we know of many traditional actions in which the celebrant is not the only one gripped by something inexplicable. Outsiders may, too, be profoundly touched by a sense of meaningfulness for which their intellect has no complete explanation, be it in a celebration with lights and noise in a snowy landscape in Central Switzerland, or in the sight of a funeral procession in a Valais mountain village. When asked, participants usually cannot say *why* they perform this or that traditional act just as they do. "That's the way it's always been done," is usually the best explanation one gets. Now, to take this fact as an indication that even the participants do not know what they are doing and hence that the entire old usage is a meaningless act of magic would be a foolish fallacy. For how many people really do know why they decorate a tree with lights at Christmas or hide eggs at Easter? Surely only very few. Nevertheless the lighted tree is a part of the Christmas celebration and decorated eggs a part of Easter. Countless people would not like to miss these practices. Hence there must be a meaning in the decorated tree and the colored eggs themselves, a meaning that exerts its effect even without being understood intellectually.

In this connection let us recall the example of the Bubikon fir tree mentioned earlier. In the symbolic power of the tree we recognized a nonmaterial value that this one tree must have held for countless citizens. In a like manner, the meaning of the lighted tree and the Easter egg lies hidden in their symbolic power as images; they are both images of meaning capable of directly addressing something within the psyche of many people.

As repeatedly mentioned, symbols or archetypal images have their roots in the archetypes of the collective unconscious. In fact, the recent investigations support the idea that traditional practices and usages have their real root in the foundations of human instinct, the

---

[163]Weiss, *Volkskunde der Schweiz*, p. 158.

image-producing aspect of which we recognize as the archetype. On the one hand, human ethology has succeeded in demonstrating the instinctual origin of our gestures, customs, and practices.[164] On the other hand, psychological research can show how religious practices ultimately have their root in the collective unconscious. This aspect of traditional practices therefore arises out of the human instinctual core, too.[165] Thus a medicine man of the Oglala Sioux Indians reports in his autobiography an extremely impressive, visionary dream which, once he had told it to his tribe, had such an effect that the events in the dream were subsequently enacted as a tribal ritual.[166] "Not only Black Elk himself, but many other members of his tribe felt infinitely better after this play. . . . The ritual was not repeated because the tribe was destroyed soon after."[167]

The direct relationship between practice and legend[168] likewise shows that it is the individual's direct experiences of the unconscious that emotionally move the community, which then takes up those experiences and enacts them as religious practices and rituals. What is recounted in the legend as an event often turns somehow into a mimicked representation.[169] Hence at a certain point in time, the wild forest and mountain demons of legend come to life in the folk tale acted out by the boys of the community. Often the practice even precedes the legend in time.[170] As we have seen, in the folk legend we are dealing with spontaneous products from the collective unconscious, with something on the order of community dreams. As with the inner connection of legend and practice, the religious practice, too, ultimately has its roots in the common emotional background of the traditional community.

The origin of usages and practices in the collective unconscious also throws light on the question of why certain actions in accordance

---

[164]See additionally Eibl-Eibesfeldt, *Der vorprogrammierte Mensch*, and Eibl-Eibesfeldt, *Menschenforschung auf neuen Wegen*, as well as Portmann's especially worthwhile essay, "Riten der Tiere."

[165]See von Franz, "The Individuation Process," p. xf.

[166]Neihardt, *Black Elk Speaks*.

[167]Von Franz, op. cit., p. 228. Lame Deer gives the same report concerning the origin of the so-called "ghost dance": "One man in the Arapatio tribe sacrificed himself in a Vision Quest, and he had a dream which instructed him to start the ghost dance." (Lame Deer and Richard Erdoes, *Lame Deer, Seeker of Visions*; see all of chapter 14.)

[168]Here we must make special mention of the research results of Hans Georg Wackernagel and Otto Höfler.

[169]Wackernagel is of the opinion that, as a rule, practices traditionally handed down show more genuine and less falsified features than the reports found in legend (Wackernagel, *Beiträge zur Volkskunde*, p. 16).

[170]Summarized from Hauser, *Wald und Feld in der alten Schweiz*, p. 82.

with traditional usage and practice become community property while others do not. If an impressive sequence of images in a dream or a fantasy arises not only from the personal unconscious but from the deeper, collective layers of the psyche, then that sequence may possibly affect other persons who hear of it. The impact can be so strong that they may feel the need to give concrete expression to this revelation from the unconscious, such as in the example of the Indian medicine man. Of course, an impression of this sort on the sensibilities of a community is made only by such symbols as are adequate vehicles for expressing a collective or archetypal constellation.

In their relationship to consciousness, the expressions of the unconscious are compensatory. They attempt to correct the natural one-sidedness of consciousness, whose attitude is inimical to life. Hence we also find in traditional practices, as in the folk legend, a balance to the collective consciousness formed by Christianity, which has diminished and rejected things archetypally feminine and natural, and things dark and lowly, in favor of the light Logos principle. Indeed, the Church has attempted to replace heathen practices with a calendar of Christian feast days. But in folk life the pre-Christian reverence for nature—indeed, even including evil—has been preserved to a great extent. The pre-Christian view of the world was often imperceptibly united with the new Christian view. A particularly noteworthy example of this is drawn from an investigation by the scholar of folklore and folk theater Oskar Eberle of Central Switzerland.[171] He demonstrated how the Three Kings found their way from a liturgical appearance in the church to a drama outside in the open. Eberle pointed out that in this drama a role was given, so to speak, to a fourth king, namely Herod, who represented evil, the demonic. Magnificent stagings must have developed out of this. In Savièse near Sitten a play about the Three Kings that involved various little villages and open country remained alive until 1892, according to reliable accounts. Unfortunately, they came to an end because all-too-frequent pub visits by the "Herod party" allowed it to degenerate beyond the acceptable.[172]

The Three Kings play shows the compensatory aspect of folk practice. The fantasy was able to find expression in folk life alongside the Christian view, adding the pre-Christian, dark, fourth element, namely the fourth king, to the Christian Trinity. Thus this practice

---

[171]Eberle, "Wege zum schweizerischen Theater," cited in Schwabe, *Schweizer Volksbräuche*, p. 19.
[172]Schwabe, loc., cit.

completed the Christian Trinity with the addition of its dark oppo-site.[173] The idea of a fourth king must have occurred to somebody; and since the fantasy obviously touched a general sensibility, the innovation was accepted by the folk. Today we recognize the uncon-scious as the source of unexpected ideas or fantasies. From this area of the soul a tendency seems to have emerged which seeks to com-plete the Christian trinitarian idea of perfection in a compensatory manner, through the addition of a fourth element. The Three Kings play is not an isolated example. We can see this tendency in folk practices in general. Alongside unconditional fidelity to the Christian faith, we find, in the traditional actions of the primal folk, a great reverence for natural, humble things. In contrast to the church view, folk thinking and folk practice still feel the foundations of Christianity—the Creation, the Mother of God—to be divine, too.[174] These foundations of life are also felt to be worthy of reverence and veneration—and they embrace animals, plants, and, finally, Mother Earth as well as the entire line of ancestors. This extension of Chris-tianity seems to have found a form in folk life shaped by traditional practice. What remained in a state of nature did not take the place of Christianity or of Christian consciousness, but rather was able to bond organically with Christian culture.

Today, however, this entire cultural heritage is in danger of not being understood and consequently being lost. Modern humanity now sees only the external forms of traditional practice. For the most part there is no longer the sense that behind these forms lies hidden a cultural achievement reaching back for generations. The natural ener-gies of the collective unconscious could be united with Christian con-sciousness by elaborating on and changing existing traditional prac-tices in accordance with ideas felt to be correct. Thus in folk life governed by practices geared to tradition, many natural, untamed aspects of the instinctual soul were integrated into daily life *without* having simply to discard the Christian heritage of moral differentia-tion. Since this union between our instinctual side and our ego-consciousness shaped by Christianity no longer appears to work for

---

[173]"[T]he quarternity is a more or less direct representation of the God who is manifest in his creation," Jung writes in *Psychology and Religion*, par. 101; Jung discusses this in detail in this same volume as well as in *Aion*.

[174]In this regard think of the veneration of Mary as a basic feature of Catholic folk piety; in Protestant areas this aspect was preserved up into the nineteenth and twentieth centuries in many places in the form of nature worship practices (see Strübin, *Grundfragen des Volksglaubens bei Jeremias Gotthelf*). Parenthetically, the dogma of the Assumptio Mariae (1950) arose on the basis of a great need among countless Catho-lics not belonging to the clergy.

the contemporary person (except when Christian ethics are surrendered entirely), this cultural accomplishment of our predecessors must be of particular interest to us. Yet in order to understand the meaning of traditional practice we have need of interpretation in this realm, too, just as in the instance of the folk legend. Only through understanding can the modern mind establish a bond with the folk knowledge contained in traditional practices. If we understand the meaning of folk life governed by these practices, we recognize the meaning of the instinctual soul's self-regulation. On the basis of this experience we may also find it expedient to take pains to find new forms of expression, so that the inner aspect of nature may likewise be an appropriate part of our daily life.

Meaningful Practices Despite "Different Times"

The fundamental changes in the industrial age have forced humanity to adapt. In the country, too, observance of the naturally given rhythms and their attendant practices have had to yield, to a great extent, to a modern economic system based on division of labor. The spirit of the times is mirrored, as Eduard Strübin emphasizes, in this decline: "Tradition has been overcome, materially through a civilization storming forward without limit, [and] intellectually through a rationalistic, progress-oriented mentality."[175] The traditional practices that have survived are noticeably altered. "Many practices are no longer naively exercised but purposively used, materialistically distorted and exploited."[176] To many people, practices that serve no material purpose seem doomed to decline entirely. However, that view does not withstand careful scrutiny. For in spite of all modernization, new traditions arise everywhere.[177] For example, in recent decades in Switzerland, Christmas has developed into an ecumenical memorial day for the dead.[178] One of the central elements of practice is the lighting of a candle on the grave of a deceased relative. Christian Hostettler sees the origin of this new tradition in the general dissatisfaction with the commercialization that has secularized, profaned, and emptied Christmas of meaning.[179] With all the clarity one

---

[175]Strübin, *Baselbieter Volksleben*, p. 288.
[176]Ibid.
[177]In regard to rural areas, see "Das Entstehen neuer Bräuche," in Gerber, *Handel im ländlichen Leben*, p. 222, and Strübin, op. cit., p. 274ff.
[178]From a survey conducted by the Swiss Society for Folklore; see Trümpy, "Entstehung und Ausbreitung eines neuen Brauchs," p. 185–89.
[179]Hostettler, "Grabschmuck und Grabpflege," p. 65.

could wish for, this example shows us how modern humanity—despite TV and the shopping mall—has certain needs of the soul and how it wants to express them. Probably very few persons who light a candle on the grave of a deceased relative at Christmas know that in following this grave cult they join in a long chain of tradition, their ancestors having observed very similar practices with respect to the dead at just this time of year. It is in the nature of archetypes that they manifest themselves again and again at certain times and in typical forms.[180]

The archetype—or simply the world of the dead—needs nourishment, that is, our attention; and the candle is an apt symbol. Conversely, somehow modern humanity is doubtless nourished or enriched in the exercise of this practice. What is sought or found on the pilgrimage to the cemetery is not something material but rather a soothing and a strength from the world of the dead. Despite all the bustle, Christmas still remains a time when the feeling life of humanity can be disturbed to the greatest degree, and when one would very much like to feel a certain stability in a community. Psychotherapists can tell many stories about that. The timing of the spontaneous (!) rise of this new practice (lighting candles on graves) at the winter season when nights are longest shows the living reality of the symbol-creating, regulative background of the psyche. Again and again I have had confirmation of the beneficial effect of this Christmas custom on people's emotional state. We are already familiar with the emotionally healing effect of a symbolic action in the example of the Indian practice that had its origin in the archetypal dream of a tribal member. In general, a practice having its origin in the collective spirit of the unconscious has beneficial effects on the unconscious itself by nourishing it with its own images, as it were. Therefore folk religious usages pacify the emotional background or, as the Chinese say, tame it.[181] Viewed psychologically, the disturbing or demonic forces (depression, moods, etc.) that influence consciousness represent contents of the unconscious that demand full attention. They behave as if they were "organs of the soul" that do not function properly if one

---

[180]Concerning the change in old practices and the origin of new ones, see Schmidt, "Brauch ohne Glaube." Schmidt very neatly discerns that the new school practices can be called "practices without belief" but not "practices without meaning"!

[181]On this see Granet, *Das chinesische Denken*, p. 310f.

does not treat them properly,[182] that is, adequately nourish them. To a very great extent, folk life takes these organs of the soul or archetypes of the collective unconscious into account through its traditional practices and usages.

Whenever and wherever people sense the reality of the soul, the hunger of the soul-dimension of life is also felt, hunger expressed in the need for symbolic images and actions.[183] One may then succeed, thanks to the symbolic bridge, in reestablishing a connection with the constants of human nature (archetypes).

> *The feeling [arises] that . . . life is spread out over generations — the first step towards the immediate experience and conviction of being outside time, which brings with it a feeling of* immortality. . . . *This leads to a restoration or* apocatastasis *of the lives of [the] ancestors, who now, through the bridge of the momentary individual, pass down into the generations of the future. An experience of this kind gives the individual a place and a meaning in the life of the generations, so that all unnecessary obstacles are cleared out of the way of the life-stream that is to flow through [the individual]. At the same time the individual is rescued from . . . isolation and restored to wholeness. All ritual preoccupation with archetypes ultimately has this result.*[184]

The traditional acts of folk life belong to a great extent to the cult involvement with archetypes.

Conclusions

Given the aspects of traditional practice we have considered, we can attempt to elucidate the underlying mode of thought. The spirit or the meaning of traditional practices will be outlined in summary.

As Leopold Schmidt has beautifully demonstrated, the significance of old practices ultimately lies in securing and preserving the order of the cosmos. "Again each year, as the children's song goes, again each

---

[182]Von Franz, *Projection and Re-collection*, p. 115. In regard to the meaning of traditional actions as nourishment for the archetypes, Jung said, "The archetypes are, so to speak, like many little appetites in us, and if, with the passing of time, they get nothing to eat, they start rumbling and upset everything." (McGuire and Hull, *Jung Speaking*, p. 358.)

[183]The Sukkudai on the Mentawei Islands south of Sumatra very sensibly call the figures and objects made for their festivals but serving no material purpose "toys for the soul." That gives expression not only to one aspect of that tribe's manner of thinking, but reveals something central in archaic, folk thought in general — the scrupulous attention paid to the reality of the soul.

[184]Jung, *C. W.* 9i, par. 316.

year the fire must be lighted, the disappearance of the ice from the river must be celebrated, the first violet must be sought, the first furrow plowed, the first grain harvested, again each year—the temporal order for the sake of the cosmic order. People copy it, this order of the cosmos."[185] Schmidt's basic thought is doubtless correct that the order in a traditional practice represents an active and daily participation in the creation or preservation of the order of the cosmos.[186] Through this continual connection with the processes and laws of nature, members of the folk community simultaneously experience their own dignity and deepest meaning, and recognize their significance as an integral part of cosmic temporal rhythms. Thus in the traditional practices pertaining to the course of a day, a year, and a life, a careful mindfulness of certain temporal conformities in nature is reflected. In folk life each time has its definite characteristics, favorable and unfavorable. In the phenomenon of the soul's geography we noted a consideration of the quality of space in the archaic mode of experience; and the primordial, folk mind takes the quality of *time* similarly into account.

With consideration of modern investigation into the unconscious psyche, this aspect of folk thought appears exceedingly meaningful. Empirical research on the nature of archetypes shows not only their local but also their temporal mode of activity. On the one hand, archetypes are structural dominants of spatial order; and on the other hand, they structure dynamic courses of events in a definite, typical manner. In antiquity these archetypal temporal laws were projected on the stars and led to astrology—and here we must use the word "projection" just as carefully as we used it in the instance of the *genius loci* phenomenon. In countless folk rules we find the planetary constellations included in daily life right up into current times. By scrupulous attention to the quality of time in folk usage and practice both in the daily alternation of darkness and light and in the annual feast and observance days, the transpersonal spiritual reality of archetypes was also heeded and taken seriously in its temporal aspect. In our contemporary way of life, by contrast, respect for the archetypal world has usually been preserved only in regard to the archetypal events in the life of the individual, namely birth, marriage, and death. When a close relative dies, for example, anyone can get time off from work, regardless of how irreplaceable he or she may be. But the

---

[185]Schmidt, "Brauch und Glaube," p. 301.
[186]Schmidt, op. cit., p. 303. See also the interesting parallel exposition in Granet, *Das chinesische Denken*, p. 310.

modern way of working and living gives less and less heed to the temporal quality of the course of the day and of the year.

We are, however, beginning to realize anew that the external rhythms of time correspond to inner human rhythmic needs which, despite re-education, cannot be made to vanish. Thus, for example, the loss of a regular day of *real* rest and reflection, or of scheduled periodic holidays and feast days is recognized by experts as codeterminant of many modern emotional disturbances.[187] For this reason the practices of agrarian and manual-labor societies, attuned as they are to natural rhythms, are by no means old hat in defiance of the modern, rational economic order. On the contrary, we must learn to experience as a reality once again the observance of a continual change in the quality of time, so that we may align our way of life to it. Research still has many laws to discover in this area, laws that, in part, have already been intuitively recognized and observed in folk wisdom.[188]

In the security offered by traditional practices concerning transitions in the course of the day and the year, as well as the transitions into new phases of an individual's life, we recognize a most important and valuable mode of correct behavior in typical human situations. Again and again we are confronted with few uncertainties that nonetheless have long been known to humanity. To cope with such novelty, the individual needs the support and the aid in orientation provided by general human experience with just these transitions. This happens externally by way of community practices. Consequently the individual does not feel alone at such times of transition but is supported by the community, be it at nightfall, at the dark time around Christmas, or at the "fateful step" of marriage.

Viewed intrapsychically, traditional practices and usages aimed at mastering transitions and making them safe embody a projection of emotional processes. "The magical practices are nothing but the projections of psychic events, which are here applied in reverse to the psyche, like a kind of spell on one's own personality."[189] For this reason, traditional practices are not only an expression but also an effect. The images given external form, whose origin lies ultimately in the unconscious, exert an effect on their creator. As images from the unconscious, they are a symbolic expression of the archetypal back-

---

[187]See, for example, Greverus, "Frankfurter Feste, von wem? – für wen?," p. 7–16.

[188]In our modern individualistic culture, so-called "biorhythms" are limited to consideration of the individual course of life.

[189]Quoted from Jung, *The Secret of the Golden Flower*, p. 103. (New York: Harcourt, Brace & World, 1931/1962).

ground; conversely, however, this background is also apprehended through the symbol. Consequently, in traditional practice, especially in a practice pertaining to a transition, the uniqueness of consciousness in the present moment is united with the immortality of the instinctual soul; and in this union the individual feels the "ground under his feet" needed for mastering life.

Summary

Investigation of folk legend and traditional practice has clarified the characteristic features of the folk way of thinking and acting. Probably the most important feature of this primordial manner of thought is the continual and careful heeding of a spiritual dimension. Be it the spiritual aspect in matter, in the landscape, or in the flow of time, we encounter the inclusion of an nonmaterial reality everywhere in folk thought. This primordial experience of certain qualitative characteristics of space and time and the need to bring life into harmony with these facts is reflected in the folk feeling of *orderedness*. By this we understand the conviction that all happenings in this world correspond to a meaningful, divine plan. The primordial, folk *Weltanschauung* does not experience the divine only as spiritualized and freed from the earthly, but also in creation itself, in the meaningful interaction of waxing and waning. Thereby the dark and the awful sides of creation are, for folk sensibility, felt to be the night or winter aspect of the divine; thanks to this conception, folk sensibility can emotionally master the fateful blows in life as being divinely ordained.

Chapter 16

Participation Mystique and Relationship

Justification

We return to the question raised earlier: What is the essence of a viable social relationship in the wake of the dissolution of *participation mystique*?[1] This is an especially important question for rural and agrarian sociology, since in rural communities people are dependent on well-functioning social relationships. For despite the change from a village community held together by *participation mystique* to the present-day municipality, village life has by no means been freed from unavoidable, close social contacts. Fundamentally different from an urban setting, the village is a place where people cannot simply avoid each other when there are antipathies and conflicts. If a generally unpleasant atmosphere prevails in a small village, the individual can scarcely avoid it, and for this very reason many have moved away. Therefore the essence of real social relationship is a distinctly pressing question particularly for smaller villages, towns, and sparsely populated areas.

In speaking of social relationship, we should distinguish between this term and the term *social contact*. The latter we take to mean the soulless manner in which people come together or live together. Purpose is the motivating force or the "glue" in social contact. Clear material advantage has taken the place of *participation mystique* as interpersonal relationship has been disenchanted or de-souled. The idea behind social contact is the modern notion of profitability. One invests time in social contacts and judges them according to cost and

---

[1]See the conclusion of chapter 13 in Part 4 of this work.

benefit.[2] Our uninvolved sort of social contact is an essential contributor to making our existence not so much a life as a business, to use Burkhardt's apt words once again.

In general terms the chapter entitled "Dissolution of *Participation Mystique*" pointed out that with the disenchantment of interpersonal relationships we have not attained a satisfying status. Key words for this were "isolation" and "alienation." The corresponding collective phenomena are "external control" and "social dichotomy." In the context of seeking the roots of social dichotomy, we discovered the intrapsychic origin of the problem. This theme led us to the conclusion that modern consciousness, having become rootless, must develop further. The result was the search to reconnect the modern, solitary consciousness with the common human pattern of behavior. We recognized the latter as the expression of the archaic man in us. In chapter 15, "Fundamental Characteristics of the Primordial Manner of Thought and Behavior," we outlined one possible approach that modern consciousness might take in order to enter again into a fruitful relationship with the bygone world of our ancestors. In that approach we familiarized ourselves with the chief characteristics of the structure of needs of the common man in us. Taking that as our foundation, we now want to examine the question of the renewal of the community. In order to keep our reflections within a social-historical context, we again take the primordial life in the village community, based on *participation mystique*, as our point of departure.

The Search for Renewal of the Community

The nature of our tradition-oriented village community is often misunderstood, because the current concept of "community" (*Gemeinschaft*) often designates entirely other forms of human social life than that in a village community. For example, the concept of community is used in communist ideologies that believe we can get at the shadow side of self-preservation instincts by submitting individuals to a *Gleichschaltung* in a "people's community," that is, by bringing everyone into line in forced conformity and "equality." But the proponents of alternative movements, too, speak of community when they form themselves into groups. In what is usually an all too idealistic way, they believe that they can create new communities if the limiting

---

[2]In a recent bulletin directed to managers, one could read the recommendation that one should cultivate social contact only with persons who could be of some use in one's professional advancement!

external conditions are right and that divisive egotism will vanish in these perfect communities. The reality of these modern forms of community, unfortunately, generally looks quite different from the way it is propagandized in slogans such as equality and fraternity.[3] This is why, in the following discussion, we must distance ourselves from both of these affect-laden depictions of community if we want to form an image of interpersonal relationships in a village community that even approximates reality.

Numerous intersecting social groupings support a village community.[4] The most prominent are, of course, the natural groupings like family, relatives, the two sexes, the married, and the single. In addition, we find quite diverse affiliations based on work and ownership, such as neighborhoods, groups sharing wells, paths, forests, and alpine meadows, as well as political and religious groupings.[5] Each individual participates in several of these social structures. The finely worked tapestry of the village community comes into being thanks to these numerous intertwinings of relationship. With this crude sketch, nothing would be farther from the mark than imagining life in a village community as idyllic, informed by altruism and brotherhood. As Arnold Niederer emphasizes in his work, interpersonal relationships in such a community are indeed most profoundly personal, but thoroughly unsentimental.[6] Thus authority relationships are not incompatible with village community. They result from the differences in birth, age, physical strength, skill, intellectual endowment, and property.[7] Correspondingly, the forms of community life are not based on appeals to brotherhood and selflessness. Various "pecking orders" are sober realities in a village community and as familiar as the rights and duties of the individual. Richard Weiss calls this an organic order, i.e., the relation of the parts among themselves is in accord with nature, is uniform, and meaningfully comprehensible.[8]

In the traditional village community with its close marriage circle, moving to another village happens infrequently. Therefore people naturally know each other and indeed have since childhood. Nobody can fool anybody; everybody knows everybody else's good and bad

---

[3]Recently the community of Longo Mai, in certain respects worthy of support for its activities, had to be publicly confronted with the nonexistence of the power devil they believed in.

[4]Details in Weiss, *Volkskunde der Schweiz*, p. 26ff., and, as an example, see Niederer, *Gemeinwerk im Wallis*.

[5]Niederer, op. cit., p. 17.

[6]Ibid.

[7]Quoted in part from Niederer, op. cit., p. 18.

[8]Weiss, *Volkskunde der Schweiz*, p. 333.

sides. People know their fellow villager's history and consequently have no idealistic illusions about human nature. Everybody has their own shadow of the past consisting of the good and the less good; and nobody can make this past disappear by the elegant trick of changing address or circle of acquaintance. Of course, the well-known disadvantage of such intimate familiarity is that a transgression sometimes marks a person for a lifetime.

In a traditional village community, however, people are not only well acquainted and consequently linked with the past of everybody else in the village but also linked beyond that with the ancestors' past,[9] which finds expression in a spiritual presence of the dead. The spirits of the dead—and the spirit world in general—are capable of bringing benefit as well as calamity and ruin. This is why the individual is intent upon paying these spiritual realities the necessary attention with the help of various rites.[10] Since time immemorial, humanity has had to experience what promotes and what threatens life in the external physical world, learning to avoid its dangers and retrieve its treasures. Likewise, humanity has also had to find a modus vivendi with the good and the evil that comes from the spirit world, which we recognize today as largely projection of the collective unconscious. Thus not only the personal past with its failings but also the current presence of demons is, for the person living in a village community, a continual and immediately experienceable reality. Here, in my opinion, we touch upon a central aspect of the folk way of life: Because the impersonal-demonic realm is a directly experienceable reality for the individual, he or she also feels the unconditional necessity not to be destroyed by these dark forces of nature, i.e., to be possessed by them. Community institutions arose reflecting this knowledge of the presence of dark powers (which we now recognize as belonging to human nature). To a large degree, the sacred and profane life of the people takes into account the reality of nature, including human nature, which consists of both good and bad; yet this happens without contemplation.

With the ascendancy of individualistic culture which, in principle, rests entirely on the field of individual consciousness, this relation-

---

[9]The community-promoting element of common ancestors naturally also plays an essential role in village communities.

[10]Marie Metrailler, who lived until her death in 1979 in the Valais' mountain village Evoléne, said of magical practices: "You might think it a simple woman's trick, a stupid practice; but it's more subtle than you think. Behind all those popular magical practices there is a lost knowledge, a forgotten science." (Metrailler, *La Poudre de Sourire*, p. 117.)

ship to our emotional background vanished. Along with it, knowledge of the destructive elements in our psychic constitution also vanished. Only in this way can one explain today's widespread belief that people can master evil, the dangerously destructive forces in the world, simply by doing good. By itself, wanting to be good unfortunately falls far short of adequately including the reality of the devilish side in us. How many devilish things have happened and still happen in the name of Good! In the same way, it is a disastrously optimistic delusion to believe that we can and must have only a particular, ideal form of society (eliminating possible opponents of such an ideal) so that genuine community can again arise on earth. Increased mobility enables us to separate from the shadow of our past;[11] and the disenchantment of the world around us has made us blind to the reality of the demonic. For this reason, a renewal of community life becomes possible only if and when individuals take it upon themselves to recognize and then to settle accounts with their own capacity for evil as an intrapsychic reality.

The contemporary search for a renewal of life in a community is justified. Ethology shows us how much the human being still has a strong herd instinct despite individual culture and therefore prizes individualized alliances and associations.[12] For this reason, the loss of an enduring culture of relationship, such as can be observed more and more today in overcrowded areas, can no longer be viewed as progress worthy of pursuit. For the signs of psychic distress that result from the uninvolved and frequently changing contacts of a modern urbanite's experiences show that urban freedom without supportive relationships cannot offer satisfaction. By "supportive relationships" we mean those relationships that are not and cannot be immediately broken off as soon as the dark side of human nature makes its appearance. The experience of the light *and* the dark side forms the foundation of an enduring relationship, and this alone gives us the feeling of security and protection. By contrast, our much-praised lack of restrictions in overcrowded areas leads all too often to a general mood that can aptly be called suburban sadness. In our age of the dissolution of relationship structures, it is probably not by chance that depression has become the most frequent psychic illness. Lack of restrictions and material advancement cannot replace sup-

[11]Separation from one's past and separation from the so-called personal shadow are related in essence.
[12]On this see Eibl-Eibesfeldt, "Ist die Versklavung durch die Technik vermeidbar?". I am indebted to Dr. Alfred Ribi for referring me to this article.

portive human relationships, relationships such as we find most distinctly in intact families, clans, and village communities.

Yet along with the great advantages of comprehensible and solidly grounded relationship structures in village communities, we are also familiar with the equally great disadvantages. Instead of security they can give a person a feeling of imposed social control. Depending on the valley, the community, the family, or even the individual, the one or the other feeling may predominate. How is that to be explained?

To tackle this question we must visualize the dissolution of *participation mystique*. The liberation of human consciousness from the constraints of our instinctual nature leads, on the one hand, to the present-day individual culture with its undeniable values; but, on the other hand, it also leads to a loosening and often the dissolution of the extended family and local affiliations. In numerous instances this process of liberation from existing ties signifies a veritable separation from each and every feeling relation to clan, community, tradition, etc. In this process of development, then, the past and the present, the old and the young, become antitheses. No longer do they form two poles of one process of life but rather come into opposition because there is no longer an emotional relationship to establish a link between them. But if the old and the new become enemies, the positive feeling of belonging to a community changes into, among other things, a predominance of the negative feeling of social control by that very community.

However, the development of consciousness need not necessarily take this relation-destroying course. Just as, for example, one son in an agrarian family can attend a modern agricultural school without finding himself opposed to the work ways of his father because of his updated knowledge, modern individual culture can enter a rural community without the automatic destruction of the local community. The decisive element in the success of an innovation or of a developmental step is, in each instance, the question of whether or not the values of the old can be integrated with the new. For only when the new is wholly separated from what has been and the latter is consequently despised as outmoded—that is, when the new no longer has any sort of inner relationship to the old—only then do what has been and what is new fall apart as opposites. Establishing a connection between these two poles is a question of relationship, and this, in turn, has to do with the domain of the soul. Because this relationship with what has been done before could be lost at every transition or step of progress, every step of progress has been regarded by the folk mind as the possibility for loss of soul. Therefore numerous folk legends tell of the necessary precautions for saving the soul from the devil of progress.[13] Consequently, the success or failure of a union between individual culture and the capacity for community is involved with the reality of the soul.

It is well known that the soul needs to be cared for. This is why we find the best conditions for a recurring, fruitful union of the two poles, "community life" and "individual culture," where the reality of the soul as well as material reality receive due consideration.

The heart of all care of the soul lies in cultivating religious symbolism, at the center of which stands the image of God. Religious symbolism forms the human capacity to comprehend; it provides the means by which an individual can grasp and cope with the compelling and divine aspects of destiny (that befall one from without and from within). If the religious symbolism of a society is an adequate expression of the divine essence, i.e., if the religious symbols are a living reality for people, they are thereby centered in a common midpoint. In such a society, the naturally given opposites are reconciled; they coexist under a supraordinated image.[14] However, this condition does not endure. A glance at the history of religion shows us how religious ideas become outdated, i.e., how with time they lose their emotional efficacy. This decaying phase of the supraordinated religious image or idea, along with its attendant arrangement of symbolic details, keeps pace with the general cultural decline; for all norms, laws, customs, and practices are ultimately dependent on the God image. All those polarities that were united by means of the supraordinated religious idea become irreconcilable opposites in the phase of decline.[15]

Christianity finds itself in this sort of phase today. The efficacy of religious symbolism is diminishing,[16] and along with it the individual's experience of the reality of the soul grows weaker. For the soul lives on the symbolic, that is, on images that express it. With the loss of living images of meaning—i.e., symbols—the relation to what is filled with meaning—i.e., spiritual life—vanishes. Then the cultivation of things pertaining to the soul is no longer meaningful. Practices shaped by religion, ceremony, or the general cultivation of relationship to the spiritual world beyond are correspondingly deemed unnecessary. But if the emotional dimension is lost as the principle that creates relationship, then only the discriminating principle of consciousness remains. Detached from the symbol-creating principle,

---

[13]For example, the legend of the Devil's Bridge in Uri.
[14]In the vernacular one then says, "The church is in the village."
[15]Details on this are to be found in Toynbee, *Studien zur Weltgeschichte*.
[16]See Strübin, *Baselbieter Volksleben*, p. 232.

which also unifies opposites, consciousness is now only capable of seeing differences that separate, be they among things or people.

Successful linkage between old and new or between community and individual culture, either in the individual or in a group, ultimately depends on whether or not the symbol-creating power of the soul is sufficiently considered. For the soul is the organ that makes possible the capacity for relationship, that subtle something that we feel as atmosphere, which someone exudes or which pervades a group. Where things of the soul can live, that atmosphere can arise; people can "get in the mood," which simply means that despite their differences, they can harmonize with or relate to each other. Seen in this light, we can understand why exclusively external modern attempts at constructing communities are doomed to failure so long as the binding principle inherent in the soul dimension is not granted due consideration. This brings us to the central question: How is this *cura animarum* to be brought about? Is attending to the reality of the soul an individual or a collective task?

Individual or Collective Reconnection?

The needs of the soul (as the organ of the potential for relationship) and the search by the modern, isolated consciousness for a relationship to the inner instinctual foundations of *participation mystique* involve one and the same thing. Since intrapsychic reality is constituted by our preconscious, instinct-guided ways of thinking and acting, we are dealing with common human nature. Yet it would be jumping to conclusions to infer, on the basis of this collective, inner nature, that collective measures could form the bridge between the deeper levels of the soul and the plane of consciousness. This is not possible because a living relationship between cultural consciousness and the collective unconscious can become a reality only on the basis of individual efforts. If detached from the individual human being, collective consciousness is just as absent as the heat from a heap of glowing coals following removal of the individual coals. The individual is the carrier of life, and hence only the individual is in a position to enter into relationship with the inner folk person who is capable of *participation mystique*.[17] The synthesis between the needs of the inner, commonly human structures and the momentary, wholly individual condition of consciousness is, for this reason, always the result of the

---

[17]The reader is referred to Jung, "The Undiscovered Self (Present and Future)," *C. W.* 10.

individual's own coming to terms with the inner collective person. Through this both the uniqueness of the individual life and the fact of membership in the collective are given their due. Since it is a matter of reconnecting individual, separate ego-consciousness to the inner faculties that are capable of *participation mystique*, the bridging action signifies a renewal of the capacity of the modern, isolated person to feel connected with others in the primordial manner.[18] Consequently, this step enables the modern person to enter into *participation mystique* at a conscious level, i.e., without dissolving spiritual and moral autonomy. *Relatedness* is the term we apply to this conscious level of archaic *participation mystique*.

In contrast to these individual efforts toward an inner synthesis, a collective reconnection to the archaic levels of the soul signifies a relapse into primordial *participation mystique*. People who are "like-minded" then replace spiritually independent individuals capable of *participation mystique*. Personal ego boundaries are dissolved in such collective movements. One is, in an intoxicating way, of one heart and one mind with those who feel and think alike. Various political and religious "paths to salvation" that promote the concept of community extol this process. But history has shown us again and again how such collective movements have a very dangerous reverse side along with their admittedly valuable aspects. That side of humanity capable of *participation mystique* does indeed take the place of related-ness among individuals capable of *participation mystique*, in the form of social cohesion; yet the price that must be paid for this more comfortable path is the sacrifice of personal discrimination and moral responsibility. The Third Reich, for example, placed before our eyes the devastating effects of a mass movement promulgating a sense of community. Held together by Blut und Boden as the origin of the Germanic race, most Germans felt themselves to be a unity. But the relapse into archaic *participation mystique* led to a loss of spiritual and moral autonomy. The result was a lasting cohesiveness of the masses that persisted even when the movement had long since become clearly and recognizably diabolical. The loss of the individual capacity to discriminate, therefore, explains why, even in the case of initially constructive mass movements, a sudden reversal into the destructive can take place without individual participants' being able to extricate themselves.

The deeper reason why a collective reconnection with the deeper

---

[18]Wherever the ego feels part of a psychically supraordinate totality, the individual can again feel a member of the whole, as a living cell in a person called humanity.

layers of the soul must ultimately be destructive is found in the following situation: Because of nostalgia for *participation mystique* with the larger group (lost during the Enlightenment), the individual would like to release his natural feeling of belonging by dismantling ego boundaries. This feeling of belonging is embodied in us in the folk person capable of *participation mystique*. But if one "loses one's head" in this endeavor—that is, if we set free the inner part of us that has remained in a state of nature *without* a solid ego-consciousness— then the natural person has no head. Since the natural person embodies our drive nature, this sort of headless regression to archaic *participation mystique* means that one has handed oneself over to the world of drives. But this fails completely to recognize the real folk person. As we have seen, the real folk person is anything but a creature of drives lacking a head. Having a precise knowledge of the dangers of humanity's chaotic drive nature, the primordial folk person is continually alert to living correctly in harmony with the whole. In the mountain folk of Uri we found this endeavor expressed symbolically in the golden ring. This ring, however, is perpetually threatened by the "It," by pure nature. For this reason the mountain folk of Uri see it as wanton to break the ring and let the "It" infiltrate. For that is the same as letting oneself be swept away by any drive and thus losing harmony with the whole. If, then, modern humanity relapses into archaic *participation mystique* in an unthinking, collective manner, we do not thereby redeem the archaic person but become only a grotesque, headless imitation. This is why newly formed community movements need some sort of guiding organ: an ideal, an ideology, a state doctrine, or a "Führer." And as a headless mass that sort of "community" is, of course, correspondingly easy to indoctrinate and to manipulate.

For these reasons the individual's forming and maintaining a relationship to inner laws is, surprising as this may sound, a further development of folk thought itself. For care of and concern for the relationship to what is one's own is an essential characteristic of the folk attitude toward life, a fact that will be discussed in greater detail in a later chapter (Part 6, chapter 19).

Summary Conclusions

We want now to transfer our understanding of the vicissitudes of the change in the individual's bond with the community to agrarian and regional development policy and planning in rural areas.

In the first place, the following fact seems to me of importance: that communities come into existence and endure has, to a decisive extent, something to do with the reality of the unconscious soul and not simply with external limiting conditions. Consequently, communities cannot be planned and built like houses.

However, it is of course equally important to respect humanity's fundamental need for community life and for relationships that contain and hold the individual. To the extent that interpersonal relationships are characterized by an atmosphere of reciprocal trust, village communities can doubtless meet this basic human need in an optimal manner. Our guiding image in rural development, therefore, will have to pay due attention to the danger that we can destroy the basic conditions favorable to relationships in a rural community both by rational, planned interventions and by a laissez-faire approach. Thus in sparsely settled regions certain tendencies toward centralization and rationalization—such as the shopping mall, the broadcast culture, or the concentration of certain public services—have an especially unfavorable influence on interpersonal contacts. Specifically, the possibilities and responsibilities for making regular personal contact in a rural community diminish—whether at the store, the milk collection station, the co-operative meeting, or in all sorts of subsidiary offices[19]—all too soon those well-known mechanisms of projection and defense arise against what has become strange or alien. If a process of general secularization is also added to this, in other words, if a mode of thought oriented solely to this world generally gains the upper hand, feelings such as envy, ill will, and dissatisfaction thrive especially well. The result is an unpleasant atmosphere typified by mutual mistrust and distance. Of course, it is not difficult to decide to move away from such a community if better material conditions can be found elsewhere. Therefore whatever promotes interpersonal relationship in rural areas must be a component in the guiding image of stronger rural autonomy.

What this means in the individual case can never be stated in general terms. In each situation the individual must decide whether or not the material savings or improvements will entail disproportionate disadvantages for interpersonal relationships in matters both large and small. These implications must be assessed in small things, for example, even in the question whether, for this purchase today, I drive to the shopping center or walk to the nearby store. Fundamentally these considerations will always commence with the question of whether or not our specific intention or project may be destructive of

---

[19]Concerning the function and significance of subsidiary offices see Ruedi Albonico, *Nebenamtlich-Neben bei?* (Fanas: Pro Vita Alpina Verlag, 1979).

structures that foster relationship. If there is that danger, the question will call for a conscientious solution. Since such problems cannot be solved with guidelines and threshold values, individuals who must take a stand on such questions are thrown back on themselves. If such problems find no solution that truly does justice to both demands—i.e., material advantage and interpersonal relationships—the individual who must make the decision is burdened with an unresolvable conflict. One wants to free oneself of such a conflict as quickly as possible; therefore arguments like "We have to do something immediately!" or "We have to decide now!" are welcome. Acting on such exhortations, however, does not permit gradual emergence of the *tertium*, the solution uniting the opposites of this specific, seemingly insoluble problem. It is not in vain that the (German) vernacular has the expression, "All haste is from the Devil"; for of course the Devil is always interested in stealing the soul, that link between the opposites. The soul can live only if individuals are ready to take the antithetical standpoints into themselves and, so long as they are irreconcilable, to endure the tension they create until a solution arises from that tension, a solution that does justice to both sides.

The significance of such an interiorization of an external problem of opposites is greatly underestimated. People do not want to see that, in the last analysis, every externally unresolvable conflict that affects me, i.e., that "gets under my skin," presents a mirror image of my own inner emotional disunion. Faust had the courage to withstand the tension; we, by contrast, prefer being able to decide immediately in all situations. But if I simply choose one side in a real conflict and thereby suppress the part of me that would have decided exactly the other way, I take the coward's escape from the suffering that would arise from the tension of opposites. The result of this attitude is an intrapsychic break, that is, a neurosis. We know the external manifestation of this condition very well. Therefore, if we are unwilling to endure the conflicts in our own soul when they are placed before our eyes by an insoluble, external problem, we fail to give soul's power the chance to reconcile opposites. Ordinarily we call this power "higher insight," that is, a kind of vision that can see opposites as a unity.[20] If the tension of conflict is not endured—if one decides on a project (= innovation) without conscientiously considering existing structures (in this case, the structures of relationship), then progress turns into the Devil who steals the soul. That is when we separate

---

[20]In this connection recall Krishna's admonition to Arjuna, the leader of the armies before the battle in the Bhagavad-Gita: "But Thou, be free of the pair of opposites!"

ourselves emotionally from our other side, which might well have chosen differently; in a one-sided decision we sever the emotional relation to the other side and hence separate ourselves from a piece of our own soul.

Viewed externally, our efforts toward reconnection with our archaic essence demand a translation of the primordial ways of thinking and living along the lines of the attempts made above. This work of translation makes it possible, both personally and in regard to society, to examine the guiding images in our way of life, our methods of research, and our politics. Where are they one-sided and how must they therefore move toward a new, more complete image of humanity? On the basis of what has been said, this new image embraces not only our consciously registered needs but also those of our entire unconscious, instinctual nature. The goal here is to offer an example of this approach by investigating where the current guiding images of the Swiss agrarian and regional policy do not adequately take these needs of the soul's archaic layers into account (Part 5) and where the missing aspects could be included in our political practice (Part 6).

A PRACTICAL EXAMPLE: REFLECTIONS ON CONTEMPORARY RURAL DEVELOPMENT POLICY IN SWITZERLAND

The foundation has now been laid. The change in the human relationship to material and social milieu has been analyzed as a phenomenon, and its consequences for our personal and social behavior have been investigated. Building upon this, we shall now examine the extent to which Swiss development policies for rural areas take these historical, social, and psychological realities into account. Even though the following reflections are limited to Switzerland, the conclusions can easily be applied to other industrial nations. For the fundamental characteristics of Swiss regional and agrarian policy are in many respects quite similar to those of other nations. This holds especially true for various countries of Western Europe.

Concerning our procedure, two additional comments are called for: First, in elaborating a holistic concept of economic development for a mountain region (according to the I.H.G.[1]), agriculture is treated as a part of the whole. This reflects the now generally accepted realization that agrarian policy must be embedded in a supraordinate guiding image directed toward strengthening rural self-reliance. Since comprehensive development policy entails interventions aimed at a particular result that must also be examined for its side effects, such procedures demand well thought-out planning based on comprehensive understanding of the situation. In the following discussion, this comprehensive sort of rural development policy,[2] increasingly common in Switzerland, will be examined. The first step will be to expose

---

[1] I.H.G. = *Investitionshilfegesetz* (= Investment Aid Law).
[2] Viewed conceptually, rural development policy embraces the "rurally relevant" aspect of regional and agrarian policy as well as land use planning.

the thinking process underlying a goal-directed or planned development policy and contrast it with so-called "folk thought." The one-sidedness or deficiencies of modern planning mentality will be discussed also. We will then highlight in summarized form the positive aspects of Swiss rural development policy and discuss inadequacies in Swiss rural development policy.

Chapter 17

The Modern Planning Mentality Contrasted with the Folk Mentality

The Intellectual Foundations of Planned Rural Development

The Goal of Development Planning

The idea of a comprehensive economic development plan is to reduce regional imbalances that have arisen out of increasing concentration of population and job opportunities.[1] As a first step, the development potentials and impediments in economically weak regions are identified through a comprehensive analysis of conditions. On the basis of this investigation, authorities formulate the development goals for future years; for this planning, experts are generally called in. Next is an examination of the mutual compatibility of the goals; and the way to accomplish this package of goals is mapped out with a catalogue of means and measures. Financial analysis and planning then anchors the whole development concept that has been worked out in the world of hard cash. The course of the process just outlined can be depicted graphically:

---

[1] On this see the comprehensive work by Brugger and Häberling, *Abbau regionaler Ungleichgewichte.*

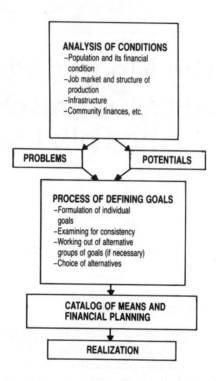

How can the intellectual foundations of this process be character-ized? Where does this method derive from? Obviously the compre-hensive rationalization of a region is a child of modern economic thought. The development planner for a region proceeds just as an industrial economist does in trying to raise the unsatisfactory profit-ability of an industrial concern. The regional planner differs from the industrial economist only in that the frame of reference is larger. This suggests the ground out of which the mentality of regional develop-ment planning has arisen—predominantly from economic common sense, and hardly at all, or only very minimally, from the folk mental-ity. Therefore rural development planning as a discipline is relatively traditionless, less because it is based on relatively little material derived from experience than because fundamentally the enlight-ened, scientific planning mentality ascribes no great significance to tradition. The process is supposed to occur strictly rationally and in accordance with the latest knowledge. Conditions are analyzed on the basis of factors relevant to development and existing conditions as

well as to the changes of only the last twenty years.[2] Likewise the
formulation of goals is generally oriented to today's concerns; the
present alone seems to be the arena of decision. What lies behind us —
history, tradition — is granted little binding force.[3] The goals of development are supposed to be solely economic growth and rationality.

Nobody can deny the solid advantages that this mentality and process have offered. Technology and rationalization have brought more
prosperity, comfort, external security, and mobility. Enabling the economically weak regions to avail themselves of this progress doubtless
appears, from this point of view, to be a worthy goal. But what effect
does the development planner's approach have on the people living
in rural areas?

Tradition and Progress

The rational, goal-directed procedures of contemporary rural development planning are faced with another reality, especially in mountainous areas. For there we find a population that to a great extent still
lives closely bound to tradition — the degree varying, of course,
according to region. The term "bound to tradition" means that human
spiritual and emotional stance which Richard Weiss has described as
volkstümlich (characteristic of the folk) — a stance that is strongly
shaped by traditional and customary mental patterns and contents.
However, the behavior patterns that contrast with a mentality believing in progress cannot be limited to certain social groups, "but rather
designates a kind of behavior in which everybody takes part to a
greater or lesser extent."[4] Consequently we must be more precise and
say that in rural areas the primordial attitude of *participation mystique*
or the *volkstümlich* attitude is more pronounced than is generally the
case with engineers, development experts, advisers, and planners.

We have become acquainted with the main features of folk thinking, including among other things the individual's experiences of
being fully involved with the native area and of having a living connection to ancestors. This imparts something enduring to the way of
life of such people, rooted in a locality and anchored in a timeless,
natural order. In a more symbolic fashion, we can also call this way of

---

[2]In this connection, the "Guidelines for Development of Mountainous Areas" (Bern,
1975) discuss the baseline period.
[3]On this see Schmid, *Standortmeldungen.*
[4]*Volkskunde der Schweiz,* p. 8.

life circular or round.[5] In this image it is not only the cycle of human life that is visible in its rational-irrational totality but also the external round of life—the economy, the community, the settlement, the language, the customs, and many other things. This circular way of life is not aimed at objective goals in the future, but rather rests in itself, which has led to the completely erroneous idea that areas and social classes that think in characteristically folk ways cannot develop from within.[6]

In contrast to this way of thinking and acting, the view of life that informs development planning is dynamic and oriented toward progress; tomorrow will be better than today. As opposed to life experienced as a great circle, this new concept is linear and loosed from the traditional milieu; mobility belongs to the modern life style. The folk way of life is bound up with the milieu and the ancestors, and hence is ultimately ordered by relationships to something more comprehensive and transcendental, while the hallmark of the planning mentality is that the order is created by human hand. To work for a better world—this is the calling of the development planner, and all energies are to be mustered to realize this goal. Weiss views this progress mentality as the upper stratum of individual thinking, for it is uncharacteristic of *volkstümlich* thinking, being a newer, more highly conscious mentality.[7] He calls it individualistic because its fundamental thought processes are no longer bound to ancestors and community.

To avoid oft-encountered misunderstandings, let us once again state explicitly that the concept of the upper-stratum, individualistic attitude does not refer to specific social strata, such urbanites or the educated. With this concept Weiss only labels a domain of spiritual-emotional behavior in every individual. Likewise, the lower-stratum attitude characteristic of the folk is not limited to a social group but is a mode of behavior in which everyone participates to a greater or lesser degree. Weiss illustrates the difference between earlier and current delimitation of the concept of *volk* ("folk") with the following diagram:

---

[5]On this see the essay by Schmid, "Fortschritt und Dauer," in *Augsätze und Reden*, vol. 2, p. 53–73.
[6]This idea can be refuted by the history of agriculture, e.g., in Hauser, "Der Familienbetrieb in der schweizerischen Landwirtschaft," and Jacobeit, "Traditionelle Verhaltensweisen und konservative Ideologien." Recall also the "innovation legends."
[7]Weiss, loc. cit.

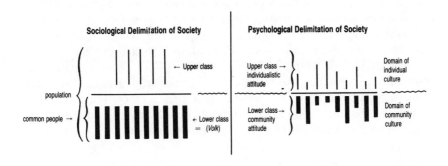

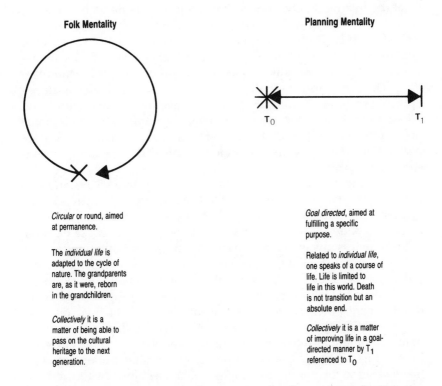

As we have seen, every modern person has been shaped to varying degrees by both kinds of thinking. Admittedly we must add that today the "circular" mentality characteristic of folk thinking is more and more being forced into the background. Consequently the individual is experiencing his existence increasingly as a course of life, and death as an absolute end. This gives rise to the feeling of restlessness, for one no longer has all the time that the folk have, embedded as they are in recurring cycles. A modern person's life can be optimally shaped or planned, using what is called "career planning." Juxtaposed with this, youth unrest and increasing "dropout" statistics are distinct danger signals. Seeing life only as a career is an unacceptable constriction of our view. But let us now leave the individual and return to the social problem of rural development.

Tradition as Only an Obstruction to Progress?

As we have seen in the preceding chapters, two antithetical modes of thought meet in development planning for rural areas. On the one hand, we have the more or less dominant *Weltanschauung* characteristic of the folk mentality, a view that can justify its mode of acting by appeals to tradition because the authority of predecessors is embodied in it. On the other hand, we have the engineers, experts, and advisors—very often people with a higher level of education—who have learned to think rationally in terms of economics and planning. Their authorities are the theories and methodologies of development planning, from systems engineering, cybernetics, and information theory to statistical guidelines for application of regional development concepts. Philosophical authorities such as Karl R. Popper or Karl Marx may also be added to this list, depending on personal inclination.

Development policy in rural areas, then, leads to a visible and palpable confrontation of these two *Weltanschauungen*. Yet the rational mentality not in accord with folk thinking triumphs in most instances. A development policy clearly pleading the cause of material progress is always more convincing; progress-inhibiting feelings for tradition must yield to it. The economist can show us mathematically, for example, that the potential for autonomous development simply does not exist for many rural areas.[8] Accordingly, these areas' development potential lies solely in improvement of their relationships with the nearest urban center, which in turn, depends on developing commuter routes and promoting specific economic currents. Such trains of thought, attuned purely to economic rationality, ultimately lead to the once autonomous rural area being "swallowed up"

---

[8]On this see the essay by Rossi, "Wirtschaftsanalyse und der ländliche Raum," p. 93–102.

in an all-inclusive economic area embracing city and country. "But such an expansion vis-à-vis the development problems of the rural area demands an initial point of view that goes beyond the traditional attitude, a point of view that does not see the rural area as isolated but rather increasingly takes into account the relations between rural and urban areas."[9] From this we see how the traditional viewpoint, corresponding more to the "circle" image—which regards the rural area as an economic and cultural unit—appears as an impediment to the "river" image of progress. In the modern view, the rural region's chance for the future lies in increasing the flow of commuters, goods, and money.

Here we clearly recognize how, informed by a rational mode of thinking and thanks to promises of prosperity, development planning promotes progressive, urban living conditions. From this vantage point, the steadfast loyalty to traditional values appears as an impediment to progress. Even if the nearest urban center lies within the very region in need of support and advancement, the rural area itself can no longer stand as an autonomous counterpart to the urban concentrations. This applies not only to the economic sector but more and more to the cultural as well. This loss of economic and cultural autonomy is, however, nothing other than an external reflection of the inner fact that the "circular" or "round" mode of folk thinking is being dominated by linear, progressive thinking. Through this, the rural area turns into an appendage of economically stronger metropolitan areas. A well-developed transportation network sees to it that the city becomes the work place for rural areas and that, conversely, the latter becomes easily accessible as the recreation area for urban districts. But imperceptibly this process of urbanization makes rural areas entirely dependent on urban population centers. Jobs, shopping centers, mass media, revenue-sharing, subsidies, legislation, and much more originate or reside in the urban center. The rural area runs the risk of a fundamental loss of identity.

Consequently city and country are no longer real socioeconomic and cultural partners. Enlightened thought, uncharacteristic of the folk, no longer has a reciprocal relationship with *volkstümlich* thinking characterized by *participation mystique*; rather, the latter is increasingly dominated by the former. The steadfastly circular or round quality of traditional *volkstümlich* life no longer rolls smoothly along on the axis of progress but rather is expected to adapt to progress by changing the circular into the linear. For the human, centering constants of

---

[9]Quoted from Rossi, op. cit., p. 103.

emotional experience do not figure in the progress mentality that seeks to be clear and unequivocal. Hence the circle and the straight line become two separate things in an "either-or" situation. Even in the image guiding the development of Swiss mountain areas, which provides for the establishment of centers in the mountain areas themselves—thus taking the autonomy of the rural area into account—the dominance of the mentality of progress finds expression.[10] The concept of "decentralized concentration" and the development slogan "concentration of investment and dispersion of gain" clearly indicate that, even in Switzerland, the well-being of things rural is seen to depend on promoting things urban. The same, of course, holds true for the agrarian sector: the salvation of agriculture is generally seen to lie, quite one-sidedly, in production quotas. The farmer is supposed to become an entrepreneur and adapt to the laws of industry and the market economy. And so in this sector, too, the modern profit mentality continually gains ground vis-à-vis the traditional, peasant mentality of permanence—despite misgivings that have been repeatedly expressed and that ought to be taken seriously.[11]

Must we now conclude from all we have said that the mode of thought and action characteristic of the folk, and with it the "circular" or "round" rural life-style, has in point of fact no intrinsic value? In the last analysis, may we, or must we, actually consider this traditional view of the world as conclusively antiquated and irreconcilable with real progress? In order to discuss these questions, we must first elucidate the basic features of a planned action. We will limit analysis to investigating regional development planning.

The Process of Planned Rural Development

Systems Theory

In regional development planning, the focal point is the relationship of human activity to the physical environment. Development planning is actually the attempt to combine socioeconomic development with land utilization planning in a comprehensive way. With

---

[10]By promoting a geographic concentration of population and jobs, the effects of economic consolidation are supposed to be achieved in developing areas. Likewise the provisions level of a region is supposed to be raised. On this see the worthwhile essay by Leibundgut, "Konzentrierte Wirtschaftsförderung im ländlichen Raum."

[11]In this connection we should mention the writings of Bach, "Bäuerliche Landwirtschaft im Industriezeitalter," and "Um eine bäuerliche Landwirtschaft."

this goal, planning must include investigation of the relations between society and environment. Since the discipline of planning regards environment and societal phenomena as an "intertwined system"[12] linked by chains of cause and effect, people have been looking for years for the most comprehensive systematic approach to fathoming the interrelationships. Thus the literature accumulates on how one could comprehend, explain, and finally predict processes of regional development using appropriate methods and procedures.

For a long time so-called "partial analysis" models stood in the foreground in regional planning and economic research, models with which experts attempted to describe external reality. These endeavors, aimed at a more or less precise depiction of a complex reality, permitted a better overview of certain relationships and a deepened understanding of the possible consequences when individual system variables were altered. As aids in understanding complex interconnections, such mathematical descriptions have their justification. They force one to think clearly and make it possible to undertake valuable prospective studies. The dangers of these sorts of procedures are, however, not inconsiderable. The fascination of grasping reality from the point of view of ideal, quantifiable possibilities can be too strong.[13] Jakob Maurer speaks of an almost desperate search for methods and techniques that enable one to comprehend the complexity of the relationships between people and the physical environment.[14] Even if today it is at best only ivory-tower systems theorists who still believe in the possibility of a complete description of reality, the attraction in reducing reality to numbers nevertheless remains enormous. We believe all too readily that we have reality in the palm of our hand when we have numbers and correlations. Then we overlook the subtlety with which thinking in terms of models can imperceptibly remove us from our feeling relationship to reality instead of putting us in touch with it. A procedure based one-sidedly on thinking generally neglects the other functions of consciousness: intuition and the sensation function, in addition to the feeling function.[15]

In recent years, theoretical research using models has been able to—

---

[12]This expression is used, for instance, by F. Vester.

[13]See the journal *Regional Science*; in general regarding the systems approach see McLoughlin, *Urban and Regional Planning*. In Swiss development policy, complicated models have generally found very little favor. See also the approach by Darbellay and Pretaz, *Grundlagen zu den Leitlinien für die Berggebietsförderung*, p. 414–29.

[14]Maurer, "Literaturnotizen zum Raumplanung," p. 149.

[15]Concerning the psychological functions in general see Jung, *Psychological Types*, C. W. 6; in relation to the activity of planning see Abt, *Entwicklungsplanung ohne Seele?*, p. 111–119.

indeed, has been forced to—accommodate the practical, political point of view. The goal of present-day research in development planning is, according to Georges Fischer, "to apprehend and to explain the economic and social dynamics of the development of sub-areas in a manner accessible to practical politics."[16] In this endeavor we are becoming increasingly aware "that it can only be assumed that numerous decisive influences, particularly of a noneconomic sort, are operative but that the extent of their influence is not yet measurable."[17] In Fischer's statements we recognize the intense search for further consciousness of a region's developmentally relevant factors and interrelationships. On the other hand, the shadow of our epistemological limitations is evident. This shadow obviously lies, first and foremost, in the noneconomic sector. When Fischer says that these influences are "not yet measurable," he speaks somewhat too optimistically. For among the factors assumed to influence development we find some that demonstrably elude rational comprehension. We must now substantiate this assertion.

Limits of Quantification

The domain where we surmise the existence of virtually unfathomed influences is the human emotional background. This unknown domain contains factors that can influence the development of a region in completely unexpected ways. In politics, advertising, fashion, and even on the stock exchange, such factors lying beyond the reach of reason are well recognized. These powers in the unconscious of all humanity are, as we know today, indeed a reality; but ultimately they can only be indirectly comprehended in the sense that we can infer their reality only from their effects.[18] Because of their unfathomability, they remain the irritating, unknown factors for every systems approach, regardless of how tightly woven or practice-oriented the investigative network may be. Indeed, empirical social research offers us methods of measuring and thus better comprehending certain sociological facts and interrelationships. Yet despite these possibilities, we still know too little about the collective unconscious that influences all sociological phenomena. Concerning archetypes (the contents of the collective unconscious), we can say only that they are extremely effective ordering factors or premises in the

---

[16]Fischer, *Praxisorientierte Theorie der Regionalforschung*, p. 5.
[17]Loc. cit.
[18]The atomic physicist is in the same plight: he too can infer the existence of electrons, etc., only indirectly, for example on the basis of changes in a photographic plate.

Atomic cloud over Nagasaki. Although no one has yet actually seen an atomic nucleus, splitting the atom is generally a known reality. Likewise the powers of the unconscious shared by all humanity are a reality and only indirectly comprehensible in the sense that we can only infer their reality from their effects.

world of our mental images. The more they sink down into the darkness of the nonobservable, the more they become completely surprising influences. We may use the expression "sink down" because we have recognized that in folk thought the world of archetypes is experienced and acknowledged as real, which makes possible a certain relation between the world-transcending consciousness and the plane of consciousness, as in legends and customs.

Consequently, the limits of what can be precisely measured can now be distinguished. The domain in which the unconscious exerts its effects begins at the point where we reach our epistemological boundaries. We can ascertain the existence of influential factors from this realm only indirectly, namely on the basis of their effects. For this reason, these factors elude the direct grasp of consciousness or even inclusion in a system. However, this does not absolve us from our scientific responsibility to take these factors adequately into account. This means that we must be duly clear about their presence and their manner of exerting effects. For an ostrich policy that, for fear of meeting something new, closes its eyes to that reality hardly leads to the kind of development planning that can do justice to human beings. Just as we have had to observe nature carefully to learn its secrets and protect ourselves from its destructive side, we cannot avoid turning our attention to inner, psychic nature to learn about these natural inner laws. Comprehensive literature on the structure and the modus operandi of the psyche already exists, especially on archetypal influences. But to a large extent our high degree of specialization has until now prevented this knowledge from becoming a part of the general knowledge of an educated person.

The Nature and Effects of Psychic Influences

As has been discussed in detail elsewhere, we can demonstrate the existence and modus operandi of energically charged centers in the individual unconscious with the aid of the association experiment. The results of the association experiment show with all the precision and verifiability one could desire that, for all persons, the reaction time between a stimulus word and the first association produced is significantly prolonged in the instance of certain stimulus words.[19] These sorts of so-called complex reactions show how unconscious factors—called complexes—influence our manner of thinking, not only in regard to reaction time but also to our manner of reacting.

In our context it is of particular significance that complexes enjoy a unique autonomy vis-à-vis the contents of consciousness.[20] They can (as in the association experiment) exert an inhibiting influence on consciousness and hinder spontaneous associations. Conversely, they can lay hold of consciousness and give rise to all kinds of possi-

---

[19] A recent work from the Federal Institute of Technology (ETH) is that of Schlegel and Zeier, "Psychophysiologische Aspekte des Assoziationsexperiments und Normdaten zu einer Reizwortliste."

[20] On this see Jung's foreword to Jacobi, Complex, Archetype, Symbol.

ble and impossible trains of thought.[21] The relative autonomy of complexes rests on their emotional nature, which they derive from an affectively charged nuclear element. This nucleus is, as empirical experience of the unconscious has shown, always an archetype. Owing to this fact, there are well-characterized and easily recognizable types of complexes that are thoroughly human and common throughout humanity.[22] As the focal points of our soul, these archetypes are recognized by modern psychology as the inner factors creating order or fate.[23] They represent those powers that were revered as gods in pre-Christian times. Then, admittedly, people experienced gods as external, whereas today we recognize the spiritual-psychical nature of these forces and experience them more from within as autonomous complexes.

As we have already seen, one of the most significant effects out of the archetypal background is the phenomenon of projection. By means of projection, inner images in the subject are superimposed upon the object world. Animate and inanimate things in the external world are thereby perceived as altered, which influences our manner or reaction accordingly. In the history of the development of consciousness, in natural science as well as in the development of individual consciousness, the mechanism of projection plays a decisive role.[24] For example, the discovery of the chemical properties of matter would never have been possible had alchemists not been fascinated by matter via projection and had they not devoted themselves to it. In his book *Psychology and Alchemy*, Jung demonstrated this aspect of projection in alchemy.[25]

Much as projection can further development, its reality-distorting effect can also become dangerous if that effect disturbs the individual's adaptation to the environment. A milieu perceived in an "optical delusion" can make us strive for what seems to have the highest value and later suddenly turns out to be illusion—whether a person, an ideology, power, riches, or any other goal. Something overpoweringly fascinating or affect-laden always has a destructive effect when, by the power of the underlying projection, a person is swept away into one-sidedness so that the other values in his or her consciousness—such as ethics and morality—are sacrificed to it. A person

---

[21]For details see Jacobi, *Complex, Archetype, Symbol*, p. 6–30.
[22]E.g., inferiority complex, power complex, father complex, mother complex, anxiety complex, etc.; see Jung's foreword in Jacobi, op, cit., p. ix f.
[23]Loc. cit.
[24]See also Meyer, "Projektion, übertragung und Subjekt-Objekt-Relation."
[25]Jung, *Psychology and Alchemy*, C. W. 12.

seized in this way by a demon or an unconscious force (via projection) loses the capacity for relatedness to the rest of the world and consequently loses humanity. Therefore, whenever projections become disturbing or overpowering, the projected content forces us to become conscious of it.

The meaning of becoming conscious of this sort of disturbing projection lies in the compensatory relation of the unconscious to consciousness. If a projection becomes disruptive and even conscious, this means that consciousness has grown too strong in a certain respect. Therefore, consciousness should develop a step further to include and respect those aspects of life that have been excluded by the one-sided point of view.

Since archetypes are experienced not only in images of meaning but also in emotion or dynamism, these ordering factors are also responsible for certain typical developmental sequences. We see this, for example, in the typical human developmental stages such as birth, sexual maturation, first love, marriage, first child, etc. In the most diverse eras and cultures we find very similar sequences of images and ideas that accompany and influence these transition phases.[26] We call these common human fantasies that rest on inherent possibilities of mental representation "mythological fantasies."[27] We surround things and persons that, in their function as carriers of projections, motivate us to some step in our development with this sort of fantasy material. A familiar example of this is the boy who has the fantasy of someday being a train engineer, ship captain, or airplane pilot. This is a "typical" fantasy preparing for and supporting the transition to adulthood, the transition to responsibility for oneself in which one must assume responsibility for one's own destiny.[28] In most instances these typical or mythological fantasies find their denouement naturally. Only in cases of disturbed development is it necessary to recognize the meaning of these development-promoting "guiding images" in order to unite them with consciousness.

But it is not solely for the individual that the unconscious weaves the mythological fantasies or "personal myths" that move one toward

---

[26] We have come to know these typical sequences of images and ideas by the name "rites de passage."

[27] On this see Jung, *C. W.* 10, p. 21ff, par. 11f.

[28] I am indebted to Dr. Marie-Louise von Franz for this example.

the fulfillment of fate.[29] Such archetypal fantasies can correspond to those of other persons since they all arise from the collective unconscious. As these individual fantasies belong to individual development, so a collective myth has its collective developmental function. For one example, we need only remember the effect of the Christian myth on the development of Western consciousness. And just as the mythological fantasies change in the individual life over the course of development, the collective myth is also subject to changes over the course of the centuries. These are, as Jung surmised, changes in the constellation of archetypes that cause or accompany the secular transformations of the collective psyche.[30]

Regarded collectively, we are in fact in the midst of a development crisis. There are numerous authoritative critical voices that emphasize again and again that the spiritual development of modern humanity lags far behind our external, material development. In our context, the necessity of regional development planning speaks for itself. The need for regional development plans indicates in itself that a certain natural development of certain regions has, in our view, come to a standstill. On the other hand, it is well known that problems of development increase in congested areas, only with different symptoms. When we are repeatedly called upon to change our attitude, expand our consciousness, etc.,[31] as the only correct approach to contemporary problems, even when doing so seems utopian, we are forced to conclude that we have lost the myth that could help us take the next step in the development of the collective consciousness. Of course, a myth as such can never be lost, for by its nature it consists of a series of images that arise from the unconscious and manifest themselves to consciousness, either from within in the form of fantasies, dreams, or visions, or from without in the form of projections. If we speak of lost myth, we mean the loss of a conscious relation to these development-promoting sequences of images from the unconscious.

---

[29]By the term "myth" (Greek "story"), we understand not only the history of a god but rather, in a larger sense, an account that gives expression to the profoundly mysterious vital relation between man and the divine. The basic feature of the myth lies in expressing man's relatedness to something transcendental and divine in the form of a story. (*Handwörterbuch des deutschen Aberglaubens*, vol. VI, p. 720.) Today we recognize the divine powers of fate as the archetypes. M.-L. von Franz's book, *C. G. Jung, His Myth in Our Time*, for example, shows the essence of a personal myth.

[30]Jung, "Flying Saucers: A Modern Myth," *C. W.* 10, par. 589–594.

[31]Thus again and again the demand is made that we must learn to think in systems (cf. Flüeler and Schwertfeger, *Die Schweiz von morgen*, p. 259f.). Vester also calls for a new consciousness which, among other things, is supposed to consist of the introduction of cybernetic modes of thought (cf. Vester, *Das Ueberlebensprogramm*, p. 14–17.) See also Pecci, *Das menschliche Dilemma*.

A search for our collective myth is meaningful not only because it might provide an aid in orientation for collective problems of development but also in order to avoid collective compulsive symptoms. Psychopathology can document that a mythological fantasy that is not voluntarily integrated into consciousness manifests itself compulsively and concretely on a "do it or else!" basis. For their part, these mythological fantasies always seek to draw energy into a new conscious condition, which is why "rites de passage" are always significant.[32] However, if the meaning of these images is no longer heeded or understood, this very same series of images is expressed in the individual in the form of seemingly senseless compulsive ideas or actions. But if one views these ideas and actions as a symbolic expression, they will always reveal a deeper meaning, a piece of personal mythology that needs to be lived consciously, not compulsively.

To illustrate this, let us take two very simple examples: a compulsive idea and a compulsive action. A woman suddenly developed a "completely inexplicable" washing compulsion. She had to wash her hands countless times every day. Only after she had virtually washed all her skin away was she ready for psychological treatment. An analysis of the unconscious processes revealed the real meaning of the compulsive symptom, namely the washing away—analyzing and thereby cleansing—her unclean, scheming way of "*handling*" situations. With this insight the destructive symptom vanished when its meaning was *consciously* accepted. Another example of a compulsive idea: An extremely extraverted businessman who had to travel often professionally and who granted himself no time for inner reflection suddenly developed agoraphobia—he was subject to inexplicable anxiety attacks whenever he intended to leave the city where he lived and worked. All exertions of will power aimed at eliminating his painful and embarrassing symptom accomplished nothing. An analysis of the meaning of his compulsive idea revealed gross neglect of his needs for rest and for introversion. His agoraphobia vanished to the degree that this man voluntarily took time for the inner needs of which he had formerly been unconscious.[33]

An essential or a mythological fantasy can prevail compulsively in the collective just as it can in the individual. Specifically, if we do not understand the meaning of the collective myth of our time, which could compensate for the one-sidedness of our general attitude, this

---

[32]Concerning the symbol as a "transformer of energy," see Jung, *C. W.* 5, par. 17, 101, 130, 450, and *C. W.* 8, par. 79–87.
[33]I am indebted to Dr. Marie-Louise von Franz for knowledge of this case.

lack of understanding leads to a compulsive compensation on the part of the collective unconscious. Instead of being an aid to orientation, the myth of our time then produces negative effects and leads to conditions of collective possession[34] just as we have seen in individual persons. Therefore it is a question (a) of seeing that collective or archetypal fantasy elements of this sort do indeed influence our manner of thinking, and (b) of recognizing where mythological fantasies can lead us to compulsive ideas.

As already suggested, we can recognize mythological fantasies both in archetypal dreams and in phenomena of collective projection. Wherever unconscious mythological fantasies are "hung" on a suitable object and provoke a certain collective fascination or reaction of affect, we are dealing with a piece of the unconscious myth of our time. Therefore we must look into the questions of whether and where the unconscious myth of our times might have established itself in development planning. This will allow us to counteract, if necessary, certain destructive aspects of this unconscious myth by becoming conscious of it. Moreover, this will aid us in orienting ourselves to the conscious realization of the developmental steps intended by the myth, steps that the collective consciousness needs to take.

Myths in Development Planning[35]

Development Planning and Projection

Let us briefly consider once again the actual task of rural development policy for which regional development schemes are worked out. According to Georges Fischer, the task lies in "taking the appropriate steps to turn undesirable future prospects—which become apparent in the 'status-quo' projections—into directions in accordance with the guiding images, on the basis of the analysis of conditions and on the facts of the case relevant to the development to date."[36] Fischer illustrates his statement thus:

---

[34]Let us also recall what was said earlier about the so-called "force of circumstances."
[35]In choosing this title, I recognize the parallel, valuable findings of the economist Eugen Böhler, who discovered elements of projection in economics and science, which he discusses in his book, *Der Mythus im Hirtschaft und Wissenschaft*.
[36]Fischer, *Praxisorientierte Theorie der Regionalforschung*, p. 13.

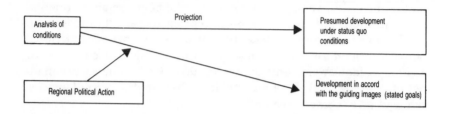

In Fischer's diagram we find the same word that previously occupied our attention: projection. Based on development so far and present conditions, a presumed development under status-quo conditions is projected into the future. Similarly, of course, the development according to the guiding image is also projected into the future. Here the word projection designates a conscious activity, namely that of a sketch of a presumed development based on a comprehensive evaluation of the situation. But even if this projection is presented as conscious action, an unconscious projection into the unknown darkness of the future also takes place. For wherever we meet with an unknown, contents from the unconscious are superimposed upon it and animate it, just as we have seen in the instance of the animated or ensouled landscape. But we do not recognize this process in which intrapsychic contents are projected; projections are met with, not made.[38] Hence we must recognize that both the image of the future under status-quo conditions and the vision of the future in a regional development plan are shaped imperceptibly by unconscious psychic factors.[39] Insofar as this is true, unconscious fantasies are superimposed upon external reality without our knowing it, and they become fascinating or at least motivating elements in regional-political actions.

This situation should make us prick up our ears. For in the projection mechanism of the human psyche we are forced to recognize that the goals of our regional-political actions arise not only out of reason but also out of the irrational background of consciousness. The guiding images projected into the future that are generally accepted among experts and politicians have their origin, to some extent, in the collective unconscious. It is archetypal images that are at work here.

---

[37]In our context we would actually have to speak of "political action in regard to development."

[38]See Part 3, chapter 8.

[39]One would have to count these factors among the so-called "autonomous variables" (see Fischer, op. cit., p. 14).

Thanks to the common human character of archetypal patterns, with their energic fluctuations, projected archetypal images can find a considerable degree of consensus. But wherever we find such projections of archetypal images in a comprehensive course of action, we no longer speak of individual projections but rather, as mentioned earlier, of an unconscious myth. Because a development plan for a region is supposed to be as comprehensive as possible, this dark, impersonal territory is suitable ground for comprehensive projections of mythological fantasy images that, in our developmentally disturbed age, must be raised to the level of consciousness. Consequently we may assume that the unconscious myth of our time is interwoven with the basic ideas of development planning.

As we have seen, contemporary development planning is informed by a rational mentality uncharacteristic of *volkstümlich* thinking. Development in general, and the science of planning in particular, are distinguished by certain ideas that have a fascination for the individual and especially the expert. Among these ideas is the almost unquestioned assumption that urban and rural areas should be better linked together. Decentralized concentration, increase in prosperity, creation of jobs, and the like—in short, material progress—have also become valid guiding images that almost axiomatically rule contemporary rural development planning. However, in the suggestive and fascinating aspects of these goals we recognize, in fact, projective elements that are mingled with reality. Since we increasingly recognize the destructive side of today's rational mentality (consider the autonomous dynamics of centralization such as depersonalization and destruction of the environment), we must concern ourselves with these individual projected elements, for they are a possessing objectification of what our consciousness lacks. Our task is to face the danger that the unconscious myth of our time is intermingled with rational guiding images for the development of rural regions. On the one hand, the myth would be rationalized during this intermingling and consequently might manifest its development-promoting tendency in consciousness but not intrapsychically in the sense of a change of attitude. On the other hand, an unconscious "mythologizing" of the images informing development signifies a disastrous condition of possession, insofar as no regulating consciousness that could impart a human scale to these energies opposes these unconscious drives. The National Socialist movement in the Third Reich illustrates, as an extreme example, the catastrophic effect of intermingling an unconscious myth with an image guiding collective development. To counteract the destructive effect of such an interpenetration of consciousness and the unconscious, we now want to attempt to identify individual mythical elements in contemporary rural development planning.

The Myth of the Creative New Beginning

Development planning in rural areas brings something new: thanks to a scheme, the doors are supposed to be opened to progress and prosperity—as far as possible and sensible. Promoting regional population increase, improving local conditions for jobs, and generally stimulating innovation are usually found in the development planner's repertoire of goals. The motivating power of many planners and politicians is often the feeling of creating a better future and promoting public well-being at the same time. Old structures and old legal conditions that inhibit development—such as small communities, complicated co-operatives, bad road systems, etc.—are supposed to vanish or be improved so that the difference in prosperity compared to the metropolitan areas can be reduced. In this endeavor it seems to be part of the nature of planning that the future as informed by planning is set above the present. Thus we often find among planning experts an inclination to place what is developing above what currently exists and not to regard the inherited, existing order very highly.[40] For it is part of the task of the expert to formulate ideas and point out how a region can develop and how the new can be created. When new regional structures are created in regional planning, it is the very idea of beginning anew that predominates. Consideration of what was appears to be of little importance; old community quarrels, for example, are regarded as illegitimate. Development planning is oriented entirely "forward" toward a better future, casting off the past.[41] Here we recognize clearly how the activity of the development planner stands under the spell of the creative, the daimon of creativity, for whom all bonds and all that arose naturally is an impediment.

This creative element has had a tremendous fascination for the Western mind, especially in recent times, as is clearly reflected in the marked increase in the literature on creativity. This can be traced back not just to the appeal of the new. Rather, to judge from appearances, humanity expects the solution to the problems of our times to come from the creative person, from the creative expert. Just recall the euphoria of planning in Switzerland in the sixties! The expectations

---

[40]On this see the essay, "Die Dämonie des Schöpferischen," in Schmidt, *Zeitspuren— Aufsätze und Reden*, p. 88.
[41]Schmidt, "Hochmut und Angst," op. cit.

of salvation that are often projected onto the activity of planning are enormous. Likewise, the temptation for the planner to identify with this projection should not be underestimated. In Switzerland we have experienced a withdrawal of some of these expectations of salvation that had been projected on the planner. At the beginning of the seventies there was something like an emotional ground swell that washed away the credulous sixties' belief in planning. Everything that had to do with regional planning was suddenly condemned wholesale. The word planning nearly became a term of abuse! In development plans as well, we have observed over and over again the phenomenon of projected expectations of salvation and subsequent disillusionment and disappointment.[42] On the other hand, in scarcely any other profession than that of the planner do we see so many examples of deflation—e.g., the thoroughly sobered planning expert who seems completely resigned. But deflation is always associated with a preceding inflation.

We recognize the mythic element of creativity in development planning. The projection of a creative, healing light has insinuated itself into the activity of planning. And in ignorance of this distortion of reality, the discipline of planning has identified to some extent with this creative spark. But since this creative, generative light is a property of the unconscious,[43] identification with this light signifies a dangerous inflation. It leads to a diabolical creative power in which the regulating conscious mind is excluded. In a condition of inflation consciousness can no longer recognize its state of identity with the archetypal background. Hand in hand with an inflation goes the feeling that one knows what is good and what is evil. And then we have arrived at the motto "The end justifies the means."[44] On a large scale, humanity experienced the demonic nature of identification with the generative in the Third Reich when, entirely unencumbered by any regard for convention, the instinctual depths of the nation, its blood and its soil were collectively affirmed as the creative.[45] And this is no bad joke: Hitler desperately wanted to become a city planner.[46]

Hence where the generative, creative light is projected onto per-

---

[42]In the period of disillusionment new expressions were coined: planning fatigue (*Planungsmüdigkeit*), planning listlessness (*Plannungsverdrossenheit*), etc.

[43]Concerning the so-called *lumen naturae*, see Jung, "Paracelsus as a Spiritual Phenomenon," *C. W.* 13.

[44]See "Gedanken über die Planung der Zukunft," in Schmidt, *Standortmeldungen*, p. 37–59.

[45]See "Hochmut und Angst," in Schmidt, *Zeitspuren—Aufsätze und Reden*, p. 138f.

[46]From Faludi, *A Reader in Planning Theory*, p. 243ff., quoted in Maurer, "Literaturnotizen," p. 92.

sons or a Führer, and where people identify externally with the projection and internally with the Luciferian light, the generative, creative becomes demonic. The generative in itself is by no means
entirely diabolical; rather, it is only the identification with the divine
spark that is diabolical. However, where this is the case and people
are seized by the creative/generative spirit, plans are made and realized in which the human measure and the individual human being
have less weight than the creative idea. Consequently, the most
apparent demonic aspect of technical planning probably lies ultimately in people's unconscious identification with the creative
godhead.

But today this mechanism of identification and projection has been
recognized and seen through to some extent and not just in the
instance of rural development planning. Today we increasingly sense
that a collective fascinated by the creative daimon is something dangerous because the limits set by a collective consciousness anchored
in tradition are lacking.[47] Thus we can understand, looking back to
our developing areas, why it is possible that suddenly some mountain village or other can completely pledge itself to progress. What
happens follows the mechanism described above: New creation is
good; to it must be sacrificed the old, impedimental structures, and of
course the planners and promoters involved in it are the "new
gods."[48] But let us not be deceived into believing that, because we
have begun to recognize the collective projection on planning and
planner, the fascinating power of the creative has ceased to exist. It
continues to live on and will be encountered again and again in projected form. It simply shifts to other areas. Today it might be overall
energy and transportation plans from which progress and well-being
are expected, or the possible saviors may suddenly be the Pope or the
President of the U.S. or even beings from outer space. Again and
again we observe the same phenomenon: We like to and quickly do
impose expectations of salvation or fantasies of the light-bringer
wherever a hook for that projection offers itself.

But what does it signify if the creative has become so fascinating
and so prominent in so strongly a projected fashion? What is the
meaning of it? According to what we have said about the phenomena
of projection, unconscious contents are encountered as projections.
As soon as such projections disturb or endanger the individual's conscious adaptation, it is necessary to become conscious of the compen-

[47]See Schmidt, "Hochmut und Angst," op. cit., p. 110ff.
[48]Here I have in mind specific regional development designs.

satory content from the unconscious. When we recognize the projection of the creative light as a mythical feature in development planning, and when it is clear that this projection should be withdrawn because of its demonic-destructive aspect, we must conclude that the creative light as a wellspring of knowledge from the unconscious should now be made conscious.

The expectations of salvation that are projected onto planning would have their origin in this light. In fact, empirical evidence of the unconscious reveals this creative, salvation-bringing light as the inner wellspring of knowledge. Psychotherapy has long since integrated this "light-bringing" knowledge of unconscious nature into its methodology for healing psychic disturbances (as in dream interpretation and the like). Likewise great minds have frequently pointed this out from their own experience. As an example let us listen to what Hans Leibundgut had to say in his address as rector of the Federal Institute of Technology on the subject of the forester's mentality: "Again and again it happens in my profession (as forester) that I must free myself from the individual question, from the individual result, and from partial knowledge, and let myself be guided by inspiration in my professional domain, the forest, not, to be sure, in the area of rapturous feelings but rather in the quiet of the life of nature and of the inner knowledge arising from it."[49]

However, this inner knowledge is no collective affair but rather is and remains restricted to the experience of the individual. When we continue to expect others to point the way, the weak light of the inner wellspring of knowledge remains hidden; and for this reason its existence is often placed in question. It is therefore the individual's task to encounter his or her own creative ground. This presupposes a strong consciousness that can grasp these contents, hold onto them, and change them so that nature's "raw product" is assimilated by the consciousness personality. We must recognize that the creative spirit must first be distilled by consciousness; it needs its opposite, namely ordering consciousness. This must give creative fires the necessary form if they are not to become destructive. But taking up this tension of opposites and carrying it to fruition can be the task only of the individual. For only the individual, not the collective, has the repository of consciousness.

We have come to know the activity of planning as the result of a mentality that is not *volkstümlich*, and have designated regional devel-

---

[49]Leibundgut, address of November 13, 1965, Federal Institute of Technology (ETH), Zürich, quoted by Hauser in the *Neue Zürcher Zeitung*, no. 147, 1979.

opment planning in particular as the result of a rational economic mentality. Now, what are we to make of the fact that we find this rational mode of thinking and acting, belonging entirely to the ordering function of consciousness, suddenly under the influence of the creative unconscious? This phenomenon has to do with the separation—indeed, the splitting—of modern consciousness from its unconscious origin. In most instances, modern people believe they are what they know about themselves, not realizing that many modes of thinking and imagining have their roots in a psychic background unknown to them. Thus it happens that they also believe that creative ideas and guiding images have arisen from the field of consciousness, the "ratio." Humanity has fallen into the role of Goethe's sorcerer's apprentice. It has eavesdropped on Mistress Nature and learned the laws of matter; and now the "energies in the broom" have become a reality. But the sorcerer's apprentice has not learned to exorcise this sinister spirit, and Mistress Nature with her regulating power seems far away.

With the split between consciousness and the unconscious—between the "apprentice and the master"—contact with the self-regulating, creative primal basis was lost. Now the apprentice faces the unleashed power of creation all alone. As humanity has lost sight of the origin of the creative spark, the creative daimon has imperceptibly been projected onto individual inventors—Edison, for example, who invented the light bulb. Thus it is no longer gods or dwarfs who show man how to make cheese or butter or even light! In the last analysis, this projection signifies human identification with the creative genius. After all, Edison is "one of us"; and thus humanity unconsciously identifies with the creative spirit, or more clearly, humanity is possessed by the creative genius. And so today we are collectively in the position of the sorcerer's apprentice. What shall we do now with this creative and innovative drive that threatens to tear us apart and endangers the world in which we live?

We assert, then, that modern consciousness has broken free from the creative ground and thereby has lost sight of its source. Consequently, it has been imperceptibly taken over by the creative daimon. The creative power now at our disposal does not have to align itself according to the yardsticks of things that have grown naturally but rather only need serve conscious intentions. Since this situation is barely recognized in planning and technological circles, we acknowledge the demoniacal qualities of the drive for progress all too little. And because being possessed by the devil of creativity or progress (Luci-fer = light-carrier!) involves more or less all of us, we must seek the answer in a personal settling of accounts with the drive for progress. Here lie the beginnings of all knowledge about projection. By reflecting on the situation, we have the opportunity to recognize that the external problems brought about by creating can more likely be corrected by the master than by the apprentice who caused them. This master as the spirit of nature or as the Spirit of the Unconscious might also, if need be, have something decisive to say about the development problems in rural areas, problems created by human beings.[50]

In summary we can state that the creative must be recognized as a feature of myth in development planning. With recognition that the creative daimon in the individual is an autonomous spirit of the unconscious, its compensatory modus operandi can have a corrective and consequently a renewing effect on consciousness. But as collective possession, this spirit brings about collective delusions of renewal, the shadow side of which cannot be seen by those possessed since they are identified with the new light.

The Myth of the Union of Opposites

Change in the Collective Hierarchy of Values

The distinction between developed and underdeveloped regions or nations arose in the course of the progress of civilization. Many rural regions became economically and culturally marginal because of the "undertow" effect of growing industrial areas. Consequently they lost their character as relatively independent extended communities and turned into so-called "developing areas" or "regions in need of development."[51] As already mentioned, one major goal of present-day counterbalancing policy consists in strengthening the economies of these "backward" areas. Regions disadvantaged in technological progress are supposed to be developed by consciously devoting attention and resources to them so that their autonomy may be maintained as far as possible.[52] This sort of regional counterbalancing policy is discussed not only in regard to a growing number of industrial nations but also in the intensified north-south dialogue.

The growing interest in the problems of economically weak areas

---

[50]Allusions along this line are to be found in my study, *Entwicklungsplanung ohne Seele?*.
[51]On this see Wiegelmann, *Gemeinde im Wandel*, p. 91, and "Richtlinien zur Berggebiet-förderung," phase 1.
[52]Preservation of the principle of federalism is a central concern of Swiss regional policy.

could be understood as an expression of a fundamental shift in the orientation of our hierarchy of collective values. Generally held in low esteem up to now, the value of such as agrarian existence or manual labor or the feminine principle is rising today in people's estimation. In the course of such rediscoveries, people are becoming increasingly conscious of the value of the country and its life-style. One result of this has been an increased political readiness to preserve economically weak rural regions as *Lebensraum*; and people are ready to provide financial support to this end.

In and of itself this inclination to pay attention to hitherto neglected rural areas is without doubt a positive one. What we must critically examine here, however, is the guiding image according to which economically weak rural and mountain areas should be developed and promoted. In this discussion we will again confine ourselves to conditions in Switzerland, but we assert that the following basic features are not specific to any one nation.

Urban Conceptions of Rural Development

As we have already discussed, current methods of regional development planning are completely under the influence of a mentality foreign to the folk. Of course the same thing is true for the overall guiding image informing the growth of developing areas. In Switzerland the general concept of development of mountain areas threatened with emigration is the principle of concentration. In a general development concept this means that growth centers are designated within an area in need of development, support, or promotion.[53] "The places selected to be growth centers are those somehow especially suited to be regional centers, in which the population emigrating from the peripheral district can be absorbed, if at all possible. Hence these are places suited for creation of sufficient opportunities for training, shopping, and earning a living, as well as for satisfying cultural and recreational needs."[54] In this endeavor, however, the purposeful application of growth-promoting support and development funds that flow into the growth centers is also supposed to benefit those segments of the population living in the surrounding communities. It is thought that improvement of the local transportation network will facilitate this, which in turn enables people living

---

[53]See Flückiger, "Gesamtwirtschaftliches Entwicklungskonzept für das Berggebiet," and especially the Federal Investment Aid Law (*Investitionshilfegesetz*) of 1 June 1974, article 10, paragraph 2.

[54]Quoted from the mandate for the Investment Aid Law of 16 May 1973, p. 27.

there to commute to the regional center.[55] Through promotion of an intraregional concentration of population as well as increased mobility, the rural regions are supposed to be able to hold their own against the undertow effect of the larger agglomerations.

In this guiding image we clearly recognize the effect of the urban mentality. Thanks to population concentration, mobility, and the possibility of increased specialization, the hitherto tradition-bound community is supposed to be incorporated into the modern economic order based on division of labor. Of course, from the standpoint of a rising standard of material well-being, this general development concept is thoroughly reasonable. Yet, as we have already mentioned, there are voices we must take seriously, voices that ask whether or not it is right that "underdeveloped" rural districts be made to resemble city areas through deliberate "urbanization." Let us take up this question and investigate whether this guiding image, which is supposed to bring more prosperity and residential appeal to rural areas, may not be so rational as it claims to be after all.

Should that be the case, it must be possible to identify somewhere the presence of unconscious mythological motifs in the guiding image of rural development. For just as with the mythological motif of the creative new beginning, these sorts of unconscious archetypal images bring about an unreasonable one-sidedness in one or another area of conscious intention, owing to their unnoticed power to fascinate. Because a mythological fantasy that seizes consciousness blinds one to the ever-present polarities of life, let us attempt to extract possible mythological motifs from the guiding image of development by observing that guiding image against the background of city-country polarity.

City-Country Polarity

At the outset of this book the concept of "rural area" was defined in Hans Elsässer's sense as an area fulfilling a combination of various geographical and socioeconomic criteria. In order to do justice to the polarity of urban and rural in its comprehensive phenomenology, we must—in addition to this list of characteristics—also take into account the cultural differences between city and country.

But first of all a fundamental question: What do *city* and *country* ultimately mean? As concepts in colloquial speech they lack the sharp

---

[55]Loc. cit., p. 8.

contours desirable in scientific terms.[56] To begin with, the variation among the many definitions of the geographers, sociologists, and folklorists has the effect of impeding understanding.[57] Moreover, contemporary developments make it impossible in many places to distinguish between city and country in the traditional sense; for in the wake of the accelerated increase in mobility and mass communication, things urban have spread out ever more widely and imposed themselves on their rural opposites, both in the way of life and in cultural expression. An urban mentality and life-style is spreading even into the remote mountain valley thanks to television, tourism, and commuting.[58] As Richard Weiss says, "The consequence of the manifold intertwinings of material and spiritual culture is that the current problem of 'urbanization' no longer has a side concerned only with population policy and economics; rather, there is also a spiritual urbanization."[59]

To recognize this progressive blurring of the geographical and sociological boundaries of city and country, people in industrialized nations speak of a "city-country continuum." By this the sociologist basically understands the intermingling of a more informal with a more formal social organization.[60] Expressed in terms of Weiss's folklore concepts, we can also speak of an increasing intermingling of a predominantly individualistic society with the more strongly community-oriented or *volkstümlich* society. What is expressed in the concept of the city-country continuum is the fact that the previous material and spiritual polarity of city and country has yielded to a mixture of rural and urban opposites. But even if the urban element is increasingly gaining the upper hand in rural areas, it would certainly be wrong to deny, in the wake of popular egalitarianism, a fundamental difference between city and country. For not only in the manner in which the land is settled but also in the way of life, fundamental differences remain between city life and the village-agrarian form of life, despite the same TV programs and the same mail-order catalogues.

---

[56]On this see Schronbek, "Das Nebeneinander 'bürgerlicher' und 'bäuerlicher' Lebensformen in einer Marktgemeinde," in *Stadt-Land-Beziehungen*.

[57]On this see the summary in Clemens, *Stadt und Umland; Zusammenstellung von Aussagen und Erkenntnissen zum Stadt-Umland-Problem*, p. 85–87.

[58]On this see the agrarian sociological study by Gerber, *Wandel im ländlichen Raum*.

[59]Weiss, *Volkskunde der Schweiz*, p. 71.

[60]After Kötter, "Stadt-Land-Beziehungen," in *Wörterbuch der Soziologie*, p. 1117.

The Spiritual Principles of City-Country Polarity

In order to contrast city and country, let us call to mind what spiritual principle has always guided the building of cities. Let us begin our observations with geography. As Walter Christaller has shown, the city has served the function not only of a political but also of an economic center for a given area.[61] Distinctly central locations have served this function for a larger region. Consequently a differentiated hierarchy of central places and areas arises, extending from the country village, structured around the church and having its particular catchment area, to the metropolis with its far-reaching zone of influence. The following diagram illustrates Christaller's theory of central places and their catchment areas in the well-known hexagonal form following the principles of economic order.[62]

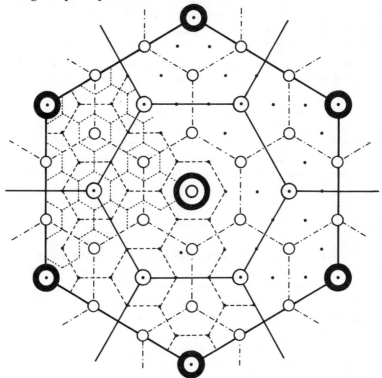

[61]Christaller, *Die zentralen Orte in Süddeutschland*.
[62]From Christaller, op. cit., p. 71; see also Blotevogel, "Die Theorie der Zentralen Orte und ihre Bedeutung für Volkskunde und Kulturraumforschung," p. 6ff.

As we can see in this basic overview, according to their size cities have an economically centering task for a specific region and hence a certain politically ordering function, too. This holds true wherever a king, a prince, or any other political force has situated its agents in a city. The function of a city for its corresponding catchment area is consequently fully analogous to the function of human ego-consciousness for the psyche or the function of the head for the body. This last analogy reminds us of the German word *Hauptstadt* and the English word *capital* (German: *Haupt* = head; Latin *caput* = head). Just as the house or the courtyard had a centering function for a family or a clan, and just as the village did for the surrounding community, the city or "principal place" (*capital, Hauptstadt*) originally also had a centering function, in which the inner opposites within its area of influence could come together under one authority. In contrast to the individual house or village, however, the city constitutes a supra-ordinate center of a common sphere of experience. Because of the limited mobility of the past, the domain of experience normally open to people constituted their cosmos, and the city or the chief place signified something on the order of the governing center on earth.

We can probably best illustrate this original significance and function of the city by referring to city culture in ancient China. We may make this comparison since we are dealing with an archetypal image. A central feature of the Chinese concept of the city is revealed, as Helmut Wilhelm has shown, in the linguistic meaning of the Chinese character for city, "*i*." "This [character] consists of a circle that represents the protective enclosure, the wall and the moat, and a kneeling man. The 'enclosing circle' surrounds a person worshipping."[63] The word "city," but also the very concrete plan of a Chinese city, with its sanctuary "as the center of the world"[64] in the center of the city, "prove to be a symbol of the highest significance, a symbol reaching beyond the threshold of perception and expressing in imagery what had been beheld there—the intuitive formulation of a darkly intimated law. Jung applied the concept of the mandala to this symbol of the center, the temple, and the sacred precinct encircled by a furrow. The tantric mandala is taken as a likeness of the heavenly city. In structure and function, the Chinese city was likewise the representation of a psychocosmic system; its layout was nothing artificial but rather inherent in the human being. The city was the place of the

---

[63]Wilhelm, "Die 'Eigene Stadt' als Schauplatz der Gestaltung," p. 211.
[64]Ibid., p. 213. The center of the world itself is, for the Chinese, in Beijing (Peking), yet the individual Chinese cities were likewise "copies of the metropolis" (p. 214).

gods and the ancestors, just as the founders of the Chinese culture had glimpsed it: a likeness and a symbol of heaven."[65]

In the primordial image of the heavenly Jerusalem, the city as the likeness of "heaven on earth" was also a living idea for us. As the center of temporal and ecclesiastical power in the Christian West, the city always embodied the higher, spiritual principle. As Alexander Mitscherlich once said, the city, with the framework that the urban setting provides, is very much a "fertile soil for the development of human consciousness."[66] Expressed more precisely, we postulate a reciprocal effect between the development of consciousness and the development of the city.

As we must assume today, human consciousness, with the ego in the center, arose out of the conflict among various, diverging animal impulses. We need only think, for example, of the primordial conflict between self-preservation and preservation of the species. The task of consciousness is a meaningful coordination and centering of the various individual drives—that is, of doing justice to the whole human being.[67] In the same way that individual consciousness had to arise for the purpose of coordination, the origin of the city may well also be grounded in the task of coordination and centering.[68] The same spiritual principle that underlies the origin of human consciousness is also at work in the origin of the city. Since antiquity people have conceptualized the principle underlying the origin of consciousness as the solar-masculine principle of consciousness, because humanity's modern, goal-directed "daytime" consciousness has so much in common with the light-bringing and enlivening-warming sun (see diagram below):

---

[65]Ibid., p. 211ff.
[66]Mitscherlich, *Thesen zur Stadt der Zukunft*, p. 12.
[67]For details I refer the reader to the specialized literature in psychology.
[68]For the student of prehistory and for the ethnologist, societies without cities are a well-known fact.

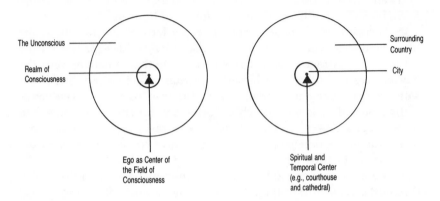

As a collective phenomenon, therefore, we recognize in the formation of the city a copy of the collective cultural consciousness, the function of which is the ordering and centering of the area it draws upon. The relationship to the "heavenly likeness," be it the metropolis of Beijing or the heavenly Jerusalem, signifies the intuitive comprehension of the necessity that humanity's ordering consciousness always be aligned with the cosmic order if it is to function correctly. The role of the heavenly city in this is to provide the guiding image for the city on earth where the opposites must be united. It is a symbol—a picture of meaning—of a center attuned to the whole, a center which embraces midpoint and periphery.

If we attempt to gain some clarity about the spiritual principle underlying the phenomenon we call "the country" or the "rural area," we get into difficulties. For what do we really mean by "the country"? When we pursue this question, we discover "that there are indeed many attempts at formulating a definition of city, but practically none for country except as they describe it in contrast to the city and have proceeded solely from that sort of mirroring."[69] In general, "the country" is not a phenomenon complete in itself, which, to some degree, can be taken in at a glance as is the city. "The country" is always the whole basis out of which individual cities and settlements arise or have arisen. One can differentiate cities, classify and group them, and establish relationships between them; in contrast, there is always only one "country," and that exists everywhere city does not.[70] In this context, the village, the hamlet, and the individual farmstead are regarded as components of the rural area.

---

[69]Quoted from Gerndt, "Städtisches und ländliches Leben," p. 37.
[70]Loc. cit.

A further difficulty posed by the concept of "the country" can be traced to a feeling tone that always resonates more or less strongly. Whenever we speak of "the country," the image of closeness to nature and distance from civilization is awakened along with the attendant affective ambivalence this triggers off in modern people. Despite the vanishing contrast between city life and country life, that network of associations entwined about the antithesis of culture and nature is still bound to our linguistic sensibility. This difference is particularly striking when we contrast the urban and the rural village life-styles. In this connection let us mention Richard Weiss's observations, even if less informed parties reproach him for holding a "wooly concept of nature" and an "affect-laden view of civilization."[71]

Following the sociologist Werner Sombart, Weiss characterized the city-country polarity in terms of the urbanites' way of life compared to that of the inhabitants of a rural community.[72] Whereas village life close to agriculture is much more subject to the realities of natural influences such as the alternation of day and night or summer and winter, urban existence liberates itself to a great extent from this bondage thanks to the technological mastery of the forces of nature. To a significantly greater degree than in the instance of the village dweller, the complex apparatus of civilization—whose own laws and tempo rule urban life—comes between the urban populace and nature in the rhythm of life. The compelling force of civilization takes the place of those conditions inherent in nature and characteristic of folk life.[73]

Given the present degree to which things urban have permeated rural areas, we must take care not to obscure the polarity of city and country with nostalgic projections, e.g., movement versus stasis, or rationality versus closeness to nature. However, despite all the contemporary confusion of opposites and all egalitarian leveling out of differences, what does continue to exist as a difference between city and country is a specifically rural or specifically urban world and way of life—a specific style of life and culture, or a specific cultural model. In the same way that we have juxtaposed the more urban mentality with the folk mentality of rural regions, we can now contrast the linear, goal-directed, progress dynamic in city life with the more circular way of life in areas close to agriculture. In doing this, however, we must emphasize that just as each person participates in both ways

---

[71]Op. cit., p. 35.
[72]Sombart, *Handwörterbuch der Soziologie*, p. 527.
[73]Based on the summary in Weiss, *Volkskunde der Schweiz*, p. 74.

of thinking and feeling, each person also participates in both ways of life, the urban and the rural. Between city life and country life there exists simply a difference in the degree of the constituent elements.

City and country are, as we see, certainly more than just geographical, sociological, or folklore concepts. When, for example, Helga Gerndt opines that as an object of knowledge "country" is nothing but a myth—i.e., as an object of knowledge it has no empirically comprehensible reality—she touches on something of the truth.[74] Beside scientific concepts of other disciplines, "city" and "country" are, fundamentally, only symbols for worlds that are material and spiritual opposites. It is, after all, the nature of symbols that they express things that are not rationally comprehensible. If ultimately the city is a symbolic expression of the centering and ordering factor that analogously underlies the formation of ego-consciousness, the country surrounding the city symbolizes that autonomous factor out of which and thanks to which this very center can arise. In the case of the human being, the opposite of ego-consciousness would be humanity's unconscious psyche.

We can now formulate the spiritual principle that underlies the idea of "rural." If the idea of "urban" is, as mentioned, informed more by the solar-masculine principle of consciousness, we recognize in village life close to agriculture more the lunar-feminine principle of human connectedness with the eternal cycles of nature. We speak of a solar-masculine principle in contrast to a lunar-feminine in part because humanity has again and again used the symbols of the sun and the moon to illustrate the contrast between the two ways of knowing: the way of conscious clarity and distance, and the way of relatedness and proximity to nature. On the other hand, we take up this symbolism because it best gives expression to what dominates the *volkstümlich* and the non-*volkstümlich* ways of life and thought. Modern thought is informed by the bright sunlight of diurnal consciousness, which makes a "masculine," clear separation or differentiation of things possible. In contrast to this, folk thought is as though informed by the changeable, faint moonlight of the night, which tends to bind opposites together. In contrast to the light of the sun, moonlight, which unites, corresponds to the feminine principle.[75] These two principles, as the roots of two modes of thought and life, have gotten out of equilibrium in our times, in that the solar principle

---

[74]Op. cit., p. 37, p. 43.

[75]Often these two are also called the logos and the eros principles. On this see Abt, *Entwicklungsplanung ohne Seele?*, pp. 187–98.

threatens to dominate all areas of life, a fact clearly reflected in the attraction of the metropolis and in the urbanization of rural communities.

Union of Opposites rather than Mingling of Opposites

Let us employ analogy as an aid in order to elucidate the chief aspect of the problems of "urban" rural development policy posed at the beginning. Starting from the disturbed cooperation of the solar-masculine, urban mode of thought with the lunar-feminine, folk mode of thought, it is not misguided to compare the status of city and country with the present-day spiritual conditions of man and woman. For a long time, a man could develop himself significantly more comprehensively than could a woman. The predominance of the masculine clearly shaped occidental intellectual and spiritual life. Now in our century a distinct tendency is emerging: a woman and women's own manner of being are becoming increasingly accepted values.[76]

However, we clearly see that if this is to happen, the spiritual blossoming needed by women is not to be understood as an imitation of the masculine essence and spirit. Hence, seeking the specifically feminine and integrating it into consciousness as a fundamental value has become the difficult task of countless women. Here it is a question of a real "deliverance" of the lunar principle (which as a metaphysical representation of the feminine has no place in the Christian patriarchal trinity[77]). As a spiritual principle it corresponds to a relationship-creating, circumambulating mode of thought, familiar to us in the method of amplification as contrasted with modern, goal-directed thought. This search for a new feminine self-concept equivalent to the masculine one, however, has become the task not only of modern woman. Becoming conscious of his own feminine side, or his own inner capacity for relatedness, has equally become the task of men if they are to be able to approach women with the understanding needed for development.[78] So much for our analogy.

We turn our focus now to the polarity of metropolitan and rural areas, wherein one pole could similarly develop out of proportion to the other. We are forced to recognize that in the measures intended to promote rural areas the uniqueness of the rural area as an autono-

---

[76]On this see Kast, "Weibliche Werte im Umbruch—Konsequenzen für die Partnerschaft," and Battegay, "Probleme der Lebensmitte aus der Perspektive der Frau."

[77]On this see Jung, "Answer to Job," C. W. 11, par. 553–758.

[78]Jung called the feminine side of the male psyche the *anima*. See "The Relations Between the Ego and the Unconscious," C. W. 7.

mous counterpart to the urban area is hardly mentioned.[79] This stems above all from the fact that in many developing areas those people who shape public opinion have a predominantly goal-oriented mentality. They are proud of their ostensible freedom of thought and feel that the primordial, *volkstümlich* thought is second-rate and inessential. Given this, we can understand the prevalence of the general opinion that rural areas must adapt themselves more and more to urban ways to counteract the urban undertow effect. The situation is reminiscent of the attempt by some women to counteract the predominance of the patriarchy by becoming more masculine. Of course, the relationships in the city-country problem are more complex than they would appear on the basis of that analogy. But thanks to the simile, we can now single out one thought: The development of rural areas cannot and must not simply mean imitating urban ways.

Therefore, along with economic and technical support in the development of rural regions, attention will necessarily have to be given to indigenous values, to the rural population's own view of itself. The following statement holds true not only for farmers but for people in the country in general when they compare themselves with urbanites: "Wherever a feeling of being second-class arises, a bad climate for the next generation prevails."[80] The rural population's feeling of being second class, especially in mountain areas, must not be underestimated. Particularly in those areas where the modern age has descended like a flash flood, its unsettling effect on the indigenous population is threatening. Richard Weiss speaks of a veritable spiritual crisis among the Alpine population.[81] Consequently we must pursue the question of what it means for rural development policy to take the rural population's view of itself appropriately into account.

Surely the first step toward realizing the specific value of rural areas will be taken when the responsible politicians, and particularly the development experts, realize that rural areas are not mere appendages of the metropolitan areas, nor can they be made into such appendages. They are, rather, autonomous counterparts to cities, having their own indigenous structure and culture. Cultural consciousness and creative accomplishment are dependent neither on urban conditions nor on large masses of people. The rural areas' potential for spiritual and intellectual autonomy is easy to document.

---

[79]See the fifth agricultural report of the Federation or the draft of the new Federal Constitution.

[80]Quoted from Hugger, "Das Nein zur Scholle," p. 21.

[81]Weiss, "Alpiner Mensch und alpines Leben in der Krise der Gegenwart."

For an example, one need only call to mind the Rhaeto-Romanic* people. As an agrarian population of now only about four thousand people, this linguistic and cultural community can point to an abundance of linguistic and cultural monuments, as the twelve-volume *Rätoromanischen Chrestomathie* of Caspar Decurtins testifies.[82] In the Catholic area of the Rhaeto-Romanic mountain country, an area with approximately two thousand inhabitants, some two thousand melodies of religious folk songs were found in 1942.[83] As Richard Weiss says so beautifully, "Here we can comprehend what is precious and exquisite in the culture of small areas."[84]

The second step consists in becoming conversant with the indigenous spiritual-cultural values of rural areas (insofar as they once were or still are alive) as we did in the discussion of folk thinking. However, this endeavor cannot be limited to only an external familiarity with this view of the world. Rather, this view of the world must be joined with our modern consciousness. As we have seen in the example of the folk legend and of customs and usages, the spiritual-cultural tradition of the rural and Alpine population reveals a *Weltanschauung* that, as modern discoveries show, is superior in certain respects to the *Weltanschauung* of rationalists. Because spirit and matter (as well as subject and object) are not experienced in primordial folk thought as separated from each other, the intrapsychic, human constants are not split apart in this view of the world. In contrast to urban-rational thought, the folk view of the world makes it possible for the psychic background to be a constant factor. Individual life is thus anchored in itself, in the community, and in the territory in which one lives. This view of the world has been reflected in structures and ways of life that corresponded not only to humanity's material but also its spiritual needs. Such a setting is capable of imparting an existential feeling of the unity of human, community, and milieu that we can scarcely have in the metropolis, despite all our comforts.

This should not lead us to the mistaken assumption that folk idylls prevailed in developing areas, at least in times past. By no means. Up until recently, poverty and need had to be counted among the characteristic features of these areas, not to mention the inestimable scourge of superstition. Surely these also are fundamental explanations why a radical switch from the folk way of life to a modern life-style was often possible. Yet despite these reservations, we must recognize that

---

*of eastern Switzerland, northeastern Italy, and adjacent areas of Austria.
[82]See Weiss, *Volkskunde der Schweiz*, p. 360ff.
[83]*Rätoromanische Volkslieder*.
[84]Ibid., p. 361.

folk thinking and experience reveal features that we miss in the urban mentality and whose absence we sense as a loss. We can characterize this lack ultimately as the loss of the lunar principle that unites individual life with what is dark and what lies beyond, and that is capable of imparting to our time-bound progress the timeless values of permanence.

At the beginning of the chapter we described a general, fundamental shift in the increasingly conscious trend toward those areas of life that the mentality of progress has excluded. In this we now recognize more clearly an unconscious need to become familiar with and to cultivate those domains of value that were left in the dark or—intrapsychically—in the unconscious. These values of a way of life that is circular rather than linear—a way of life in which people are as they always have been, not living provisionally with an eye to a better future—these represent the constants in human life and the nightside of our existence. Just as we need the night to balance the day externally, so also do we need it internally. In addition to the urban progress mentality, we must rediscover the folk values of permanence; the feminine-lunar epistemological principle must take its place beside the masculine-solar principle of knowledge. In other words, the unconscious must be able to take its place beside the world of consciousness as the other, equivalent pole of reality that operates as an independent counterpart to consciousness. The unconscious motivating force for the development of things that have remained natural is, consequently, a deep interest in the values of permanence, of the earth, and of nature. From out of this nether realm we infer the possibility of a regulating sluiceway to the river of progress that is today a torrent threatening to hurl us over ever more dangerous cataracts. Consequently in the fantasy that motivates the development planner we recognize a common unconscious myth representing a contemporary inclination to develop and cultivate the "other side." Basically the task is that of bringing to consciousness this other side (as the world of the lunar principle). In the expert it is the inner other side; and in people living in the country it is the value of the naturally structured world in which they live. With Albert Hauser we clearly recognize the essence of this as lying in the relationship-promoting aspects specific to the rural area—namely, the bond with the community, rootedness in nature, embeddedness in a tradition, and the connection to a transcendental realm experienced in folk thinking.[85] Our economic and planning mentality will have to integrate the complementary values of the folk mentality. For we see that the one-sidedness of rationalization must be made whole by the enduring values of human instinctual foundations. Values such as self-sufficiency, thinking in terms of cycles, decentralization, "small is beautiful," etc., are a part of this. Yet here, too, nothing will happen unless individuals recognize these values and draw the necessary conclusions.

In developing, cultivating, or making conscious the inner values of the *volkstümliche Weltanschauung*, we begin to discern a counterforce of equal value to progress, mobility, concentration, and the profit mentality. Valuation of a decentralized way of life, in which being is more important than doing, becomes conscious and is no longer carelessly disregarded. In this light, an advisor or engineer entrusted with rural development can hardly continue, one-sidedly, to urge people in rural districts to believe they must employ urban planning technology to imitate urban ways. Insofar as that advisor or engineer has gained some understanding of his or her own needs for permanence—needs once unconscious—and has been able to unite this inner world with the world of progress, to that extent is he or she able to make an externally constructive contribution. That contribution would be the making conscious of the indigenous values of a region and, as far as possible, uniting the new with what already exists rather than replacing what exists with something new.[86]

However, becoming conscious of indigenous values should not lead to the view that rural regions should be protected from things urban and serve primarily as recreation and relaxation areas. Just as we are getting away from role stereotypes in the relationship between man and woman, with both sides expanding the entire spectrum of their existential possibilities while preserving the differences between man and woman, we must likewise see the city-country relationship from both of their standpoints. For the population of rural areas, consequently, it is a matter of taking in and incorporating the urban opposite without imitating it and thereby giving their own differentness second-class status. Conversely, the task facing people in metropolitan areas is that of recognizing the value of the folk sense of belonging and having ties, and of approximating their urban life-style to it in an appropriate way, always mindful that the polarity of city

[85]Hauser, *Ueber die Nutzung von Böden im Grenzertragsbereich—sozioökonomische und kulturelle Aspekte*, p. 48.
[86]For further thoughts on this see Röpke, *Die Gesellschaftskrise der Gegenwart*, p. 311–50.

and country is a tension of opposites *within* the human being. At the practical level of development planning, it means recognition of the fact "that urban and rural areas are inseparably interwoven with each other functionally, but that they have to some extent differing tasks to perform, corresponding to natural requisites, their situation in the region as a whole, and the status of socioeconomic development. Particularly for the rural area, functions must be recognized and correspondingly recompensed, functions that cannot be immediately justified in terms of the mentality of economic success."[87] This refers, among other things, to their overall balancing function relative to overcrowded areas.[88]

We can now summarize the second characteristic of the myth of development planning. In consciously turning attention to those regions that have been disadvantaged by our economic growth, we have recognized signs of an increasingly distinct shift in our general mentality. In the development of "backward" rural and mountainous areas we see the signs of a new countertrend that seeks to take into account and upgrade the split-off opposite to growth and progress. This compensatory tendency must, however, be consciously recognized and integrated into consciousness exactly as it is in the case of unconscious human creativity. For if one does not recognize and integrate the compensatory, upgrading tendency of an ignored opposite, compulsive phenomena begin to appear. Then the consequence is not the reconciliation and union of opposites recognized as being of essentially equal value (such as folk and urban, or tradition and progress). Instead, where the unconscious tendency toward upgrading the split-off opposite is not recognized, we get a monstrous *mingling* of opposites. Today we recognize this mingling of opposites in the phenomena of the urbanization of rural areas or in the bizarre "country look" in the metropolis. And we see with especial clarity the compulsive mingling of the urban-rural opposites or of two poles in general in the phenomenon of *possessive mobility*.[89]

One aspect of the unconscious myth of our times that has been neglected by progress and rationalism is the pole of permanence and naturally evolved things, which holds an attraction for modern

---

[87]Ringli, *Die Gesamtverkehrskonzeption als Herausforderung an die nationale Raumplanung in der Schweiz.*

[88]On this see the Konrad Adenauer Stiftung publication, *Entwicklung ländlicher Räume.*

[89]In the compulsive mobility of many people themselves we recognize simultaneously an unconscious flight from as well as a search for their own depths—compulsive mobility as flight from and search for themselves! [*Possessive mobility* refers to the paradoxical phenomenon characterized by both the desire for freedom from and the longing for attachments (e.g., "roots"), hence a mingling of opposites—TR.]

humanity and draws attention to this realm. But if this counterpole indeed is to be upgraded or "developed," we must examine whether our means to that end are suitable. In our examination, we have recognized that rural areas cannot be appropriately "upgraded" exclusively with urban development methods because doing so fails to bring these regions into a relationship of true partnership with urban areas. Only when we acknowledge the tendency of the collective unconscious, working through its attractiveness to provide a counterpole that would compensate our one-sided urban thought—only then can the significance of unconscious fantasies or of the unconscious myth have a function conducive to development. But since the individual alone has the possibility of becoming conscious of the facts of a situation, the meaning of the unconscious myth of our time can therefore only be recognized by the individual. Consequently it is the task of the individual to recognize the value of permanence as the equivalent counterpole to progress and to bring the two realms into a fruitful relationship with each other. However, recognizing folk thinking and urban thinking as equivalent opposites in our way of understanding the world ultimately means a renewal of our *Weltanschauung,* in which consciousness and the unconscious, progress and permanence, work together in constant union.

From what has been said, we must draw the conclusion that, basically, behind the efforts directed toward the external development of areas that have been left behind, there is an inner task that must be recognized and solved, a task parallel to the external one, so that efforts to develop external things will not be impaired by subjective inadequacies.[90] For only where the disturbing veil of projection is removed does a true capacity for relatedness arise. By a "true capacity for relatedness" we mean that we can agree with our counterpart both emotionally and intellectually without losing our identity and without our counterpart's wanting to adapt to our views.[91]

---

[90]As an example of this see my study, *Entwicklungsplanung ohne Seele?*
[91]See Kast, "Weibliche Werte im Umbruch—Konsequenzen für die Partnerschaft," p. 140.

Chapter 18

Swiss Rural Development Policy

Positive Aspects

The Will to Federalism

Swiss domestic policy is carried by an idea of federalism seen in scarcely any other country; that is, while Switzerland does not strive for centralization of decision-making power, it seeks the preservation of a federal state with extensive cantonal autonomy. With increasing population density in all parts of Switzerland and concentration of job opportunities in high-density areas prompting emigration from agrarian regions, a federal-level, counterbalancing policy aimed at strengthening economically weak parts of the country became necessary. As a consequence, geographic and economic sectors disadvantaged by an economy based on division of labor benefitted from sizable advancement measures provided by new laws and ordinances.[1] Our first task is to highlight the will to federal solidarity with the economically weaker areas of the nation. Swiss counterbalancing policy need have no qualms about being compared with that of other nations, both in the areas of agrarian and forest policy, as well as in policies aimed at reducing regional imbalances. Let us remember this later when we dwell on the inadequacies of the Swiss concept of strengthening rural self-sufficiency.

---

[1]Based on Article 31 bis, paragraph b and c of the Federal constitution.

Promotion of Collaboration and Deliberation

With the creation of the federal investment aid law (I.H.G.) for mountain regions in 1974, a decisive step was taken in Switzerland toward assisting those areas threatened with emigration, especially with the introduction of a *regional* frame of reference. The "region" was recognized as a level between the community and the canton. This recognition offered the possibility of bringing the decision-making power and administration back as close as possible to those affected. That communities were encouraged to participate actively and were supported in working out a regional development concept is of inestimable, perhaps decisive, significance in three respects:

1. *in promoting collaboration among communities and thereby also promoting their ability to express themselves vis-à-vis the cantonal and federal governments;*

2. *in returning responsibilities to the region, responsibilities that in recent years had been delegated by the communities to the canton;*

3. *and in re-evaluating development to date, the current situation, and the common guiding image according to which future individual decisions would be made. (There is incalculable value today in pondering what is important in an age of seemingly limitless possibilities!)*

With the stimulus to establish regional secretariats supported by the federal government, an additional foundation stone was laid in the creation of a regional consciousness. In the course of time, the self-reliance of a region gains an external, visible framework through this sort of organ for coordinating and executing a regional development concept. To these positive aspects in Swiss development policy for regional autonomy we now must add a list of deficiencies. Let us begin with a critique of the planning mentality.

Shortcomings

One-Sided Development Concept

Decentralized Concentration

Up until recent years it was primarily the great material distress in rural areas, especially in mountain areas, that forced people to emigrate. Consequently public measures aimed at reducing the depopulation of these rural districts began with the issue of material need through improvement of usable income, agricultural production, and residential desirability. In recent years, however, the reason for emigration has shifted. More and more it has been less material need and more the attractiveness of the urban life-style that has led to people's leaving their native community in the country or in the mountains. Proceeding on the assumption that this trend might well continue to increase in future years, improvement in living conditions in mountainous areas threatened by emigration was planned along the following lines: By means of goal-directed support and promotion of regional centers, the advantages of the city could be brought more and more out into the country, as we have already discussed in chapter 2.

In the mandate for the Investment Aid Law (*investitionshilfegesetz*) we read the following as the rationale for the concept of regional concentration: "Regional centers are capable of meeting the need for an urban atmosphere, at least in part. Here the unemployed members of the work force from surrounding areas would be absorbed in order to prevent their emigration from the mountains into the large, populous, urban centers of the plains."[2] The surrounding communities, thus disadvantaged, could be supported in regard to the so-called absolute necessities, which include the water supply, schools, and development of transportation. In particular the expansion of commuter facilities between outlying communities and the regional center was accorded great importance. Through this, opportunities for wage-earning and consumption would be improved.

Without a doubt it makes sense to support the formation of a regional center where no adequate one exists. However, if the principle of concentration of investment with broad distribution of benefits is elevated to the level of a guiding image in general, it becomes extremely questionable. For a concept such as this is based on exactly those principles that facilitate the worldwide process of population agglomeration—mobility and concentration. This development concept is supposed to raise the rural area's competitiveness by creating an urban atmosphere, at least in the regional centers. What is contradictory in the concentration principle becomes more clearly visible if we call to mind that land-use policy should basically be a policy of compensation. So divorced from *volkstümlich* thought, the currently widespread and overvalued urban mentality and life-style—among whose features we find mobility and concentration—is supposed to be countervailed by a policy of equalization. The following example

---

[2]Mandate of 16 May 1973, p. 8.

illustrates how senseless this principle of concentration—not unreasonable in itself—can become when it is singled out as the sole, highest principle of support and development of rural areas.

As in many other regions, authorities initially intended to promote the process of concentration of the Inter-Cantonal Region of Wil,[3] which overlaps the Cantons of St. Gallen and Thurgau. The focus was on the centrally located town of Wil, to which access was to be improved. The justification for this was that Wil's already strong growth rate needed to be accelerated in order to assert itself over the cities of St. Gallen and Winterthur. The communities of the so-called *Winterthurgau*, on the other hand, were singled out as recreational areas. A development concept of this sort did not, of course, promote the independence of the surrounding communities. On the contrary, furthering the process of concentration meant an accelerated bloodletting for the rural population. Fortunately the surrounding communities, under the leadership of the president of the community of Fischingen, vehemently and successfully fought against this concentration concept.

To avoid possible misunderstanding, let us once again emphasize that the principle of so-called "decentralized concentration" in itself is not to be condemned. In remote districts there is certainly no dispute about developing and supporting central points and supplying them with the necessary infrastructure. But when promotion of a particular center aggravates an existing decline in attractiveness within a region and consequently accelerates emigration from rural communities, the concept of decentralized concentration becomes questionable. For the argument of "preserving the competitiveness vis-à-vis the next-larger unit," as we have seen in the case of Wil versus St. Gallen and Winterthur, arises out of a one-sided viewpoint that takes into account only the well-being of one place and not that of the region's overall structure. Even the city of Zürich advocates increasing its attractiveness (by improved urban transit, etc.) in the name of decentralized concentration, that is, in order to become more competitive than Paris, Vienna, Frankfurt, or Milan. Without its opposite, every principle becomes senseless at some point, including decentralized concentration, which we can also designate as the principle of rationalization or progress.

The basic principle of decentralized concentration for the purpose of strengthening rural independence really makes sense only if

---

[3]Here regional development did not fall under the terms of the Investment Aid Law; rather, it had to do with a so-called "regional planning" area.

decentralization as a principle takes its place beside the principle of concentration as a coequal.[4] In its own right, of course, regionalizing is a process of concentration. Individual communities come to some common agreement on an issue. But there is a fundamental difference between whether regionalization is intended as a first step toward dissolving community autonomy, or whether, thanks to regionalization, community autonomy is strengthened in that, for example, the Federation or the Canton grants political weight to a region through decentralization of tasks. In a comparable way, promoting concentration in a rural area can be called sensible only if the principle of concentration has relative validity. That is, this principle is appropriate only if its application works toward an effective decentralization—a concept that we must briefly discuss.

As mentioned earlier, the human being feels held and contained when in a social unit that is comprehensible. To be active and to have a sense of responsibility to oneself in such a setting makes possible not only an optimal blossoming of the individual, but also guarantees that the supraordinate social unit will thrive. Decentralization as a principle on which to build society does not of course mean "building society and the economy exclusively on nothing but small units, but rather a gradated structuring of social systems resting on subsystems of varying sizes appropriately distributed."[5] The functioning of the decentralized domains of responsibility and activity are guaranteed from below upwards, through what is called the *principle of subsidiaries*. By this we understand "that the higher level should assume only those tasks that the respective lower levels can accomplish either not at all or only inadequately. But the principle of subsidiaries also means, for example, that the state should not undertake the work of the economic system."[6] Accordingly, decentralization as a principle informing the support and development of rural independence does not mean exporting the urban, short-term profit mentality, known today, for example, in the "marketing of intact regions." Naturally this has nothing to do with the fundamental concerns for independent development worked out earlier. Thus when we speak of decentralization in this context, what is first and foremost intended is a re-

---

[4] As was done, for example, in the development outline for the Canton Uri.
[5] Bach, "Die Akualität der Gesellschaftslehre Othmar Spanns," in Bach, *Um eine büuerliche Landwirtschaft*, p. 21–33.
[6] Ibid., p. 27.

delegation of decision-making ability and power to the rural regions, as well as provision of appropriate job opportunities.[7] What that could mean will be discussed in Part 6.

In summary we can say this: If regional concentration and rationalization is all that is considered in supporting and developing rural areas, without paying attention in equal measure to the value and the meaning of decentralization, this sort of equalization policy brings about a one-sided strengthening of the existing trend toward overvaluation of things urban. We have already demonstrated in other respects how abundantly the seeming rationality of such catchwords as "concentration" and "increased mobility" are nourished by mythological energies and cannot hold their ground against true rational examination. Therefore a demythologization of this one-sided concept of development is called for.

Rationalizing away Relationships

In numerous realms, development of rural areas is understood to mean publicizing and carrying out sensible mergers and improvements of all sorts. Some examples will illustrate how the relationships and bonds of the people living in those areas are unscrupulously destroyed in this process.

As a means toward structural improvement in rural areas, the general guiding idea held by many authorities is that small units should be abolished in favor of larger ones: mergers of communities, consolidation of schools, large central cheese factories, abolition of water cooperatives, road corporations, and the like. What may be thoroughly justified in the individual instance can under certain circumstances lead to absurd creations when raised to the level of general principle. Rationalization and consolidation go forward for the sake of principle without attention being paid to the overall balance. The values of what Dahrendorf calls "ligatures," or relationships in plain English, constitute part of a holistic judgment. To achieve certain administrative advantages, which are often only minor, countless people's relationships are impoverished by rationalizations of this sort. They lose some of their sense of identity or belonging. For example, the community may assume administration of the central water supply or roads and paths; or the local authority may have a full-time official

---

[7]The current (1982–83) debate on the division of responsibilities between the Federation and the Cantons is a step in this direction.

who takes over all the responsibilities that were previously assumed by members of the village community as honorary offices, often "in turn," i.e., in rotation from one to another.

The short-sightedness of experts who have wholly embraced the principle of "cutting the cord" in order to construct "reasonable" and "rational" mergers and consolidations was recently illustrated in a meeting of landowners in a community in eastern Switzerland. The meeting was concerned with presenting information on a possible merger of landholdings. The plans were shown and discussed. A young farmer asked if they couldn't keep at least their favorite plots of land. But the engineer wouldn't hear of such "sentimental attachments" because such an arrangement would not permit a technically optimal solution.

This engineer should be kept after school and have it made clear to him that it is precisely those "sentimental attachments" that give the human being the feeling that "home is where the heart is." Only where this feeling lives do people gladly stay, even if the conditions of their life remain ever so uncomfortable. For it is then meaningful to them to live there despite all the inevitable negatives. They just simply like their land, their farmstead, their village. In contrast to this, where people are arbitrarily transplanted or "have the cord cut," they no longer know where they belong or what contains them. Then it is only a short step to emigration or to change of job. We need to open the other eye of the one-eyed philanthropist who would like to give the rural population a technically optimal solution. That is the eye that can recognize the values of relationship. To stay with our example of land consolidation, it would then be a matter of adapting technology to human and not the other way round. One or two favorite plots of land would remain in the farmer's possession, and the remainder would be merged into larger plots. Then we would not have an economically and technically optimal solution but rather an optimal overall balance, in which the satisfaction and *joie de vivre* of those involved plays a role.

On the basis of our examples we can single out an essential deficiency in our present-day conception of rural development. In the attempt at rationalization, rural development policy takes the relationship side of life far too little into account. Thereby we probably lose the best trump card that rural areas have: the countless emotional bonds of the people in rural, agrarian areas who have a folk mentality. These are the ties to the land, the community, and to tradition, as well as the respect for the dead and the timeless powers of the cosmic dimension. Disregarding these relationships signifies nothing less than a false evaluation of the attitude and mentality of the rural population, since it is, after all, these very same ties that have given rural life its particular quality since time immemorial. These emotional ties are the roots of independent folk culture, which have grown deep regardless of the size of the folk group; we need think only of the overwhelmingly rich culture of the Lötschen Valley with its mere 1,500 inhabitants![8] The quality of life nourished by emotional ties cannot be supplanted by an increase in material well-being, regardless of how great it is. However, if we advocate urban lack of ties and goal-directed rationality as the highest value, and if we plan change solely with the goal of liberation from progress-inhibiting commitment, then we propagate a corresponding uncertainty in the sense of identity and belonging.

Therefore present-day, one-sided development policies, geared to strengthening rural independence and aimed at external, material progress, absolutely must be supplemented by their missing dimension. What is lacking is careful attention to the spiritual and emotional human needs. It is well known that humanity does not live on material well-being alone; rather, above and beyond this, humanity wants to experience existence as meaningful. But that is only possible if we feel contained in a network of emotional relationships. Emotional relationships give us needed nourishment, existential meaning, and quality of life. Yet as everywhere else, it is true here that only those who know and take seriously their own spiritual and emotional needs are in a position to perceive and attend to this reality in their external activities. Only on the basis of one's own experience can the value of emotional bonds be recognized and consequently advocated. Here we are confronted with nothing less than the counterweight to the ever more demonic drive for progress and mobility, with its well-known consequences for rural areas and for agriculture. But insofar as we continue to promulgate only a rationalistic liberation from *volkstümlich* ties, thereby irresponsibly destroying our emotional bonds, and if we continue to place high value on materialistic externals at the expense of the spiritual-emotional dimension,[9] the logical consequence will continue to be migration from the less prosperous rural areas toward metropolitan wealth.

---

[8]Details on this can be found in Anneler, *Lötschen*.
[9]See, for example, Flückiger, *Gesamtwirtschaftliches Entwicklungskonzept für das Berggebiet*, as well as the *Grundlagen für die Berggebietsförderung*, the fifth *Landwirtschaftsbericht*, and the *Leitbild des Bauernverbandes*.

One-Sided Methodology

In addition to the one-sidedness in the development concept for our rural areas, there is a no less weighty bias in the process of realizing these goals, since all efforts at rural development rest on the scientific-statistical method. Rural areas are compared with urban districts using the "performance criteria" of population, income, job market, production, infrastructure, and public finance. Doubtless this analytical procedure is fully justified in laying the foundations for equalization policies. With such analyses, the extent and the development of regional imbalances can be clearly documented; and consequently they make it possible to institute effective countermeasures. However, if we reckon with all those values we have come to know in the course of this study of folk attachments and ties, the one-sidedness of this basically reasonable procedure can be described: It consists in detaching the values of rationality from an all-encompassing understanding of the human being. This means that our contemporary methodology and research in the field of rural development ignores an entire category of phenomena because those phenomena do not lend themselves to the mentality behind the research methodology being brought to bear.

With the statistical method of the natural sciences, differences can be made visible; for the purpose of knowledge, opposites are contrasted with each other. But what falls through the cracks of this procedure is the domain of the emotional relationship between the opposites discussed in the preceding chapter. Whether we mean the relationship of human to environment or the relationship of people to one another or even the relationship of humanity to the beyond, methodology in rural development is currently constituted as if considerations of this sort were nonexistent or at least irrelevant. An impressive amount of research in empirical sociology and psychology show how highly significant these emotional relationships are for people and human social life, and consequently also for human decision making, e.g., in the case of emigration.

Like a film in comparison to reality, a statistical truth without the entire relational atmosphere at work in an area is only a dry fragment of reality. For this reason, judging a situation when the subtle relational dimension has not been taken into consideration is not entirely realistic; every rural development policy that rests on such an analysis consequently takes into account only a part of human existence.[10] A procedure intended to improve the conditions of rural life that is limited to material needs will necessarily fall victim to the human emotionality that has been excluded. For a method that rests only on statistics despite every greater subtlety cannot establish a real relationship to that domain lying beyond supply and demand. As the English say, "You can't carry water in a sieve." Where the moved and the moving emotional substance cannot be grasped as a reality, this neglected side will again and again inundate the soulless image in the form of an emotional eruption. When we read on the wall of a "restaurante" in mountain village in Tessin

> God protect us
> From avalanches
> From forest fires
> And from planners

what is reflected is not only local vexation at the planner's way of doing things but also a very general displeasure with technocrats who create structures that completely fail to take into account that "folk" side of humanity which is bound to things in *participation mystique*.

Summary and Conclusions

Criticism of contemporary rural development policy in Switzerland leads to three general observations. First, study of the mentality informing our rural development policy has shown us that it derives practically in toto from the rational mode of economic and cause-effect thinking. Goal-directed, linear planning mentality, which considers things with an eye solely to their utility and productivity, appears to stand in irreconcilable opposition to the circular mode of thought and experience geared to a sense of continuity that is characteristically *volkstümlich*.

The analysis of our seemingly quite reasonable development plans shows how—via projection—our rational guiding images get mingled with mythic images from the archaic-folk level of our psyche. As we have also seen, this mingling of mythic fantasies with the activity of rational planning produces distinctly nonsensical results by externally concretizing certain images that should provoke modern people

---

[10]Practically speaking, recent studies in this area also take the dimension of social psychology into account only from the viewpoint of social technology. See Robert Abt, "Praxisorientierte Potentialbestimmung für nichttouristische Entwicklung in Bergregionen," Nationalfondsprojekt "Regionalprobleme Schweiz," Bern, 1980.

to take a step in *inner* development. It is precisely because a planned development in a rural area is concerned with the inscrutable future and with interconnections one cannot take in at a glance—a condition especially conducive to projections from the unconscious—that we must demand that the expert learn to distinguish between consciousness and the unconscious psyche that produces images. To continue to deny the influence of the unconscious on development planning and on similar activities must, therefore, be clearly and distinctly called *obscurantism*, the consequences of which may well be incalculably negative for the way we shape our future.

Second, if we look back to the beginning and call to mind the overall statement of the problem, we can now see more clearly why the opposites of spirit and matter, as well as subject and object, could fall out of relationship with each other, and why our modern loss of this unitary view has made a holistic rural development policy impossible. Where the only principle served is the principle of consciousness, which makes discrimination possible and assists in dissolving our ties to nature, appreciation for the other principle gets lost—namely the principle of our unconscious emotional relationships and hence our capacity for them. Rational mergers into larger units (concentration) as well as intensified dynamic forces and increased levels of exchange (mobility) belong to the principle of consciousness. In contrast to this, the principle of unconscious emotional relationships such as we have gotten to know in the folk way of life provides nourishment from the here and now in a more natural manner. But in order for this "root principle" to manifest its effects, a certain connectedness with the earth is necessary. An equalization policy that one-sidedly serves only the principle of consciousness and thereby damages those roots of the unconscious soul makes, for this very reason, no true contribution to the diminution of regional imbalances. On the contrary, through a concerted action that one-sidedly emphasizes and promotes the values of liberation from constraints, the contrast between "boring and backward" rural life and "attractive" city life is only aggravated. Where relationships are viewed as unimportant, meaning can no longer be drawn from one's immediate surroundings. This attitude empties rural life and closeness to the earth of their meaning.

Finally, on the basis of our observations, we must consider our contemporary rural development policy anew. The present outline for strengthening rural independence is inadequate. It does, after all, take too little into account those aspects that still powerfully shape rural and small-town areas, continuity and respect for relationships. Therefore the need for development of a new basic outline for rural development that includes these factors forces itself upon us.

PART 6

A GUIDING IMAGE FOR THE SUPPORT AND PROMOTION OF RURAL INDEPENDENCE WITH INCLUSION OF SOCIAL REALITIES

Prerequisite for the Guiding Image: Recognition of the "Unknown Other"

Every intervention intended to improve the conditions of rural life, commencing with local soil improvement and reaching all the way to regional development planning, is based on an analysis of existing conditions. All subsequent steps depend on this initial study. There is extensive technical literature on the procedures of recording, grouping, and interpreting the relevant data. However, in these methodological approaches to a systematic understanding of external data, what recedes into the background to the point of being meaningless is the subject of all knowledge, that is, the psyche.

On the basis of the fact that the psyche, as the beginning and the end of all knowledge, receives hardly any consideration in the disciplines of engineering and planning, we would have to assume an unproblematical nature and consequently its insignificance for a process of cognition. However, this is by no means the case. The decisive contribution to the discovery of the problem of human epistemology is made by the discovery of an unconscious realm of the psyche independent of consciousness. This fact has been elucidated from various sides in the course of our discussion here. But if the psyche, as the subject of knowledge, also exists in a dark form not immediately accessible to consciousness, then it follows that all our knowledge must be incomplete to a certain degree.[1]

Jung has pointed out that,

> between "I do this" and "I am conscious of doing this" there is a world of difference, amounting sometimes to outright contradiction. Consequently there is a consciousness in which unconsciousness predominates, as well as a consciousness in which self-awareness predominates. This paradox becomes immediately intelligible when we realize that there is no conscious content which can with absolute certainty be said to be totally conscious,[2] for that would necessitate an unimaginable totality of consciousness, and that in turn would presuppose an equally unimaginable wholeness and perfection of the human mind. So we come to the paradoxical conclusion that there is no conscious content which is not in some other respect unconscious.[3]

From this we can see how far conscious statements may claim only relative validity because their very contents are at the same time conscious and unconscious, that is, conscious from one particular viewpoint and unconscious from another.[4] "As is the way of paradoxes, this statement is not immediately comprehensible. We must, however, accustom ourselves to the thought that conscious and unconscious have no clear demarcations, the one beginning where the other leaves off. It is rather the case that the psyche is a conscious-unconscious whole."[5] Hence in every act of cognition there lies a "system-dependent" obscurity of which we are, however, generally not the least bit aware.

This psychological fact confirms for us the familiar observation from empirical sociology that in a complex situation we see, first of all, what we are accustomed to recognize, expect to recognize, or we want to recognize.[6] Therefore whatever we do not know in our inner world is likewise overlooked in the outer world or is perceived in distorted form. The analysis of any situation of complexity—such as confronts us in a rural area—therefore gains greater objectivity if the

---

[1]Details are to be found in Jung, "On the Nature of the Psyche," C. W. 8, p. 159ff.
[2]"As already pointed out by E. Bleuler, *Naturgeschichte der Seele und ihres Bewusstwerdens*, pp. 300ff," as Jung notes.
[3]Jung, "On the Nature of the Psyche," p. 187, par. 385.
[4]Jung, op. cit., p. 200, par. 397.
[5]Loc. cit.
[6]On this see Atteslander, *Methoden der empirischen Sozialforschung*.

party responsible takes pains not only with external data but also with his or her own "lens," that is, the individual organ of knowledge and especially its dark domain.

In our context, we cannot attempt to discuss every individual area of darkness or shadow that consists of forgotten or repressed contents. Since Freud's time voluminous literature has arisen on this subject, literature to which I refer the reader.[7] What must interest us in the present context, however, is that realm of our soul which quite generally leads a shadowy existence in our modern cultural consciousness. As we have seen, this collective dark realm is our capacity to experience in the archaic mode of *participation mystique*. Consciousness has gradually freed itself from its bondage to nature and drive and today has usually severed the connection completely. The consequence of this is modern humanity's loss of relationship to that inner "dark realm" out of which the light of consciousness has developed. Consequently we fall victim to the pernicious idea that we are simply what consciousness knows of itself.

With the separation of modern consciousness from the natural realm (i.e., from our ancestors' mode of experiencing), we have lost essential values such as elemental emotionality and creative power,[8] the capacity for *participation mystique*, and our ancestors' entire heritage stored in our instinctual underpinnings. In the chapter of folk thought, we discussed the values of psyche's "dark realm" in detail. But something else is even more important. Not only do we forfeit something valuable; with this separation we also lose the knowledge that, on the basis of our psyche's participation in pure nature, we likewise participate in evil,[9] in nature's destructive power. Hence through splitting off the dark realm of pure nature in us, we experience a double loss in that we lose not only the values of that dark realm but also the knowledge of our constantly present capacity to do abysmal evil just as nature herself can.

In becoming generally unconscious of the dark aspect of our nature, we project our shadow onto others. We cannot deny that the human being can perpetrate terrible things, but it is always the others who do

---

[7]A very instructive summary of the problem of the personal shadow is to be found in von Franz's essay, "The Process of Individuation," in Jung, *Man and His Symbols*. Concerning the shadow problem of planners, experts, etc., see my study, *Entwicklungsplanung ohne Seele?*, p. 266–68.

[8]An index of the degree to which we are cut off from our emotional background is the extent of a person's inability to express himself simply; emotion is, after all, the greatest simplification of expression! (See von Franz, "Die Erlösung des Weiblichen im Manne," p. 18.)

[9]Details on this in Jung, particularly in "The Undiscovered Self," *C. W.* 10.

them. What is true in world politics on a large scale we find on a small scale in regional and agrarian politics, too. Scientists and experts believe they do only good with their plans, programs, and designs; the devilish fruits of their work arise only because of greedy politicians, real estate agents, financial institutions, or foreigners. Conversely, the opponents of state intervention point their finger at the experts and technocrats whose fault it is that, in their opinion, the world we live in is going to the devil. And so each blames the other as the culprit; each side is profoundly convinced of their own innocence and rectitude, and does not notice that for this very reason the culprit is the third party, who has the last laugh. By simply dumping our ever-present capacity to do evil on the other person, "our lack of insight deprives us of the capacity to deal with evil."[10]

Today more and more people—especially young persons—feel they are lacking something; and for the most part they are seeking somehow to reestablish a connection with the split-off, natural part of the psyche. But the often predominant opinion—that simply by canceling out all the restrictions of the prevailing order one can again live naturally and in paradise—is a dangerous fallacy, for it carelessly underrates the reality of evil. In the last analysis it is precisely the uncanny, destructive power of blinding affect and the overwhelming power of the world of drives themselves that awakened the culture-creating need for a strengthening of consciousness.[11] Sinking back into the womb of nature, out of which our modern cultural consciousness has developed through laborious confrontation and struggle, is, for this reason, a misleading alternative.

The great task of our time, therefore, consists not in relapsing into the dark natural realm of our psyche, but rather—as C. G. Jung has attempted to present in his work—in two things: first, in seeing the existence of this "unknown other" in us, which means experiencing it; and second, in letting this other reality also live in us so that we do not become its victim, which means that we give it human proportions.

As we have seen, it is not a question of a new social program to improve the world, but rather of the urgently needed, albeit unpleasant task of the *individual*. For recognizing and acknowledging the "unknown other" in us means perpetual conflict; and having a conflict means being painfully suspended between opposites. Only by

---

[10]Jung, "The Undiscovered Self," *C. W.* 10, par. 572.
[11]Without the profound need in late antiquity for moral mastery over human animal drives, Christianity and Mithraism could not have spread.

consciously accepting and enduring our own dual nature, with all the suffering that it entails, can an objective attitude arise. Then, for example, we no longer fall so easily for the trick of our inner devil, who tempts us to this or that power play and moreover, makes us believe we did it for noble, selfless, and idealistic reasons. We may assume that the catastrophic consequences of such unconscious devilment are generally well known. But even a compassionate smile at the folk mode of thought, at the view of the world held by our ancestors "who didn't know any better," is hardly appropriate any longer when we take a look at our own world of inner ancestors.

In acknowledging the unknown other in our psyche, a side of ourselves that harbors simultaneously the most precious things and the greatest dangers, we create the precondition for shaping a guiding image for rural development. Those who have come to know the value of things primal and close to the folk mentality in themselves will also have an eye for those worthwhile external things that lie outside the achievements of our contemporary progress mentality. And those who have made the inner acquaintance of their own perpetually lurking potential for evil will surrender the naive idea that it is possible to destroy the roots of devilish machinations and mechanisms externally, say by altering inadequate collective conditions.

As we have seen, the change from the primordial mode of thinking and living characterized by *participation mystique* to the rationalistic and individualistic life-style is reflected externally in increasing regional imbalances. In the same way, the break between locally shaped and locally customary structures and modern rootless constructions and arbitrary zones reflects externally our general psychic dissociation of consciousness from the unconscious. Now if the image that guides the strengthening of rural independence were to take either side—aligning either with maintenance and preservation or with further rationalization and concentration—the split would only be widened. Only if our guiding image takes a compensatory stance vis-à-vis the existing trend—itself the result of one-sided attitude of consciousness—is there any possibility for a new equilibrium. Compensatory means making a conscious one-sidedness complete and consequently whole. Therefore a guiding image for strengthening regions threatened with emigration, an image compensatory to the existing trend, must not be informed solely by the principles of the calculatedly rational and rootless planning mentality, but rather it will also have to embrace the values of the primordial, folk view of the world in addition to those of our modern cultural consciousness.

If we recognize and acknowledge the "unknown other" in us in the manner we have outlined, we will, first and foremost, become more modest in our practical work in the realm of rural development, for after all we must see that we have lost the relationship to an entire domain of reality in our psyche. If we find persons in the world about us who stand closer to the primordial, folk mode of experience, thanks to a rural life-style, we will become more receptive to the "unknown other" in the external world. We will seek dialogue with those persons, who have become questioners, and thus lose the arrogance of expertise. Whoever thus comes into relationship internally and externally with the reality of the "other world" typified by a folk mentality and *participation mystique* will pay necessary attention to this realm in practical activities, too. From this will arise the understanding we need in order to grasp why the primordial, folk view of the world must be included in an image guiding the development of rural areas. In view of the fact that both modern physics and modern psychology confront us with the truth of the relativity of opposites, we must also broaden our view and act in accordance with a guiding image in which this relativity or, more precisely, the relationship between the opposites, is honestly acknowledged and taken seriously, whether opposition is between consciousness and the dark world of the unconscious, between subject and object, or between the spiritual interior world and the material external world.

The Parameters of the Guiding Image: Respect for the Subtle Network of Relationships

Basic Principles

The aim of Part 6 of this work is to draw up a guiding image for rural development, a guiding image that does justice not only to the current ideas of our conscious world but also includes the "unknown other." The current ideas about rural development are well known: amelioration of the material conditions of life through raising the income level and improvement of residential desirability. Now in order to understand and include the needs of that side of the human psyche which is capable of *participation mystique*, we must once again briefly review the essential features of the archaic-folk mode of experiencing.

The central value in the *volkstümlich* or folk way of life is, in my opinion, the unconscious relatedness to four realms that, taken together, comprise all aspects of life:

1. *the relationship to matter and thus also to the land;*

2. *the relationship to the spirit and thus to all the things of the beyond, such as the dead;*

3. *the relationship to the community and thus to its tradition and its customs;*

4. *the relationship to oneself, that is, to one's own activity and therefore the responsibility not to behave wantonly.*

If we depict this fourfold relationship in the form of a cross, we have an orienting compass in the center of which stands the person of the folk mentality who relates through *participation mystique*:

The folk person is united with all of these domains. Through them he or she feels on the one hand at home and on the other hand bound or obligated to them by relatedness. As long as this subtle network of emotional relationships is intact, we can speak of a bond to place and to community. Whether this place be the north-facing slope of the Schächen Valley in Canton Uri or the village of Schattenhalb in the Bernese Hasli Valley, as long as these various emotional relationships are to some extent intact, people love the place where fate has placed them, even if in the winter they must again and again see how the farms and homesteads on the other side of the valley bask in the sun.

If the network of relationships is intact, people leave their ancestral homes only if they absolutely must, that is, if, for example, they are forced to make a life elsewhere. We find this frequently confirmed in Swiss mountain areas. For example, although the Schächen Valley and the Isen Valley, both in Canton Uri, present natural conditions under which production is not at all favorable, we find a surprisingly good familial succession in agriculture compared to other similarly situated mountain valleys.[1] One could more easily find two than none willing to carry on the family farm. Various recent studies have shown that the network of relationships in these valleys has remained intact to a great extent. The people there—and not just the farmers—feel a pronounced bond with the soil. They cultivate community life and a community spirit in the form of active, neighborly self-help and in vital community organizations such as theater groups. They have a direct and living relation to their tradition and religion as well as to the sense of their own responsibility, which is reflected in continuing the practice of the call to prayer from the alps.

In recent years, however, behavior has changed even in those mountain communities, and nearly everywhere we find a loosening or questioning of emotional ties. Due primarily to schooling and to the mass media, the individual has become more conscious of education, job, and advancement, among other things; and the conse-

---

[1]See Abt, *Das Aufrüstungsprogramm für die Urner Land- und Forstwirtschaft*, p. 11.

quence of this has been the imperceptible loosening of the traditional bonds and attachments that used to be primary codeterminants of one's actions.[2] In almost all instances, planned interventions and overall economic development schemes enhance this trend. Hence people consider attachment to one's surroundings to be a static attitude and as self-satisfaction standing in the way of modern "developing society."[3] As an exponent of a mentality particularly fond of planning, Karl Marx expressed this to an extreme degree when he lamented the French peasants' unenergetic attitude: "One plot, one peasant, one family; next door another plot, another peasant, another family. . . . Thus the great mass of the French nation is built by simple addition of quantities having the same denominator, as a sack of potatoes makes up a potato sack."[4] Of course one cannot make a revolution with people like that. Hence Marx advocated the formation of large-scale agricultural operations, severing the peasants' bonds to their individual plots. Even if Karl Marx's ideology is not the official state doctrine among us in the West, various of our "four-year development plans" have nevertheless moved us into a certain proximity with the well-known five-year plans in the U.S.S.R.

How do things stand today? Does the materialistic mode of thinking and acting—that, as we have seen, very closely resembles Marxist ideology—really give us the promised happiness on earth? Let the following moving incident serve to illustrate one consequence of contemporary "liberation" from every sort of attachment: While on vacation in a mountain village, a young family lost one of their children in a hiking accident. After the cremation, the parents were given the urn and faced the problem of where they could give their beloved child its final resting place. They had not yet established any real relationship to the suburb of a metropolis where they lived, and the possibility of a job-related change of residence was not impossible. Thus the cemetery of the suburb where they lived was out of the question. Moreover, neither the father nor the mother had any relationship to their native villages. As a temporary solution, the urn found a place in a clothes closet in their flat. The parents were painfully aware of something in that mountain village where the accident had taken place. They saw how the cemetery up the mountain was a part of the community and that in the evening candles were lit on graves of those who had recently died. They recognized how the connectedness in

---

[2]See Jaeggi, *Probleme der Planung im ländlichen Raum*, p. 202.
[3]On this point see the chapter entitled "Triebkräfte der Landentwicklung" in Planck and Ziche, *Agrarsoziologie*, p. 348ff.
[4]Quoted in Planck and Ziche, op. cit., p. 333.

this must give the people a feeling of being contained and held safe in something more comprehensive. Naturally there will be those critics who smile condescendingly at this example and say that we have prosperity in place of a cemetery, while that mountain village is suffering a population loss through emigration. I know that, too. I also understand that mountain villages are no postcard idylls but rather places in which, like everywhere else, there exist internal tensions, class stratifications, and power structures. But above and beyond such facts as these, I can only add one thing: When I heard of this incident, it moved me profoundly and opened my eyes to what we have lost with the thoughtless destruction of our soul ties in favor of a one-sided worldview oriented solely to the here and now.

We neither want to nor can we turn back the wheel of time. No planner can breathe new life into symbolic structures that have lost their vitality and hence their function. But we can learn something from the disadvantages of an exaggerated urge for freedom and mobility. In rural development particularly it would seem obvious not only to support and promote modern things but also to strengthen the awareness of the values that still exist, i.e., our soul's living ties and bonds. (Here we may continue to use the word "soul," even if a noted sociologist[5] instructs us that the word "soul" is old-fashioned.) An increased consciousness of those aspects of the quality of life still found in varying degrees in rural areas but lacking in urban settings is certainly meaningful to compensate for the current tendency to view our rural population one-sidedly as "worse off" and "under-privileged."

For our guiding image this means insight into the significance of the subtle network of relationships. Moreover, it means that in all our planned interventions for supporting, developing, and promoting rural areas we must scrupulously weigh those bonds of the soul that might be destroyed against what our intervention could bring in terms of actual improvement—whether we are considering consolidation of landholdings, formation of a region, an action to root out all the old fruit trees in an area, a major investment in tourism, or any other planned structural alteration. In contrast, whenever we simply dissolve and destroy naturally evolved structures and with them the bonds of the soul, we export the urban process of reducing people to nobodies, or *"Verniemandung,"* as was once spray-painted on an urban

---

[5]Jaeggi, *Probleme der Planung im ländlichen Raum*, p. 205.

concrete wall. When this happens there can no longer be any talk of developing the *indigenous* potential in a rural area.[6]

In order better to understand this domain of the soul as a limiting condition for our guiding image, let us turn our attention to each of the four bonds characterizing the folk mentality.

The Relationship to Matter

In the relationship to a specific environment there exists a fundamental difference between that of a native and that of an engineer, planner, or other expert from outside. Especially for the natives in rural areas the surrounding world is a *vis-à-vis* that has arisen naturally, which has grown over the course of time to be as it presents itself at the moment of observation; even what is useless and not purposeful has its history, its memories, its significance. In contrast, the same world appears fundamentally different to the outside expert, who must be concerned with technical and economic improvements. For that expert the very same stuff belongs to the local "inventory" which must be assayed and evaluated for to its utility. The landscape, the soil, the buildings, the institutions, yes even the inhabitants, are examined and assessed for their utilitarian suitability in the expert's eyes. However, we must clearly understand that this distanced, technocratic mode of thought is being adopted more and more by the rural population.

In most cases of planned rural development, improvements are conceived by outside experts on the basis of this sort of actual assessment. Depending on the project, such improvements are then realized immediately or must first be presented to a larger segment of the population for their appraisal. Now here is the decisive point: If material advantages are predominant in a project, the probability is great that a supporting majority will be found. In the view toward the possibility of a better future, structures that have arisen naturally over time are degraded to the status of secondary factors. They are limiting conditions at T_0, so-called time-zero; and these baseline conditions must, if necessary, be "reconstructed" to some degree in the direction of a general increase in prosperity according to the goals established. Here a group of houses, there a landscape, must be sacrificed to some

---

[6]J. K. Galbraith wrote of the value of attachments and ties in his book, *The Affluent Society* (German ed., *Gesellschaft im Ueberfluss*, p. 302ff.) without, however, recognizing the reality and meaning in this context of the unconscious structures.

sort of technical improvement.[7] With this kind of ahistorical and unrelated, but factual, viewpoint, there arises a break in the continuity of
what has been. Those things that, like the annual rings of a tree
trunk, have evolved over the centuries in the space we inhabit, that
have their own character and a structure specific to their locality,
suddenly lose their meaning.

We recognize this break in relatedness to the matter around us most
distinctly in architecture. Alongside historically shaped and self-
contained villages fitting meaningfully into the landscape, we find
"functional" architecture with its drawing-board face proliferating
like a cancer, boring but practical, the sort one can find the world
over. This contemporary architecture is a visual correlative of the
unrelated mentality that informs our planning. Contempt for everything that has arisen over time was expressed probably most inci-
sively by the "great" architect Le Corbusier. He said, "The core of our
cities, with their churches and cathedrals, must be broken to bits and
replaced with skyscrapers. . . . Il faut recommencer à zéro [We have to
go back to square one]."[8]

To the degree that the new, the modern, progress, and a better
future become the only valid norms, not only does our understanding
of the value of what has arisen naturally vanish, but our relationship
to the here and now disappears, too. The prevalence of development
in linear time estranges humanity from our existence in space and
from the ever-recurring cycles of waxing and waning. The more
tomorrow dominates, the more provisional and hence restless today
becomes. Therefore, whenever a rural development policy speaks
only of progress and linear time, a process of inner estrangement is
promoted, a dissolution of the emotional relation to our surroundings. But this is precisely the most counterproductive thing that a
policy intended to slow the flight from the country could attain.
Those who no longer feel emotionally bonded with their surroundings become drifting sand that can be blown to whatever place has
the greatest power to attract.

Therefore a truly realistic development policy will strive to respect
human relatedness to the established environment as it supports and
promotes innovation, either by reducing emphasis on the idea of a
better future or by abandoning radical alteration of existing structures. Taking into consideration our subtle, emotional relationship to

---

[7]See also Schwabe, *Verwandelte, verschandelte Schweiz? 100 Beispiele aus dem 19. und 20.
Jahrhundert.*
[8]Quoted from Hauser, "Verwandelte, verschandelte, entartete Schweiz," p. 2.

matter ultimately means paying attention to the commonly unconscious needs of the territorial, animal soul upon which so much of our
physical well-being depends. In most instances of rural development
this means defending the claims of the unconscious soul vis-à-vis a
one-sidedly materialistic viewpoint. That viewpoint arises frequently
out of short-term advantages that prompt us to modify landscapes
and structures that have arisen naturally.

In this age of gigantic destruction of the environment for utilitarian
purposes are such thoughts not purely utopian? Perhaps they are.
But there are also hopeful signs that human attitudes toward our
material foundation are changing. This is exemplified in the statement of principles of the "Zürich Mountain Area," which, with its
approximately 35,000 inhabitants, corresponds roughly to the Canton
Uri in terms of population.[9] "The basis of the development concept
for the 'Zürich Mountain Area' region consists in defending and promoting existing values, without, however, encouraging a forced
growth. In particular this means: . . . preservation of the landscape
and of the structure of communities as it has taken shape over the last
generations. The landscape shall be preserved as a genuine, i.e., non-
mechanized and non-commercialized, recreational area."[10]

That the principles of the region known as the "Zürich Mountain
Area" were not empty words was proven recently by the community
of Fischental in the Zürich Oberland. A showman wanted to erect a
"Disneyland Recreation Center" on a 12.5 acre plot zoned for industrial use.[11] The numerous visitors to such a center would indeed have
brought business and jobs into the mountain community, but not
without extensively compromising an intact landscape as well as
existing structures. Against these considerations the showman was
ultimately unable to find a majority to support his project; preservation of the charming landscape took precedence. In reaching this
decision, application of the principles cited above played no small
role.

Certainly this example is a rare case; and certainly countless political decisions will still be made in which people will neglect the needs
of the soul in favor of material advantages during the evaluation
phase. Every change in general human attitude takes years, genera-

---

[9]The region includes fifteen communities from the Cantons of Zürich, St. Gallen, and
Thurgau, and has easy auto access to the city of Zürich for recreational purposes
(about 40 km).
[10]Quoted from Abt, "Entwicklungsconzept für die Region 'Pro Züricher Berggebiet,'"
Part 1, p. 11.
[11]See the *Neue Zürcher Zeitung*, 9–10 February 1980, p. 52.

tions; but it is always individual cases like the one mentioned from which the "multiplier effect" can proceed to form a new, general attitude to the space in which we live.

Relationship to the Spirit

It is peculiarity of numerous modern persons that they lead a life geared totally to their physical existence. In contrast to this, the life of our ancestors was not nearly so limited, being almost endlessly extended "backwards"−via the living relation to their predecessors in their reverence for tradition and ancestral spirits−and "forwards"− via a conscious orientation of earthly existence toward a spiritual life after death. This moored their brief earthly life in eternity. The link to the objective spiritual dimension was the experience of the reality of the soul and consequently the continual concern with the soul's well-being. Every community had what was needed to care for the soul as the most central institution, a statement that holds true today only to a quite limited extent.

The relationship to this spiritual dimension began to wane with general enlightenment, at the time when the world was being disen-chanted or de-souled. The objective spirit came to be viewed as a subjective phantom and the soul as subjectivity itself, insofar as its existence was not totally denied. Spirit was identified with intellect and the objective spirit equated with the sum of human intellectual attainments. What thus remained to humanity was only material exis-tence. With the loss of the dimension of the objective spirit, the inti-mation and the significance of consciousness-transcending constants was also lost. Modern humanity now believes only in itself, that is, in the world of human consciousness and in the possibility of somehow creating a better world with the help of progress. Through this pro-cess of secularization our thought and action is no longer directed toward something beyond our consciousness, i.e., to something objectively spiritual. Consequently the driving energy and urge to freedom on the part of our consciousness have lost their moorings in any comprehensive context of meaning. Loss of this relativity ulti-mately signifies the loss of moderation. Wherever consciousness loses the sense of the larger context, people are ready to adapt their entire way of life to this or that "liberation or development movement."

We can deplore this process of spiritual impoverishment, but we cannot revoke it. Where the soul as the link to the objective spirit has been lost, the experience of the efficacy of the spiritual dominants− whose all-embracing center has been represented by the god-image since time immemorial—also slips away. But if the experience of this realm of reality has disappeared, well-meant appeals to relate more to the beyond and to cultivate religious rites are of mighty little help. For the objective spirit can again become an experienceable counterpart only where a soul relationship can be established. Whether or not this relationship is sought depends on the extent to which a person is compelled to do so by the circumstances of life and is ready to accept the reality of the soul and take its stirrings seriously. Since time immemorial it has been the events of the soul that have given humanity indications of the objective spirit. Neither from the pulpit nor from the TV screen has the divine revealed itself to us but rather out of the depths of our soul. As C. G. Jung formulated it: "God has never spoken to man except in the soul and through the soul, and the soul understands, and we experience it as something having to do with the soul. Whoever calls that psychologizing denies the eye that sees the sun."[12]

In general even the cool rationalist, when faced with impending danger, is ready once again to seek and to cultivate a direct relation to the objective spirit. As we know, illness, war, and imminent death force countless people to their knees. The following document illustrates for us how a major threat causes our relationship to our ancestors and to the Almighty to be revived. When the Swiss Federal Assembly elected Henry Guisan general in 1939, the Assembly's president, H.-F. Valloton, turned to the newly elected Guisan with the following words:

> *Tell the army that it is not alone, but that all Swiss—men and women, young and old, the living and the dead—are keeping watch at the borders. We entrust to you, General, the protection of our people and our country that we all love boundlessly and that we will never, under any pretext or conditions, surrender to an intruder. May God bless your lofty task, General! God preserve our fatherland and protect our army!*[13]

What finds expression here is the direct acknowledgment of and appeal to the powers of the beyond, not by just any idle dreamer but by the highest ranking political figure of the time. Words like these make a deep impression and were doubtless highly significant in the psychology of defense. They mediate the relationship to a spirit that

---

[12]Jung, *Letters*, 15 VIII, 1932; *Briefe I*, p. 132.
[13]See Bonjur, *Geschichte der schweizerischen Neutralität*, vol. 4, p. 45; and as very beautifully expressed in a broader context see Scheuber, *Ein Urschweizer erzählt*, p. 67–77.

can move and inspire. Through them a momentary existential crisis can be seen in a different light or context of meaning and consequently be more readily mastered. Of this spiritual aspect Henry Guisan said: "I am proud that I, too, am permitted to protect something of the spirit of our country. In the hour of decision everything depends on this spirit alone. I will do everything to cultivate it also in our military training."[14]

It is probably not in vain that there is so much talk today of *animation rurale*. We all sense ever more distinctly how little enthusiasm can ever arise for a common project from dry statistics, whether for a regional development plan or a more localized undertaking by a group of individuals. A one-sided scientific attitude lacks the soul's relationship to a living spirit that allows a feeling of unity to arise above and beyond special interests and the force of circumstances. But naturally only human beings who are themselves concerned for their soul can establish and inspire this relation to the living spirit, and consequently only such people can really contribute anything when it is a question of "animation" (*anima* = soul).

The image guiding the development of our economically weak rural regions must aim at assuring and improving the conditions of material existence *without* destroying something else that is essential in the process. Promoting material development must not promote human hubris. For ultimately what good is increased prosperity if the devil of progress kidnaps the soul, that is, if in the process the soul's relatedness is lost? The soul is the link to the spirit, to a spiritual aim in life, to the real meaning of life; therefore where things of the soul atrophy because of a rationalistic view of the world, the relationship to the objective spirit is lost. Since the time that we have de-souled the world, "we no longer understand the language of the dwarfs," as a legend from Solothurn tells us.[15] In fact, with the loss of our relationship to a spiritual reality, we are also threatened with the loss of our capacity to understand the subtle stirrings of our inner nature. Consequently our capacity for relationship to meaning—inherent in our nature—atrophies, thus degrading our existence to a meaningless statistical unit. But if we no longer see meaning in life, the material conditions under which our soul languishes are also a matter of indifference.[16] Therefore in our guiding image for rural development, the necessary respect for the soul's existing bonds to the objective spirit

---

[14]Quoted from Scheuber, op. cit., p. 73.

[15]Pfluger, *Solothurner Sagen*, p. 241–243.

[16]Von Franz, "The Process of Individuation," in C. G. Jung (ed.), *Man and His Symbols*, p. 224.

must have its place, something that we can by no means take for granted. For unfortunately, he is no isolated case, that "clever" young agrarian engineer who made the cynical comment when he saw a burial ritual in a mountain village: "It's like among savages." Fundamentally, such "enlightened" arrogance is tragic, for it reflects how completely this man has split off his consciousness from his archaic capacity for *participation mystique*. With this sort of attitude we can rationalize very independently and efficiently in rural areas; but by despising the spiritual dimension we also injure that subtle fabric of relationships to the world beyond, as has already happened and continues to happen in countless villages and developing countries.

Relationship to the Community

The nature of and the change in the rural village community were treated in detail in Part 4 of this book. At the end of our discussion the question was posed about what brings about the feeling of belonging in a village following the dissolution of *participation mystique*. Discussion of this question revealed the significance of the "liberated" ego's reestablishing its bonds with the deeper levels of the soul capable of *participation mystique*. In addition to this inward-directed task, cultivating external, interpersonal relationships in the village was found to be important. In that discussion brief mention was made of those things in the domain of village structures that promote this social contact: the school, little shops, the milk collection station, and part-time office-holding were examples of this. One conclusion for our guiding image for strengthening rural independence was that the framework favorable to relationships still existing in many rural areas must not be thoughtlessly sacrificed to innovation and rationalization. Here further study is necessary to find out which structures in a community especially promote interpersonal contact.

What are the structures conducive to relationship? The temptation would be great to apply something like factor analysis to all the things that would have to be included. And then there would be the equally great danger of slipping into a formalized policy of conservation on the basis of such definitions. This can be illustrated with the example of road building. As we know from experience, good automobile routes between rural communities and urban centers increase not only commuting to work but also increase leisure time mobility. Conversely, rural communities increasingly become residential and recreational areas for city dwellers. But all this breaks up village cohesiveness. We cannot, however, demand that road building in rural areas be prohibited. Something similar could also be said about television or, more generally, about raising the level of prosperity; for both have a destructive effect on village life. Here, too, general pronouncements and courses of action help little to clarify what "structures conducive to relationship" really are supposed to be. Even in a prosperous household with a TV, relationship to people can be cultivated. Only one thing is decisive for our guiding image, and that is to take into consideration the fact that there are areas of village life which, under certain circumstances, play a very important role for social life. In addition to village autonomy, these include, first and foremost, the village school, a village pub, and last but not least, a spiritual center. To illustrate what we have said, let us take the example of the village school.

Relationship structures were unscrupulously destroyed in the schools of many Swiss communities, especially. In near all rural areas, one-room village schools were abolished — usually on the initiative of jurisdictional superiors — and consolidated in suitably situated places. Often this took place in the conviction that the children would be better educated.[17] On the other hand, such considerations took little note of the fact that the children became estranged from their village or their mountain valley at a very early age because of their daily commute. This was particularly true for certain mountain villages in the Italian part of Switzerland, where a consolidation point for the central elementary school was chosen at the mouth of a valley, for example in the Muggio Valley or in Val Calanca. Every one-sided advocate for centralized elementary schools should experience at least once how deserted a remote mountain village in Tessin feels on a frosty November morning when the fathers have left for their commute to work and the small school children have left for their distant school. What young mother would feel really contented and contained, or would argue in favor of making a home in such a place? Moreover, there is the multiplier affect — having no school in the village lets the typical village manner and the traditions borne among children wither away, which further undermines the feeling of belonging to one's native place. The end of the village school also means the end of a local school board and local school activities in which the various local families regularly get together. And in all those instances where a village school teacher might have had a wide

---

[17]In some instances, a temporary lack of teachers was the precipitating factor in school consolidation.

range of interests, not having a local school means not having a chorus or perhaps not having a theater group, depending on the interests of the teacher.

On the other hand, various examples in Switzerland show how it is certainly possible to support a village school even in small communities. An example of this is the school in the small community of Göscheneralp in Canton Uri. Barely fifty people live there year-round. The (approximately) ten children in this community go down to the village of Göschenen to school during the summer as long as the road is open, but in the winter they have their own school up on the mountain. Thanks to the cooperativeness of the school authorities of the Canton Uri, one of the women living in Göscheneralp—a trained kindergarten teacher—was given the opportunity to continue her training by taking individual courses and qualifying as a primary teacher. Today this woman is able to run the one-room school in Göscheneralp on her own. Surely this is an example pointing the way to a relationship-promoting policy intended to strengthen rural independence.

In the same way, we could honor the significance for village social life of such institutions as the village store, the village pub, agricultural establishments, cooperatives, societies, etc. But, as already emphasized, in our guiding image it cannot be a question of this or that rigid policy of preserving existing structures. In this context it is critical that both sides be looked at in every innovation: What are the advantages? What are the disadvantages? The latter are often of a spiritual, emotional nature as illustrated in our example of the elementary school. If this sort of intangible disadvantage weighs heavily, people may have to accept a material sacrifice and, perhaps, forego certain possibilities of rationalization. Ultimately this is the touchstone that will show whether people are ready to preserve relationship-promoting conditions that are regarded as especially important, but limiting.

As the last chapter of our observations we now come to the fourth relationship of the *volkstümlich* person, the relationship to one's own actions.

Relationship to Oneself

The idea is widespread that life in a village community and the free development of the individual are irreconcilable opposites. In fact, many young people do indeed emigrate from rural communities because they want to escape village social control and shape their lives freely under urban conditions. Here we have the rural community with its way of life prescribed by custom, lacking the possibility of self-development; there, by contrast, we have the urban society with its freedom of individual development. Is this contraposition valid, or is this an instance of a misleading oversimplification?

As we have seen in the chapter dealing with the discoveries of modern psychology, we must severely relativize the possibility of the freedom to choose. If we believe that the choice (assuming external freedom of choice) of partner, job, or of something quite ordinary is possible solely on the basis of consciousness, we are in error. For every choice is the reflection of our total psychic constellation at the moment. In other words, in the process of making a decision, both the unconscious and consciousness have played a role. Numerous psychological test procedures are based on this fact.

The more we are influenced by individual affect-laden concepts, the more often we make decisions that do not come out of our entire being. Despite degrees of external freedom, this does not make us freer by any means. On the contrary, absence of external bonds exposes us to the broad spectrum of compulsive impulses from within the psyche. In precisely the same way that we can only attain degrees of external freedom when we attempt to relate to the laws of external nature, our freedom from inner psychic compulsions also depends on whether or not we succeed in relating correctly to our instincts, that is, to the laws of our inner life. To a great extent we have lost our relation to the vital, inner foundation because of prevailing, fundamentally extraverted attitudes. The result is that we increasingly disregard inner laws. But those who no longer live in harmony with their inner nature become divided against themselves and therefore no longer live at peace with themselves. That is to say, they become internally dissatisfied, or more precisely, they become neurotically dissatisfied. Those who live contrary to the inner laws of life in one way or another suffer again and again from "inexplicable" disturbances from the inner world—e.g., from ominous presentiments, disagreeable fantasies, and burdensome moods, or they get carried away and make "stupid decisions" of one kind or another in the objective world. Despite external freedom, this naturally leads to a feeling of no freedom. Hence those who believe they will attain greater freedom only through dissolving external attachments deceive themselves. The feeling of freedom, the feeling that one can actualize oneself in life, is by no means dependent only on the external limiting conditions under which one lives, but certainly rests just as much on the individual's capacity correctly to relate to the laws of inner nature.

Between folk thought and enlightened thought we have been able to discern a fundamental difference in the relation to the laws of human inner nature. Since *volkstümlich* or folk people do not consider themselves nature's rulers but rather experience again and again its superior power, they need to take many precautions in order to assert themselves against nature. This holds true not only for external, physical nature, but also for the inner drive nature with its affects, desires, and aggressions. This is why folk thought is characterized by scrupulous respect for the underlying drive nature with all its laws.

The proper way to deal with this drive nature is evident in folk life in the form of Christian and magical rituals and ideas. By their nature they are symbolic—we need only remember the golden ring or the sign of the cross. But since symbols are never consciously thought up but rather are spontaneous products of the unconscious,[18] both arise from the same realm—the power of drives *and* the countervailing power that opposes the drive and gives it a meaningful form. This is no contradiction, for the essential element of our unconscious background is this polar structure, in the sense that drives (as the biological aspect) and their limitation (as the so-called spiritual or cultural aspect) belong to the nature of the unconscious.[19] We experience this drive-limiting principle as that unknown something in the psyche which engenders and marshalls the images on its own, as in our fantasies and dreams. We call this unconscious principle *spirit* because we can observe that these inner images and sequences of images are ordered in a most ingenious manner, namely for the purpose of self-regulation. Because of this meaningful content we do not simply speak of images but of "images of meaning" (German, *Sinnbilder*, "pictures/images of meaning") or of symbols. Symbols, consequently, are the expression of a drive-regulating spirit, a spirit that strives to bring the multiplicity of drives into a unitary structure. Konrad Lorenz speaks of a "parliament of instincts"; the symbol-shaping function in humans corresponds to the president of such a parliament.[20]

The symbolism of rituals, myths, sagas, and legends handed down from our forebears is, consequently, something like a visible precipitate of the drive-regulating spirit. In the same way that the drive structure of our predecessors is rediscovered in our inheritance, we

---

[18] I.e., revelations or intuitions.

[19] In the animal kingdom it is by no means the case that drives such as aggression, sexuality, etc., are limitless; they are held within certain bounds by counterimpulses, e.g., the attack inhibition when the enemy assumes a posture of submission, periodicity in sexual activity, etc. C. W. 8, par. 88–113.

[20] Loc. cit.

also find there the limitation of our drives. This consists of a spiritual inheritance consisting of "pathways" for the symbolic function of the psyche, which permeate all (individual) drive limitations.[21] "The mind, as the active principle in the [psychic] inheritance, consists," as Jung says, "of the sum of the ancestral minds, the 'unseen fathers,' whose authority is born anew with each child."[22] If the entire store of symbols in folk heritage forms our external cultural inheritance, the archetypal structures that shape and order the inner, visible images in a specific, meaningful manner are our inner spiritual inheritance.[23] As long as such symbols are vital, they function as *agentia* against the unbounded forces of the drives. In other words, these images are capable of imparting a proven human measure to the drives. But if symbols lose their spiritual efficacy, their efficacy in limiting the drives also dwindles. Therefore to a person for whom symbolic truth is no longer real (in the sense of having an effect), making the sign of the cross in order to exorcise a devilish compulsion makes no sense at all.

The decline in the efficacy of symbols, of which religion has always been the custodian, is characteristic of our scientific age. The extent of the individual's and society's loss of living symbols can scarcely be estimated, for with it the relationship to our spiritual inheritance has been lost. That means that we no longer understand the spirit of our ancestors, the spirit that could capture the energy of drives in effective forms and thus make culture possible. If this symbol-creating function loses its relationship to contemporary life, the inner connection between drive and drive limitation is lost, too. However, since the biological drive and its spiritual limitation are both dynamic principles (otherwise they could not counterbalance each other), both the drive and the drive-limitation become boundless in their unrestricted possibilities for action. Loss of moderation is, in every instance, the visible consequence of the loss of the symbol. Today this has become generally recognizable in licentious, biological compulsion and in loss of the human measure in spiritual ideas, ideologies, and development projects and plans of all sorts.

If, therefore, we lose our relationship to the symbolic dimension,

---

[21]Loc. cit. Therefore it is not a question of inherited ideas but rather of "the inherited *possibility* of ideas, of 'pathways' gradually traced out through the cumulative experience of our ancestors. To deny the inheritance of these pathways would be tantamount to denying the inheritance of the brain." (Jung, *C. W. 8*, par. 99.)
[22]Jung, *C. W. 8*, par. 101.
[23]This spirit is manifested probably most impressively in the archetypal dreams of small children. See Jung, "Children's Dreams Seminar."

our relationship to our spiritual inheritance also slips away from us. Fundamentally that means the loss of what stands behind the symbolic world of our ancestors, namely the supraordinate principle of spiritual meaning or order, which can impart meaningful form to individual drives in accordance with the whole. We use the concept of God for the spiritual authority that as a coordinating and regulating principle opposes the polymorphism of our primitive drive nature.[24] If our relationship to this spiritual principle of order is lost, individual drives not only become boundless but they endlessly hurl us back and forth, since individual drives and that which limits them do not work together. Consequently the individual is pulled, driven, hounded first by this and then by that, and finally falls into a completely meaningless, mindless busy-ness. The feeling associated with this is lack of freedom.

The idea that life in a tradition-directed village community makes the self-actualization of the individual impossible is, therefore, surely an untenable oversimplification. For the feeling of freedom, and hence the feeling of having the freedom to develop, rests to a very great extent on the inner freedom from feeling driven, and this, in turn, depends on the extent to which a person lives with the reality of the soul, that is, with living symbols. The living symbol is the repository within which we can apprehend the drive-regulating principle of order and through which we feel connected to the central meaning. Where this is the case, we have the possibility of self-actualization.[25] For the spirit that imparts meaningful form and order to the drives strives for optimal development of the individual.[26] This may well be the reason why, despite social and material limitations imposed on freedom of mobility in village societies with active religious images and rites, we do not find only dull people forced into conformity. On the contrary, we continually encounter impressively independent characters with healthy, critical common sense.[27] In contrast, enlightened individual culture devoid of symbols has tended to produce mass phenomena, as Eduard Strübin convincingly showed in his study of the folk life of the rural part of the Canton of Basel.

---

[24]Jung, loc. cit.

[25]Meister Eckehart captured this in words very beautifully: "Therefore God created the entire world: so that the soul would be born and, in turn, the soul in God. The innermost nature of every seed means wheat, and all metals mean gold, and all birth mankind." (After Büttner, vol. 1, p. 186.)

[26]For this reason Jung called this spirit the principle of individuation which, as is evident from what has been said, does not effect an asocial, egocentric development.

[27]A recent, pertinent document on this topic very much worth reading is the memoirs of Marie Metrailler.

But let us not lose sight of the other side. The relationship between village society and the possibility of personal development can also become irreconcilably antithetical. This occurs when religious life and with it the entire hierarchy of community values petrifies into dogma.[28] Then only set formulas and clearly defined things have any significance for social life. When this happens, the individual experience of and profound emotion aroused by the reality of the soul's autonomous activity either is restricted to what dogma permits or is even wholly suppressed. To remain true to the reality of the soul and consequently to the inner meaning of life, the individual must then, under certain circumstances, emigrate internally or externally. But this signifies a loss for everybody. The individual must part from familiar surroundings, and the village community loses the spiritual fertility of an inspired individual. As a consequence, the village hierarchy of values, always one-sided in some regard, can no longer be compensated by the symbol-forming activity of the unconscious psychic background—that is, it cannot be made whole. As everywhere in nature, it is always the union of opposites only that leads to the birth of something new and consequently to living renewal. Therefore separating the unorthodox from the orthodox is always injurious to the preservation of a life-promoting village atmosphere.[29] And since the unorthodox compensations coming from the unconscious soul can be registered only by the individual as the carrier of life, every rigid collective attitude vis-à-vis someone who thinks differently leads not only to the opposition between individual and collective but also to the ossification of village culture.

A break of this sort between community and the individual has already precipitated countless waves of emigration, for example in the period following the Reformation. Protestantism as the expression of an unorthodox, individually directed relation to the Godhead could not be reconciled with Catholicism as the embodiment of the experience of a spirit uniting all people. Instead of a renewal of the Catholic church by inclusion of the unorthodox protestant standpoint, a split developed with effects extending all the way down into the village community. Many families chose or were forced to leave their ancestral homelands as a consequence of the irreconcilability of the two religious viewpoints. What holds true on a large scale for our Christian *Weltanschauung* also holds true on a smaller scale for every

---

[28]As is well known, materialistic *Weltanschauungen* and dogmae can be proclaimed with religious zeal as universal.

[29]In this connection let us recall the significance of cultivating the village *Fastnacht* (Shrove Tuesday) as a sort of fertility rite.

community. A village's excessively rigid orthodox stance toward "social deviants" or "protestants" in the original sense of that word is disastrous for the perpetually necessary spiritual renewal of community life. These reflections make it obvious that understanding the spiritual-emotional aspect of village renewal and consequently also of rural development policy can be just as important as the material dimension.

With this we leave the question of a possible antithesis between community life and the possibility of individual development and take up again the primordial, "volkstümlich" relationship to oneself.

With the Enlightenment the events of the soul were devalued to the level of insignificance. With rejection of the reality of the symbol-creating soul as an organ of perception, the relationship to the drive-regulating spirit was also lost. Consequently the relation of the individual to oneself—that is, to individual, spiritual development in accordance with a supraordinate model or pattern—was also lost. We no longer know that intensely personal responsibility we encountered among the mountain folk of Uri, that responsibility of the individual not to behave wantonly towards those transpersonal powers. We no longer know that self-evident obligation on the part of the individual to treat properly the overpowering spiritual forces which can confront the individual at any moment, such as we have seen in countless folk legends. Nor do we any longer recognize the serious consequences of wantonness, for the offender as well as the community. Generally, the image of the world held by our ancestors has, for us, turned into something completely incomprehensible.

With the development of modern, enlightened thought, the feeling of personal responsibility for dealing correctly with overwhelming powers has dwindled. Likewise in the wake of this change in attitude, the imaginal knowledge of our ancestors toward this reality has seemed to become superfluous. Along with this our ability to comprehend, by which we can bring the dynamic energies of the unconscious down to human proportions, has imperceptibly been lost. Because in one way or another we all fundamentally have a premonition of this calamitous state of affairs but do not acknowledge the truth of it, we usually prefer to deny the reality of the unconscious totally, although recent history shows us most distinctly how unconscious powers can set the entire world afire whenever regulation of unconscious dynamics falls away.

Because we have collectively lost almost all our experience of the efficacy and significance of the drive-regulating spirit, we become increasingly vulnerable to countless material and spiritual compulsions—such as *Sachzwang* (force of circumstances) and compellingly stubborn, affect-laden demands of all sorts. (The archaic identity of many people with these phenomena is often so perfect that one might think there had been no cultural development between a person of this sort in the twentieth century and an ancestor of five thousand years ago.) We are hopelessly exposed to these modern compulsions because we lack an extra-worldly standpoint by which the phenomena of this world can also be seen *sub specie aeternitatis*. But having such a standpoint means nothing other than sensing a living relation to such a moderating spirit.

The connecting link between the ego and the principle of order transcending consciousness is the human soul. For in it the forces working from out of the depths of the unconscious are portrayed, "that is, it [the soul] creates symbols, pictures, and is itself only a picture. In these pictures it transmits the powers of the unconscious to consciousness. In this way it is both container and mediatrix"[30] an organ for perceiving the spirit of the unconscious. Since today we can scarcely grasp things symbolically any more, we have lost an essential part of our capacity to adapt to existing realities. Specifically, we no longer notice that the function of images that arise within is to regulate our compulsiveness. Rather we believe we must realize these inner images only externally. Over and above this, we do not recognize that our guiding images for development are unconsciously mingled with archetypal images because in the usual situation we simply do not notice that images arise from within, that ideas "occur to us." Consequently we let ourselves be driven concretistically by these images instead of letting ourselves be guided by the meaning that becomes visible in these inner images. Hence because our relation to the drive-regulating, inner center common to all people is lost, all our modern, purely rationally conceived plans and improvements have an uncoordinated effect. In this sense, the widespread fascination for centers and centralization might be drawing its energy from an archetypal idea constellated in the collective unconscious—from just that inner spiritual center that we must internally realize as such, and not merely externally, concretely, and hence compulsively.

In light of this, the relatively short life of political guiding images speaks for itself. Because we have lost our relation to the supraordinated regulating principle, individuals are seized not only by certain activated biological drives, they are also tossed back and forth endlessly by archetypal ideas whose meaning they do not properly understand. First we decide the hope of the future lies in this guiding

---

[30]Jung, *C. W.* 6, pars. 402–406 and pars. 419–421.

image or in that ideology; disappointment then follows; and then in its place another idea appears by which we are swept away.[31] Because people come to identify unconsciously with compelling ideas of this sort, the concretization of such ideas is correspondingly limitless. The end then justifies the means, whether in realizing an ideology or in carrying out certain rational plans for improvement and reorganization; and unfortunately no heed is paid to the individual.[32] That the individual feels increasingly controlled externally — unfree — in this situation can no longer be argued away; and of course such external direction by the demons of the unconscious affects the rulers and the ruled in equal measure.

A principal concern of contemporary rural development policy is the independence of the rural population and the provision of comprehensive bases for demonstrating political will, for example by means of regional development schemes. In the light of what has been said above, we can no longer consider these intentions apart from the individual's feeling of freedom. For wherever people no longer feel free, the will to autonomy vanishes. Since feelings of being unfree are associated with compulsiveness, it is no surprise that problems like a demanding attitude toward the state undermine the freedom of the individual and communities. Specifically, if our inner feeling of freedom is lost, our external freedom is no longer worth much. With that, our desire to be able to live with a personal sense of responsibility also dwindles. Consequently we are glad to hand over our decision-making authority to the next higher level, demanding in exchange comprehensive welfare services provided by the state along with new laws and regulations. And thus we quickly find the scapegoat that increasingly robs us of our freedom. The interconnection between an inner greediness that has become boundless and our increasing loss of external freedom is, however, seldom seen.[33]

---

[31]Let one example stand for many: "Nous avons accepté, il y a une quinzaine d'années, avec une sorte d'enthusiasme aveugle, l'idée d'un abandon des 'zones marginales' non rentables. Nous envisagions avec optimisme le grand déplacement des hommes de la terre vers les villes, pour en faire des artisans efficaces de la croissance économique." ["It has been some fifteen years since we have accepted, with a sort of blind enthusaism the idea of abandoning the 'marginal areas' as unprofitable. With optimism we envisioned the great movement of people from the land to the cities in order to make them effective artisans of the economic faith."] (Jean Vallat, speaking on the occasion of the centennial of the National Agronomic Institute, Paris, in *Bulletin der Ing.-Agronomen*, Winter 1977.)

[32]". . . to whom Philemon and Baucis must be sacrificed 'involuntarily.' *Faust* II, Part V, verse 11268ff. Here one might call to mind the "city fit for cars" according to which countless cities were rebuilt and, in part, are still being rebuilt.

[33]I am indebted to a conversation with Regierungstrat Josef Brücker for these ideas.

Therefore, since the will to autonomy has something to do with the feeling of freedom, and the latter in turn is dependent on the experience of inner freedom and consequently on the reality of the soul, our guiding image for supporting and furthering rural autonomy will have to pay due attention to the relation of the individual to the background formed by the soul. In the next chapter we shall discuss further what that might mean.

Chapter 20

The Whole Person as Guiding Image

In the light of the practical significance of *volkstümlich* thought for rural life, such as we have sketched it, a realistic rural development policy can no longer leave this reality out of consideration. Therefore we cannot avoid basing our policy for strengthening rural independence on a broadened image of humanity—an image that attends both to the needs of the individualistic, non-*volkstümlich* side of humanity and also to the folk aspect of the human psyche capable of *participation mystique* and usually unconscious.

This new, expanded image of humanity corresponds to the state of contemporary knowledge of human nature. According to what is known today, the human being is not simply a rational creature, "that you can count on," but rather a highly complex and ultimately inscrutable psychological phenomenon, for the psyche does consist of far more than just consciousness. Consciousness is simply a small part of the total psychic reality, namely the youngest result of a developmental history extending over eons. The individual stages in this psychic development are found in the genotype of every human being, namely in the archetypal modes of imaging common to all people. On the one hand these archetypal modes are shaped by the experiences of our ancestors. On the other hand, we can find all the prehuman developmental steps in the unconscious structure of our psyche, much as the animal, autonomic, and elemental stages of development can be demonstrated in our body.

Human ethology shows us the *animal* aspect of our psychic modes of behavior. The *vegetative* aspect becomes visible in the light of psychosomatic research, especially if we think of the interrelationship between the autonomic nervous system and the collective unconscious. Finally, our entire *elemental* psychic reactions are illustrated, for example, in the use of language that utilizes the images of the four classical elements (earth, water, wind, and fire): "having a stone on one's heart," "waves" of feeling, a "breath" of inspiration, the "fires" of love. Despite the faith in progressive ideas, we can never free ourselves from this common human background. For these patterns of instinct are so deeply ingrained in us that we cannot expect to be able to change fundamental psychic structures through education in a few generations, structures that have taken shape gradually over the course of thousands of generations. In folk thinking the lower powers of nature — i.e., the elemental, the vegetative, and the animal — have always been regarded as divine; to find examples, we need think only of the veneration of the four elements and of the vegetation numen,[1] or of the superhuman knowledge of helpful animals in folk tales. Here we recognize that these lower structures in us are basically overpowering factors of fate.

The extent and the significance of our psychic background become more clearly visible if we remember how long our unconscious, spiritual-psychic regulating mechanisms had already been operative before modern consciousness arose. Specifically, if we place the developmental history of humanity along a time line and if we transfer this time line to the minute markings on the face of a clock, we get more or less the following picture: If the interval of one hour is assigned to earth's planetary age of around four billion years, elemental life dominates the entire first half hour. Vegetative and animal life dominate almost the entire second half hour; and only in the last two seconds has homo sapiens been in the picture! We shall not make our comparison yet more pointed by logging the appearance of modern, enlightened consciousness on this scale. Our rough sketch may suffice to point out the approximate extent of the unconscious deposits in our psyche. In its unfathomably deep channels, the life of all our predecessors right back to the lowest levels of our development has again and again proven its worth and adapted to changing limiting conditions in the best possible way.

With the empirical proof of the powerful influence that the entire unconscious background of our psyche exerts on the ways human beings conceptualize and act, we can no longer shape our development policy as though humanity consisted only of the ideas and wishes that happen to be momentarily conscious. For of course this wholly other aspect of our being, this immeasurable dark domain of our nature, is also continually alive in our background. If we pay it no

---

[1]On this see, e.g., Caminada, *Die verzauberten Täler*.

heed, if we are not ready to admit that psychically we are also elemental, vegetative, animal and archaic-primordial creatures, the background domain of our psyche unfailing reacts with disturbance. The same holds true, as is well known, for our body; if we are not appropriately concerned about its elemental, vegetative, and animal "background"—that is, about air, water, food, warmth, sleep, and movement—our body bills us with illnesses of all sorts and thus gains the necessary attention by force. On the basis of these reflections, it is essential that we keep this broadened image of humanity in view in questions of rural development.

Of course it is most uncomfortable for the scientific mode of observation to have to acknowledge a realm that we cannot get a grip on. But practice compels us to widen our field of vision. Let the potential doubter be reminded here of the situation we described at the very beginning: Our rationally designed overall concepts of rural development are torpedoed precisely from the unconscious background of the human psyche—on the one hand by emotions of all sorts, and on the other by the force of circumstances (*Sachzwang*) which we have also recognized as a spiritual-emotional background phenomenon.[2]

For decades we have known about an unconscious reality independent of consciousness. Why indeed have our applied social sciences not long since given due attention to this critically important discovery? The reason may well be that comprehensive acceptance and inclusion of this background confronts us with a distressing situation. Because this unconscious domain of the soul in us is informed by non-Christian, natural elements almost exclusively—that is, by things that our Christian consciousness has banished to Hell—recognition of this unconscious domain signifies nothing less than our consciousness's encounter with powers which heretofore we have excluded from our generally accepted *Weltanschauung*. Here we are speaking of the hellishly overpowering forces of our natural drive nature, in the face of which we naturally feel an absolutely justified fear. But today we can no longer deny the presence of these unconscious powers. They confront us in the unprecedented threat to our time, casting a shadow over everything that has existed up until now—the threat posed by the human "beast."

We can no longer deny the existence of our non-Christian background even in the applied social sciences. However, in most instances we lack the necessary ability to comprehend that would allow these lower forces to exist without inundating our discrimina-

---

[2]See Part 4, chapters 13 and 14.

tive consciousness with emotionality and wild delusions. Moreover, this non-Christian, unconscious realm of nature consists, as does nature in general, of light and dark, of good and evil. With the recognition of this background in us, we would also have to confess to our capacity for devilry. Seen from this vantage point, it is certainly easy to understand why so many scientists resist looking this dark domain squarely in the eye. People are afraid of their own inner contradictions, which could become visible and prompt a revelation that usually strips us of numerous illusions about ourselves and our activities.

The fear of taking cognizance of this inner reality could possibly be overcome if we recall the mandate of scientific research. New discoveries never result from dogmatic adherence to theories and articles of faith but rather only from unprejudiced observation of the facts. Therefore it is unavoidably necessary that the individual researchers in the domain of the applied social sciences should endeavor to make the requisite observations concerning the existence of the unconscious background of the psyche and how it exerts its effects. Continued obstinate insistence that the "sun turns about the earth" must be labeled as absolutely untenable in the light of our modern state of research.

The problem now consists in including the background realm without falling under the power of blind emotionality or wild fantasy. Since an effective capacity to comprehend these powers from the human realm of darkness is obviously of the greatest significance for rural development policy, we must take up this question.

As we have already explained, the non-Christian background of our soul consists of a drive force arising from the material substrata and a drive-regulating spiritual side. We have thoroughly attended to our material side through the natural sciences. Compared to this, we have fallen under the power of the disastrous view that the drive-regulating, spiritual aspect of the unconscious is identical with the intellect. This has led to modern human inflation, to our being filled with a spirit to which we have no right. The consequence is, paradoxically, that consciousness becomes unconscious. "This always happens when consciousness takes too many unconscious contents upon itself and loses the faculty of discrimination, the sine qua non of all consciousness."[3] The enlightened mind today is generally unconscious of the reality of an objective, supraordinated spirit able to join together individual drives in a meaningful pattern and, by its imper-

---

[3]Jung, *Psychology and Alchemy,* C. W. 12, par. 563.

sonal nature, giving organic form to human social life. The result is that the scientific spirit, with discoveries in natural science and the pursuant material progress, has found knowledge to be a powerful counterforce to Christian faith. In this conflict between knowledge and faith, faith becomes the underdog. The consequence is a general ebbing of the efficacy of our religious forms, the visible and palpable expressions of the living spirit capable of posing a counterbalance to the drives' lack of moderation. Moreover, because today (as already mentioned) we equate the drive-regulating spirit with intellect, which does not have the effect of regulating drives, modern humanity increasingly lacks the countervailing spiritual force that could give our barbaric acquisitiveness a human measure and thereby ultimately a meaning. The sinister increase of unbridled venality sufficiently demonstrates this. We have noticed in general that our environment and our social life suffer immeasurably from this. But now we believe somewhat naively that we might subdue this dragon of acquisitiveness with development strategies worked out by our intellect and force it into a meaningful form. We do not notice that we are dealing with a divine power in the case of this *mater saeva cupidium* (Nietzsche), namely with the death-dealing side of Great Mother Nature.[4] In doing this, humanity arrogates divine power to itself. Instead of serving the drive-regulating spirit and distilling its meaning from the images it arrays within our psyche, we identify with these inner images. Mingled with intellectual deliberations, we then fabricate monstrous, mystically rationalized guiding images, thanks to which we hope to subdue the monster of our immoderation.

This disastrous identification with the spirit of the unconscious is, therefore, the root of both the contemporary euphoric belief we can do anything *and* our feeling of powerlessness. Euphoria prevails among those who still believe we can still construct something better by progressing from error to error and by employing yet more ingenious development strategies; resignation reigns among those who sense these intellectual gymnastics do not really advance us toward solving the actual, sinister conflicts. In which direction might it then continue?

In my opinion, the only possible first step out of this dilemma is that of sacrificing the disastrous opinion that with our reason we are the light of the world, and that if only we planned things rationally, a lot would be put in order. So long as we identify our intellect with the regulating spirit and believe that, thanks to our cleverness, we can get

---

[4]Details in Jung, *Symbols of Transformation*, C. W. 5.

a grip on the growing imbalances, we will also remain unable to understand the moderating spirit of nature. Only by sacrificing our identification with the spiritual principle and by beginning to observe the inner events with a truly critical eye can this spirit manifest itself as our objective counterpart. Thus when individuals accept the depth of their own souls through introversion and take them seriously, they relate to that which is common to all. Thereby the individual regains something of that context and of that secret and irresistible power that usually imparts the feeling of belonging to the whole.[5] This is the prerequisite for understanding real human needs, the needs of the whole person and not just the momentarily activated desires that all too often lead to a one-sided development inimical to life.

But since inflation from identification with the divine spirit carries something pronouncedly elating and elevating, what we have said here may well not encounter great love among planning and development experts. For whoever identifies with the principle of consciousness becomes the "sun hero," the great, knowing, "night-flying" expert who, with clever ideas, promises to bring the world a new sunrise—if people would only see it! This is the prototype for modern, inflated experts and ideologists who believe they know how the alarming problems of our worldwide imbalances are to be solved.[6] The downfall of these sun heroes generally follows when their ideas, concepts, guiding image, or social program have proven unsuitable. The radiant experts then become cynics and moreover fail to notice that, in their rise and fall, the archetypal lives of such divine heroes have "lived" *them*; as human beings, however, they could not take root. To become conscious of this calamitous identification with the divine light bearer and to sacrifice this identification is, therefore, a prerequisite for a policy on a human scale.

The place of the "knowledgeable experts" must be assumed by unprejudiced people who are ready to let the conflicts in society and planning work on them, despite all their expert knowledge, and to renounce the pretension that sooner or later the solution can be brought about exclusively through knowledge. We will then have to recognize that the external, insolvable conflicts that concern us are fundamentally a reflection of our inner fragmentation, the fragmentation of modern people torn between their drives and their desire to limit those drives, between acquisitiveness and the desire to set limits

---

[5]Jung, *Symbols of Transformation*, C. W. 5.
[6]In psychology we use the term "puer aeternus" for this typical phenomenon (see von Franz, *Puer Aeternus*).

by means of planning, between the forward-striving belief in development and the restraint that gives form and meaning. Those who are ready to suffer the insolvability of certain inner conflicts in this manner thereby accept the superior strength of their own discordant intrapsychic nature. Within this tension a real standstill ensues and with it a receptivity to the stirrings of the drive-regulating spirit of the unconscious.[7] This inner principle of order can reconcile the antithetical tendencies in us as it has done since time immemorial.[8] We call the expressions of this inner principle of order a sudden idea, an intuition, or a revelation. When associated with consciousness they provide the possibility of a creative solution, which always means an acausal expansion of consciousness that comes by leaps and bounds, the birth of a new, more comprehensive viewpoint. The external tension of conflict can also find a creative solution synchronistically in certain circumstances.[9]

This brings us to the end of our study without our having said in detail that everything must be done from a social viewpoint in order to strengthen rural independence. The central concern of this study was not a new recipe, i.e., a new handbook for supporting and promoting rural areas. Rather, it has been the attempt to delineate the spiritual background of our increasing regional imbalances. Proceeding from that, we demonstrated how ultimately we can work on this problem only if we are concerned with the premises underlying our thinking that have led to these imbalances. Then we can recognize that the external imbalances are a reflection of the one-sidedness in our generally accepted views. The real contribution toward dismantling external imbalances therefore begins with the internal dismantling of the prejudice that one consists only of what one knows. From a position that recognizes the whole person as the guiding image, decisions will consequently be made that are appropriate to the collective whole externally as well. For the whole person is rooted in the animal, the vegetative, and the elemental realms; and such an approach ultimately takes into account the totality and unity of the invisible background of the world.

---

[7] For the practice-related aspect of this assertion I must refer the reader to my investigations in *Entwicklungsplanung ohne Seele?*.
[8] Jung called this inner center the self; on this point see the dream series of Wolfgang Pauli in *Psychology and Alchemy*, C. W. 12, part 2.
[9] Details on this point are in the section on synchronicity and planning in my work, *Entwicklungsplanung ohne Seele?*.

Chapter 21

Summary and Conclusions

Our investigation of Swiss policy intended to support and further rural areas has shown how little the political goals and measures take our primordial side capable of *participation mystique* into account. Paying adequate attention to these largely unconscious spiritual-emotional needs will have to be the task of a future rural development policy.

If we examine the constitutional mandate for Swiss agrarian policy, we see that, fundamentally, the mandate already demands such a comprehensive vision of the material and the spiritual-emotional viewpoint. In Article 31 bis, No. 3b of the Federal Constitution we find the principle of "maintaining a healthy agrarian class and a productive agriculture in the service of providing for the country." That this constitutional article should be and, in fact, is understood in that sense is shown, among other ways, by the course in agrarian policy recently published by the Swiss Farmers' Union. There we find the application of article in the demand that it be the concern of agrarian policy to see "that, on the one hand, the agrarian family be able to achieve an income on a footing of equality, and that, on the other hand, the ethical, spiritual and social values of the agricultural class be cultivated."[1] Hence maintaining a healthy agricultural class entails the cultivation of nonmaterial values, as outlined, for instance, in the relationship to oneself (ethos), to the spirit, and to the community. The nonmaterial dimension must, of course, not simply remain an

---

[1] Swiss Farmers' Union, "Gesunder Bauernstand und leistungsfähige Landwirtschaft," p. 32; similar statements also on p. 14.

empty formula.[2] On the basis of our discussion, the nonmaterial domain of human existence should form part of the evaluation of a situation and consequently part of the process of setting goals simultaneously and in equal measure. Continued division between the solid, material domain of agrarian policy and a realm of "spiritual-emotional edification" that is often indulged with a smile is no longer permissible, given our current knowledge of the inseparability of spirit and matter. To be rather graphic: it wouldn't occur to anyone to look first with the right eye, then close it and look with the left. But that is precisely what we do when we do not unite the "view with the eye of concrete perception" with the "knowledge of a spiritual-emotional reality."

In extending the constitutional principle for Swiss agrarian policy to the area of regional policy, the same would have to hold true. The goal of a policy intended to strengthen rural independence would be the "maintenance of a healthy rural population and of productive economic structures in our rural areas." As in the text concerning agrarian policy, this statement of principle refers first to the human being as a whole and secondly to the economic and material conditions. For all practical purposes, the second part of this principle commands all the attention in agriculture as well as in regional policy. The issue of the "healthy person," by contrast, is pursued hardly at all. But what does "healthy" indeed mean in this context?

In an article by Bruno Glauser[3] I found a paraphrase of the adjective "healthy" that seems to me fitting. In his article he quotes the view held by the Paï-Tavyteräi Indians in northern Paraguay:

> *For us Paï, health is a condition that we call "tekoresai"; so that this "condition of being healthy" will be assured, various things and relationships must be present; they all belong to the "condition of being healthy" and constitute it: the plants and trees, taken individually, as medicaments; but also all plants and trees taken together, as medicaments; water, words truly expressed and carefully weighed; good nutrition; not acting without consideration for others; the virgin forest; the animals in the bush, the fish, harmony, the village community; talking with others and carrying on conversations; maintaining our way of life; our own culture and nature; the feeling of strength that is given us by*

---

[2]In the Farmer's Union report cited, this is, unfortunately, the case. Also in the Fifth Federal Agricultural Report the spiritual dimension is hardly mentioned at all.

[3]Quoted from Glauser, "Indianer in Not," *Schweizerisches Rotes Kreuz*, no. 5, July 1, 1981, p. 17f. I am indebted to Marie-Louise von Franz for bringing this article to my attention.

all the things I have mentioned; holding our community together; living peaceably and in security on our land; our life together, in the family and in the village community; the festivals.

From this description it is clear how the "condition of being healthy" ultimately is a feeling for life. Consequently since this realm cannot be grasped with intellectual feats of reason alone, research and policy in rural development will also have to develop a sensorium in order to take this domain of emotional health and well-being adequately into account. Only in this way can the mandate to maintain a healthy agrarian class and a healthy rural population really be fulfilled. In contrast, an exclusive consideration of measurable quantities such as wage comparisons, productivity, regional national income, or status of the infrastructure must be labeled as untenably one-sided.

In juxtaposing the folk or *volkstümlich* mentality and modern planning mentality we have stated that the folk ways of thinking, feeling, and acting must by no means simply be called outmoded. On the contrary, we have to take cognizance of characteristics of this view of the world that, in certain respects, do more justice to the objective facts than do our enlightened ways of thinking. Hence as sociologic thought comes to terms with the discoveries of modern physics and psychology, concepts and behaviors typical of primordial folk thinking are again suddenly recognized as meaningful and faithful to reality. For this reason development policy for rural areas in particular must investigate more carefully the practical knowledge stemming from the primordial, *volkstümlich* mode of experience for its contemporary relevance. The thought and action in this view of the world hold empirical value that must be conveyed to modern consciousness. The value lies essentially in the fact that *volkstümlich* thought is erected on a tradition in which the intrapsychic dimension has been able to function actively in daily life. In the legends, usages, rules and customs—indeed, in the entire folk culture—the unconscious, common human background has always been able to collaborate in structuring and regulating life. The ability of the instinctual foundation to collaborate is the reason that we feel "instinctively" well when we come into contact with structures, usages, or stories of archaic folk. Consequently, their practical knowledge actually contains for us some "know-how" about the right way to include the spiritual-psychic dimension in daily life and, by extension, in rural development policy.

For the empirical knowledge of the folk to enter into a fruitful union with the worldview of the Enlightenment, modern society must first see the value of this opposite pole. But this can only happen through

intense involvement with the folk view of the world. Here it is critical
to find a suitable method of making the knowledge of the folk accessible to rational understanding. In our investigation of folk legends and
usages we have become familiar with the fundamental features of a
viable approach. It is primarily a question of expanding the imaginal
expressions of folk knowledge found in legends, usages, rules, etc.,
using amplification—thus elucidating them so that the meaning of
this empirical knowledge becomes comprehensible to our modern
mentality. Only in this way is there a possibility that our progress-
oriented age will not lose the living relationship to the world of our
ancestors. This procedure is the only way to preserve folk culture
from internal decay. To counteract further loss of rural independence,
we must, therefore, support and promote a comprehensive elucida-
tion of the meaning of the symbolism in folk culture. This must be the
task of experts who have both personal experience in understanding
symbols and expert knowledge at their disposal in areas such as
folklore, agrarian sociology, or folk literature. In this undertaking
special attention should be given to translating the findings written in
scientific language back into a language commonly understood. In
my opinion we are concerned here with a research and educational
task of the first priority. If the modern school system has tremen-
dously diminished the value of folk thought and folk life, it is necessary today to rectify this devaluation by giving these values back the
attention they deserve in science and in the schools.

Recapitulation

The starting point of this work was a complex of three issues: the
rural-agrarian social problem, the disturbed city-country relationship,
and contemporary rural development policy. As became evident in
the course of our study, all three areas are characterized by a problem
of opposites. As the essence of our observations concerning the rural
social problem, we found how the primordial, rural-agrarian feeling
for life—involving attachment to the community, landscape, tradition, and the transpersonal dimension—stands in seemingly
unbridgeable opposition to the principles of progress—reason and
liberation from attachments of all sorts. The relation between the
rural-agrarian population and the urban-nonagrarian population is
also greatly disturbed, since both rest to a large degree on a mutually
distorted view, that is, on a mixture of defensiveness and fascination
or on over- and undervaluation. In the center of the third area of
study (current policy intended to support and promote rural areas) a
problem of opposites appeared, too. Material hardship seemed to

have no tangible relation to the spiritual-emotional dimension of life; and so-called individual culture appeared to be ever less easily reconcilable with the interests of the community.

In Part 2 the problem of opposites was viewed in the light of the development of Western culture. In that context we demonstrated that the questions posed can not be treated only externally. The change in our predominant collective mode of thought and action must also be included in our investigation. This approach finds support in the contemporary state of knowledge dealing with social change.

By sociohistorical and sociopsychological investigation of the change in the relationship of human and environment (Part 3) as well as of interpersonal relationships (Part 4), we were able to show that the dissolution of humanity's inner attachment to environment and the primordial, closed social unit stands in direct relation to the rise of an individual ego-consciousness. To the extent that ego-consciousness has freed itself from the general human capacity for *participation mystique*, the individual's sense of connectedness to a locality and a community has also slackened. The result of this development is our modern capacity for geographic and social mobility. The reverse side of this progress is the increasingly palpable feeling of general estrangement. Nostalgia as a cultural mood is an expression of this fact. Therefore the roots of the external problem of opposites, which was our starting point, are to be sought in an intrapsychic dichotomy, namely in the split between ego-consciousness and what has been called the collective unconscious. For this reason the next question concerned what can be done to renew a viable relationship between human and environment, as well as among people themselves to reverse the dissolution of the inner feeling of membership or belonging. For life in rural communities threatened by emigration, the issues of attachment to the soil and locality and the "atmosphere in the village" are often as important as the material conditions of life.

In Part 5 contemporary Swiss rural development policy was scrutinized in terms of the insights gained into the significance of nonmaterial phenomena. The essay concludes with a sketch of a guiding image for regional and agrarian policy that includes human spiritual-emotional needs. The quintessence of the entire book is to make visible an image of humanity consisting not only of basic biological but also of fundamental spiritual structures that must be given scrupulous attention. Making the whole human being the center of a future guiding image is the need of our age, both for our personal way of life and for our political actions, if the gulf between human and environment as well as between people themselves is not to grow even wider.

Bibliography

Abt, R. 1975. *Arbeiterbauerntum in Schächental* [Farmer-workers in the Schächen Valley]. Thesis, Folklore Institute, Zürich University.

Abt, Theodor. 1972. *Welches sind die Ueberlebenschancen des kulturellen Erbes im Lötschental?* [What are the Chances for the Survival of the Cultural Heritage in the Lötschen Valley?]. Thesis, School of Agriculture, Federal Technical University, Zürich.

_____ . 1978. *Entwicklungsplanung ohne Seele* [Regional Development without Soul]. Berne and Frankfurt a/M: Peter Lange.

Abt, Theodor, et al. 1979. *Aufrüstungsprogram für die Urner Land- und Forstwirtschaft* [Rearmament Program for Agriculture and Forestry in Uri]. School of Agriculture, Zürich University.

Adelmann, I. and G. Taft Morris. 1968. An econometric model of socio-economic and political change in underdeveloped counties. *The American Economic Review* 68.

Adler, A. 1973. *Ueber den nervösen Charakter* [On Nervousness]. Frankfurt: Fischer Verlag.

_____ . 1931. *Menschenkenntnis* [Understanding People]. Leipzig.

Albonico, R. 1979. *Nebenamtlich – Nebenbei?* [Additional Responsibility – Incidental Significance?]. Fanas.

Alverdes, F. 1937. Die Wirksamkeit von Archetypen in den Instikthandlungen der Tiere [The efficacy of archetypes in the instinctive actions of animals]. *Zoologischer Anzeiger* 119.

Ammann, A. 1964. *Tannhäuser im Venusberg* [Tannhäuser in the Mount of Venus]. Zürich.

Andrey, R. 1972. *Adam und sein Revier: Der Mensch im Zwang seines Territoriums* [Adam and His Domain: Mankind and the Territorial Imperative]. Munich.

Anneler, K. 1918. *Lötschen*. Berne.

Aron, R. 1953. *Deutsche Soziologie der Gegenwart* [Contemporary German Sociology]. Stuttgart.

Atteslander, P. 1969. *Methoden der empirischen Sozialforschung* [Empirical Methods in Social Research]. Berlin.

Bach, H. 1967. *Bäuerliche Landwirtschaft im Industriezeitalter* [Peasant Agriculture in the Industrial Age]. Berlin.

_____ . 1981. Um eine bäuerliche Landwirtschaft [On peasant agriculture]. *Schriftereihe für Agrarpolitik und Agrarsoziologie* 30. Linz.

Bachofen, J. J. 1862. *Das lykische Volk und seine Bedeutung für die Entwicklung des Altertums* [The Lycian People and Their Significance for the Development of Antiquity].

Bächtold-Stäubli, H. 1927–1942. *Handwörterbuch des deutschen Aberglaubens*]Dictionary of German Superstition]. 12 vols. Berlin and Leipzig.

Barnes, H. E. 1948. *Historical Sociology: Its Origins and Development*. New York.

Basler, E. 1972. *Strategie des Fortschritts* [Strategy of Progress]. Frauenfeld and Stuttgart.

Battegay, R. 1967–1972. *Der Mensch in der Gruppe* [The Person in the Group]. Berne.

_____ . 1979. Probleme der Lebensmitte aus der Perspektive der Frau [Problems of midlife from woman's perspective]. *Neue Zürcher Zeitung*, Dec. 2–9.

Bell, D. 1973. *The Coming of Post-Industrial Society*. New York.

Benvenuti, B., B. Galjart, and H. Newby. 1975. The current status of rural sociology. *Sociologia Ruralis* 15: 3–12.

Birket-Smith, K. 1946. *Geschichte der Kultur* [History of Culture]. Zürich.

Bleek, B. and B. Lloyd. 1911. *Bushman Folklore*. London.

Bleuler, E. 1931. *Naturgeschichte der Seele und ihres Buwusstwerdens* [The Natural History of the Soul and of Its Emergence into Consciousness]. Berlin.

Bodenstedt, A. 1981. Housewives in rural households. Multigraphed paper presented at the 9th European Congress for Rural Sociology, Helsinki.

Böhler, E. 1965. *Der Mythus in Wirtschaft und Wissenschaft* [Myth in Economics and Science]. Freiburg i.B.

Bolliger, A. 1941. *Die zürcherische Landwirtschaft an der Wende des 18. Jahrhunderts* [Zürich Agriculture at the Turn of the 18th Century]. Zürich.

Bonderer, E. 1964. *Bildungsprobleme der Bergbevölkerung* [Educational Problems of the Mountain Population]. Berne.

Bonjour, Edgar. 1970. *Geschichte der schweizerischen Neutralität* [History of Swiss Neutrality]. 5 vols. Basel.

Boos, W. 1977. *Intelligente Bakterien: Chemotaxis als primitives Modell von Reizleitungssystemen* [Intelligent Bacteria: Chemotaxis as a Primitive Model of Stimulus Transmission System]. Konstanz: Universitätsverlag.

Braun, R. 1960. *Industrialisierung und Volksleben: Die Veränderungen der Lebensformen in einem ländlichen Industriegebiet vor 1800 (Zürcher Oberland)* [Industrialization and Folk Life: Changes in the Way of Life in a Rural Industrial Area before 1800 (The Zürich Oberland)]. Erlenbach-Zurich.

———. 1965. *Sozialer und kultureller Wandel in einem ländlichen Industriegebiet im 19. und 20. Jahrhundert: Zürcher Oberland unter Einwirkung des Maschinen- und Frabikwesens im 19. und 20. Jahrhundert* [Social and Cultural Change in a Rural Industrial Area in the 19th and 20th Centuries: The Zürich Oberland under the influence of Mechanization and the Factory System in the 19th and 20th Centuries]. Erlenbach-Zürich.

Brenner, Charles. 1955. *An Elementary Textbook of Psychoanalysis*. New York: International Universities Press.

Brepohl, W. 1952. Die Heimat als Beziehungsfeld [Home as relationship network]. *Soziale Welt* 4.

Brugger, B. 1939. Die Landflucht der Begabten [The talented flee the country]. *Allgemeine Zeitschrift für Psychiatrie und inhr Grenzgebiete* 112.

Brugger, E. A. and G. Häberling. 1978. *Abbau regionaler Ungleichgewiche* [Reducing Regional Imbalances]. 3 vols. Double dissertation, Zürich University.

Büchli, A. 1958–1966. *Mythologische Landeskunde von Graubünden* [Mythological Study of Customs of Graubünden]. Aarau.

Büttner, H. 1909. *Meister Eckeharts Schriften und predigten* [The Papers and Sermons of Meister Eckehart]. Vol. 1. Jena.

Buff, Eva, et al. 1978. *Migration der Frau aus Bergregionen* [Migration of Women from Mountainous Regions]. Zürich.

Caminada, C. 1961. *Die verzauberten Täler. Die urgeschichtlichen Kulte und Bräuche im alten Rätien, Olten und Frieburg, i. B.* [The Enchanted Valleys: Ancient Cults and Customs in Old Rätia, Olten and Frieburg i. B.] Olten und Frieburg i. B.

Capra, F. 1976. *The Tao of Physics*. Shambhala.

Christaller, W. 1968. *Die zentralen Orte in Süddeutschland. Eine ökonomisch-geographische Untersuchung über die Gesetzmässigkeit der Verbreitung und Entwicklung der Siedlungen mit städtischen Funktionen* [Central Places in Southern Germany: An Economic and Geographic Study of the Laws of Distribution and Development of Settlements with City Functions]. (Reprint of the 1933 ed.) Darmstadt: Wissenschaftliche Buchgesellschaft.

Cicero, T. 1959. *De Fato IV*. Translated by Karl Beyer. Munich.

Clemens, H. 1961. *Stadt und Umland: Zusammenstellung von Aussagen und Erkenntnisse zum Stadt-Umland-Problem* [The City and Its Environs: Anthology of Statements and Insights on the Problem of the City and Its Environs]. Hanover.

Cohen, J. M. 1980. Integrated rural development: Clearing out the underbrush. *Sociologia Ruralis* 20, 3.

Coombs, P. and M. Ahmed. 1978. *Attacking Rural Poverty: How Nonformal Education Can Help*. Baltimore.

de la Caudra, J. L. 1977. De proportio sesquitertia in Psychologie und Naturwissenschaft [On the *proportio sesquitertia* in psychology and natural science]. *Analytische Psychologie* 8, 2.

Cysat, R. 1969. *Collectanea pro chronica lucernensi et Helvetiae*. Edited by J. Schmidt. Luzern.

Dahrendorf, R. 1979. *Lebenschancen: Anläufe zur sozialen und politischen Theorie* [Vital Opportunities: Approaches to Social and Political Theory]. Frankfurt a.M.

Darbellay, C. 1980. *Charactéristiques socio-économiques des communes rurales et montagnardes; leur signification dans l'aménagement régional et local* [Socio-economic Characteristics of Rural and Mountain Communities: Their Significance in Regional and Local Order]. Dissertation, Zürich University.

———. 1980. *Agriculture et Société* [Agriculture and Society]. Charrat.

Degh, L. 1975. Stadt-Land-Unterschiede in den USA [Differences between city and country in the U.S.]. *Stadt-Land-Beziehungen. Verhandlungen des 19. Deutschen Volks. Kongresses* [Relations between City and Country. Proceedings of the 19th German Folklore Congress]. Göttingen.

Dönz, A. 1972. *Die Veränderungen in der Berglandwirtschaft am Beispiel des Vorderprätigaus* [Changes in Mountain-Area Agriculture Exemplified in the Vorderprätigau Region]. Dissertation, Federal Technical University, Zürich.

Dreizel, H., ed. 1972. *Sozialer Wandel* [Social Change]. 2nd ed. Neuwild-Berlin.

Dünninger, J. 1969. Tradition und Geschichte Kontiuität? [Tradition and history of continuity?]. In H. Bausinger and W. Brückner, eds., *Geschichtlichkeit und Dauer als volkskundliches Problem* [Historicity and Permanence as Folkloric Problem]. Berlin.

Eberle, O. 1956. Wege zum schweizerischen Theater [Approaches to Swiss theater]. In *13. Jahrbuch der Schweizerischen Gesellschaft für Theaterkultur* [Thirteenth Yearbook of the Swiss Theater Society].

Egli, E. 1943. *Erlebte Landschaft* [Lived Landscape]. Zürich.

———. 1970. *Natur in Not* [Nature in Distress]. Stuttgart.

———. 1977. *Geborgenheit im Raum. Zum Begriff Heimat* [Containedness in Locale: On the Concept of Home]. Schaffhausen.

Eibl-Eibesfeldt, I. 1973. *Der vorprogrammierte Mensch* [Preprogrammed Mankind]. Vienna.

———. 1976. *Menschenforschung auf neuen Wegen* [Human Research along New Paths]. Vienna.

———. 1977. Ist die Versklavung durch die Technik unvermeidbar? [Is technological enslavement unavoidable?]. *Aerztliche Praxis* 29, 73.

Eliade, M. 1961. *Mythen, Träume und Mysterien* [Myths, Dreams and Mysteries]. Salzburg.

———. 1976. *Die Religionen und das Heilige* [Religions and the Sacred]. Darmstadt.

———. 1977. *Die Schöpfungsmythen* [Creation Myths]. Darmstadt.

_____ . 1978. *Histoire des croyances et des idées religieuses* [History of Religious Beliefs and Ideas]. Paris.

Elsässer, H. 1977. *Der ländliche Raum—eine Aufgabe der Raumplanung* [Rural areas—a task for regional planning]. *Der ländliche Raum.* Publications of the Institute for Village, Regional and Rural Planning, no. 28, Federal Technical University, Zürich.

Ernst, F. 1949. *Vom Heimweh* [On Homesickness]. Zürich.

Escher, W. 1947. *Dorfgemeinschaft und Silvestersingen in St. Antönien* [The Village Community and New Year's Eve Caroling in St. Antönien]. Thesis, University of Basel.

Ewald, K. W. 1980. *Der Landschaftswandel. Zur Veränderung schweizerischer Kulturlandschaften im 20. Jahrhundert* [Change in the Landscape: Concerning Man-Made Changes in the Developed and Cultivated Land in Switzerland in the 20th Century]. Report No. 191 of the Federal Institute for Experimental Forestry, Birmensdorf-Zürich.

Faludi, A. 1973. *A Reader in Planning Theory.* Oxford.

Fischer, G. 1973. *Praxisorientierte Theorie der Regionalforschung* [Practice-Oriented Theory of Regional Research]. Tübingen.

Fischer, R. 1982. *Das Selbstbild von biologische wirtschaftenden Bauern* [The Organic Farmer's Self-Image]. Zürich.

Flückiger, H. 1970. *Gesamtwirtschaftliches Entwicklungskonzept für das Berggebiet* [Holistic Economic Development Outline for Mountainous Areas]. Bern.

Flüler, N. and R. Schwertfeger. 1971. *Die Schweiz von Morgen* [Switzerland Tomorrow]. Zürich.

Flütsch, E. 1976. *St. Antönien: Kulturlandschaftliche Aspekte einer Walsergemeinde* [St. Antönien: Aspects of a Wallais Community in Terms of Developed and Cultivated Lands]. Dissertation, Zürich University.

Fourastie, J. 1963. *Le grand espoir du XXe siècle* [The Great Hope of the 20th Century]. Paris.

Frank, A. G. 1972. Sociology of Development and Underdevelopment of Sociology. In James D. Cockcroft, et al., eds. New York.

von Franz, M.-L. 1962. Ansicht einer Psychologin [A psychologist's view]. *Forum Alpinum.* Zürich.

_____ . 1962. Concerning the religious background of the *puer aeternus* problem. *The Archetype. Proceedings of the 2nd International Congress of Analytical Psychology.* Zürich.

_____ . 1974. *Number and Time.* Evanston: Northwestern University Press.

_____ . 1970. *Puer Aeternus.* New York: Spring Publications.

_____ . 1972. *C. G. Jung: His Myth in Our Time.*

_____ . 1972. *Creation Myths.* New York.

_____ . *Projection and Re-Collection.* LaSalle: Open Court.

Frazer, J. G. 1910. *Totemism and Exogamy.* London.

_____ . 1911. *The Golden Bough.* 3rd ed. 12 vols. London.

Freyer, H. 1926. *Der Staat* [The State]. Leipzig.

_____ . 1955. *Theorie des gegenwärtigen Zeitalters* [Theory of the Present Age]. Stuttgart.

Fuchs, F. P. 1977. *Bauernarbeit in Appenzell-Innerhoden* [Peasant Work in Appenzell-Innerhoden]. 2nd ed. Publications of the Swiss Folklore Society, No. 61, Basel.

Galbraith, J. K. 1959. *Gesellschaft im Ueberfluss* [The Affluent Society]. Munich.

van Gennep, A. 1909. *Les rites de passage.* Paris.

Gerber, F. 1974. *Wandel im ländlichen Leben.* Dissertation, Federal Technical University, Zürich.

Geiger, P. Weihnachtsfest und Weinachtsbaum [The festival of Christmas and the Christmas tree]. *Schweizerisches Archiv für Volkskunde* 37, 229ff.

Glauser, B. 1981. Indianer in Not [Indians in distress]. *Schweizerisches Rotes Kreuz* 5.

Granet, M. 1963. *Das Chinesische Denken* [Chinese Thought]. Munich.

Greverus, I. 1972. *Versuch zum Heimatphänomen* [Essay on the Phenomenon of 'Home']. Frankfurt a.M.

_____ . 1979a. *Auf der Suche nach Heimat* [The Search for Home]. Munich.

_____ . 1979b. Frankfurter Feste: Von Wem, für Wen? [The Frankfurt Festival: By whom and for whom?] *Notizen des Institutes für Kulturanthropologie und europäische Ethnologie* 8. Frankfurt a.M.: University of Frankfurt.

Guntern, J. 1979. *Volkserzählungen aus dem Oberwallis* [Folk Tales from Oberwallis]. 2nd ed. Basel.

Hauser, A. 1961. *Schweizerische Wirtschafts- und Sozialgeschichte* [Swiss Economic and Social History]. Zürich.

_____ . 1972a. Entmythologiseierung der Landwirtschaft [Demythologizing the landscape]. *Agrarpolitische Revue* 204.

_____ . 1972b. *Feld und Wald in der alten Schweiz* [Field and Forest in Old Switzerland]. Zürich.

_____ . 1973. *Bauernregeln* [Peasant Rules]. Zürich.

_____ . 1975. *Ueber die Nutzung von Böden im Grenzertragsbereich – sozio-ökonomische und kulturelle Aspekte* [On Land Utilization in Marginal-Yield Areas – Socio-Economic and Cultural Aspects]. Federal Research Institute Series No. 5, Tänikon.

_____ . 1976. Leitideen des Bauerntums im Wandel der Zeit [Historical perspective on guiding ideas for the peasantry]. *Die Grüne* 45. October 29, 1976.

_____ . 1978a. Der Familienbetrieb in der schweizerischen Landwirtschaft [The family farm in Swiss agriculture]. *Zeitschrift für Agrargeschichte* 26, 2.

_____ . 1978b. Verwandelte, verschandelte, entartete Schweiz [Transformed, disfigured, debased Switzerland]. Multigraphed. Zürich: Federal Technical University.

_____ . 1980. *Waldgeister und Holzfäller. Der Wald in der schweizerischen Volkssage* [Forest Spirits and Woodsmen: The Forest in the Swiss Folktale]. Zürich.

_____ . 1982. Bäuerliche Leitideen im Wandel der Geschichte [Guiding peasant ideas in the course of history]. *Festschrift für Hans Bach: Agrarpolitik, Landentwicklung und Umweltschutz [Festschrift* for Hans Bach: Agrarian Policy, Land Development and Environmental Protection]. Vienna and New York.

Hechter, M. 1975. *International Colonialism: The Celtic Fringe in British National Development 1536–1966.* London.

Hediger, H. 1946. Zum Raum-Zeit-System der Tiere [Space-time systems in animals]. *Schweizerische Zeitschrift für Psychologie und ihre Anwendung* 5.

Heisenberg, W. 1945. Wandlungen in den Grundlagen der Naturwissenschaften [Changes in the Foundations of the Natural Sciences]. Leipzig.

Heitler, W. 1961. *Der Mensch und die naturwissenschaftliche Erkenntnis* [Mankind and Natural Scientific Knowledge]. Braunschweig.

_____ . 1972. *Naturwissenschaft ist Geistewissenschaft* [Natural Science Is a Science of the Spirit]. Zürich.

Hellpach, W. *Geopsyche: Die Menschenseele unter dem Einfluss von Wetter und Klima, Boden und Landschaft* [The Soul of Man under the Influence of Weather and Climate, Land and Landscape]. 4th ed. Leipzig.

Heusser, H., ed. 1976. *Instinkt und Archetypen im Verhalten der Tiere und im Erleben des Menschen* [Instinct and the Archetypes in Animal Behavior and Human Experience]. Wege de Forschung, vol. 80. Darmstadt: Wissenschaftliche Buchgesellschaft.

Hirzel, J. C. 1816. *Synodalrede von 1816* [Address to the Synod, 1816]. Zürich.

Hocart, A. M. 1936. *Kings and Councillors.* Cairo.

Hofer, J. 1688. *Dissertatio medica de nostalgia.* Basel.

Holzmann, H. 1948. *Wipptaler Heimatsagen, Oesterreichische Volkskultur* [Legends from Wipptal, Austrian Folk Culture]. Vienna.

Hoselitz, B. 1981. Main Concepts in the Analysis of the Social Implications of Technical Change. In H. Winkel, ed., *Wirtschaftliche Entwicklung und sozialer Wandel* [Economic Development and Social Change]. Wege der Forschung, vol. 493. Darmstadt: Wissenschaftliche Buchgesellschaft.

Hostettler, Christian. 1979. Grabschmuck und Grabpflege [Funeral jewelry and care of graves]. *Schweizerisches Archiv für Volkskunde* 415.

Huber, E. 1893. *Schweizerisches Privatrecht* [Swiss Civil Law]. Vol. 4. Basel.

Hugger, P. 1970. Das Nein zur Scholle [Saying nay to the soil]. *Regio Basiliensis* 11, 1.

_____ . 1972. *Hirtenleben und Hirtenkultur im Waadtländer Jura* [Pastoral Life and Culture in the Waadland Jura]. Basel: Schweizerische Gesellschaft für Volkskunde.

Ilien, A. and U. Jeggle. 1978. *Leben auf dem Dorf. Zur Sozialgeschichte des Dorfes und Sozialpsychologie siener Bewohner* [Village Life: On the Social History of the Village and the Social Psychology of Its Inhabitants]. Opladen.

Isler, G. 1971. *Die Sennenpuppe* [The Alpine Doll]. Basel: Schriften der schweizerischen Gesellschaft für Volkskunde, vol. 52.

_____ . 1977. Zur Erlösung des Weiblichen in den Alpensagen [Redemption of the Feminine in Alpine Legends]. Multigraphed lecture. Basel: Psychologische Gesellschaft.

Jacobeit, W. 1969. Traditionelle Verhaltensweisen und konservative Ideologie [Traditional behavior and conservative ideology]. In H. Bausinger and W. Brückner, *Kontinuität? Geschichtlichkeit und Dauer als volkskundliches Problem* [Continuity? Historicity and Permanence as a Folkloric Problem]. Berlin.

Jaffe, A. 1979. *Apparitions: An Archetypal Approach to Death, Dreams and Ghosts.* Irving, TX: Spring Publications (original German ed., 1958).

de Jager, H. and A. L. Mol. 1972. *Grundlagen der Soziologie* [Foundations of Sociology]. Cologne.

Jäggi, U. 1965. *Berggemeinden im Wandel* [Changing Mountain Communities]. Bern.

_____ . 1966. *Probleme der Planung im ländlichen Raum* [Planning Problems in Rural Areas]. Zürich: Publications of the Institute for Local, Regional, and Rural Planning, Federal Technical University.

Jakobi, J. 1959. *Complex, Archetype, Symbol in the Psychology of C. G. Jung.* Princeton, NJ: Princeton University Press (original German ed., 1957).

Jakobsen, H., M.-L. von Franz, and W. Hurwitz. 1968. *Timeless Documents of the Soul.* Evanston, IL: Northwestern University Press (original German ed., 1965).

Jöhr, W. A. and H. W. Singer. 1969. *Die Nationalökonomie im Dienste der Wirtschaftspolitik* [The National Economy in the Service of Economic Policy]. Göttingen.

Jöhrin, R. 1980. Parastaatliche Organisationen im Agrarsektor [Unofficial organizations in the agrarian sector]. *Zeitschrift der Schweizerischen Gesellschaft für Agrarwirtschaft und Agrarsoziologie* 2 [Journal of the Swiss Society of Agricultural Science and Agrarian Sociology]. Zürich.

Jung, A. 1962. Psychologie vegetativer Neurosen [The psychology of vegetative neuroses]. *Der Archetype/The Archetype: Proceedings of the Second International Congress for Analytical Psychology.* Zürich.

Jung, C. G. 1954–1980. *The Collected Works of C. G. Jung.* Princeton, NJ: Princeton University Press.

————. 1975. *Letters.* 2 vols. Edited by G. Adler and A. Jaffe. Princeton, NJ: Princeton University Press.

————. 1962. *Memories, Dreams, Reflections.* New York: Pantheon Books.

Jung, C. G., et al. 1964. *Man and His Symbols.* London: Aldus Books.

————. 1938–1941. *Seminar on Children's Dreams, 1938–1941.* Multigraphed and privately circulated. Zürich.

Jung, C. G. and K. Kerenyi. 1963. *Essays on a Science of Mythology.* Princeton, NJ: Princeton University Press (original German ed., 1951).

Jung, C. G. and W. Pauli. 1951. *Naturerklärung und Psyche* [Psyche and Explanation in Nature]. Zürich. (Contains Jung's essay, "Synchronicity: An Acausal Connecting Principle," which can be found in *Collected Works* 8:417–531. Princeton, NJ: Princeton University Press, 1960.)

Jung, E. 1957. *Animus and Anima.* Zürich: Spring Publications (original German ed., 1955).

Kast, V. 1974. *Kreativität* [Creativity]. Dissertation, Zürich University.

————. 1979. Weibliche Werte im Umbruch [Revolution in women's values]. *Analytische Psychologie* 10, 2.

Kaufmann, G., ed. 1951. *Stadt-Land-Beziehungen: Verhandlungen des 19. Deutschen Volkskunde-Kongresses* [City–Country Relations: Proceedings of the 19th German Folklore Congress]. Göttingen.

Kerenyi, K. 1951. *The Gods of the Greeks.* New York: Thames and Hudson.

————. 1959. *Asklepios: Archetypal Image of the Physician's Existence.* New York: Pantheon Books (original German ed., 1947).

Keyes, R. 1973. *We the Lonely People.* New York.

Keyserling, H. 1928. *Das Spektrum Europas* [The Spectrum of Europe]. Heidelberg.

Konrad-Adenauer Foundation. 1974. *Entwicklung ländlicher Räume* [The Development of Rural Areas]. Schriftenreihe des Instituts für Kommunalwissenschaften [Publications of the Institute for the Study of Local Government Administration]. Vol. 2. Bonn.

Konrad, G. and K. Szelenyi. 1977. Social conflicts of under-urbanization. In M. Harloe, ed., *Captive Cities.* London.

Kötter, H. 1969. Stadt-Land-Beziehungen [City–country relations]. *Wörterbuch der Soziologie.* Stuttgart.

Kromka, F. 1981. Selbst- und Fremdbild der deutschen Landwirte [German farmers' image of self and others]. *Agrarwirtschaft* 30, 8.

Kühn, H. 1929. *Kunst und Kultur der Vorzeit Europas: Das Paläolithikum* [Art and Culture of Prehistoric Europe: The Paleolithic]. Berlin.

Kunkel, J. H. 1970. *Society and Economic Growth: A Behavioral Perspective of Social Change.* New York.

Kunz, G. and C. Lerch. 1979. *Geschichte der Landscaft Oberhasli* [History of the Oberhasli Landscape]. Meringen.

Künzli, A. 1966. *Karl Marx: Eine Psychographie* [Karl Marx: A Psychological Biography]. Vienna.

Lame Deer. 1972. *Lame-Deer, Seeker of Visions.* New York.

Layard, J. 1942. *Stone Men of Malekula.* London.

————. 1945. The incest taboo and the virgin archetype. *Eranos Jahrbuch* 12. Zürich.

————. 1967. *Institutionen im Primitiven Gesellschaften* [Institutions in Primitive Societies]. Frankfurt a.M.

Leibundgut, H. 1965. Inaugural address. Zürich: November 13, 1965, Federal Technical University.

Leibundgut, J. 1977. Konzentrierte Wirtschaftsförderung im ländlichen Raum [Concentrated economic development in rural areas]. *Publications of the Institute for Village, Regional and Rural Planning* 28. Zürich: Federal Technical University.

Lewis, K. 1972. *Principles and Practices of Town and Country Planning.* London.

Locher, T. 1978. *Bindung und Freiheit im bäuerliches Leben* [Attachment and Freedom in Peasant Life]. Dissertation. Zürich: Federal Technical University.

Lorenz, K. 1973. *Die acht Todsünden der zivilisierten Menschheit* [The Eight Mortal Sins of Civilized Humanity]. Munich.

———. 1973. *Die Rückseite des Spiegels: Versuch einer Naturgeschichte menschlicher Erkenntnis* [The Backside of the Mirror: Essay on the Natural History of Human Knowledge]. Munich.

Lüthi, M. 1966. Märchen und Sagen [Fairy tales and legends]. *Volksmärchen und Volkssage.* 2nd ed. Bern and Munich.

———. 1973. *Es war einmal . . .: Vom Wesen des Volksmärchens* [Once upon a time . . .: On the Essence of the Folk Tale]. Göttingen.

———. 1979. Warn- oder Leitbildsagen [Admonitory or guiding-image legends]. *Volksliteratur und Hochliteratur.* Bern and Munich.

Lütolf, A. 1976. *Sagen, Bräuche und Legenden aus den fünf Orten Luzern, Uri, Schwyz, Unterwalden und Zug* [Sagas, Customs and Legends from Five Places: Lucerne, Uri, Schwyz, Unterwalden and Zug]. Reprint of the 1862 ed. Hildesheim.

Man and Biosphere. International, interdisciplinary, and practice-oriented UNESCO project. *Bulletin of the Man and Biosphere Project* 2, June 1980.

Marti, H. 1958. *Urbild und Verfassung* [Archetype and Constitution]. Berne.

Marx, K. 1969. Zur Kritik der politischen Oekonomie [Criticisms of political economy]. *Marx-Engels-Herke,* vol. 13. Berlin.

Maurer, J. 1974. *Literaturnotizen zur Raumplanung* [Notes on regional development]. *Publications of the Institute for Village, Regional and Rural Planning* 29. Zürich: Federal Technical University.

———. 1973. *Grundzüge einer Methodik der Raumplanung* [Fundamentals of Methodology in Regional Development]. Zürich.

Medweth. W. 1957. Die Kärntner Sage. Eine soziologische Studie über heimatliche Lebens- und Kulturformen, aus Kärntner Volksüberlieferung [The legend in Kärnten: A sociological study of local forms of life and culture based on folk traditions in Kärnten]. *Kärntner Museumsschriften* 17. Klagenfurt.

Meier, C. A. 1954. Projektion, Uebertragung und Subjekt-Objekt Relation [Projection, transference and subject-object relationship]. *Dialectica* 8, 4.

———. 1968. *Die Empirie des Unbewussten* [Empire of the Unconscious]. Zürich.

Messmer, E. 1976. *Scharans, eine Gemeindestudie aus der Gegenwart* [Scharans: A study of a present-day community]. *Publications of the Swiss Folklore Society,* 59. Basel.

Métrailler, M. 1980. *La poudre de sourire.* Lausanne.

Meuli, K. 1975. *Gesammelte Schriften* [Collected Papers]. Basel and Stuttgart.

Meyer, K. 1965. *Weltgeschichte im Ueberblick* [Overview of World History]. 3rd ed. Zürich.

Mitscherlich, A. 1971. *Thesen zur Stadt der Zukunft* [Propositions Concerning the City of the Future]. Frankfurt.

Müller, J. 1926–1945. *Sagen aus Uri* [Legends from Uri]. 3 vols. Basel.

Müller, K. 1981. *Räumlicher Wandel wirtschaftlicher Entscheidungsprozesse* [Geographic Change in the Processes of Economic Decisions]. Berne.

Nationalfonds-Forschungsprogramm Regionalprobleme: Ausführungsplan [National Fund Research Program for Regional Problems: Actualization Plan]. Berne: 1978.

Neidhardt, J. G., ed. 1932. *Black Elk Speaks.* New York.

Neumann, E. 1953. *Kulturentwicklung und Religion* [The Development of Culture and Religion]. Zürich.

———. 1954. *The Origins and History of Consciousness*. Princeton, NJ: Princeton University Press (original German ed., 1949).

Newby, H. 1981. Die Herausforderung der ländlichen Soziologie heute [The challenge of rural sociology today]. *Zeitschrift für Agrargeschichte und Agrarsoziologie* 29, 2.

Niderberger, F. 1978. *Sagen aus Unterwalden* [Legends from Unterwalden]. Reprint of the 1924 ed. Hildesheim.

Nussbaumer, J. 1963. *Die Lebensverhältnisse der Bauernfamilien in Homburgertal* [The Living Conditions of Peasant Families in the Homburg Valley]. Dissertation. Zürich: Federal Technical University.

———. 1976. Brennpunkte bäuerlicher Lebensgestaltung [Foci of organization in peasant life]. *Die Gründe* 45, Oct. 29.

Ogburn, W. 1950. *Social Change with Respect of Culture and Original Nature*, 2nd ed., revised. New York.

Olsen, P. 1979. Public policy and the politics of agriculture: organization inaction. *Rural Sociology* 44, 2.

Ostander, S. and L. Schröder. 1975. *PSI*. Berne, Munich, Vienna.

Parsons, T. 1966. *Societies: Evolutionary and Comparative Perspectives*. Englewood Cliffs, NJ.

Pauli, W. 1976. Naturwissenschaften und erkenntnistheoretische Aspekte der Ideen vom Unbewussten [The natural sciences and epistemological aspects of ideas of the unconscious]. In H. Heusser, ed., *Instinkte und Archetypen im Verhalten der Tiere und im Erleben des Menschen*. Wege der Forshung, vol. 80. Darmstadt: Wissenschaftliche Buchgesellschaft.

Peccei, A., ed. 1979. *Das Menschliche Dilemma* [The Human Dilemma]. Vienna.

Pestalozzi, H. 1805. *Geist und Herz in der Methode* [Spirit and Heart in Method].

———. 1806. *Gespräch über Volksaufklärung und Volksbildung* [Conversations about the Enlightenment and Education of the Common Folk].

Peukert, W. 1965. *Sagen. Einführband zu den europäischen Sagen* [Legends: Introduction to the European Legends]. Berlin.

Pevetz, W. 1974. *Stand und Entwicklungstendenzen der ländlichen Sozialforschung in Oesterreich 1960–1972* [Status and Developing Tendencies in Rural Social Research in Austria 1960–1972]. Vienna.

Pfenninger, K. 1981. Raumplanung gegen Landwirtschaft [Land-use planning against agriculture]. *Zürichsee-Zeitung* 288, Dec. 11.

Pfluger, E. 1975. *Solothurner Sagen* [Legends from Solothurn]. 3rd ed. Solothurn.

Piot, J.-C. 1982. Les limites de l'interventionisme dans la politique agricole suisse [Limits of interventionism in Swiss agricultural policy]. *Jubiläumsschrift zum hundertjährigen Bestehen des Bundesamtes für Landwirtschaft* [Jubilee Volume for the Centennial of the Federal Agriculture Office]. Berne.

Planck, M. Gibt es eine vernünftige Weltordnung? [Is there rational world order?] *Föhre*. Berne.

Pop, M. 1971. Problemès généraux de l'ethnologie européenne [General problems of european ethnology]. *Actes du Premier Congrès International d'Ethnologie Européenne*. Paris: G.-P. Maisonneuve et Larose, 1973.

Popper, K. R. 1979. *Die beiden Grundprobleme der Erkenntnistheorie* [The Two Fundamental Problems of Epistemology]. Tübingen.

Portmann, A. 1956. *Biologie und Geist* [Biology and Spirit]. Zürich.

———. 1956. Das Lebendige als vorbereitete Beziehung [Living matter as prearranged relationship]. *Eranos Jahrbuch* 24. Zürich.

Psychology Club of Zürich. 1935. *Die kulturelle Bedeutung der komplexen Psychologie* [The Cultural Significance of the Psychology of the Complexes]. Berlin.

Rambaud, P. 1981. Organisation du travail agraire et identités collectives [The organization of agricultural work and collective identities]. Paper read at the Eleventh Congress for Rural Sociology, Helsinki.

Redfield, R. 1947. The folk society. *American Journal of Sociology* 52, Jan.

Reinle, A. 1976. *Zeichensprache der Architektur* [The Sign Language of Architecture]. Zürich.

Renner, E. 1967. *Eherne Schalen. Ueber animistischen Denk- und Erlebnisformen* [Bronze Bowls: On Animistic Forms of Thought and Experience]. Berne.

_____ . 1976. *Goldener Ring über Uri* [The Golden Ring above Uri]. 3rd ed. Zürich.

Rentsch, B. 1954. *Neuere Probleme der Abstammunslehre* [Recent Problems in the Doctrine of the Origin of the Species]. Zürich.

Reuter, H. 1963. *Geschichte der religiösen Aufklärung im Mittelalter* [History of Religious Enlightenment in the Middle Ages]. Reprint of the 1875 ed. Aalen.

Ringli, H. 1974. *Gesamtverkehrskonzeption als Herausforderung and die nationale Raumplanung in der Schweiz* [Overall traffic plan as a challenge for national land use planning in Switzerland]. *Publications of Institute for Local, Regional and Rural Planning*, DISP no. 48. Zürich: Federal Technical University.

Roepke, W. 1942. *Gesellschaftskrisis der Gegenwart* [The Contemporary Social Crisis]. Erlenbach-Zürich.

_____ . 1966. *Jenseits von Angebot und Nachfrage* [Beyond Supply and Demand]. Zürich.

Rossi, A. 1977. *Wirtschaftsanalyse und der ländliche Raum* [Economic analysis and rural areas]. *Publications of Institute for Local, Regional and Rural Planning*, no. 28. Zürich: Federal Technical University.

Roucek, J. 1981. Die Entwicklung des Begriffes "sozialer Wandel" [The development of the concept of "social change"]. *Wirtschaftliche Entwicklung und sozialer Wandel*. Wege der Forschung, vol. 493. Darmstadt: Wissenschaftliche Buchgesellschaft.

Rüegg, W. 1978. *Bedrohte Lebensordnung. Studien zur humanistischen Soziologie* [Endangered Order of Life. Studies in Humanistic Sociology]. Zürich.

Satori, P. 1932. *Das Buch von den Glocken* [The Book of the Bells]. Berlin and Leipzig.

Seattle. 1982. *Wir sind ein Teil der Erde. Rede vor dem Präsidenten der USA im Jahre 1855* [We are a part of the earth. Address of Chief Seattle to the President of the United States in the year 1855]. Olten.

Scheuber, J. K. 1965. *Ein Urschweizer erzählt* [A Dyed-in-the-Wool Swiss Speaks]. 2nd ed. Lucerne.

Scheuchzer, J. J. 1705. Von dem Heimwehe [On homesickness]. *Naturgeschichten des Schweizerlandes* [Nature Stories of Switzerland]. Zürich.

Schilpp, P. A. 1949. *Philosopher-Scientists*. Evanston, IL.

Schlegel, J. H. G. 1835. *Das Heimweh und der Selbstmord* [Homesickness and Suicide]. Hildburghausen.

Schlegel, M. and H. Zeier. 1982. Psychophysiologsische Aspekte des Assoziationsexperimentes und Normdated zu einer Reizwortliste [Psychophysiological aspects of the association experiment and norm data on a stimulus word list]. *Analytische Psychologie* 13, 2.

Schmid, H. A. 1942. *Die Entzauberung der Welt in der Schweizer Landeskunde* [Disenchantment of the World in the Study of Swiss National Customs]. Basel.

Schmid, K. 1967. *Aufsätze und Reden* [Essays and Addresses]. 2 vols. Zürich.

_____ . 1973. *Standortmeldungen* [On Location Reports]. Zürich.

Schmidt, G. 1935. *Der Schweizer Bauer im Zeitalter des Frühkapitalismus* [The Swiss Peasant in the Age of Early Capitalism]. Vol. 1. Berne.

Schmidt, L. 1977. Brauch ohne Glaube [Customs without belief]. *Ethnologia Bavarica: Studienhilfe zur allgemeinen und regionalen Volkskunde* 5. Würzburg and Munich.

Schronbek, G. R. 1975. Das Nebeneinander "bürgerlicher" und "bäuerlicher" Lebensformen in einer Marktgemeinde [The co-existence of "urban" and "peasant" lifestyles in an economic community]. *Stadt-Land Beziehungen* [City–Country Relations]. Proceedings of the 19th German Folklore Congress 1973. Göttingen: Verlag Otto Schwartz.

Schwabe, E. 1975. *Verwandelte, verschandelte Schweiz? 100 Beispiele aus dem 19. und 20. Jahrhundert* [Transformed, Vandalized Switzerland? 100 Examples from the 19th and 20th Centuries]. Zürich.

Schweizerischer Bauernverband. 1982. *Gesunder Bauernstand und leistungsfähige Landwirtschaft* [A Healthy Farmer Class and Productive Agriculture]. Course in agrarian policy from the Swiss Farmers' Union. Berne.

Schwind, M. 1950. Sinn und Ausdruck der Landschaft [The meaning and expression of the landscape]. *Das Wesen der Landschaft*, Wege der Forschung vol. 39. Darmstadt: Wissenschaftliche Buchgesellschaft, 1973.

Senti, A. 1974. *Sagen aus dem Sarganserland* [Legends from the Sarganserland]. *Publications of the Swiss Folklore Society*, vol. 56. Basel.

Sonderegger, S. 1973. *Appenzeller, Sein und Bleiben. Zum Wesensbestimmung des appenzellischen Menschen* [Born and Bred an Appenzeller: Toward a Characterization of the Essence of the People of Appenzell]. St. Gallen.

Sooder, M. 1943. *Zelleni us em Haslital*. Basel.

Sparks, G. 1982. *The Wounded Finger: Anchorage for Soul and Sense in Technology*. Thesis for the C. G. Jung Institute. Zürich.

Staedeli, H. P. 1969. *Die Stadtgebiete der Schweiz* [Swiss Urban Areas]. Dissertation. Zürich University.

Stebler, F. G. 1981. *Am Lötschenberg: Land und Volk von Lötschen* [On Mount Lötschen: The Land and People of Lötschen]. Original edition 1907. Visp.

Strüblin, E. 1952. *Baselbieter Volksleben* [Baselbiet Folk Life]. *Publications of the Swiss Folklore Society*, vol. 8. Basel.

_____ . 1959. *Grundfragen des Volkslebens bie Jeremias Gotthelf* [Fundamental Questions Concerning Folk Life in the Works of Jeremias Gotthelf]. *Schweizerisches Archiv für Volkskunde* 55.

Stutz, J. 1960. *Sieben mal sieben Jahre aus meinem Leben* [Seven Times Seven Years from My Life]. Original edition 1853. Winterthur.

Suzuki, D. T. 1968. *The Essence of Buddhism*. Kyoto.

Swiss Federal Council. 1973. *Botschaft an die Bundesversammlung über Investitionshilfe für Berggebiete* [Message to the Parliament on Investment Aid for Mountain Areas]. May 16.

Swiss Federal Parliament. 1976. *5. Landwirtschaftsbericht* [Fifth Agricultural Report]. Berne.

_____ . 1974. *Eidgen/ssisches Investitionshilfegesetz (IHG) vom. 1. Juni 1974* [Federal Investment Aid law (IHG) of 1 June 1974).

Szondi, L. 1944. *Schicksalsanalyse* [Analysis of Fate]. Zürich.

Toennies, F. 1979. *Gemeinschaft und Gesellschaft*. Reprint of the 8th ed. 1935. Darmstadt: Wissenschaftliche Buchgesellschaft.

Toynbee, A. 1979. *Menschheit und Mutter Erde. Die Geschichte der grossen Zivilisationen* [Mankind and Mother Earth: The History of the Great Civilizations]. Düsseldorf.

_____ . 1949. *Studien zur Weltgeschichte* [Studies in World History]. Zürich.

Tuchfeldt, E. 1977. *Gefärdete Marktwirtschaft* [The Endangered Market Economy]. Berne.

Urzidil, J. 1969. *Väterliches aus Prag und Handwerkliches aus New York* [Ancestral Reminiscences from Prague and Work Memories from New York]. Zürich.

Vallat, J. 1977. Rede gehalten anlässlich des Centenaire de l'Institut National Agronomique de Paris [Address given on the occasion of the centennial of the National Agronomy Institute, Paris]. *Bulletin der Ing.-Agronomen.* Winter 1977.

Vester. 1972. *Das Ueberlebensprogramm* [The Survival Program]. Munich.

Wackernagel, H. G. 1959. *Altes Volkstum der Schweiz* [Old Swiss National Characteristics]. 2nd ed. *Publications of the Swiss Folklore Society,* vol. 38. Basel.

Wahlen, F. T. 1971. Stellung und Rolle der Landwirtschaft in der heutigen Gesellschaft [The place and role of agriculture in contemporary society]. Address on the occasion of the centennial of the Agricultural School, Federal Technical University, Zürich. *Bulletin des SVIAL,* no. 160. Zollikofen.

Waldvogel, K., et al. 1981. *Landwirtschaft im Kanton Schaffhausen.* Schaffhausen: Cantonal Agricultural Office.

Wallerstein, I. 1974. *The Emerging World System.* New Yoirk.

———. 1978. *The Capitalist World-Economy.* Cambridge.

Warshay, L. H. 1964. Breadth of perspective and social change. In G. Zollschau and W. Hirsch, eds., *Explorations in Social Change.* London.

Weber, M. 1947. *The Theory of Social Change and Economic Organization.* New York.

———. 1922. Wissenschaft als Beruf [Science as a vocation]. *Gesammelte Aufsätze zur Wissenschaftslehre.* Tübingen.

Weber-Kellermann, I. 1965. Erntebrauch in der landwirtschaftlichen Arbeitswelt des 19. Jahrhunderts aufgrund der Mannhardtbefragung in Deutschland von 1865 [Harvesting Customs in the World of Agriculture in the 19th Century Based on the 1865 Mannhardt Survey in Germany]. Marbach.

Weiss, H. 1981. *Die friedliche Zerstörung einer Landschaft und Ansätze zu ihrer Rettung in der Schweiz* [The Peaceful Destruction of a Swiss Landscape and the First Steps Toward Saving It]. Zürich.

Weiss, R. 1946. *Volkskunde der Schweiz* [Swiss Folklore]. Zürich.

———. 1951. Heimat und Humanität [Homeland and humanity]. *Schweizerisches Archiv für Volkskunde* 47.

———. 1957. Alpiner Mensche und alpines Leben in der Krise der Gegenwart [The alpine persona and alpine life in the contemporary crisis]. *Die Alpen* 33.

———. 1959. *Häuser und Landschaften der Schweiz* [Swiss Houses and Landscapes]. Erlenbach-Zürich.

Wetter, A. 1981. *Auswirkung des Strukturwandels in der Landwirtschaft auf die Besiedlung der landwirtschaftlichen Räume und die Wirtschaftliche Tätigkeit* [The Effects of Structural Change in Agriculture on the Settlement of Agricultural Areas and on Economic Activity]. Thesis, Institute of Rural Economics. Zürich: Federal Technical University.

Wikmann, K. 1937. *die Einleitung der Ehe* [The Introduction of Marriage]. Abo.

Wilhelm, H. 1961. Die Eigene Stadt als Schauplatz der Gestaltung [One's native city as the theater of incarnation]. *Eranos Jahrbuch* 29. Zürich.

Winkel, H., ed. 1981. *Wirtschaftliche Entwicklung und sozialer Wandel* [Economic Development and Social Change]. Wege der Forschung, vol. 493. Darmstadt: Wissenschaftliche Buchgesellschaft.

Wiswede, G. and T. Kutsch. 1978. *Sozialer Wandel* [Social Change]. Erträge der Forschung, vol. 86. Darmstadt: Wissenschaftliche Buchgesellschaft.

Wolfram, R. 1962. Weihnachtsgast und Heiliges Mahl [The Christmas Guest and the Sacred Feast]. *Volkskunde* 58, 1.

Wüthrich, W. 1979. *Vom Land – Berichte* [Reports from the Country]. Zürich.

Zapf, W., ed. 1969. *Theorien des sozialen Wandels* [Theories of Social Change]. Cologne-Berlin.

Ziche, J. 1970. *Das gesellschaftliche Selbstbild der landwirtschaftlichen Bevölkerung in Bayern* [The Social Self-Image of the Agrarian Population in Bavaria]. Inaugural address, Technical University, Munich.

Zingerle. 1850. *Sagen aus Tirol* [Legends from Tirolia]. Innsbruck.

Zwingmann, C. 1962. Das nostalgische Phänomen [The phenomenon of nostalgia]. *Zur Psychologie der Lebenskrisen*. Frankfurt a.M.

Index

Marx, Karl, 58, 59, 63, 160, 276, 333
Masculine principle, 304, 305, 308
Mass media, 332
Materialism, 46, 54–56, 93
Matter
    animation of, 107
    desouling, 86–90
    ensouled, 83
    essence of, in physics, 94–95
    meaningful behavior of, 105
    relationship of archetype to,
      101–103
    relationship of psyche to, 103–105,
      107, 212
    relationship to, 32–33
      and guiding image, 331, 335–338
    vs. spirit, 53–54, 101, 121, 211
Mechanization, and agriculture, 15–17,
  22
Medicine, and psychophysical
  interconnection, 105
Mentality
    modern planning vs. folk, 271–311
    of a population and landscape,
      117–120
Metropolitan area, vs. city, 3nn
Microphysics, 93–95, 98, 106
Migration, process of, 3–12, 40, 55, 71,
  320
    and agriculture, 15, 17, 27, 31–32
    and legend, 206
    in birds, 134–135
Milieu
    animation of, 110, 117
    as symbol, 141–152
    ensouled, 83–90, 111
    levels of experiencing, 112–117,
      283
    -man relationship, 109–126,
      156–157
    solidarity with, 132
    (*see also* environment, landscape,
      place)
Milieu theory, and Skinner, 61
Mobility, 71, 159, 187, 190, 196, 297,
  309, 310, 315, 318, 323, 334, 341, 347
Modernization, 12, 63
    and agriculture, 17
Money economy, 159, 187
Moods, 65
Mother-child relationship, 162

Mother Earth, 132, 192, 217
Myth, 85, 101, 189
    creation, 148
    (*see also* folk legend, legend,
      saga)
Natural phenomena, inexplicable,
  84
Natural laws, 102
Nature, 14, 150–151, 327, 356–357
    and spirit, in saga, 211–214
    animation of, 121
    conservative facts of, 9
    degradation of, 89–90
    forces of, 8, 201–202
    laws of, 12
    spirit of, 147, 358
      and dwarfs, 214–223
Neurosis, 266
Newspapers, and dissolution of
  participation mystique, 183–184
North America, settlement of, 118–119
Nostalgia, 128–129, 133–134, 136–137,
  151, 191, 303
    as cultural mood, 34, 129, 152, 365
Nuclear physics, 105, 106
    (*see also* physics)
Nuclear weapons, 74
Object, and subject, relationship,
  103–107, 195
Observer, relation with observed, in
  physics, 95–96
Oneself, relationship to, and guiding
  image, 331, 343–352
Ontogeny, 162
Opposites, 328, 364–365
    in social structure, 64
    myth of union, in planning,
      295–311
    soul as link between, 266, 310
    splitting, 51–53, 321, 323
Overview, 43
Paradox, 209, 228, 326
    (*see also* opposites)
Participation mystique, 83–90, 142, 161,
  162, 169–171, 226, 244, 273, 322, 327,
  329–330, 331, 341, 353, 361, 365
    and homesickness, 129, 136–140
    and relationship, 255–267
    dissolution of, 168, 173–188, 195
    limits of, 189–192
Peasant culture, 19–21